Europe's Destiny

Europe's Destiny

The Old Lady and the Bull

Attila Marján

Translated by Péter Szücs

Foreword by André Sapir

Woodrow Wilson Center Press
Washington, D.C.

The Johns Hopkins University Press
Baltimore

OCT 29 2010

EDITORIAL OFFICES

Woodrow Wilson Center Press
One Woodrow Wilson Plaza
1300 Pennsylvania Avenue, N.W.
Washington, D.C. 20004-3027
Telephone: 202-691-4029
www.wilsoncenter.org

ORDER FROM

The Johns Hopkins University Press
Hampden Station
P.O. Box 50370
Baltimore, Maryland 21211
Telephone: 1-800-537-5487
www.press.jhu.edu/books/

Library of Congress Cataloging-in-Publication Data

Marján, Attila.
  Europe's destiny : the old lady and the bull / Attila Marján ; translated by Péter Szücs.
    p. cm.
  Rev. and translated ed. of: Európa sorsa : Az öreg hölgy és a bika. Budapest : HVG Kiadó, 2007.
  Includes bibliographical references and index.
  ISBN 978-0-8018-9547-0 (hardcover : alk. paper)
  ISBN 978-0-8018-9548-7 (pbk. : alk. paper)
  1. European Union countries—Economic policy. 2. European Union countries—Economic conditions. 3. European Union countries—Social policy. 4. European Union countries—Social conditions. I. Marján, Attila. Európa sorsa. II. Title
  HC240.M2447   2010
  330.94—dc22

                                                              2009054218

Originally published as *Európa sorsa: Az öreg hölgy és a bika*
by HVG Kiadó Zrt, Budapest, 2007

 **Woodrow Wilson
International
Center
for Scholars**

The Woodrow Wilson International Center for Scholars is the national, living U.S. memorial honoring President Woodrow Wilson. In providing an essential link between the worlds of ideas and public policy, the Center addresses current and emerging challenges confronting the United States and the world. The Center promotes policy-relevant research and dialogue to increase understanding and enhance the capabilities and knowledge of leaders, citizens, and institutions worldwide. Created by an Act of Congress in 1968, the Center is a non-partisan institution headquartered in Washington, D.C. and supported by both public and private funds.

Conclusions or opinions expressed in Center publications and programs are those of the authors and speakers and do not necessarily reflect the views of the Center's staff, fellows, trustees, or advisory groups, or any individuals or organizations that provide financial support to the Center.

The Center is the publisher of *The Wilson Quarterly* and home of Woodrow Wilson Center Press and *dialogue* television and radio. For more information about the Center's activities and publications, including the monthly newsletter *Centerpoint,* please visit us on the web at www.wilsoncenter.org.

To my masters

Contents

Foreword

It is obvious that much has changed in Europe and in the world economy in the past fifty years. But what is perhaps less obvious is the sheer magnitude of the changes. Three facts stand out.

First, in the late 1950s, the newly born European Economic Community —the ancestor of today's European Union—and geographical Europe were very different entities. The six original member states then accounted for less than half the population of geographical Europe and a little more than half of its gross domestic product (GDP), excluding the European part of the Soviet Union and Turkey. Today, with its twenty-seven members, the EU is almost identical to geographical Europe.

Second, in parallel with the gradual achievement of congruence between the European Union and geographical Europe, the latter's relative importance in the world has steadily eroded. Fifty years ago, geographical Europe still accounted for nearly 30 percent of the world's GDP (measured at purchasing-power parity). Today, its share is only slightly above 20 percent. Put differently, the EU's success in increasing its share of world GDP in the past fifty years has been entirely attributable to its successive enlargements. Yet when considered as a unit, the EU is still the largest economy in the world, on par with the United States, which has also lost a bit of ground during the past fifty years. The big winner of the past fifty years is Asia, whose share of world GDP has increased from less than 20 percent to more than 30 percent. Lest we may think that this is a new age, we should remind ourselves that China and India together accounted for about half of the world GDP until the early nineteenth century and still held a 30 percent share in 1870. History will record that their combined share reached an all-time low of roughly 10 percent precisely when the European Economic Community was founded. Today their share stands at more than 15 percent.

Third, the European Union's geographical widening has been accompanied not only by a remarkable deepening of its economic integration—from the original customs union, to the single market, and now the single currency—but also by a severe widening of income disparities among its member states. Its six original members had fairly similar incomes. In the late 1950s, their GDP per capita ranged from 80 to 120 percent of the EU weighted average (measured at purchasing-power parity, and excluding Luxembourg). By contrast, today the disparities among its twenty-seven members are huge, with a per capita GDP ranging from 40 to 140 percent of the EU weighted average (excluding again Luxembourg).

So what do the next fifty years hold, economically speaking, for the European Union? Is it bound to succumb to internal tensions due to the large economic disparities among its members, to stop its process of widening and deepening, and to decline on the world scene? Or will it draw strength from its economic diversity, renew itself, and still be a leading world player?

I take it for granted that Asia's income levels will continue to catch up with those of Europe and the United States, and therefore that its weight in the world economy will continue to increase toward matching its share of the world's population, which is expected to remain at about 60 percent between now and 2050. Consequently, the economic weight of Europe and the United States can be expected to continue to decline—but by how much will depend on productivity growth and demography.

As far as the European Union is concerned, its future also depends on whether its enlargement continues and on whether it can better organize itself politically, economically, and socially. As Attila Marján thoroughly discusses in this volume, all this boils down to whether the EU can articulate a clear vision for its future. He points out, rightly, that the EU is at a crossroads—that it must make political choices and decide whether it wants to become a political union or remain a collection of cooperating nation-states.

Yet it must be recognized that there is currently very little appetite among EU members for a major institutional initiative. The failure of the treaty establishing a Constitution for Europe and the difficulty getting the subsequent Treaty of Lisbon ratified bode ill for attempts at new treaty changes in the near future.

At the same time, the recent global financial and economic crisis has clearly exposed a number of weaknesses in the EU's institutional design, which if not addressed could put Europe on a path of lingering economic and political difficulties. Economically, there is a risk that, by compounding protracted demographic and economic problems, the crisis will result in a spiral of near stagnation, rising public debt, and declining innovation. Politically, the EU risks being blamed for having fostered a liberalization agenda in the past rather than being praised for having promoted a coordinated response to the global crisis when it struck.

It is difficult to predict whether Europe will simply muddle through or find a clear and bold vision. But what is certain is that unless it can rise to the challenges of global change, the world will soon again be dominated by two superpowers, China and the United States.

André Sapir
Professor of Economics, Université Libre de Bruxelles
Senior Fellow, Bruegel, Brussels

Acknowledgments

I would like to thank all the people who allowed me to interview them and with whom I had many lively discussions during the preparation of this book. I would like to especially thank Ambassador Egon Dienes-Oehm for his readiness to exchange views. I would also like to thank Ambassador Peter Gottfried for agreeing to be the professional consultant for the book, and Ambassador Tom Glaser and his wife Ros for proofreading the translation. I also thank my wife, Eva Szell, for proofreading the original text. Finally, I would like to express my gratitude to Samuel Wells of the Woodrow Wilson International Center for Scholars, whose encouragement and help have been instrumental throughout the process of publication.

Europe's Destiny

Chapter 1

Overview: An Old Lady in the Mirror

Europe, nicknamed the "old continent" in the Western world—but obviously not so old for the Chinese—is trying to find its place in this rapidly changing global age, just like America and the new Asian powers. What are its chances of securing its achievements of peace, stability, prosperity, and a relatively important geopolitical status? And why do many think that Europe, this part of the world that was once so mighty, now resembles a fragile old lady looking in the mirror and thinking of the good old days? Is there any truth to what these doomsayers claim? What are the real challenges that Europe is facing? In this first section, I try to summarize them.

Baron von Munchausen and the European Onion

The pressing issues and dilemmas that Europe faces are not always specific to the old continent. Nor should Europe's destiny been seen as only a regional issue, because its course of development is intertwined with those of other regions of the world, particularly with that of the United States. Some of the challenges on the two shores of the Atlantic are very similar, though of course many are quite different. Europe is in many ways more intensively challenged by the forces of geopolitics and economics than is America.

In this sense, the 2008–9 global financial and economic crisis should not blur the long-term picture of the deeper underlying issues that Europe must address, such as demographic trends, energy dependency, the vigorousness of its economy, and the uncertainty of the political and institutional framework of the European Union as a regional alliance. This book, and this chapter by way of an introduction, seek to focus on these more profound trends, which will inevitably define Europe's longer-term course, and to some extent that of the rest of the world.

Europe's Not Completely European Destiny

The success or the failure of Europe, the biggest capitalist market and the cradle of Western culture, would have serious consequences for the whole world, especially for its closest and natural ally, the United States. Europe's destiny matters to non-Europeans as well.

In these turbulent times, the future of Europe has become a standard topic of conversation, which is a positive development, even if the tone of public discourse is best described as anxious. This debate takes place almost exclusively in Europe, as if the rest of the world would not be very interested in the fate of Europe. This book intends to help remedy this situation by discussing the most important themes related to the future of the "continent of the past," and thereby to raise awareness of Europe's challenges and options in the United States and all over the world.

Strangely, when in 2008 I spent some time in the United States, which had then just been hit by the financial and economic crisis and the then-probable failure in Iraq, I could feel a sense of decline among the American people similar to what one could detect in Europe. Until recently, Europe—at least its mainstream political and intellectual spheres—traditionally looked to the United States as a model, or at least as its most important competitor, but the United States devoted less and less attention to Europe after the fall of the Berlin Wall and the emergence of China.

In 2009, however, things started to change somewhat between the United States and Europe. Politicians who are more pro-European became more influential in the United States. The latest crisis, which has proven to be the biggest in several decades, along with the political change in the United States, seemed to pull the two cousins of the West closer to each other on several fronts, including climate change and financial regulations.

The post–Cold War era of U.S. unipolar global dominance proved to be very short, and now America needs to be more open toward the rest of the world. This means that the United States and Europe share not only a sense of alarm about their international standing and competitiveness but also a less one-sided interest in the other region's situation.

Europe Is a Value, but Its Future Is in Doubt

Europe is a value—not only for Europeans, but also for the whole world. It is because of centuries of suffering, revolutions, fruitful trade, and cultural ties—or, at times, fierce fighting and wars—with other cultures, and of achievements on a universal scale in science, ideology, and the arts, that Europe has become the wonderful, globally cherished place it is today. Europeans must sometimes be reminded of how lucky they are to be living in peace, security, and prosperity on their beautiful continent with its ancient yet vibrant cultures and glorious cities filled with historical treasures. To be walking down a street in Dubrovnik, Prague, or Venice and be surrounded by history is something that they may seem to take for granted. And this is only the tip of the iceberg. For more than five decades, Europeans have not had to follow war news nervously, and east of the former Iron Curtain, they no longer need to talk differently inside and outside their homes for fear of the secret police.

Europe is a value for all the world's people—for the Japanese tourist clicking away with his camera in Budapest, spending his few days of vacation in Western Europe; for the young Californian Internet millionaire searching for her roots in the archives of Warsaw; and for the Texan couple strolling along the Champs-Elysées. In this respect, the testimony of retailers is mostly infallible and points to Europe's value on the global market. If you walk into a shoe shop or a pastry shop anywhere in the world, look at the prices and the goods on the shelves, and you will see the quintessential value judgments of the local culture. In the United States and Canada, a label reading "made in Italy," "made in France," and the like commands a premium price tag of a certain percentage above other products. Europe is still chic.

America is a value in most parts of the world. Besides being the world's leading power, the United States is also a symbol of the global New World, making it a prime target for the rage and despair of those who cannot accept this world. Today's power balance is best symbolized by the fact that many equate "globalization" with "Americanization." Americans also love symbols; perhaps their most important symbol is the Statue of Liberty—a gift from the French people that evokes the European enlightenment—standing just off Manhattan, the heart of the global world. Asia and other regions of the world of course also have particular values, with their unique cultures and traditions, and their hard-working people. Still, Europe is my home; it is where I feel at ease and at home. And I believe there are many others out there who feel the same way—along with the Europeans, perhaps those living around the world whose ancestors came from Europe, who particularly value Europe's unique contributions to humanity.

In Greek mythology, Europa's destiny—after hardships and conspiracies —changed for the better. Zeus, who—as always—was up to no good, disguised himself as a white bull and abducted the young Europa, flying her from Asia Minor to what is now the European continent, where they had three children and lived happily ever after. Such miracles do not happen today. Instead, the European continent should try to imitate the legendary Baron von Munchausen, who pulled himself out of the mire by his bootstraps. Because—it is sad but true—Europe, just like Venice, is sinking. Or to be more precise, in this era of globalization, the rest of the world is emerging economically and politically at an increasing rate. The future of Europe is in doubt. And at the center of Europe's concerns are the challenges and options rooted in the continent's most ambitious socioeconomic project, the creation of a stronger international profile and the quest for integration and unification embodied in the European Union.

How can the European Union be described in a nutshell? The aggregate population of the EU's twenty-seven member nation-states is almost half a billion, more than that of the United States and Russia combined. The EU is the world's biggest single market and still—though not for long—its largest trading bloc, accounting for roughly one-third of the world's gross domestic product, surpassing even that of the United States. The euro, the continent's single currency, is the second most important global reserve currency. However, in the coming years Europe's situation will change dramatically and start going downhill. Extrapolating current growth trends, by 2050 the EU's share of world production will fall by 50 percent, as will Japan's, while the United States may even improve its position. The real winners will be China and India, with Brazil following closely in their footsteps, overtaking Italy by 2025, France by 2031, and Germany by 2036. By 2041, China will have become the world's biggest economy; and by 2032, India will outperform Japan. By 2050, Europe's active labor force will have shrunk by 50 million to 60 million, if there are no further enlargements of the EU's membership or major waves of immigration.[1] And with respect to EU enlargement and to immigration, the question is how European public opinion will respond to these two pressing phenomena and what tensions they could create in the future.

The fact that Europe is growing more slowly than the rest of the world is not the only problem the continent must face. In some cases, there are objective reasons for Europe's inaction; Europeans have no way of influencing the population cycles of other continents. But the real problem is that even in areas where something could be done to avoid falling behind the rest of the world, Europe seems impotent because it cannot make the right choices.

At the beginning of the third millennium, Europe finds itself at a crossroads, while desperately trying to defend its position on the international scene and overcome its internal economic and social difficulties. Therefore, Europe must choose a viable model to follow. And this choice is much more complex than whether there should be a political union, such as a United States of Europe, because—theoretically—a political union could be created on the basis of different socioeconomic values, that is, models. One escape strategy could be to press on with widening integration; another could be to deepen it, by setting up a "two-speed" Europe, with a unified "core" and less closely integrated "periphery."

Antiglobalization sentiments and protectionist efforts seem to be on the rise, especially since the latest crisis hit Europe and the world in 2008. Europe seems unable to engage in reform; and Europeans seem unable to grasp the huge challenge that China and India—which are growing and modernizing at an amazing rate—pose to their continent. Europeans do not seem to understand that swift economic and social reforms will be unavoidable if Europe is to preserve its strength and role. In the face of the challenges of globalization, the European model must be reformed; if Europe keeps lagging behind its competitors economically and technologically, in the long run that could seriously undermine not only its international role but also its social order. The future could easily reveal that none of these strategies is effective. Europeans must, therefore, ask themselves three questions: How long can European integration (with popular support for it at a historic low) serve as a panacea for, or at least help, their ailing continent? What are the problems that even integration cannot solve? And what is integration good for, anyway? To be able to answer these questions, Europeans must first explore the challenges of the global and continental economy and society.

The European Onion

The challenges that Europe faces are like an onion with three separate but enwrapped layers. We must peel off these layers one by one to find out what problems Europeans must confront and then to find the cures for them. Peeling onions is not a pleasant pastime; it brings tears to one's eyes, but it is something Europe can no longer put off doing.

The external layer of the European onion consists of *global* challenges. These include growing international competition, the emergence and improving performance of competitors, the shifting balance of power, and the danger of giving the wrong (protectionist) answers to globalization.

The middle—*pan-European*—layer contains problems that affect all of Europe but are not linked to the EU's decisionmaking, regulatory, or institutional issues. These include the sustainability of the European model, poor competitiveness and productivity, the aging population, social tensions caused by immigration, and increased energy dependency.

Finally, the inner layer is the *EU* layer itself—the challenges related to European integration and the European Union. Basically, these are problems linked to the EU's institutions, decisionmaking procedures, and lawmaking, and thus to the political uncertainties surrounding the future of the "European project."

Thus, these three layers can be separated. But they are—undoubtedly—enwrapped together in the one European onion.

In addition to choosing a future model for Europe, another set of difficult issues that Europeans must face is what role they want European integration via the EU to play, how they will define it in the future, and what challenges the EU can and cannot solve.

The European continent competes in the global cutthroat race, which is not only economic in nature. Europeans must give serious thought to their continent's historic opportunities, the dangers looming ahead, and the potential ways out. They can no longer avoid asking these kinds of questions: How should Europe proceed from here? What will happen to the Europeans? Is the "Chinese menace" something of which Europe should be wary? Why would Europeans think of Europe and the EU as their own? Do they need European integration at all? Why do they think that the EU does not function properly? Will the euro disappear? Why is competitiveness falling on the continent, and how can this trend be reversed? Will Europe be able to overcome the global financial and economic crisis? Is there a need for a European Constitution and, if so, who needs it? Is the aging European population really a disastrous problem, and will Europe just die out? Is immigration the only cure for an aging Europe? Will terror spread in Europe? What will happen to the European social model, and why are immigrants and students throwing Molotov cocktails on the streets of Paris? What number should one dial if one wants to talk with Europe? Will there ever be a political union, a United States of Europe? How far can Europe enlarge without collapsing like history's great empires? Is it a realistic fear that, in a few decades' time, Europe will have become an open air museum on the axis of modernization and growth, midway between the United States and Asia? Or will Europe become an important player in the new, postcrisis world order? Is Europe's aspiration to become the leading rule setter for the postcrisis era realistic, or should it be happy to survive the crisis and remain relatively stable as a bloc? What strategy should Europe follow if it wants to clear its historic hurdles?

Having asked these questions, one can pose the most important question of all: What will have become of Europe in fifty years' time? And, as corollaries: Will Europe be able to lead the world by example, or will it sink without hope in the stormy high seas of history? What principles and values will define political policy on the continent and in the daily lives of its citizens? Will Europe be degraded in a world of Sino-American dominance, or will it be able to play a more prominent role in a multipolar world order? What should Europe's policy be toward America, China, India, and Russia?

To be able to answer these questions, we first must have a clear idea about Europe's situation. Let us start peeling the layers off the onion.

First, what can we see in the onion's *external* layer? The last few decades have brought a dynamic expansion of world markets and the emergence of new economic powers. In such an age, only those regions and countries that can harness international trends can be successful. Europe seems to be wary of this world. Some "old" EU member states even accuse new members of unfair competition. Where does this lead?

In recent times, the pace of global competition among the world's traditional economic and political powers has picked up enormously. In addition, new economic powers—particularly China and India—have emerged, claiming their piece of the global pie. And along with their increased contention, the competing countries are interlinked in thousands of ways in the global marketplace. Having said that, it should come as no surprise that the number one economic policy objective of today's superpowers is to strengthen their competitiveness. Only time will tell which region emerges victorious and what is the winning policy mix. The odds are uneven. But one thing is certain: If Europe is serious about achieving better competitiveness and bigger growth while at the same time preserving its unique socioeconomic model with an aging population, it had better get its act together and pick up its game.

For the time being, Europe is not doing too badly statistically, but the figures reveal alarming trends. In 1950, the level of development of the three biggest continental countries (Germany, France, and Italy) was about one-third of that of the United States. By 1991, these nations had significantly reduced this gap, lagging a mere 20 percent behind America—only to fall behind again; by 2004, the gap had widened to about mid-1970s levels, as if Europe had been at a standstill for the last quarter century.[2] The real problem was that, following the first upswing, the big continental countries were unable to carry out the restructuring necessitated by their global challenges. During the years of plenty in the 1960s and 1970s, the continental European socioeconomic model based on redistribution, high taxes, and welfare institutions was reinforced. This model, however, crippled the flexibility, innovation, and adaptability of economic operators, which led to reduced productivity and—contrary to the model's aims—greater unemployment.

A peculiar phenomenon observable in the continental European societies was that as they grew richer, the available workforce shrank. These countries, especially Germany, found themselves in a difficult situation, because their economies were mainly based on their traditionally developed industries, and this became more of a disadvantage with the global revolution of the services sector in the early 1980s. It became clear that the era of national economic strategies, like Germany's, based on big international industrial firms had come to an end. Because these big multinational companies are the movers and the shakers as well as the beneficiaries of globalization, they are quick to relocate to countries offering cheaper labor—leaving their erstwhile national patrons in the lurch. Conversely, the United States, the United Kingdom, and Ireland were keen to adapt to the changing environment and thus make their economies service oriented and information technology focused, one of the key guarantees of innovation and maintaining a competitive edge. Moreover, their stock exchange–based financial and corporate management systems proved to be better suited to the fast-changing conditions of increasing globalization.

The current difference between the United States and the EU in per capita gross domestic product is fundamentally attributable to three factors: the EU's one-third or shorter working hours, one-third or lower employment rate, and one-third or lower rate of productivity. In the EU, the number of working hours per worker has been falling steadily since the 1970s, while it stayed unchanged in the United States, partly because of more flexible employment solutions and massive immigration. And we could continue: Europe's competitiveness hovers at the U.S. level of the 1970s; the last time the level of employment stood at 64 percent in the United States was back in 1978; and the money Europe devoted to research and development in 2004 corresponds to America's research and development expenditures in 1979.[3] One out of three Americans has a college or university degree, whereas only every fifth European can claim the same, and American postgraduate education is generally more developed. The United States and the European Union are the world's two largest traders, with a combined global share of more than 50 percent, but the United States is better placed in markets where future growth will be concentrated.

It is also important to understand that although Europe measures itself against the United States, always trying to catch it up, America gives little thought to Europe. America is busy racing along so as not to be overtaken by the global pack, led by China. Europe has its job carved out: It has much catching up to do, but the train it is running after is moving ever so quickly. And Europe should not be triumphalist about the idea that America has been written off with the credit crunch and the global financial and economic crisis of 2008, which are indeed the worst since the Great Depression. First, this idea is not true; and second, Europe is not immune to the crisis's consequences—nor is China, for that matter. But let us look more closely at China's burgeoning positive prospects.

China has yet to become a financial superpower, but its economy boasts an astonishing growth rate. Undoubtedly, it will play a key role in the global economy in the coming decades. Many believe that the world's economic prospects are already largely being determined by the pace of growth behind the Great Wall of China. Let me illustrate this argument with some facts. In 2004, China replaced the United States as Japan's biggest trading partner. In 2005 China had overtaken the United States in the consumption of basic "agrifood" and industrial products.[4] The Chinese economy has a firm place among the top five economies of the world, but its dynamism is what is really breathtaking. The United States remains the world's biggest consumer of crude oil, and there are ten times as many cars in the United States as in China, but the gap is shrinking fast. In 2005, China led the United States in the number of television sets, mobile telephones, or refrigerators sold. An even better indication of the Chinese economic boom is the fact that Chinese companies have begun buying American companies. Who would have thought even a few years ago that a Chinese firm would buy the personal computer division of IBM? India is another serious contender with which Europe and the rest of the world must increasingly deal.

Forecasts until 2050 predict a growth rate of 1 to 2 percent in Europe, 3 to 3.5 percent in the United States, and 6 to 8 percent for Asia's emerging economies, which will bring about a drastic shift in the status quo.[5] Arguably, size is not everything, but the greater a region's economic power, the more say it has in world affairs. It will be a symbolic turning point when global economic and business standards no longer come from the European Union–United States–Japan trio but from China. The day when, for example, the latest generation of mobile electronic gadgets starts operating in accordance with Chinese standards from Singapore to Los Angeles will mark the beginning of the Chinese era.

I vividly remember watching in horror as the terrorist-hijacked planes crashed into the Twin Towers of the World Trade Center. Those who say that the September 11, 2001, terrorist attacks on New York and Washington marked the start of a new era are right in many ways, but I still think that this is an exaggeration in some ways. One thing is certain: Global-scale terrorism and the fight against it have become part and parcel of our everyday life. The main target of terrorists is the United States, but Europe cannot feel very safe either. For both Americans and Europeans, protection against terrorism requires more and more resources, while people must endure more and more insecurity. And along with the menace of terrorism, Europeans are increasingly anxious about the escalation of climate change.

Second, let us now start peeling off the onion's middle—*pan-European* —layer and focus on problems that affect all Europeans but are not linked directly to the EU. These include the future of the European socioeconomic model, competitiveness, the aging population, immigration, and energy dependency.

The generation that has had the good fortune to grow up in Europe in recent decades is probably one of the luckiest in history. However, the generous, caring nanny state and the security and prosperity to which this generation has grown accustomed have been somewhat eroded by recent developments, and it has become clear that the system's munificence needs to be trimmed. The million-dollar question is: Will Europe muster enough courage to push through the necessary reforms, and what will happen to the "European model"?

It is important to stress that there is no single socioeconomic model for Europe's development designed in and controlled from the European Union's headquarters in Brussels. Instead, Europe has a complex system of somewhat similar national models, which are the result of a long process of evolution. This patchwork of models can only be analyzed if we compare it with the corresponding American and Asian models. Thus, in today's developed Western world, we can distinguish two main socioeconomic models: the Anglo-Saxon model based on free market competition, and the continental European model based on social cohesion. A key trend of recent times has been the reinvigoration of the Anglo-Saxon model and the convergence of the social-cohesion and market-based models. Nevertheless, the 2008–9 financial and economic crisis in the United States made it evident that some of the basic principles of the American version of the Anglo-Saxon model need to be overhauled, in particular the regulation and supervision of the financial sector. The fundamental institutions of the two models are rather similar; both are built upon private property, a market economy, and the rule of law. The difference between them is that, in the continental European social model, the state plays an important role in redistributing wealth and caring for its citizens.

The Anglo-Saxon model's liberal cornerstones are free competition, market and individual freedoms, deregulation, liberalization, prices and wages set by free market forces, and a limited role for trade unions and the state. This model is characterized by low taxes and big income gaps. Conversely, the continental European social model, which is of primarily German origin, is firmly rooted in a belief in the welfare state, where the freedom of competition is balanced with social cohesion and solidarity. In this model, the state plays a central role, and accordingly the redistribution of wealth reduces differences between various social classes, which looks reassuring at first sight but raises the question of whether a generous welfare state is sustainable in the new global circumstances.

Almost all European countries, even with their slightly differing social models, are sitting on a demographic and pension time bomb. Europe's population is aging at an alarming rate, making its pension systems unsustainable. There are several reasons for this. The postwar baby boom generation is nearing retirement, and its life expectancy has improved significantly due to advances in modern medicine. Currently, there are four active workers for every retiree, but by 2050 this ratio will drop to one to two. In the coming decades, Europe's population will change dramatically, both in terms of its size and age structure, as a result of the falling fertility rate (1.5 births per woman, while a minimum rate of 2.1 is required to maintain the population) and the rising average life expectancy. The number of people of working age (between fifteen and sixty-four years) will drop from the current 310 million to 250 million in 2050. The size of the population above sixty-five years of age will double, to more than 120 million.[6] This quickly aging population foreshadows a disaster for the EU member state budgets unless their welfare systems are radically reformed. Due to the costs of supporting a growing number of inactive people, the developed industrial countries could see their credit ratings drastically lowered.

Aging has an impact on the whole economy. During the course of the last four decades, Europeans have grown accustomed to increasing prosperity guaranteed by a growing labor supply and rising productivity, which will no longer be present in an aging society. Productivity must improve to compensate for the shrinking number of active workers if nations are to realize their economic growth objectives. Without the necessary reforms, aging will cut Europe's growth potential, now about 2 percent, in half by 2040. The negative consequences look even gloomier in Japan, while the United States will preserve its relatively high potential growth rate of 2.5 percent.[7] Clearly, in the absence of radical reforms, Europe's welfare system cannot be sustained. With the current demographic trends, there are several alternatives for financing traditional pension systems: raising contributions, lowering pensions, or postponing the retirement age. But none of these is an easy or popular solution.

To what extent can a rising immigration rate serve as a panacea for Europe? Theoretically, immigration could partly offset low productivity and longer life expectancy. Conversely, immigration policy and control is a bit of a hot potato in several countries, even now with the current relatively small numbers of foreigners. It is commonly known that foreign immigrants make up 4.5 percent of the population in Europe and a mere 1.5 percent in Japan. Unless there is a sudden swing in public opinion and political will in favor of immigration, the aging of the population will be irreversible. Naturally, these issues cannot be judged on purely economic grounds, because —as recent events in France have shown—social integration is proving quite a headache for both political leaders and society as a whole. Economic necessity and social peace are the two objectives that a wise immigration and integration policy must be able to reconcile.

A finger reaching out and pushing the red button—this is what the worst-case scenario of the recent past boiled down to. Thankfully, our parents' worst nightmare never materialized, and the nerve-racking power struggle of the Cold War ended without a nuclear cataclysm. Then, recently, Europeans did see a finger reach out and push a red button after all—except that this button did not trigger a bomb but closed a gas pipeline supplying energy, heating, and security. Millions of Europeans sat glued to the small screen, finding themselves asking the same question all over again: What will happen if they do not find a solution? For a moment, Europeans felt vulnerable again, and maybe even began wondering whether they did use too much energy unnecessarily. In fact, at the moment, Europe can only supply internally about 50 percent of its energy demand, and this rate of self-sufficiency will drop to 30 percent by 2030. For the remaining 50 percent, the continent depends on imports.[8] What does the future hold for Europe in this field? It is unlikely that new energy sources will be discovered in significant quantities in Europe, and hence energy conservation through more energy efficient vehicles and buildings seems to be the only way to ease the continent's energy troubles. The trends, however, clearly show that Europe's energy dependence will further increase. Moreover, due to the demand generated by the booming Chinese and Indian economies, energy prices will keep rising in the next few decades. Thus, Europe is vulnerable. The EU's member states must join forces, but whether they will be able to do so remains to be seen.

Third, we have come to the onion's last, *internal* layer: the dilemmas and challenges related to the European Union and European integration. These are primarily decisionmaking, regulatory, and institutional problems, along with the need to deal with the uncertainty surrounding the future of the "European project." They include the fragmentation of the supposedly single internal market, the contested macroeconomic rules, the future of the euro, and the economic impact of further EU enlargements.

Europe is not as cheap as Asia and not as business friendly as the United States; thus, it must identify its strengths. Europe should make the most of what it—theoretically—has: the world's biggest single market. But does an obstacle-free single European market really exist? Although most of Europe does use the same currency, the internal market is not yet completely single; there are still many obstacles and shortcomings. And in addition to its economic image, Europe must also build a political image. We cannot yet talk about a common European foreign policy, and often we cannot even talk about common foreign policy actions. There is in practice no such thing as common European public life; an EU member state's domestic politics is almost completely isolated from those of other member states, and citizens have yet to develop a strong European identity. The public has very limited knowledge of European integration, and the situation is far from rosy as far as the European Union's popularity is concerned. The question is whether, in such circumstances, there will be enough courage and a window of opportunity to move toward a political union; but, if the answer is yes, will it not lead to the breakup of the Union?

In discussing Europe's layers of challenges, I deliberately chose an onion and not, say, a rosebud for the purposes of my comparison. I felt that there are more than enough books out there that talk about the—unquestionable —successes of European integration and that do not venture beyond a static description of where things stand at the moment. Admittedly, rolling in rose petals is more enjoyable than peeling onions, but in this book I seek to probe into the future and face the threats it holds for Europe. Accordingly, I focus more on the challenges and less on the successes. I do so not out of skepticism; on the contrary, I am guided by my genuine concern. I also attempt to propose solutions to the dilemmas for which so many in Europe are searching.

The European Union's Dilemmas

To illustrate the EU's dilemmas, let me briefly describe three of them. The first dilemma concerns the euro, the EU's single currency, which is a success story of European integration and thus has become a key, tangible symbol of Europe. However, the shortsighted attitude of some EU member states has harmed the credibility of the euro's stability. A number of recent political statements and analyses have raised the possibility of some countries leaving the euro zone, arguing that the Economic and Monetary Union's strict rules, by enforcing stability versus growth, actually impede growth. Such a move would be detrimental to both the member state deciding to leave and to those staying in the euro zone. The abandonment of the single currency could set off a major financial crisis for several participating countries. Outside the euro zone, the burden of financing public expenditures and the national debt would grow drastically, and the protective shield of the European Central Bank would disappear. The unilateral withdrawal of Germany or more than one big country from the euro zone would inevitably lead to the euro's death, which would in turn have disastrous consequences for the European economy as a whole.

The second dilemma concerns efficiency versus equality. The European Union is the world's most sophisticated and complicated decisionmaking system, which was originally conceived a half century ago as an elite club of six founding nations that spoke a common language (or—to be precise— four languages). Yet fifty years later, and now with twenty-seven member states (and still growing), the same system is proving rather cumbersome, which poses the dilemma of efficiency versus equality. Compromises are difficult to forge, deals are difficult to make, it takes too long for all the EU's members to give their approval, and it takes ages to translate all EU documents into its twenty-three official languages.

With the question of the EU's continuous enlargement, the third dilemma—of the EU's "deepening," promoting closer integration and even political union, versus its "widening," allowing enlargement with more diverse member states but thus also more complexity vis-à-vis integration— becomes increasingly acute. To deal with this dilemma, a two-speed Europe, which already exists in some areas (the euro zone; the Schengen

Agreement, which eliminates all internal border controls between its signatories; certain parts of the Common Agricultural Policy), could become institutionalized and pervade more and more policies. A true two-speed Europe could be declared openly as a result of a political breakthrough, or it could gradually and quietly come into existence through the repeated application of "enhanced cooperation." For this third dilemma of deepening versus widening, then, Europe must face these key questions: Will EU enlargement breed a two-speed Europe? Will the forerunners ever embark upon the venture of a political union? Will the EU ever be able to stomach a huge, poor, and Muslim Turkey? If there is two-speed integration in the EU, what model will those in the vanguard choose, and how will the "core" relate to the "periphery"? What will be the shared values and objectives of the "core countries"? Will they decide to cooperate because of market challenges and for fear of international competition, with protectionist intent, and be willing to defend themselves even against those countries on the periphery? Or, on the contrary, will their main motivation be their desire for faster reforms, market opening, and a more proactive role in global competition?

The fundamental questions raised by these three dilemmas boil down to the following: Will there be a true, single European market and a modern European model guaranteeing prosperity for citizens and competitiveness for businesses? In other words, can Europe reinvent itself? Will the European Union, a "hermaphrodite" displaying both federal and interstate traits, muster sufficient courage to embark on the road to a political union and a multispeed Europe, and will it be able to weigh the advantages and pitfalls of doing so? Or will Europe instead crumble under internal and external pressures? Will there ever be such a thing as a European identity and a European Olympic team? Or—more absurdly—will the time ever come when the question "Would you give your life for Europe?" will no longer sound as ridiculous as it does today? And, last but not least, to what extent will the hundreds of millions of citizens of the European nations be receptive to the political elite's great ideas for the continent's future?

All these concerns about Europe's future may bring to mind the fall of the Roman Empire—a core in long agony, finally swept away by its periphery. There are indeed a few similarities between the two historical cases, but in fact they are vastly outnumbered by the dissimilarities. The key difference is that the danger Europe now faces is not that of a thriving culture and civilization being overrun by barbaric hordes, bringing about an economic-social-cultural ice age, but one that is—ironically—far greater: No one wants to conquer and subjugate Europe anymore. The center of the globalized world has shifted elsewhere, while the "old continent" finds itself abandoned and deserted, watching the world speed by and brooding over its past glory.

Many believe that Western civilization, and with it Europe, is hopelessly on the decline. One can only hope that this is not how things will evolve. If Europeans want to avoid this gloomy scenario, they must understand two things. First, protectionism, through attempts to close Europe's gates to or demonize globalization, is doomed to fail. And second, they must accept and come to terms with losing some of Europe's weight in the changing world. Instead of chasing unrealistic ambitions in vain, Europeans must redefine themselves; they need a more modest identity and need to focus consciously on what they are best at. There are still many areas where Europe— the cradle of Western civilization—can lead the world by example. Let us see how.

The End of Liberalism?

In his best-selling book *The End of History and the Last Man,* Francis Fukuyama argued that the end of the Cold War also marked the end of history.[9] He claimed no less than that liberalism with its economic and political institutions has won the final battle; no ideology or worldview will ever be able to dethrone it. But fifteen years later, I am asking the question: Has the rule of liberalism come to an end already? Liberalism has many critics, who increasingly often resort to physical violence. Just think of the hysteria surrounding summits of world leaders.

Those opposing liberalism, though they may be extremists, can now be so loud and often successful in public life only because both the political elite and society as a whole look at liberalism as a husband would look at his wife when he has become bored with her. Liberalism has always been around, sitting quietly in the corner, but nobody gets excited by her any more. She gave birth to two beautiful girls, Prosperity and Democracy. Of course, her first-born son—Free Market Competition—is a real rascal, who has grown into a menacing man and now prefers being called Globalization.

If one defines "globalization" as the intensification of international trade, economic, and social relations—and I believe this is all it is, and nothing more, no matter how some pundits and politicians play with this word— then we must see that it is no spring chicken. The only novelty is that these processes have accelerated and now happen on a much more global scale. It is fashionable to blame all things bad on globalization. But the problem is not that there is too much globalization but that there is too little. It is much more understandable when the developing world demonizes globalization than when Europeans do the same. As long as Europeans called their earlier version of globalization "colonization," it was all right; but now that their once-despised former colonies in formerly remote parts of the globe are growing in strength and are even setting the terms for them, they are suddenly appalled.

The lesson to be learned is this: Without their aging mother, the children would be doomed. Without liberalism—that is, economic, political, and social freedoms—there can be no democracy and prosperity in Europe.

You could, of course, say that it is possible to build a sort of quasi-capitalism and perform economic miracles without liberalism. For prime instance, economic growth in China is at dizzying heights, and skyscrapers are mushrooming in downtown Shanghai. But the truth is that the Chinese economic miracle could not have happened without capitalism based on private property and freedom in the liberal Western world. China would not have the know-how, the major markets, the examples of modernization to follow, or the trade links if the Western world had not built a liberal world order over the centuries with blood, sweat, and tears—with which China is now trying to integrate in its own peculiar way. The success of the Asian tigers—Hong Kong, Singapore, South Korea, and Taiwan—often follows the same pattern: a mélange of a totalitarian political regime and economic liberalism. Undoubtedly, this model has contributed to the modernization of these countries; more prosperity sooner or later leads to more democracy. Yet naturally, these Asian societies, with their communal cultures, will never have the same attitude toward democracy as the individualistic Western cultures.

The tornado of globalization and China's enormous shadow have left even the most fervent believers in free competition shaken in their faith. Here, it is not George Soros and his militant antiglobalist sentiments I have in mind.[10] I am alluding to liberal economists' views that China's huge economic potential forces us to reevaluate our faith in the beneficial effects of global free competition.[11] Or I am thinking of Thomas L. Friedman—author of the multiple award winning *The World Is Flat*—who, seeing the influx of talented information technology specialists from India, wonders whether David Ricardo was wrong after all and that international free trade does more harm than good.[12]

In fact, there are several dangers inherent in liberalism, especially in the short run, and also in rising global competition—markets, professions, and jobs hitherto protected could be at risk; and some social groups may be forced to give up their privileges. So it is no wonder that the knee-jerk response of political protectionism exists worldwide, and is quite strong in some countries. Former French president Valéry Giscard d'Estaing, who could hardly be accused of Francophobia, writes in his self-critical book *The French:* "When the leading British-American economic press characterizes France as 'an agricultural country with strong protectionist traditions,' I believe they are right."[13] In fact, the ghost of Jean-Baptiste Colbert still seems to haunt the corridors of Parisian government offices. And to be fair, I must note that during the Doha Round of world trade liberalization talks, the main stumbling block was the United States' unconstructive attitude—the Americans figure that they can best capitalize on their superior economic and political might if they negotiate separate bilateral trade deals with different regions of the world.

There are, however, fundamental differences in economic philosophy, which are more important in the long run than the behavior of individual countries in specific cases. Let us step back now, put aside our emotions, and take an objective look at what we could lose if we gave up on liberalism. But to be able to do so, we must first make a historical detour.

It may sound bizarre, but this is not the first liberalism-based age in the history of humankind. (At this juncture, I must point out that I mean "liberalism" in a strictly economic sense. This original definition of liberalism would encompass a wide range of shades on today's political palette, from the reformed left-wing economic policy in Britain epitomized by former prime minister Tony Blair to moderate American conservatism. Liberalism in society comes in many different shapes and sizes, and I do not wish to delve into the question of how to define it. For our purposes here, let it suffice to define liberalism as the "ideology" of the capitalist model based on free market conditions, societal freedom, and the rule of law. The key concepts are freedom, individual, property, enterprise, competition, and free markets.) As I was saying, there has already been a world order that is liberal in an economic sense, based on the freedom—liberalization—of international trade and finance, which existed during the period from the second half of the nineteenth century until World War I.

Of course, with regard to that period, we cannot talk about a number of things that we today identify with freedom. Nonetheless, the world order of that period could justly be called liberal or—in many respects—even globalized. This golden age from 1870 to 1913 was similar to the post–World War II era, when liberal economic policy became the rule of thumb in the developed world, leading to an unprecedented upsurge in international trade. These two periods were unparalleled not only in the intensity of their global trade but also in their growth rate, and thus prosperity. Some even say that the most intensive period of international integration has not been the past two decades, which have come to be known as the age of globalization, but rather those between the turn of the nineteenth and twentieth centuries and World War I. This period had its foundations in free trade and currency exchange rates based on the gold standard. The free trade agreements that were concluded during that period by and between leading European countries would be considered modern even by today's standards. And the prices of the products that were then listed on commodity exchanges (e.g., wheat) converged at roughly the same levels on both sides of the Atlantic, for the first time in history.

It may seem unbelievable, but during that period, the links between capital markets of strong economies were more intensive than today. The liberal world of the time was built on the then-dominant British economy, which placed immense sums of capital abroad. If the United States, today's superpower, were to be as "global" in international money markets now as Britain was then, its foreign investment would total a net $20,000 billion. Of course there are thousands of other differences between the two periods, such as the geopolitical situation and the role of technology. But we are more interested in the similarities: a global world order based on liberalized economic relations.

A question naturally arises: If this world order brought prosperity, growth, and development never seen before, then why did it come to an end and why did it lead to a dreadful war claiming 8 million lives? There were several interrelated factors. The benefits of the golden age were unevenly distributed among the European powers and the different social classes. There were losers, both countries and classes, that wanted their slice of the ever-growing pie—and wanted it then and there. The political awakening of the working classes and growing nationalism proved to be an explosive mixture, which was used and abused by the elites unable to keep a lid on increasing internal social tensions. That World War I broke out was not the fault of the liberal economic world order, intensifying international relations, or growing prosperity. It was the fault of the political elite, or—to put it differently—of certain states that could not find the right answers to the challenges of an age bringing rapid social and economic changes. Does this sound familiar? I will return briefly to this earlier period of economic liberalism and what we can learn from it in the closing chapter.

In the end, the first liberal-global world disintegrated, and it made way for Nazi and communist dictatorships, the Great Depression, and voluntarist-perfectionist lunatics. Another 40 million people had to die for humankind to realize that things do not work like that. The more fortunate half of the world could return to its liberal roots and set up organizations destined to establish global free trade and regional free markets. The less fortunate half of Europe, which got a raw deal at Yalta, having found itself on the wrong side of the table, had to wait another half century until it could abandon an experiment doomed to failure from the beginning, but not before wasting five decades trying to make the command economy and party-state work. The ideology of, and daily life under, totalitarian regimes was extremely antiliberal. Communism tried to do away with fundamental capitalist values such as private property and free competition, just as it tried to dispose of everybody—eventually millions—opposed to it.

Many people—unfortunately, including a number of reputable politicians—think that the market is a jungle and the role of civilization is to tame it. I happen to believe that they are gravely mistaken; history has proven repeatedly that when politics seizes control over markets, prosperity and democracy suffer. Of course, you could cite the contrary examples of Attila the Hun, Alexander the Great, and Napoleon. How many countries in history emerged as great powers through wars, conquests, and pillaging, laying the foundations for their strength and importance for centuries? Well, those times are gone, once and for all. At the beginning of the third millennium, the human world has become so refined and complex, we have come to possess such dangerously powerful weapons, and our population has grown to such a critical size that violent solutions—that is, wars—are no longer simply morally wrong but could also jeopardize the whole world as we know it.

Today's world is a truly global one. Sooner or later, the opponents of liberalism or globalization must understand that—to paraphrase Winston Churchill—democracy may not be perfect, but we have not come up with anything better yet, and the same holds true for free economies, free enterprise, and free competition. There are two levels of economic liberalism: domestic and international. Domestic liberalism means the freedom to do business, nonintervention or a low level of intervention in market mechanisms, and the sanctity of private property. This has become the reality in most countries; capitalism is the dominant universal model, only questioned by radicals on the far left. International liberalism, an obstacle-free global marketplace, has been largely completed, or is developing by leaps and bounds, even though it is much more complex than liberalism at the domestic level. However, international liberalism—which, as I have explained above, is essentially globalization—is much less accepted. In fact, as also suggested above, globalization—the theme of the next chapter—is widely regarded as something negative.

There is no need to mince words. Adversaries of the European Union are right in saying that the EU is, in a way, a step toward globalization, because it is a regional alliance founded on the liberal platform of what have come to be known as the EU's "four freedoms"—to travel or live freely, to invest freely, to trade freely, and to provide services or to establish firms freely in another EU country. The EU's four fundamental freedoms are the antithesis of the four fundamental obstacles to economic and human relations, guaranteeing the free movement of goods, persons, services, and capital. Moreover, along the way, other fundamental values—such as social solidarity and environmental protection—have also come to shape the EU's policies. In the 1950s, Robert Schuman, once the French foreign minister, who is regarded as one of the founding fathers of European integration, wrote this about the aims of creating the European Coal and Steel Community—the forerunner of the European Communities and the EU: Europe can embark upon unification through the gradual elimination of trade obstacles, the rational coordination of production, investments and exports from different countries and—finally—the guaranteed free movement of persons and capital.[14]

The EU is often accused of being a red tape factory churning out rules by the hundreds. But one should understand that, quite frequently, it makes rules in order to dismantle obstacles and ensure the freedoms that are vital for economic relations, despite the protectionist intentions of its member states. Say what you will, but Europeans should strive to keep it this way.

In 2007, a financial and economic crisis started to suffocate the world economy. This led many people to rethink free market principles. Then in March 2008, Josef Ackermann, chief executive of Deutsche Bank, said that he did not believe anymore in the market's self-healing power. This statement was seen as a turning point, a real paradigm change in Europe.

In late 2008, the former chairman of the U.S. Federal Reserve, Alan Greenspan, admitted that he had put too much faith in the self-correcting power of free markets. "Those of us who have looked to the self-interest of lending institutions to protect shareholders' equity, myself included, are in a state of shocked disbelief," he said.[15] He acknowledged that his belief in deregulation had been shaken.

Greenspan noted that the immense and largely unregulated business of spreading financial risk widely through derivatives had gotten out of control, and he agreed that the multi-trillion-dollar market for credit default swaps needed to be restrained: "This modern risk-management paradigm held sway for decades, but the whole intellectual edifice, however, collapsed." But he added: "Whatever regulatory changes are made, they will pale in comparison to the change already evident in today's markets, those markets for an indefinite future will be far more restrained than would any currently contemplated new regulatory regime." During a hearing before a committee of the U.S. Congress, he was asked whether he feels that his ideology pushed him to make decisions that he wishes he had not made. "Yes, I've found a flaw. I don't know how significant or permanent it is. But I've been very distressed by that fact," he replied.[16] So America seemed to follow suit in the ideological shift.

Greenspan's successor at the Federal Reserve, Ben Bernanke, had no time for ideology. "There are no atheists in foxholes and no ideologues in financial crises," he said in the middle of the 2008–9 global financial and economic crisis.[17] World-famous economists like Joseph E. Stiglitz now proclaim the end of the "neoliberal" era[18]—and by the way, the 2008 winner of the Nobel Prize in Economics, Paul Krugman, was already arguing in the late 1980s that free trade was passé after all.[19] Government intervention and nationalization were on the rise in 2008 all over the world to save the financial sector, and people were asking for a new Keynes. Is this really the end of liberalism, then? No. Governments must act in extreme circumstances, but it does not mean the rebirth of socialism. Americans voted for Barack Obama basically to repair past mistakes and to bring a change into U.S. politics, but this did not mean the dismissal of free market basics either. Anyway, liberalism is much more than some would depict it as being—such as blind hope in the benefits of no regulation of the financial sector or in the market's perfect capability to self-correct. For me, liberalism is not the perfect ideology, and it encompasses not only the principles of free entrepreneurship and free competition but also that of control over and punishment of wrongdoers.

The heyday of right-wing free market enthusiasm, of Thatcherism and Reaganism, may well be over, and the pendulum has swung again to the left. Yet the more sophisticated a system is—for instance, the modern financial sector—the less such blunt ideological dogmas as the omnipotent self-control power of markets hold true. The global mantra that financial markets always allocate resources perfectly was never true anyway. Any dogma becomes counterproductive at some point. Having said this, liberalism has not been surpassed. Appearances can be deceptive; liberalism may be under constant attack, but it is still holding out and is not about to go under. The enthusiastic faith in government regulation and intervention will fade away. Within a few years, once the 2008–9 global crisis is well past, the pendulum will start swinging back, and praising the market will no longer be a suicidal or extremist stance. I am certain that this day will come soon. In the meantime, Europe must control its protectionist instincts and avoid overreaction. Anyway, it is not Europe's task to revive the idea of liberalism; all it must do is make sure that it does not set sail in search of happier havens.

Chapter 2

Global Problems: The External Layer

Climate change, the global demographic shift, the rise of Asia, the dramatic effects of globalization on Western social systems, increasing competitive pressure, the more and more anxious middle classes in Europe and in America—all are common issues in the headlines today. This chapter explores these issues and reflects on their significance for the future of the old continent and how Europe should deal with them.

Global Trends

To forecast future developments in Europe, the broadest underlying trends —such as environmental and demographic changes and the availability of basic resources—first need to be briefly examined. Then it is useful to touch on how the forthcoming changes in the global economic and demographic environment could affect the geopolitical order.

Can We Trust the Forecasts?

We have learned to take forecasts with a large pinch of salt, especially when they relate to the distant future, even if they come from acknowledged academics, research fellows, or futurologists. And although these forecasts today use strictly scientific methods, often mathematical models analyzing vast amounts of data, they cannot free themselves from the present. A seemingly unprofessional but actually illustrative example is the visual design and operating principles of the "technology of the future" for computers, weapons, and spaceships in old science fiction movies. Thus George Lucas, when producing episodes one to three of the *Star Wars* films twenty years after the original movies, had to "dumb down" their visual design to the level of the first parts of Luke Skywalker's tale. In other words, we are held captive by the present and often commit the mistake of extrapolating today's trends into the future in a linear fashion.

But humanity, being the curious and endeavoring species it is, cannot live without the excitement of wanting to know what the future holds. To err is human. There have been many erroneous predictions throughout history—some feared global suffocation from the smoke of the steam engine, some believed that humankind had invented everything there was to invent, and one gentleman (whom I will talk more about later in the book) went as far as predicting the end of history at the end of the Cold War. Paul Kennedy, another eminent thinker and author of the best-selling book *The Rise and Fall of the Great Powers,* published in 1987, in a recent light-hearted interview rated his own geostrategic forecasts as "below average." Two decades ago, he predicted the survival of the Soviet Union and the weakening of the United States. He was right on one point, however—he, too, saw China as the superpower of the future.[1]

Demography

Despite the limitations of forecasts, I must try to make some predictions on global social and economic trends pertinent to the topic of this book. Undoubtedly, demographics is a key area of consideration for futurology. There are numerous forecasts on population change; for instance, according to the United Nations, if the current pace of growth continues, the world's population will have shot to 40 billion by 2100, to 204 billion by 2150, and to 1.3 trillion by 2300.[2] These are obviously absurd figures, but projecting current trends hundreds of years ahead into the future yields such calculations. In addition to the population's size, its age composition could also be a major headache: in three hundred years' time, when every second person will be more than sixty years old, and one out of six people will be over eighty, compared with today's one out of every hundred. Of course, this model disregards potential revolutionary improvements in medicine and genetic engineering, which may as much as double current life expectancy.

There are less pessimistic forecasts as well, which calculate that the world's population will level out at around 10 billion in 2050 and hover around the same level afterward. In 1800, the world supported only 1 billion people, while humankind's current daily birthrate of 200,000 means that by 2013 there will be 7 billion of us sharing planet Earth. Out of every 100 babies, 57 are born in Asia, 26 in Africa, 10 in America, and only 5 in Europe. Optimistic scientists reckon that the present exponential population growth will slow down and even come to a halt. They enumerate a number of reasons for this prediction, the most important being the worldwide spread of birth control and unforeseeable factors, such as pandemics or wars. What can we deduce from these forecasts? The world's population will surely grow, but it is difficult to say by how much. Yet, however steep the rise will be, it seems certain that its bulk will not be in Europe.

Since the beginning of time, there have been 100 billion people born into this world. At the time of Christ's birth, only 300 million people populated the six continents, every sixth person lived in the Roman Empire, and the average life expectancy was twenty-four years. It sounds unbelievable but, in the mid–seventeenth century, there were still only 500 million Earthlings living an average thirty years. Then came a dramatic change—the Industrial Revolution—and, during the two hundred years that followed, the global population trebled. The second half of the twentieth century, the age of globalization, also brought a "population big bang," with less than fifty years required for the number of people inhabiting the world to double. About one-fifth of this population explosion came from India and one-tenth from China, which indicates that India will surpass China in the foreseeable future. By 2050, around 85 percent of the world's population will live in a so-called developing country. The population of these countries will increase threefold, while in Hungary and Italy it will fall by a quarter, and in Russia and Ukraine by a third.

Another noteworthy demographic trend is the acceleration of urbanization and the emergence of the megalopolis. In the early twentieth century, townsfolk numbered a mere 150 million; a century later, 3 billion people live in urban areas. Cities have always been one of the driving forces behind the development of human culture and modernization (Jane Jacobs, the late urbanist, went as far as to say that cities and not countries are the real engines of economic growth in the world[3]), but modern urbanization is more than that. Hundreds of millions of people are moving from rural areas to cities or their suburbs to escape extreme poverty, and these disadvantaged people have not the slightest chance of integrating into the life of the urban middle class. The global urban population is growing at three times the rate of the rural population and, during the course of 2007, the world's *urbanites* began to outnumber its *villagers*. In the next thirty years, population growth will be concentrated almost exclusively in cities; according to forecasts, by 2015 there will be twenty-three megacities with more than 10 million inhabitants, enormous conurbations of environmental pollution and urban poverty.

A snowballing global population could have unforeseeable consequences. Therefore, the developed countries—including those in Europe, of course —must counter the escalating situation by spreading modern birth control techniques and making them an established habit. The most terrifying consequence of overpopulation could be wars sparked by clashes over the possession of increasingly scarce resources. Have you ever thought about the fact that small wars have claimed 20 million lives since World War II, which killed 40 million people? Of course, in today's world order, an armed conflict between global superpowers is unthinkable, but the 20 million victims should serve as a memento that, in human history, periods of war have lasted longer than times of peace. The Cold War is over, but not all nuclear warheads have been disarmed. There are still close to 30,000 deployable warheads out there, two-thirds in Russia and one-third possessed by the American army—and in the wrong hands, a single one could prove fatal. But enough gloomy antiutopian thoughts. Let us return to reality and the problem of the shortage of resources.

Resources

It may be surprising, but I will not first turn my attention to oil. Another natural resource—water—is literally vital for survival and is becoming an increasingly precious asset. Agriculture is the biggest consumer of freshwater, because it must supply foodstuffs to a global population that is growing exponentially. Logically, water use in agriculture is increasing exponentially as well. It is therefore not accidental that water is becoming as much of a security issue worldwide as oil. Forecasts are alarming; global water use will double by 2050 and, by 2025, two out of three people (roughly 5 billion) will not have access to enough potable water. Already, now, some of the biggest rivers—such as the Amu Darya, the Colorado, and the Yellow—run dry in some seasons, and they may be soon followed by the Ganges and the Indus. China, India, and the United States, the world's largest grain-crop-farming countries, use more of their subterranean water reserves than are being replaced, and thus the water table is being depleted at a fast pace. If water shortages cause grain crop yields to drop, China will need to import more, causing price hikes in the world market, and the poorest countries will find it difficult to feed their starving populations.

Water is thus a sensitive resource, and the rivers carrying it cross many borders, occasionally those between countries with a history of tensions, which can easily incite another conflict. Diverting a watercourse in one country can have substantial effects in another one downstream. No wonder that Boutros Boutros-Ghali, the then–UN secretary-general, predicted twenty years ago that the water carried by the Nile River would be the main bone of contention in a water-hungry Middle East. One of the great fiascos of the modern European powers and the biggest test of European integration to date erupted in this very region during what came to be known as the Suez Crisis of 1956.

I will discuss the consequences of the depletion of energy resources and the astounding pace of growth in energy demand in chapter 3, but here let me share a few figures with you to illustrate my point. Between 2000 and 2030, the world's energy use will increase by one and a half times due to rising demand in developing countries. In the same three decades, Asia's energy needs will more than double. Such a stupendous increase will rearrange the international power balance as energy-importing countries become more and more dependent on energy-rich countries. The prosperity of the European Union and the entire European region will hinge on the supply of energy from third countries. Oil consumption goes up by 2 percent every year, which means 120 million barrels a day in 2020, when half the oil will come from countries with considerable problems of domestic instability. A growing hunger for energy and the resulting carbon emissions will have a huge impact on the environment and the Earth's climate. Scientists reckon that carbon emissions could almost double between the turn of the millennium and 2020.[4]

The Environment and Climate

One of the toughest questions bearing down on humanity is whether the environment will be able to cope with pollution, deforestation, and other curses of civilization. Humankind has always influenced its own environment; the difference is that today's huge human population—which will only become bigger in the future—is doing so by means of energy-intensive technology. I have noted the polluting role of megacities; London, for example, produces 23 million metric tons of industrial and communal waste and sewage each year. The list of related problems and dangers is endless. In the last hundred years, forest areas have dwindled by half, every tenth tree species is on the brink of extinction, while three-quarters of the world's fish stock suffers from overfishing and is unable to recover—and so on and so forth.

One of the hottest global environmental issues is climate change, also known as global warming. Over the eons, the Earth has warmed up and cooled down several times before, as its orbit around the Sun has changed. In other words, climate change is a natural geological phenomenon. The problem stems from the fact that the impact of human activity is of such magnitude that it alters the natural course of spontaneous geological processes and tampers with the mechanisms of the biosphere. Industrial and household emissions have skyrocketed in recent decades, and we have no reason to believe that this trend is going to change. This could amplify self-induced and negative processes, which could further aggravate global warming. Statistics now reveal that global warming is indeed happening, and we can already see its first consequences: rising sea levels and desertification. Forecasts for global warming in the coming century vary between 1.0 and 3.5 degrees centigrade, which may sound insignificant to a layperson but is in fact uncomfortably high.

The inhabitable part of the Earth is a complex ecosystem that has evolved over the course of billions of years and rests on the fragile symbiosis of millions of living creatures and inanimate factors. Overpopulation is contributing to a quick deterioration in the condition of our ecosystem, but it is difficult to assess the role of human expansion in this deterioration. Nonetheless, one can safely say that humanity is to some extent responsible for climate change and could play an important role in slowing down the further worsening of the situation or in stopping it altogether. The European Union's member states signed the Kyoto Protocol, which intends to cut global emissions of greenhouse gases. The EU members and the protocol's other signatories have pledged to reduce their emissions by 8 percent by 2012 relative to 1990 levels. Despite American efforts to throw a spoke in the wheel of Kyoto, with Russia's decision to join the pact, it finally entered into force at the beginning of 2005. Unfortunately, the European emissions trading scheme designed to help member states meet their commitments turned out to be a washout. Nevertheless, the old continent remains a model for environmentally conscious development. Europe has nothing to be ashamed of; it has done its best to forge a platform for international cooperation to counter climate change and environmental pollution, and it is not its fault that its noble attempts have more or less failed. Having a clear conscience, however, will not stop soil erosion or glaciers from melting.

A much-awaited climate change report by Nicholas Stern, a former senior economist at the World Bank, was published in October 2006. The report predicts that, by 2050, climate change could reduce world economic output by as much as £6 trillion, which roughly equates to the total gross domestic product (GDP) of the European Union. Due to the increase in temperature of 2 to 3 degrees centigrade forecast for 2050, some countries could face a drastic drop in rainfall, while others could be flooded by melting glaciers. The result could be the biggest wave of migration ever seen in history and, in the coming few decades, humankind will face the threat of an enormous economic and social cataclysm comparable to the world wars of the twentieth century or the Great Depression.[5]

"We, the human species, face a planetary emergency," said Al Gore, former vice president of the United States, who joined European politicians in their efforts to set an ambitious timetable for a global climate change deal in 2007 in Bali. But even these joint forces were not enough, and thus it seems that Europe must proceed alone, at least for a while.

Technology

Technological progress is fundamentally positive; I would not want to give the impression that innovation, knowledge, and technological progress only do harm. Far from it. Science and technology have been advancing with giant strides in recent decades; scientists have made more discoveries since World War II than in all the years since the beginning of human civilization. Technological and scientific progress will continue at breakneck speed, which could yield solutions that would be considered science fiction today. Moon travel could become available to everybody, we could project pictures onto the retina, heart transplants could become a routine operation like a tonsillectomy, and God knows where the limits of genetic engineering or nanotechnology may lie. You may have heard about Moore's Law, laid down by Gordon Moore decades ago, which stipulated with an eerie precision that microchip capacity would double every eighteen months. During a recent presentation in Munich by a marketing director, I was shocked to hear that a computer that comes standard with the latest BMW 7 Series automobile has 1,000 times the capacity of the computer that the U.S. National Aeronautics and Space Administration used during the first lunar landing. We can now read about the so-called Carlson curve, which predicts a similar pace of progress in the area of gene technology. If current trends continue, by the end of the decade, a single day will be sufficient time to synthesize a DNA chain containing the entire human genome.

European governments and companies spend less on research and development than their counterparts overseas, which is believed to be one of
the reasons behind the growing gap in technological progress between the
two sides of the Atlantic. Grand schemes are elaborated to address this gap,
but they are worth precious little as long as researchers and companies prefer the United States and the superior conditions it offers. The soaring
progress of medicine and genetics, for example, will probably boost average life expectancy, putting social care provision under considerable strain
as more retired people become dependent on fewer active workers.

The North/South Divide

Let us now focus on the individual. How will he or she live in decades to
come, and what dangers will he or she face? First of all, it must be said loud
and clear that, despite all the alarming figures and gloomy forecasts, the
luckier half of humankind inhabiting the Northern Hemisphere, also known
as the developed world, has never lived in as much prosperity and security
as it does now, at the turn of the third millennium. Moreover, growth and
progress are reaching more and more developing (i.e., less-developed) regions of the world, mainly in the Southern Hemisphere, bringing wealth and
improved living standards. On a global level, however, the problem is that
a substantial and growing part of the world's population, mainly living in
Africa, is unable to break out of a hopeless state of poverty. The problem is
not that these people live under worse conditions than they did fifty years
ago, because they do not. The problem is that their poverty is perpetuated
in a globalized world of improving living standards, exacerbated by the fact
that more and more of them live in the centers or outskirts of jam-packed
cities, where social problems created by high population density and scarcity
of resources can easily turn into disasters, such as epidemics, famines, and
armed conflicts.

Analysts occasionally underestimate future trends in the developing
world, known as the global South. In 1990, for example, UN analysts predicted that the number of people suffering from HIV/AIDS would not reach
25 million by the turn of the millennium. In reality, the number of HIV in-
fections rose to 36 million, with more than 25 million in Africa alone. In
Zambia and South Africa, every fifth adult, and in Botswana every third,
carries the deadly disease. Viruses and pandemics do not spare the rich
North, but with its high-standard medical care and an extensive technological arsenal, it is better equipped to protect its citizens. What can the world

and Europe do with a continent like Africa, with its prevailing poverty and a population decimated by diseases? The European Union is the world's biggest provider of financial assistance and aid to developing countries. In 2005, its development aid budget totaled €43 billion, which was more than half of all global aid to these countries but still only represented a few tenths of a percent of the EU's GDP.[6] Is that sufficient? Of course not. It is not that the sum is too low, but that most of this aid is used for "emergency repairs" instead of tackling the roots of the problems. As the saying goes, instead of handing out fish, aid programs should hand out fishing nets and teach people how to fish.

A Clash of Civilizations?

There is a Hungarian saying that a lot of good people can get by with a little space. Nevertheless, goodness is a subjective notion. "Good" is sometimes interpreted as "similar." What is different is seen with suspicion and perhaps as even dangerous. When more and more different people compete for a given set of assets, conflicts can be easily sparked. Hostility toward different peoples, cultures, and groups runs through human history, and these hostile sentiments often lead to aggression. This is not surprising; the ancient reflex of "us and them" is programmed deeply into our instincts, as fans at any soccer match demonstrate. In his award-winning book *The Clash of Civilizations,* Samuel Huntington predicts that the Judeo-Christian and Muslim cultures will be unable to live peacefully side by side, and thus a clash between them is unavoidable. In the new millennium, especially since the September 11, 2001, terrorist attacks on the United States, Huntington's prediction seems to be proving true.[7] Clashes between religious fundamentalism and terrorism are not a newfangled phenomenon, but they have come to set the climate of public life worldwide and serve as tangible proof of the unavoidable clash of cultures. European countries, particularly those with a sizable Muslim minority, must allocate substantial resources to combating terrorism and maintaining social peace.

According to some forecasts, in fifty years' time the world will be divided into three groups. The first group will be the vanguard of "globalization," accounting for three-quarters of economic output and half of the global population, with a middle class growing in strength and wealth. The second group will be a backward, fundamentally Muslim "world," accounting for a third of the global population but only 5 percent of economic output and consumption. Finally, the third group will comprise fall-behind countries, making up 15 percent of the global population and producing one-fifth of global GDP. If you have automatically put the European countries in the first group, you are wrong. Europe, along with South America, will be in the third group. Other analysts predict that, in addition to its economic decline and comparative loss of competitiveness, Europe will experience a slow erosion of its European cultural identity, an increase in its Islamization through continuous cultural relativism, a break with liberal principles, and a rejection of globalization.

Futurology—Once Again

The Reverend Thomas Malthus, the eighteenth-century economist who is considered a pioneer of futurology, prophesied two hundred years ago that farming would be unable to keep up with the pace of population growth, and that this would send devastating waves of famine around the globe. By projecting the trends of his time into the future, Malthus arrived at false conclusions. Naturally, he could not foresee the impact that new farming machinery, artificial fertilizers, or genetic engineering would have on improving the efficiency of agriculture. Although the world has seen famine, fundamentally, the trends are pretty much the opposite of what Malthus foresaw—despite the population explosion, there is a glut of food. People in the developing world are starving not for financial reasons but because of production and capacity problems.

Contemporary thinkers can sometimes get it awfully wrong; not a single social scientist would have predicted the collapse of the Soviet Union. Who would have imagined that the former western movie star turned U.S. president, Ronald Reagan, and his aggressive armaments policy would bring the Russian bear to its knees so quickly? Nevertheless, some global trends remain unquestionable and certain. As we have seen, these trends usually do not favor Europe, but Europeans must learn to live with them and take them into consideration when defining future European strategies.

Globalization

It is a dull Sunday afternoon in Brussels when my mobile telephone suddenly starts ringing. It is my eighty-three-year-old grandmother calling from a small town in Hungary. "I am reading one of your books, but there is this one word I cannot understand. First I asked your mother and father to explain it to me, but I was still not sure what it meant exactly. We have tried searching the Internet but without much success. I have even called your sister in Budapest, but she was not much help either. So I figured it is best to call and ask you directly." At this point, I ask her what the confounded word is. "Globalization," she says.

People talk a lot about globalization, but usually as a distant and mysterious danger looming ahead and casting a shadow over our future, as an intangible manipulation directed from the dark boardrooms of multinational corporations. We do not realize that we are inside globalization, caught up in it up to our ears, taking part in it every hour of every day. That is why it is such a difficult concept to define, and why there are so many interpretations and misinterpretations of its significance.

The concept of globalization and references to it became trendy in the 1990s, but—as I have said—the concept is understood in many different ways. Globalization means that economic actors and the man in the street cannot disregard events taking place in the far corners of the world because countries, companies, people, and events are increasingly closely interlinked. The liberal definition of globalization is the cross-border integration of economic activities. If one thinks about it, this definition could just as well apply to the European Union. In his amazing book *Why Globalization Works,* Martin Wolf quotes David Henderson, a former senior economist of the Organization for Economic Cooperation and Development, and his definition of globalization: the free movement of goods, services, labor, and capital, which creates a single market where foreign investors and workers are treated equally with domestic ones, without any discrimination.[8]

Dear reader, if you have not noticed so far, let me tell you now that you are an active participant of a historic experiment: The European Union is the manifestation of globalization in Europe. Has Brussels really pulled the wool over our eyes? Are we saddled with all the dreadful consequences of globalization—now institutionalized—and must we really live in fear for the rest of our lives, as many suggest? Naturally, the answer is no, but let me take a short historical detour before explaining why.

Globalization, and the liberal economic policy accelerating it to unprecedented speed, is—despite all criticism to the contrary—the guarantee of international stability and calm. In the last fifty years, international economic relations have become considerably stronger, leading to the creation of several international economic organizations, including the European Union. The volume of international trade and financial transactions has been growing at a tremendous pace. In such a world, any national power that opts for introversion and the traditional policy of territorial expansion over economic cooperation is gravely mistaken and unavoidably ends up on the losing end. I recently visited Serbia, and it felt like traveling back in time; Slobodan Milošević's insane war policy has left what was once Eastern Europe's most prosperous country in ruins and excluded from the international community. If Saddam Hussein had stuck to selling oil and had not started running amok twenty-five years ago, Iraqis could be living as well as their Saudi neighbors. Countries that are interconnected by millions of economic ties become enemies much less easily than isolated ones. This is particularly true if different countries are connected not only by trade but also by a network of international companies, production chains, and common standards.

Globalization is not only a guarantee of international stability; it also ensures domestic stability and the democratic process. In a democracy, the elite abstains from oppressing the weaker majority, those who have less money, power, and ability to defend their interests—in other words, "the people." Once the foundations of democracy have been laid, globalization is an important way of guaranteeing that the elite will not snatch power from the people through an antidemocratic restoration of the ancien régime. In underdeveloped social systems, the behavior of the local elite in possession of goods and assets is largely determined by the power of the public and the elite's fear of democracy. That is why it makes such a big difference for the elite as to what form and shape democracy finally takes and whether it remains within tolerable limits, for example, in terms of taxes on capital goods. International financial integration and well-oiled international financial markets make it easy for investors to withdraw their funds from a country, which in turn makes it harder for the local democracy to metamorphose into a populist, antielitist system. The elite tolerates democracy more easily when it feels safer, reducing the chances of an elitist coup d'état, a violent overthrow of the democratic order.

Another feature of globalization is that an explosion in international trade can facilitate democratization. Every country specializes in the trade of those goods that it has ample resources to produce. Rich countries naturally specialize in capital-intensive products and services, while poor countries focus on labor-intensive products such as clothing or agricultural produce. As the volume of international trade grows, the significance and value of the relevant resources for the country's prosperity also increase. This means that in poor and typically antidemocratic countries, the prestige and social significance of labor and workers increase, which in turn forces the local elite to guarantee greater freedom for the common people. Before a country becomes involved in international trade, the opposite is true; the lack of capital and huge oversupply of workforce preserves and reinforces the social power of the capitalist elite. As international economic, political, cultural, and institutional ties become more intensive—in other words, with globalization—it gets more difficult to dismantle democracy and oppress the people. (Acemoglu and Robinson take a new approach in their book and provide an interesting insight into this issue.[9]) Of course, this is all theoretical, and real life is much more complicated; globalization does help, but it would be a mistake to believe that it is a panacea for all of humankind's troubles. Globalization cannot do wonders overnight, especially—and it is time to refute yet another misconception—because it has been going on for many centuries.

A Short History of Globalization

Do not get me wrong. It is not the history of globalization that is short, only my summary of it. Three and a half millennia ago, there were more than half a million autonomous political entities (we can generously call them "countries") on Planet Earth. Today, there are fewer than two hundred. Something monumental must have happened; independent political entities began to establish closer and closer relations and to merge at an increasing pace. I would not like to commit the mistake of extrapolating this truly impressive trend and conclude that the emergence of a global political entity and world governance is unavoidable.

In addition to difficulties in politics and power there is another, even more important counterargument: In today's age of "turboglobalization" (on which more just below), the political framework is no longer a crucial issue. As long as the political system does not impede the forces driving globalization, primarily economic actors and increasingly individuals, a radical reform of global political governance is unnecessary. This means that nation-states play a shrinking role in shaping global conditions, although several fundamental international rules such as the world trading system and the international financial framework are still set by governments. For instance, it is hard to believe that, in the late nineteenth century, there were hardly two neighboring cities where the linear measures "inch" and "foot" meant the same. This created a lot of inconvenience and extra costs, which had to be addressed. Back then, they did not set up a standardization council; instead, they resorted to political and military means, and the unified German state was born.

However bizarre it might sound, for a long time, it was the state's political framework that paved the way for globalization because only empires, nation-states, and kings were strong and powerful enough to integrate and unify the patchwork of global political, economic, and cultural relations. But kings started losing power to the markets. British economists concluded as early as the seventeenth century that globalized capital markets not only make government intervention superfluous but also render it ineffective and even impossible. Governments' efforts to set the exchange rates of their national currencies or interest rates are not only unproductive but also detrimental. The—now widely accepted—theorem that global capital markets restrict governments' coercive power was first formulated twenty-five years ago. However, as governments' coercive power is rolled back, their economic power expands. Instead of coercion, governments can use globalized capital markets within the framework of private legal contracts—ideally— to the benefit of their citizens.

As economic actors with various activities, governments can benefit from globalization. They are compensated for their loss of power by the potential profits available for them as "regular" players in the money markets. By the eighteenth century, the globalization of capital markets had reached a relatively high level. The first international treasury bonds to be issued in a foreign currency date back to the 1730s. They were issued in London in pounds sterling and raised much more money for the Holy Roman emperor Charles IV than previous bonds issued in the national currency and thus only traded domestically. Even the head of what was then the world's biggest empire had to accept orders from foreign capital owners, just as any of us would need to do from our creditors today.

Globalization—the integration of political, cultural, and economic entities when geographic distances disappear—began well before the nineteenth century. From time to time, key events added new momentum to the process. For example, during the age of explorations in the fifteenth century, the Earth suddenly became round. Navigational technology and the mapping of the Earth shrank the world and extended Western ideology, paving the way for the Renaissance and later the Enlightenment. And today's "Information Revolution" is not the first one either; the "Internet" of the past was the printed book, without which neither the Reformation nor the scientific revolution and Industrial Revolution would have taken place.

Oddly, the first global world order was created during one of the least civilized empires in history, under Mongol reign. The enormous Mongol Empire was merciless in guaranteeing the security of its trade routes connecting China with the Middle East for the first time in the thirteenth century. Goods, services, persons, and money began moving between the developed China and the undeveloped Middle East more intensively and freely than ever before. But knowledge and technology knew no borders and spread all the way to medieval Europe, which opened Europe's eyes to the fact that there was a more developed East far beyond the neighboring Muslim world. Europeans began building ships big enough to go and explore the world at large.

As we have seen, globalization was propelled mainly by trade and geopolitical self-interest rather than enlightened ideas or technological progress. The foundation of the East India Company four hundred years ago marked a milestone not only in the history of colonization but also in globalization, especially because these two notions were inseparable for a long time. For Europe, conquering the Americas before China or any other power was a historic opportunity. However, the vast American continent was conquered by two very different Europes: the hard-working and trade-oriented Anglo-Saxons who landed in the north, and the eager-for-gain Iberians in pursuit of gold who explored Latin America. These two groups of conquerors created two very different Americas, and they benefited very differently from this godsend. The Chinese opium wars of the mid–nineteenth century were symbolic of the global conflict between an expansive West and a defensive East; Great Britain, the master of the first global world order, wished to enter the huge Chinese market, but China resisted. The global power, Britain, struck at the introverted, regional, medium-sized power, China, which centuries earlier had missed a crucial window of opportunity at the time of the Earth's "rounding off." China decommissioned its fleet, closed its gates, and let Europe "globalize" the world. We are witnessing the second age of globalization, which is happening at breakneck speed. Thomas Friedman calls it the "flattening out of the Earth."[10] I prefer to call it "turboglobalization."

Turboglobalization

The last one or two decades have brought a cataclysm in the world order unseen since the Industrial Revolution. New actors have appeared on the global scene: China, India, and Russia have integrated into the global fabric. China has begun to quickly build a capitalist economy and has joined the World Trade Organization, India has abandoned the self-sufficiency model that proved to be a dead-end street, and Russia has slowly recovered from the shock of the collapse of the Soviet Union and is now pocketing windfall profits from soaring oil prices. As a consequence, over the last ten years, the world economy has seen the entry of 700 million new workers in industry and services, which represents an astounding 50 percent increase in the global workforce. And all this has come at a time when information technology has been developing at a dizzying speed and communication costs have been falling at an unprecedented rate, opening the way for relocating thousands and thousands of jobs to the far end of the world, where labor costs are low, through outsourcing.

As a result of these dramatic changes over the course of just a few years, China has become the world's workshop, India has become its service center, and Russia has become its energy supplier. The developed world can respond to these formidable changes in two ways. It can press on with the counteroffensive, or it can seal its doors and fail. But more of that below, for now let us focus our attention on the level of unprecedented global integration, most of which is yet to come. By 2030, another 1.5 billion workers will have entered the global labor market, most of whom will have skills and qualifications comparable to those of Western workers in the lower segment of the labor market.

What has happened? What was the cause of this explosive change in globalization in the 1990s? The first shock wave came from the West, in two different forms. First, with the end of the Cold War, market liberalization policies became dominant, which brought about substantial liberalization not only in trade but also in capital movements and financial intermediary institutions. The creation of the internal market was a prime example of this.

Second, the staggering pace of progress in technology, especially in computer technology and communications, further shrank the world with elemental force. The international financial system was quick to follow; technological revolution and legal liberalization paved the way for money—the most mobile of all assets—to start moving at an astonishing speed between the far ends of the world in the form of credits, shares, bonds, and hedge transactions. The second shock wave came from the East as the two giants, China and India—together, "Chindia"—joined the global game. Dirt-cheap communications, billions of dollars moving in a split second, international liberalization, and the huge markets and enormous supply of labor of the two gigantic new contenders proved to be an inflammable combination—and the fusion torch of turboglobalization was ignited. Thus globalization came to symbolize various different concepts in a short period. First it meant liberalization, then it began to mean intensifying international competition, and now it seems to be synonymous with China.

Why is this latest globalization different from earlier ones? First of all, the extent and pace of integration of world markets are unprecedented. Today, trade accounts for 20 percent of the world's GDP, compared with 15 percent in 1994 and 8 percent in 1913, at the end of the previous age of globalization. The nature of world trade has also changed considerably. Developed countries used to sell "sophisticated" products to undeveloped countries in exchange for "unsophisticated" (i.e., low-value-added) goods. This is no longer the case. China makes and exports all sorts of products, including cutting-edge technology. The breathtaking progress of digital technology has broken down production processes and services into their constituent units, which has made many services internationally marketable or outsourceable. One would figure that sooner or later all economic activities will move to countries or regions with low labor costs. Yet, although financial services are among the most mobile, they are still concentrated in a handful of large centers, such as New York City, London, and Tokyo, where salaries tend to be the highest. This is because of the presence in only these cities of locally available, uniquely qualified specialists. In some less-advanced sectors, market proximity plays a bigger role; according to calculations, moving a factory from a region of 100,000 inhabitants into one with 10 million consumers can yield a 40 percent efficiency gain, so distance can still matter. China and India are the world's most populous countries, but their purchasing power remains relatively low. Where they have a competitive edge is in labor costs, because their wage levels mean that companies using their workers pay a fraction of Western payroll costs. However, the middle classes of China and India are growing rapidly, which provides a further incentive for outsourcing. The role and power of multinational companies in the world economy keeps increasing, just as research and development is becoming more and more important in corporate strategies.

Turboglobalization relies heavily on technology; there is a vast amount of global and mobile capital readily available for companies, investors, and people with good business ideas. Capital has become truly international; in 1995, foreign-owned financial instruments accounted for 57 percent of the world's GDP, up from 18 percent in 1980.

In the latest age of globalization, production has become as mobile as capital, and businesspeople have had to learn newly coined words, such as "relocation" and "outsourcing." Relocation implies that production is relocated lock, stock, and barrel to another country, where wages are lower; in outsourcing, only part of the workflow is relocated to another part of the world. Outsourcing is one of the biggest driving forces behind globalization; spreading out work geographically is like dividing a factory into divisions and moving them to different parts of the globe. The customer service telephone call centers of India are a perfect example of how this works.

There, about a quarter of a million English speakers answer the calls of customers from all over the world, but mainly from the United States. This is more than a multinational company that is present in several countries but without real cross-border production, because individual subsidiaries in practice operate independently. Outsourcing is the globalization of all globalizations—it is microeconomic globalization that really integrates and interlinks. Thus, turboglobalization is slowly but surely relocating the center of gravity of the world economy; the future has a dragon's smile.

Economic Globalization

It can safely be said that economic globalization is the principal component of the complex phenomenon of globalization. One can approach economic globalization from many angles, and one can try to measure it through many quantifiable phenomena. The most important ones are the extent of transnationalization, the expansion of world trade and foreign direct investment, market concentration, the volume of mergers and acquisitions, and the volume of cross-border production (outsourcing). One way of measuring the level of transnationalization in the world economy is to look at the share of foreign trade in the GDP of different countries.

On this basis, it can be concluded that transnationalization has been expanding at an increasing pace since World War II. The share of exports in the GDP of developed countries grew from 12 to 20 percent between 1965 and 1988, and since then this trend has only sped up. We must, however, realize that transnationalization is primarily the sign of merging among developed economies, and only recently did a handful of developing economies jump on the bandwagon. European economic integration has played a particularly important role in this process, as have growing transfers between Western Europe, Japan, and the United States. The acceleration of transnationalization since the 1980s has been largely driven by giant multinational companies.

The volume of world trade has also been growing dramatically, accounting for 5 percent of global GDP in 1950, 10 percent in 1973, and 18 percent in 1998. The volume of financial transfers not directly related to actual trade in goods is rising even faster. Foreign direct investment became the engine of the world economy from the mid-1980s on. Here are a few figures to illustrate the order of magnitude of such capital. In 1970, operating capital moving in the world economy totaled roughly $12 billion; by 1990, this measure had increased by a staggering eighteenfold, to $211 billion. Corporate mergers broke all previous records in 2000, both in Europe and overseas. In that same year, the total value of mergers of European and American companies amounted to $320 billion, with $224 billion coming from European acquisitions in the United States and $88 billion from American acquisitions of European companies. In the early 1990s, foreign subsidiaries employed 18 million workers; ten years later, this figure had trebled, to 54 million.[11] The stock market crash of 2001 brought a temporary setback in international capital investments and acquisitions, only to see them bounce back to 2000 record levels by 2005. We will have to wait and see what follows the 2008–9 global financial and economic crisis.

Undoubtedly, multinational companies have played a key role in global economic growth, in knowledge transfer, and in spreading new management models and a global business culture—and this role will probably continue to become more significant. A survey shows that the impact of the U.S. business cycle on the German and European economies has been falling since the 1990s; multinational companies have become more intertwined with the spread of microglobalization.[12] Globalized capital markets and global companies provide more and more of the momentum of the world economy. Since the 1990s, capital markets have been playing an increasing role in transmitting growth factors. Due to their size and global coverage, multinational corporations can elaborate long-term strategies that are independent of downturns in the business cycle, and thus the international commitment of corporations acts as a buffer, cushioning the exposure of national economies to the booms and busts of the global economy.

Globalization brought a qualitative change in the traditional international division of labor between the global North and South. New trends reshuffled international conditions; as a result of the major drop in shipping and communication costs, production chains could be shortened and the international division of labor could be deepened. Vast economies with an abundant supply of cheap labor (China, India, and Brazil) opened up, and together became more powerful than the previous wave of developing economies in the 1970s and 1980s (South Korea, Taiwan, Singapore, Hong Kong, Malaysia, and Thailand). Finally, through the foreign subsidiaries of multinational companies and with the help of advanced technology, the workforce and work itself became mobile. The international production and service provision workflow systems of multinationals encompass the globe as a meshwork pulsating twenty-four hours a day and seven days a week. Companies are no longer connected by management boards and markets but by information flowing through fiber-optic cables and work processes intertwined in millions of ways. Let me illustrate: Parts of the new Boeing

787 aircraft are made in China, Japan, Italy, England, France, and four American non-Boeing factories.

Globalization, unquestionably, has affected the development of financial systems and international financial relations to a greater extent than any other factor. As a result, the rules, principles, and decisionmaking mechanisms that govern the financial world have changed fundamentally in the last fifty years. The integration of international financial markets is now so intense that key financial products are traded around the clock and around the world by countless market actors. The role of exchange-rate systems has also changed considerably. The Bretton Woods system was based on fixed but readjustable rates, which allowed for small corrections within the system. The exchange rates of the three big currencies of today—the dollar, euro, and yen—float freely. Since the integration of markets, capital market rules have gone through almost global harmonization.

At the same time, the developed world has accumulated an enormous stock of savings in the form of pension funds or investment funds (some with assets far exceeding the GDP of a medium-sized country), which will go anywhere in the world in search of better returns on investment and risk diversification. Huge financial conglomerates with a global reach have been created, and these entities are present on several continents, providing banking, stock exchange, and insurance services. The volume and composition of capital flows to developing and emerging regions has changed; the volume of capital flowing to these regions as a ratio of their GDP has gone up remarkably since the early 1980s. The share of foreign direct investment within capital flows has risen, while that of loans has dwindled, which helps the more organic interconnection of national economies and companies, contrary to lending, which creates precious little economic linkage between lenders and debtors. There was a proliferation of financial services, with a new investment or hedging instrument added to the range of available ones almost weekly. This proliferation was followed by new global and international forums, international rules, and standards.

Economic globalization—as we have seen—began many centuries ago, often as a result of war, conquest, or empire building. Then, slowly but surely, it became obvious that trade was a more rewarding way of going about things. An ever-expanding global economic system was created, with its center of gravity in Europe in the nineteenth century and in the United States in the twentieth, which will probably shift to Asia and America in the twenty-first. Corporations and information play an increasingly central role in the process of economic globalization, to the detriment of the traditional nation-state. Nevertheless, we should not be misled into believing that the role of the nation-state has vanished altogether; states retain an important role in shaping the rules of the game and monitoring their observance.

A New Global Institutional Framework for Economic Governance

Globalization has changed how people, institutions, and corporations behave in numerous ways, often by making them unpredictable. Globalization is, however, not an unstoppable tidal wave against which governments are defenseless. Not at all. Governments can do a lot for or against globalization. The leading national powers are fundamentally proglobalization, and consequently the integration of the world economy continues relentlessly. Although, obviously, the influence of governments on global trends is diminishing, in certain areas they are holding on to their full and exclusive powers. Turboglobalization leaves governments with little time to revamp frameworks; market developments can make global institutions obsolete overnight. The global institutional architecture built after World War II was instrumental in consolidating the new world order, managing new conflicts, and spreading democracy and prosperity globally.

With the end of the Cold War and—more important—as turboglobalization has exploded, the time has come for urgent repairs to this institutional framework. These reforms are particularly pressing at a time when the multilateral approach of world trade liberalization seems to be faltering with the deadlock in the Doha Round of World Trade Organization (WTO) negotiations. The WTO is basically a universal institution; every country active in world trade is a member. Its decisionmaking is, thus, also universal; every member takes part in the negotiations and must give its assent to all decisions. Admittedly, this is all very democratic, but decisions made this way are watered down because they are based on a common denominator agreeable to all, not to mention the time required to reach a consensus.

The other key "globalizing organization," the International Monetary Fund, is facing the most serious crisis of its existence. Not only has the Bretton Woods currency system it was set up to manage been gone for thirty years, but the IMF's loans to developing countries are not as sought after as they once were; its lending is at a twenty-five-year low, and falling revenues have pushed it to the brink of a financial crisis. How could this happen? Oddly enough, poor countries are currently financing rich ones—mainly, China, with its immense surpluses on one side, and the United States, with a similarly immense deficit on the other. And private investors moving easily in well-oiled global capital markets are also able and willing to finance poor countries if they so wish.

However, the IMF's decreasing loan volume and falling revenues are by no means its biggest problems. Its structure and decisionmaking mechanisms are from an age long gone. Thus, Europe and the United States dominate its governance and decisionmaking; Belgium has more votes than India, the Netherlands has almost as many votes as China, and Europe controls 32 percent and the United States 17 percent of all votes. The decision was made in September 2006 to increase the voting rights of China, South Korea, Mexico, and Turkey starting in 2008, but India and the Latin American countries left out of this round of vote reallocations opposed the proposal. Nonetheless, Europe's prospects in the IMF—at least for voting rights —are not very bright; it has been suggested that European countries' votes should be halved to 16 percent. These figures are symbolic of a changing world. But the IMF needs more than a recalculation of votes; its entire function needs rethinking if it is to avoid marginalization. One obvious function for a reformed IMF would be preventing global economic crises.

Europe must also rethink its international representation. In the WTO, the European Union is a member in its own right, represented by Commission officials, which is only logical because EU trade policy is managed from Brussels. Why not have a single representative in the Group of Seven (the seven most developed industrial countries), the Group of Eight (the Group of Seven plus Russia), and the IMF for the EU—or at least the euro zone? This question has been on the table for quite some time, but so far its logical answer has always been rejected. Other new formations could appear, such as the Group of Four for financial cooperation, which was launched in 2006 as a pilot scheme and has the United States, China, Japan, and the euro zone as its members. Although it could reduce the role of Canada and the United Kingdom, it is necessitated by changing conditions. The significance of certain international economic organizations and groups keeps shrinking; thus, the World Bank is not really the world's bank, and Group of Seven meetings stir little excitement apart from antiglobalization protests. Besides economic and financial institutions, the global security network must also be reformed, taking into account new realities.

In the years 2008–9, during the global financial and economic crisis, it became evident to everyone that a globalized, incredibly interconnected world needs some global rules. This is especially true for those sectors that are most interconnected—and the first candidate is the financial sector, where the trouble started. In postwar economic history, this was the first crisis that started in the West; earlier, economic turmoil always came from emerging or developing economies. This fact shows how serious this current crisis was. The job of the West now is not to teach the rest of the world how to correct deficiencies and apply Western ways, but something much more difficult: to repair its own system, to render it viable. Otherwise, protectionism will come hastily and take the stage. Western governments—in cooperation with the other players—now have a great responsibility to set global rules for global capitalism, in fact, to set the basic global principles for the post–turboglobalization era, the era of G20 following G8.

Information and Telecommunications

During my traineeship at the European Commission ten years ago, I tried surfing the Internet for the first time. With an Austrian colleague of mine, we used an early version of Netscape to cruise the global information highway, where there were—in retrospect—surprisingly little traffic and only a handful of rather primitive Web sites to visit. Recently, somebody asked what I thought was the greatest achievement of the new millennium. "Google," I answered, without the slightest hesitation. It looks like I am not alone in this opinion. The Web site Brandchannel surveys 2,500 advertising experts and students every year about which brand made the biggest impact on their life in the given year. In 2006, Google topped the list, with Apple as runner-up and Skype (the Internet-based telephony firm acquired by eBay in 2005) as third. In fact, this was not a first for Google; it had already found itself at the top of the same list in 2003.

People tend to identify technology with information and communication technology (ICT), and, although this is incorrect, for the sake of simplicity and because we live in the age of the Information Revolution, I use this oversimplified definition here. Inventions and advances in biotechnology and nanotechnology could also have a major impact on the economy or on the whole of society, but ICT has a horizontal impact, transforming the economy, governance, and every area of life, and therefore it merits our special attention. The microchip is to us what the steam engine was during the Industrial Revolution; the Internet is today's railway.

However, an ICT fever should be avoided. History has seen other technological revolutions comparable to today's that gave progress and globalization new impetus. The first transatlantic telecommunication cable was laid on the ocean bed in 1866, which—among other things—enabled stockbrokers to learn about overseas indices in one day instead of ten. As a result, the price gap between similar financial products available on the London and New York stock exchanges narrowed by 70 percent overnight. The symbolic quintessence of globalization is exactly this: a product costs the same at the far ends of the world. And this 70 percent narrowing in the price gap was bigger than what the appearance of the telephone and the Internet would later bring about. From a global economic point of view, the greatest effect of the ICT revolution at the end of the last century was the profound transformation of the financial sector. The two fast-moving and thriving service sectors provided the right mixture to create an information and financial network covering the entire globe, which was to become the circulatory system of a global financial market with electronic stock exchanges buying and selling around the clock and financial conglomerates providing Internet-based services simultaneously on five continents.

In the early 1990s, the American technology sector was in crisis. Cheap Asian semiconductors were carving out an increasing slice of the market, while computers were mostly found at the workplace but underutilized even there. Then a group of engineers at the University of Illinois developed a small piece of software that greatly simplified surfing on the World Wide Web by eliminating the need to enter complicated command lines; instead, it provided a graphical user interface that the user could navigate with the help of a handheld "mouse," simply clicking on the desired destination. The Internet was born, which triggered an unprecedented wave of investment. The Internet gold rush (known as the dot-com boom) came and went, leaving millions of small private investors stripped of their savings once the stock market frenzy passed. Having the benefit of hindsight, we can now see that all that glitters is not gold. Or as Bill Gates put it: During a gold rush, the smart thing to do is not to join the gold diggers but to sell them shovels. Yet when the dot-com bubble burst, not all capital and intellectual investment went down the drain; some of the good things it had brought survived.

Although the billions that telecommunications companies poured into third-generation mobile telephony concessions proved to be a premature investment, the first third-generation services were launched with a few years' delay. The dot-com firms promising miraculous profits vanished, but e-commerce (online retailing) keeps developing with giant strides, and hundreds of millions of young people now use the Internet daily. Last but not least, the fiber-optic cables laid at enormous cost survived, and we can use them to communicate with the other end of the world (long-distance call rates have fallen from \$2 to 10¢ per minute).[13] Fiber-optic cable capacity will soon reach a level where it will take only a few seconds to send online all the texts that humans have ever written. I believe that this has also been one of the factors in Google's success.

Information technology is also a means of democratization. Internet access opens up the world; the World Wide Web knows no boundaries, geographical or political. No wonder that China only granted access to Google on the condition that it agreed to voluntary censorship. However, such restrictions are becoming a thing of the past. For long centuries, information had been the privilege of the great and mighty; today, almost all information is just one click away. And we can not only learn about facts and other people's opinions but also communicate our own opinions to the rest of the world. People seem to be taking advantage of this opportunity; a new blog (Web log, or online diary) is started every second. The Internet has revolutionized our daily life, a bit like the television did half a century ago. But the Internet is far from reaching its limitations, because only 10 percent of the world's information is available online and only 1 percent of Sub-Saharan African households have a fixed-line telephone. Maybe they will never need a landline. Mobile surfing seems to be the way of the future.

Culture

Globalization as a force for unification and standardization causes the world to shrink and brings common norms and behavioral patterns, which can endanger diversity and differences because open competition rewards dominance over the weaker. As corporate management culture becomes Americanized, so do global culture and daily life. "Americanization" is a simplified term, but its use is justified by global acceptance. Dominant powers are well placed to spread their own culture. At the peak of its power, the British Empire spread many behavioral patterns, although fundamentally in its own colonial area. American culture, however, has a truly global scope of impact—for two reasons. The United States is the leading power of a truly global age and has at its disposal the new invention of mass media. In addition to the dominance of gigantic financial holdings, global media concerns are the root of most of politicians' and citizens' anxieties. Both groups fear that profit-oriented media empires will brainwash people worldwide and contribute to the decline of alternative or national (non-American) cultures. Critics of global media argue that transnational media conglomerates narrow the range of available cultural goods instead of enriching it, by siphoning off funds from local media. Global commercial media overshadow public service programs, reduce the presence of political publicity, and weaken the cohesion of political communities by treating them as consumers rather than citizens.

The inclination to imitate others is deeply embedded in human nature, and it has often come in handy. If an individual or the members of a group see a good example, they tend to follow it. Problems arise when cultural patterns are forced upon people, as by Mao Zedong in China during the infamous Cultural Revolution. Voluntary imitation of a cultural example is a strong urge, especially if the example is at the global level and reinforced by the mass media. France is the main European champion of stopping this cultural globalization and, in fact, advocates of preserving alternative cultures are right in many ways. European culture, however, is stronger than many think, and though it may need some protection or special attention, its strength and depth will save it from marginalization. It is not in the area of culture that Europe needs help the most.

There is another reason why one should not despair that cultural globalization is inevitable. If we look back at history, we will see that this is not the first time that a culture has become globally dominant. Just think of religion. On a historical scale, Christianity took the world by storm and—linked with the massive political institutions of the Roman Empire—created a global cultural and institutional framework spanning millennia. Islam followed closely in the footsteps of the Roman Empire, taking over the role of the dominant religion in the regions it conquered. Or we can take more profane examples from the more recent past; the Enlightenment, Romanticism, and postmodernism all brought with them fashionable trends dictating values for some time in certain parts of the world. Much of Europe's strength comes from its cultural diversity. The cohabitation of dozens of cultures on one continent is what makes Europe such an exciting place, but unfortunately, in the long run, it can also make it economically uncompetitive, unless it does something about its fragmentation. Abandoning Europe's cultural diversity is not an option; even if it were possible (which it is not), it would be counterproductive. A sensible compromise strikes a balance between inspirational diversity and efficient unity.

We can trust European culture to identify with globalization and face the challenges it presents. Most European peoples have survived many disasters and various cultural shocks. They have shown that they can both dictate and adapt to trends, if need be. Europe has been home to the Protestant work ethic as well as the ideas of the Enlightenment. Supposedly, there are two kinds of people: the explorer type, the rolling stone, always moving on to see more of the world; and the inventor type, who is too lazy to get moving and prefers to stay put and create the things he or she needs. Europe has plenty of both types, so its people need not worry—especially because fear is a bad counselor.

Fears, Refutations, and Real Dangers

Still, many have globalization-related fears. I would like to dispel some of these fears, or at least allay them, and to discuss some real dangers. At the beginning of this chapter, I described the democratizing effect of globalization, which disproves the often-cited criticism that globalization kills democracy. Similarly, populist comparisons envisage the increasing power of blood-sucking multinational companies that act as the vanguards of globalization, surpassing governments in strength and defying democratic principles. Multinational corporations—the accusations go—unscrupulously exploit the resources of poorer countries, including their workers, who will become impoverished just like their jobless Western counterparts. There is only one thing more evil than a capitalist: a moneyed capitalist—critics say. Money capital moves huge sums with no real products or production behind it; only money, securities, swaps, options, and the Lord knows what else changes hands. If we look behind the childish anger of such criticism, we will see that financial globalization is not without dangers. Finally, another common criticism concerns the state and its weakening role: States are squeezed off the level playing field by the forces of globalization, and thus they can hardly fulfill their social tasks.

Are multinationals really the tyrants of the age of globalization? Let us not confuse apples and pears. States are trustees of public power—they can levy taxes, wage wars, or send people to prison; this is their job and obligation. One can hate international chains and giant conglomerates, but a cashier at Tesco will not ask us to pay taxes, and Coca-Cola will not enlist anybody to fight a war against Pepsi. Multinational firms may cheat their customers and exploit their employees, but they cannot make us do things we do not want to. In many ways, multinational companies drive forward technological and product development, and therefore it is absurd to claim that they impede progress. It is also relatively easy to refute accusations that multinationals exploit poor laborers in poor countries. Naturally, investors seek out cheaper labor, but launching production creates value, a part of which always stays at the place of production. Workers in poor countries may get worse treatment and lower wages than their Western counterparts, but to be realistic, we must always compare their situation with local conditions. The goods produced increase prosperity, which slowly but surely spreads through the country. And these are vast sums we are talking about; in 2001, roughly 11 percent of the world's GDP was produced by foreign subsidiaries of multinational companies. I am not saying that these firms cannot do harm to society, but—and this is an important distinction—they only become harmful when they do not operate by market rules, turn into monopolies, form trade-distorting cartels, or lobby their governments to delay liberalization in an attempt to protect their markets.

Are states really losing ground due to globalization? In many ways, yes. But this has not affected society negatively at all. International best practices and competition have often forced states to consolidate their democratic institutions and improve the standard of social services. Nor should states be portrayed as innocent victims of globalization; they consciously opted for trade liberalization and a common economic space in Europe. Globalization is happening as much by choice as by itself. We must see clearly that countries as well as societies needed globalization as the obvious instrument of modernization and growth.

Figures speak louder than general statements, so I will let them do the talking. If the role of states has really weakened, then their size (not their area, but the magnitude of state spending in relation to GDP) must have gone down as well. In fact, the opposite is true. Over the course of the twentieth century, state spending (as a percentage of GDP) increased steadily in the West, from 24 percent in 1937 and 28 percent in 1960 to 42 percent in 1980 and then 45 percent in 1996. The huge leap between 1960 and 1980 is particularly noteworthy and will be analyzed below, just like the fact that, in 1996, public spending in Sweden was double that of the United States (64 percent and 32 percent, respectively), although both countries started off from below 20 percent in 1937. One more illustrative figure to back up my argument that the state's role is as robust as ever is that the tax revenues of countries belonging to the Organization for Economic Cooperation and Development totaled 38 percent of GDP in 2000, a substantial increase from 25 percent in 1965. I will elaborate on this point in more detail below, but here let me assert my views on the size of the state: The problem is not that the state is too small but that it is too big. Gulliver the state is held back by scores of Lilliputians, actors of the free market—companies, consumers, and consumer groups. That is not a problem; quite the contrary.

There is one real danger related to globalization: timing. Problems arise when market developments and government action are out of sync, that is, when markets are too quick and governments are too slow. Occasionally, governments or the International Monetary Fund act too quickly, or some developing countries open their financial markets too hastily. This is what happened in Asia in 1998, for example, sending local currencies downhill, triggering an economic crisis in the region, and making a serious dent in the IMF's reputation. The problem of timing can manifest itself in many areas of the economy, but most especially in sectors where market development is fastest. Today these sectors are information and communication, and finance. Following the liberal flourishing of the nineteenth century, the world plunged into a crisis of overproduction, and more recently the dot-com bubble burst in the face of the West, although the two events cannot be compared in their severity. To trivialize the social tensions that are increasing with globalization would be dogmatism on my part. The relocation of production to Asia is a real danger for the working and middle classes of the West. The "anxious middle class" has already appeared in the United States, while in Europe, antiglobalization sentiments are something of a fashion in some circles of society and politics. Both theoreticians and governments would be making a big mistake if they were to sweep this problem under the carpet.

Now let us briefly examine the most nimble of all sectors, the financial world, and look at the dangers when governments act too slowly. A potential crash of increasingly globalized financial markets is not a negligible hazard. The situation is best compared with a contagious disease in a crowded room, where everybody is quickly infected. Today's financial markets and institutions are similarly crowded; banks, stock exchanges, and investment funds are interconnected by millions of links, and markets are extremely concentrated. If there is a problem, all actors will be affected, and a "financial epidemic" could wreak havoc. More than a third of interbank money movements (in the form of loans) are cross-border transactions between banks in different countries. Therefore, the collapse of a large bank in one country can easily have a domino effect in the entire region. Recently formed gigantic financial conglomerates—which are banks, insurers, fund managers, and investors all at the same time—only increase the danger of such a scenario. One shock can send several large financial groups into bankruptcy, which can have serious macroeconomic implications.

To make things worse, there is no systematic and organized monitoring of these firms at either a European or a global level. In a crisis situation, communication and coordination are hampered by conflicting interests, while supervisory authorities are frequently unable to work together. Once again, markets are ahead of the state; banks are international, but supervisory bodies are still national. Reinsurance firms (insurers backing the risks of commercial insurance companies) play a key role in the stability of the financial sector. The reinsurance sector is astonishingly concentrated; 60 percent of reinsurance deals are covered by five companies, three of which are European. Large-scale terrorism is making life more difficult for both insurance and reinsurance firms. In the securities market, cross-border stock ownership and stock exchange concentration increase vulnerability to a "financial epidemic," and a stock market scare can sweep around the globe in no time. Hedge funds have become major market actors in recent years. (Hedge funds invest huge sums in order to reduce risks for market players but, due to their size, they pose a risk for the whole system.)

Such intense growth raises concerns about the accumulation of huge potential risks in the hedge markets and, due to insufficient transparency, we cannot know for sure whether the system could handle a large shock. Another relatively new market is that of the so-called credit derivatives, which has been growing at a breathtaking pace and which is also a cause for concern, experts claim. In the age of global financial liberalization from 1970 to 2000, about 100 financial crises erupted in developing countries, and fewer than 50 in developed ones. Of these 150 crises, 30 involved banks, 90 involved currency, and 30 involved both. These crises set the affected countries back in their development, sometimes plunging them into desperate poverty. During the 1998 crisis, for example, Indonesia's debt went up by 50 percent of GDP. In the summer of 2006, the Amaranth Advisors Hedge Fund lost $6 billion in investors' money in just one week.

Hedge funds, credit derivatives—they sound gruesome. But there is no need to understand the intricate details of how they work; it is sufficient to know that they handle tens of trillions of dollars, grasp their significance for the stability of the global financial world, and appreciate why it is important to have timely supervisory instruments in place. It is no wonder that the world's three biggest financial supervisory bodies (the Federal Reserve and the Securities and Exchange Commission in the United States, and the Financial Services Authority in the United Kingdom) have issued a statement calling for the global coordination of financial supervisors as a means of guaranteeing international financial stability. (See the 2008–9 crisis.)

The problem of timing appears in another, non-sector specific dimension as well. This is the short-term/long-term contradiction of globalization. But what does this mean exactly? In the short term, there will be losers from globalization in Europe and the Western world. Factories, and production with them, will move to China, India, or Romania, and workers will lose their jobs. Cheap but high-quality products will flood the markets, and thus European firms will have to cut costs, typically by reducing wages. Rich countries could be home to more and more poor people if the shocks of globalization come too fast and, let us face it, they will come too fast. There is not a single politician or trade union leader who would be happy to sit down with a German factory worker to discuss this issue openly, which is totally understandable.

The lesson here is that globalization creates major problems if it happens faster than governments can act. The West, and within it Europe, must not shun globalization and the global community. On the contrary, they must assume the short-term losses to be able to remain competitive in the long run. If things work out well, in a few years' time the unskilled European worker will only exist in the pages of almanacs, because the few left will surely be unemployed. Many feel this coming, which explains the rising concern and anxiety. Recently, the head of a French company about to re-locate to Romania told his workers that he was willing to stay in France if the workers were willing to accept Romanian wages. A German company only canceled plans to shift production to Hungary because its workers agreed to a workweek five hours longer without any compensation. But Eastern Europe is not comparable to China in terms of wages, especially because in the new EU member states, the average income has been going up steadily since accession. Losses and tensions will be largely limited to a handful of low-added-value sectors and bring one-time costs. Conversely, according to the European Commission's 2006 forecasts, the positive effects of globalization could translate into €800 million annually between 2005 and 2050. One precondition would be that governments will not shy away from globalization and seal the borders. Western governments must look ahead and be proactive; they must invest in their citizens and arm them with the skills required in areas where Europe has a chance of competing with Asia.

The Bastard Children of Globalization: Climate Change, Terrorism, and Poverty

Globalization has its bastard children—climate change, terrorism, and poverty—major international problems that are routinely blamed on it. But if we look behind the scenes, it turns out that these problems would exist anyway.

Global warming has already been discussed above, and we have seen that the situation is not yet catastrophic but could become so, unless China does something about its growing hunger for energy sources and makes a serious effort to curb its carbon dioxide emissions. Is global warming attributable to reinforced international economic cooperation, more intense global trade, multinational companies—that is, to globalization? Partly yes, but only insofar as it has revved up the world economy. Globalization has nothing to do with the United States' refusal to sign the Kyoto Protocol. Likewise, China's amazing growth has only partly been caused by its more active participation in the world economy, and its use of outdated, environmentally unfriendly technologies cannot be blamed on globalization either. Just the opposite: The transfer of advanced technology and pressure by the international community will make China adopt greener technological solutions. Climate change is a global issue, but not a consequence of globalization; nonetheless, it requires a global answer. Europe can cut its carbon emissions as much as it wants, but it will not do much good unless China and the United States follow suit.

Similarly, the United States can reduce its oil consumption by as much as it wants, but as long as Brazilian farmers keep felling tropical rainforests, then on the whole we have not done much to stop global warming. Some influential American economists calculate that it would cost the United States about 1 percent of its GDP to comply with Kyoto targets. This 1 percent may look like a lot at first thought, but increasingly frequent and devastating hurricanes and dropping farm yields will probably cost much more.

Several measures could bring Europe closer to achieving its objective; thus, a single European energy policy would be a much better means of combating climate change than the current practice of EU member states pursuing uncoordinated national energy policies. The lack of a single European energy policy and market does little good for competition, efficiency, or efforts to reverse global warming. The problem should be tackled at its root. First, global energy use will continue to rise, and hence energy efficiency gains are needed. Second, energy production must be greened. As a last resort, an international tax could be levied based on a country's level of development, with developed countries paying the highest tax. The taxes collected this way would go to a fund, which could help poor countries purchase climate-friendly technology.

Climate change fills us with anxiety, but let us admit that it is dwarfed by the fear of terrorism. There have always been evil people blinded by their anger; it is not fair to blame the proliferation of terrorism on globalization, although it does make terrorists' lives easier. They can communicate more easily, and they have access to a wealth of information on the Internet quickly and legally, like everyone else.

Today's predominantly Muslim megaterrorism has evolved into a global issue since the September 11, 2001, terrorist attacks on the United States. The first suicide bombing of the modern Muslim world was perpetrated in 1983 in Lebanon by extremist Shi'ites, killing 241 U.S. and 58 French soldiers. This bombing targeted military personnel, unlike today, when innocent tourists and passersby fall victim to attacks designed to intimidate and terrify the world. For a while, suicide bombing was an exclusively male and religious business, but this no longer holds true. Wafa Idris, the first female suicide bomber, detonated a bomb in her backpack in Jerusalem in January 2002. Since then, many others have followed. Another recent trend is that the attacks are frequently committed by secular organizations and outside the Middle East.

If the West is to come up with the right answers to the megaterrorism problem, it needs to expose its roots and understand the reasons leading to it. Solving the underlying causes is the only viable solution. American military and antiterrorist action has weakened Al Qaeda but cannot handle the fact that terrorists in recent years have not been or have only loosely been linked to the most notorious terrorist organization. They are often young Muslims raised in Western countries with little religious education who resort to bloody terrorist acts due to their frustration with society. An average European terrorist cell is made up of ten to fifteen men of fifteen to thirty years of age born into and raised by nonfundamentalist local families, who are first operation oriented and only second ideologically motivated. About 70 percent of cell members join because of their former friends, and only 10 percent are organized by fundamentalist Muslim schools or organizations. The terrorist's average age is falling as more and more young people are tempted on Internet chat rooms by the image of these groups oozing with false heroism. The 2005 London Underground bombers regularly met in gyms and went on rafting trips while cultivating their radicalism to perfection.

Such terrorist networks are impossible to destroy with the kind of heavy artillery used to wipe out Al Qaeda. Some analysts believe that, in 1997, Al Qaeda had a three-phase plan: In Phase 1, find a large number of potential terrorists and train them in Afghanistan; in Phase 2, spark a clash between the Muslim and Christian worlds, starting with the attacks on the Twin Towers and quickly followed by the U.S. invasion of Iraq; in Phase 3, as the United States and the West in general get sick and tired of fighting terror-

ism and are worn out by the war of attrition on the eastern fronts, their retreat opens the way for Jihadist forces to take power. This plan builds on de-
pleting the U.S. Treasury, a bit like Ronald Reagan did with the Soviet
Union. In this respect, the estimated cost of America's war on terrorism is
roughly $1 trillion, while Al Qaeda has spent only a few million.

The terrorist threat has incurred costs not only for the federal government
but also for the corporate world, particularly in New York City. The Bank
of New York has installed two backup computer systems (perfect dupli-
cates): one 40 miles and one 600 miles from its headquarters at 1 Wall
Street. Some say that even these colossal sums are insufficient, especially
for external action—in Iraq, for example. During the Cold War, U.S. military spending amounted to 7.5 percent of GDP (compared with 33 percent
during World War II), but currently it hovers around 4 percent. I personally
do not think that this is the biggest problem. It is important to understand
that the United States and the West have suffered disadvantages that are hard
to express in financial terms, such as the shaken trust in society and feeling
of insecurity or the falling number of researchers and scientists settling in
the United States due to stricter visa rules. Six years after the collapse of the
Twin Towers, there has still not been a breakthrough in the war against terrorism; organizations recruiting men and women for violent acts retain their
appeal among young Muslims.

U.S. antiterrorist policy has been under heavy criticism for being exaggerated and not focused—particularly the intervention in Iraq, which
plunged transatlantic relations to their lowest ebb in quite some time. Following the 9/11 terrorist attacks, *Le Monde*'s headline read "We Are All
Americans." After the Iraq intervention, this enthusiasm swung over into
bitter anti–United States sentiments. EU member states were divided on the
issue, which was further deepened by U.S. secretary of defense Donald
Rumsfeld's remarks on an "old" and a "new" Europe, angering both Paris
and Berlin. According to a 2006 *Financial Times* poll, Europeans considered the United States a greater threat to global security than China or Iran.

Groups responsible for specific acts of violence, and thus receiving most
of the media attention, might not be considered Islamist in the traditional
sense and are much more like secular gangs, but this does not mean that radical Islamists do not pose a serious threat to liberal Western values. In the
eyes of radical Muslims, liberty, equality, and tolerance are not fundamental values at all. In the long run, this contrast will surely lead to tensions between the two cultures, especially because Islamist political forces have
been reinvigorated after suffering brief transitional setbacks (e. g., Egypt,

Jordan, Pakistan, Saudi Arabia, and Syria). The proliferation of terrorism has a much greater impact on the liberal Western world than does the loss of human lives and physical damage. Serious thought must be given to such questions as how liberal Western people can be, to what extent they can tolerate multiculturalism, and to what extent they can put up with having their liberties curtailed.

The key to handling the situation would be to have a carefully formulated multilayer social, foreign, and public order policy mix. First, this mix would manage the problems of frustrated Muslim communities living in Western countries and thereby tame the potential hinterland so receptive to terrorist propaganda.

Second, this policy mix would accept pragmatically—under certain circumstances—that in the majority of Arab states Islamist forces are part of the political spectrum (as election results demonstrate time and again) and would try to make the most of bilateral relations on that basis. Of course, in the long run, it would be nice to see conditions change in these countries and politics replace religion as the dominant force of public life. An aggressive elite that defines itself on ideological grounds and becomes too influential can be a serious danger, but a direct and immediate refusal to recognize it is not always the most expedient solution.

Third, this policy mix would offer an effective and amply funded counterterrorism policy suited to the fast-changing character of terrorism. Throughout the course of history, we have had to learn that the intensification of economic relations brings about an improvement in political relations. It is a promising trend—which should not be overrated, however—that the value of so-called Islamic bonds (securities that comply with Islamic law and its investment principles, which prohibit the charging or paying of interest) held by American and European investors doubled in 2006 to €3.6 billion.

The effectiveness of European antiterror policy will largely depend on whether the "old continent" can pursue a more united and consistent foreign policy. United action is especially important vis-à-vis countries and regimes posing a potential terrorist threat. Before 9/11, what is now called the war on terrorism was waged on a fundamentally national level by police and intelligence forces. Cooperation between member states in this field began only a few years ago and remains limited.

As to how to go on from here, there are several suggestions—some ambitious, some utopian, like the idea of a common European intelligence service focused on counterterrorism. Former Spanish premier Jose Maria Aznar even suggested that NATO should be the key organization of the war on terrorism since, with the Cold War out of the equation, terrorism is the biggest global security risk.

In a famous *Wall Street Journal* article, Eliot Cohen claimed that the fourth world war has begun (the third being the Cold War).[14] Yet I am convinced that, despite all the regional wars and the frequent terrorist acts, on the whole the world has never been as safe as it is today. Since 1945, the world has never been as peaceful as today. Who remembers the 1 million lives claimed by the Iraq-Iran war in the 1980s or the 100,000 people that died in an armed conflict in the small central American state of Honduras? Today, we have no postcolonial problems, which were the cause of most wars after World War II and led to France and Great Britain waging more wars in the modern age than any other two countries in the world. Today, an armed clash between major powers is almost unthinkable, but this has only been so recently. Why, then, do we feel so unsafe and insecure in this safest of all worlds? The answer is simple: because of the global media. The pictures of a conflict are broadcast throughout the world ten minutes after it breaks out. The global media work like a giant magnifying glass, often bringing grist to the mill of terrorists; as we watch the bloody pictures in horror, our optimism and confidence slowly wane.

Joschka Fischer made a remarkable point: What the Arab world needs— and at the end of the day, the West as well—is their own counterpart to Jean Monnet, the great architect of European unity.[15] An integration process in the Middle East would be the best guarantee of prosperity and peace in the region and therefore of safety for Europe and America. Europe started its integration when visionary leaders pooled steel and coal capacities after the devastating World War II. The Arab world could start its regional integration by pooling water and energy resources. Europe could play an instrumental role—if not in finding a new Monnet, but at least in providing know-how for the creation of a prosperous, increasingly integrated region.

Another important and often-discussed issue is whether globalization impoverishes the world? The answer is a resounding NO. According to official World Bank statistics in 1990, there were 380 million people in China living on under a dollar a day. Ten years later, this number had dropped to less than half. If this trend continues—and we have no reason to believe otherwise—in 2015, only 16 million Chinese citizens will have to live in such miserable conditions. The number of people living on less than a dollar a day in India, Pakistan, and Bangladesh fell considerably between 1990 and 2000, although not quite as drastically as in China. In Sub-Saharan Africa, however, globalization has only had a negative impact, if any; the number of Africans struggling to survive on less than a dollar a day increased from 230 million in 1990 to 310 million in 2001 and is expected to reach 340 million by 2015. Between 1961 and 1999, average daily food intake rose globally by about a quarter and by 40 percent in developing countries.[16] The Food and Agricultural Organization reports that while in 1970 about 35 percent of the population of developing countries was starving, by the turn of the millennium this percentage had dropped to less than half that.[17]

In the developed world, the average life expectancy went up from fifty-five years in 1970 to sixty-four in 2000. In 1900, Sweden had the highest life expectancy; the average Swede lived fifty-six years. In 1950, the average life expectancy in developing countries was about two-thirds of that of the developed world. By 2000, this had reached 82 percent, despite the terrible HIV/AIDS pandemic sweeping across the African continent. In 1970, one out of ten babies born in a developing country died; thirty years later, "only" every eighteenth newborn is lost.[18]

Different parts of the world develop at a different pace, and these differences will only be amplified with turboglobalization. Likewise, differences in standards of living have increased astonishingly; citizens of the world's wealthiest country live seventy-five times better than those living in the world's poorest state. The difference between the far ends of the scale was only tenfold a century ago. The gaps keep widening and are becoming increasingly obvious as a result of the work of the global media, analysts, and interest groups. The fundamental reasons for this growing gap are the explosive growth of developed countries and the bad policies of the countries falling behind. In many parts of the world, globalization is hardly felt or people only feel the disadvantages it allegedly causes. According to a World Bank study, developing countries playing an active role in globalization doubled their GDP between 1980 and 1997, while developing countries not involved in globalization only managed to raise their GDP by 10 percent.[19]

As stated at a press conference by Kofi Annan, the UN secretary-general from 1997 to 2007, it is a mistake to believe that people in the most difficult situation are the victims of globalization. The problem of the developing world is not globalization but rather that its benefits are hardly felt. Globalization has not yet reached countries in some regions, and these are exactly the countries facing the greatest difficulties. It is not globalization that the developing world needs to fear. On the contrary; being left out is what could have disastrous consequences and leave them in a "Friedman-ian" gray, desperate, globalization-free zone without any hope of jumping onto the train of development.

The End of Globalization?

The World Trade Center attacks; the Enron collapse; the stalled Doha Round of trade talks; the global subprime mortgage, then financial, then economic crisis—what are they? Some say these catastrophes are milestones along the road leading to the grave of globalization—potentially staggering blows to the global liberal world order. Following the terrorist attacks on the World Trade Center, the world's biggest superpower reinforced its borders and shut the door on the world. As a result of the Enron scandal, the world's biggest economy—corporate America—lost its credibility. The failure of the Doha Round—which was supposed to facilitate global free trade —marks the dawn of protectionism. For some, these three events thus foreshadow the end of globalization. But is this really a likely scenario? *No*— even though I could continue listing failures, such as the bursting of the dot-com bubble, overoptimistic forecasts of the arrival of the digital age leading to huge flops on the stock market, growing economic protectionism in Europe, and so on and so forth.

In the aftermath of 9/11, the United States introduced drastic security measures, which became a major obstacle to trading. Stricter controls of containers in practical terms meant that authorities in developing countries had to check each and every container before shipping, which—as you can imagine—proved to be a time-consuming and laborious task. Port authorities have since introduced modern risk assessment tools that have reduced the ratio of containers checked from 100 to 8 percent and cut waiting time to a quarter without additional risk. Technological improvements have made their way into other areas of port services, and thus have increased security and accelerated international trade. Nor has the cooling of United States–European Union relations caused by disagreements over the war on terrorism significantly harmed globalization. Though political relations between Berlin and Washington fell to the level of postwar years, in 2003 American firms invested $7 billion in Germany, much more than in the previous year, and American investments even grew in France. Similar trends were also observable in the other direction; in 2003, French investments in Texas alone exceeded American investments in the whole of Asia, including China.[20]

Enron Corporation, once the largest U.S. energy company, caused the biggest corporate scandal in U.S. history when in 2001 it was discovered that, in the previous four years, its profits were inflated through creative accounting techniques and the firm was unable to service its debt of $61 billion. Willful fraud by senior executives (who made sure they sold off their stocks at a good price before the company collapsed) cost many small shareholders their life savings, and thousands of Enron employees lost their pensions as the corporate pension fund vanished into thin air. In addition, the scandal caused the dissolution of Arthur Andersen, once one of the "Big Five" accounting firms, when it turned out that its auditors were involved in the fraud. Enron's vice chairman committed suicide, and even the White House was incriminated. The Enron scandal triggered a chain reaction; in the weeks that followed, dozens of serious international companies admitted to cooking their books and reports. Parmalat was for Europe what Enron was for America; at the end of 2003, a €8 billion hole was discovered in the Italian dairy and food giant's accounting records.

Civic capitalism is based on the respect of contracts and ultimately on trust. Without trust there is no business, no cooperation, no credit, no investment, no stock market, no capitalism. With Enron and other scandals, trust seems to have disappeared. Markets went wild, and the state had to intervene—introducing strict management rules, clarifying auditors' responsibilities, and implementing conflict-of-interest rules. As the hysteria subsided, confidence was restored; and following the bursting of the dot-com bubble, the stock market revived.

The World Trade Organization has been the chief institutional driving force of globalization. It was under the aegis of the WTO and the General Agreement on Tariffs and Trade that the world's countries agreed to make trade freer and cheaper, fundamentally through a gradual reduction of customs tariffs and duties. Negotiations—referred to as "rounds"—have never been easy: the so-called Uruguay Round lasted eight years. But as a result, average industrial tariffs fell from 5.7 to 3.6 percent in the EU and from 4.6 to 3 percent in the United States.[21] The Doha Round has been dragging on for years now, but there is a good chance that it will end in failure and no agreement will be reached on the further reduction of tariffs. This would halt the trend of market access getting cheaper—the process of globalization, if you like. Developing countries would like to see massive European and American agricultural levies reduced, while Europe would like easier access to the closely guarded industrial and service markets of developing countries. The United States may leave the negotiating table and conclude bilateral agreements on reducing customs duties, and the EU might even follow suit. The idea of multilateralism may be injured, but tariffs will continue to drop.

Moreover, I disagree with speculations that the 2008–9 U.S. financial and economic crisis (with the U.S. trade deficit also having reached historic highs) will cause America's free trade network to collapse. The theory goes that, so far, the United States has been able to encourage the better half of the world to pursue trade liberalization by promising its partners continuous and high-volume presence on its markets. This situation is no longer valid because the United States has reached the limit of its importing capacity, and thus the greatest guarantee of free trade has been lost. The other reason behind the proliferation of protectionism to the detriment of free trade is that natural resources are running out, fueling competition for control over energy sources. Of course, globalization is attacked for many other reasons; there will always be people opposed to it on various grounds.

It is true that, finally, the WTO's Doha Round broke down in 2008. This nevertheless should not mean the end of multilateralism or the end of the WTO. Collective efforts for trade liberalization must be kept, although probably the rulebook should be renewed. Regional preferential trade agreements will be part of reality for the foreseeable future, and therefore the WTO should learn to live with them and do all it can to render them compatible with existing multilateral rules and principles.

The recent failure of the world trade talks is nothing compared with the potential dangers of the financial crash that started as American mortgage credit troubles in 2007. Yet one must be aware that economic crises are an integral part of capitalist history. The history of capitalism is the history of booms and busts. The first financial storm in the Western world dates was in 1632, when the Holy Roman Empire debased its coins, which triggered a pan-European panic. Then, in 1637, came the tulip boom-and-bust crash in Holland, where foolish speculators pumped up the price of tulip bulbs to the sky. In 1720 came another huge crash, the one we know as the South Sea bubble. Eight more crashes took place in the eighteenth century, and some twenty in the nineteenth century, mostly in Europe and some in the United States. The biggest crises took place in the twentieth century, thirty-three altogether; the best known of these are the stock market crashes of 1929 and 1987. The 1929 crisis, followed by the Great Depression, had horrendous consequences, both economic and political, while the impact of the

1987 stock exchange crash was much smaller, although the fall of share prices was the biggest since 1929. The financial sector was shaken, but the nation's economy and society did not feel too much pain. The 1987 crash saw the infamous Black Monday, and no one knew how much it was caused by weak fundamentals and how important psychology was in the ensuing havoc. "A crisis is all about human emotion, greed, and fear," says a senior Wall Street investment analyst, quoted by the *Financial Times*. Global interconnections can channel hysteria extremely efficiently and quickly.

In 2007, a huge calamity started in the financial markets, and the trouble escalated within a few months, eliminating millions of jobs and endangering huge industries like American car manufacturing. Many have asked, Why has this happened? As the majority of economists, like Martin Wolf, see it, the Western world has become complacent, which is a natural consequence of every golden era.[22] A long period of steep and continuous growth, low inflation, low interest rates, endless consumer spending, and a rising standard of living increased optimism and risk taking. Those in Western society—especially Americans—started to believe that nothing can go wrong and that everything is possible.

As the trouble unfolded in 2008 and 2009, American mortgage institutions kept telling people that immovable property prices can never go down, only up. This is, of course, a lie. Thus, it is not surprising that huge housing bubbles emerged in the Western world (interestingly, these bubbles were bigger in the United Kingdom, Spain, and Australia than in the United States), which, coupled with heavy reliance on (extremely overvalued) securitized financing, made a deadly cocktail. The American mortgage business collapsed, and Fannie Mae and Freddie Mac, the two giant U.S. mortgage institutions, had to be bailed out with government money. This, however, did not save the—once so mighty—American investment bank industry, which practically evaporated within a few hours. Losses were measured in trillions, and governments pumped trillions back into the system to save at least those who had not fallen at the first shot. Short selling was banned in most markets, financial giants were nationalized, and central banks for the first time in history acted in a completely coordinated way. But still, in October 2008, within a week the leading stock markets fell 20 percent and the world was preparing for a long period of no growth.

As a result of this huge global financial and economic crisis of 2008–9, Enron (and its European equivalent, Parmalat) and Doha are now distant, unimportant history. The new story is this global crisis, which has been compared several times to the Great Depression. Although this comparison is false, the gravity of the situation is significant. The new crisis—in the view of many analysts—does not only show the weaknesses of free market capitalism but also foretells the inevitable decline of the West. The simple enumeration of arguments and counterarguments put forward by American and European economists and political scientists along with politicians would fill hundreds of pages. In the meantime, governments are busy helping their shaky economies with massive cash interventions. The United States is in the lead with its nearly $800 billion federal stimulus package, and interestingly the Europeans, who are rhetorically much more state dependent, are very much lagging behind. They have spent only a few tens of billions on revitalizing stimulus packages. Obviously, the new intellectual hyperbole is the crisis and its societal and political consequences.

The global crisis sparked a bitter naming and shaming quarrel between the EU and the United States, because Europeans blamed American mismanagement and negligence as the primary source of the global trouble. For the first time in modern history, Americans found themselves on the defensive in a debate related to financial services. The French president and the whole German government were furious about this American plague that had immediately infected the European economy. Whoever was to blame, whoever started it, by mid-2009, the crisis had become a more and more European one. Though, in the United States, GDP sank by about 2.8 percent, in the euro zone it fell by 4.2 percent. In 2009, the EU's biggest economy, Germany, was paralyzed by the recession. The Irish economic miracle evaporated, and unemployment in Spain rocketed to 20 percent.[23] Some of the new EU member states were devastated, with a decrease of more than 10 percent and sometimes lingering political havoc.

In May 2009, U.S. president Barack Obama announced that he saw the light at the end of the tunnel, and thus the economy was starting to come back to life. These statements always have to be taken with caution these days. Nevertheless, it is already clear that the global crisis of 2008–9 has not shattered the Western economies, let alone Western societal models. I think economic and political analysts will have to find a new scoop soon. Capitalism will survive, though new rules will be set to tame the financial markets. Yet this crisis is beyond doubt the toughest challenge that globalization has ever faced. The leaders of the world, like the global economy, have entered unchartered territory. It is extremely important to handle this turbulence and the overhaul of the system in the right way—not only to preserve globalization, which is beneficial for the world, but also for the sake of the world's long-term geopolitical stability.

Some claim that globalization is an ideology: the ideology of the global village, free and unlimited world trade, and global equality. This ideology became obsolete with the emergence of Asian powers, when the self-defense reflexes of the Western countries put an end to globalization ideology, leaving nothing but survival and outsourcing. However, I do not believe that globalization is an ideology. It is more the relentless integration of world markets and everything it brings with it. Others argue that America and then Europe became the prisoners of their own free market, liberal ideology, on which the post–World War II West was built, and that they are now caught in the web of this almost-religious liberal utopia without realizing that the rest of the world is surpassing them.

I see no need to look for ideology behind every trend. Thus, I do not consider ideological attacks conclusive. The countries of the West need to remain pragmatic and prepare for the emergence of Asia. The world does not seem to be in a mood to abandon globalization and the liberal model, as it did in the early twentieth century. The situation is different today—there is no added value in turning away from globalization, there is no territorial rivalry between the great powers, and different parts of the world are connected not only politically but also by thousands of microeconomic ties. These ties are priceless; tearing them up would have serious implications. In 2005 and 2006, we saw that the global volume of outsourcing began to decline from the record level of $85 billion in 2004. Could this mark the end of turboglobalization? No, because the decline is only due to the fact that the average term of outsourcing contracts has fallen from ten to four years. The value of these contracts seems to have dropped, but their number has risen and they are increasingly flexible.

As we have seen, globalization began a long time ago. But it still has not reached all parts of the Earth; there are still many gray areas on the map. The phenomenon of globalization is strongest in the form of economic integration between neighboring countries, as is best demonstrated by European integration. Nevertheless, the importance of the "neighborhood factor" is decreasing with the rapid development of information and communication technologies.

Europe's Role

Globalization exists in two forms, both for the European Union's member states and third countries with close economic ties with the Union. For Europe, globalization means "Europeanization," a sort of regional globalization, with its power concentrated in Brussels, mainly in the hands of the European Commission, the EU's peculiar government-like institution. One distinctive feature of the Commission is that it hardly ever makes decisions; instead, it makes proposals to the European Council and thus to the members' national ministers, who then decide. The other is that the Commission can only be considered an executive government on the basis of the EU treaties; it does not have the power of the purse. In the twentieth and twenty-first centuries, we have become used to the tax-collecting state doing much of the redistribution. The Commission has many competences, but it does not dispose of huge sums of money.

By dismantling economic hurdles, the European Union—this libertarian universe built on the four freedoms (see chapters 1 and 4 for explanations of these)—plays a major role in reinforcing globalization, on both European and global levels. Paradoxically, most of the time European lawmakers legislate to deregulate—in other words, to remove the remaining obstacles from the single market. It is wrong to look at the EU as a redistributing, caring entity just because its common policies (the policy of reducing regional disparities, the Common Agricultural Policy, or the cohesion policy) are redistributive in nature. It should be remembered that the funds financing the common policies, that is the EU's budget, are no more than 1 percent of the Community's total national product.

The European Union helps its member states become successful players of "global globalization" by pooling their resources, economic weight, and political clout and acting in unison on the global scene—provided, of course, that they are willing to do so. Mario Monti, a former EU commissioner, said at a conference in 2007 that the EU must help globalization to survive by setting and enforcing reasonable rules for the global game. What better occasion to start doing it than the global financial and economic crisis?

In the fall of 2008, this United States–originated crisis spread all over Europe with a deadly force. In just a few days, five large banks crashed, Iceland went bankrupt, France acknowledged being in a recession, huge quantities of money were pumped into banks to save the financial system, and emergency meetings at the highest levels were called. Europe needed to find an answer—a coordinated one. History teaches us that Europe as a community in times of trouble can do much better than in normal days with regard to setting policies. This was also true this time. (However, in the meantime, there were individual initiatives sometimes driven by protectionist instincts, such as the French invitation to overseas sovereign wealth funds to become coinvestors in a newly established vehicle conceived by Nicolas

Sarkozy to stop French companies being bought up by foreign predators. And of course the concrete market interventions, such as bailing out or nationalizing banks, have been done by individual member states themselves.) European leaders used the Group of Twenty summit in November 2008 to urge the United States to back reforms of the world's financial system. As I mentioned above, the European Union members of the Group of Twenty— France, Germany, Britain, and Italy—were irritated by the way the United States has handled the crisis. While France held the EU's rotating presidency, Nicolas Sarkozy urged the U.S. president-elect to help reshape the world's financial framework, but he made clear the frustration of European leaders, saying at a press conference that "this is a global crisis and we have to remember where it started. The time when we had a single currency— the dollar—one line to be followed, that era is over." The message was clear.

At a special European summit, the EU agreed on a list of reforms, including setting up supervisory colleges to regulate the thirty biggest banks and rules on the operation of credit-rating agencies. The EU also wants to strengthen the International Monetary Fund's role in monitoring cross-border risk and issuing early warnings and to raise its $250 billion fund base, as well as instituting new accounting standards and increased transparency. Inside Europe, huge tax cuts were announced and plans for balanced budgets were dropped. The EU has effectively agreed to suspend fiscal rules during these "exceptional circumstances" to allow member states' borrowing to rise.

Looking at the broader picture, what we see is probably the end of the unipolar era. The war in Iraq has undermined America's diplomatic stance, and the 2008–9 global financial crisis has undermined its economic position. In the meantime, China has been steadily rising. Make no mistake: America's relative decline does not mean Europe's rise. But there is a window of opportunity for Europe to have a bigger influence on the United States, at least for a limited time. The best way Europe can use this opening is to play a prominent role in setting the global rules—for economic governance, climate issues, and the like—for the next era of the globalized world.

International Competition:
Is Europe Losing Its Place at the Top Table?

Competition has been part of humanity since the beginning of time. Empires, countries, warlords, politicians, companies, inventors, and businesspeople have always battled for power, land, influence, or dominance. The first half of the twentieth century brought the fiercest form of competition yet: the two bloodiest wars in the history of humankind. The nerve-racking competition of the Cold War brought global peace—Pax Americana—as well as economic competition, coordinated by international institutions, and accelerating international integration, that is, globalization.

Since World War II, competition has been peaceful and fundamentally limited to the sphere of the economy but, due to turboglobalization, it is increasingly difficult to define clearly who is competing with whom. When globalization was dictated by nation-states, the formula was easier: One country competed against the other. Today, when globalization is in many aspects fueled by multinational companies, how could traditional definitions of geopolitics describe the fight between DaimlerChrysler and Toyota over the Chinese market? Large multinational enterprises are owned by millions of investors, among them pension funds. The success of a Japanese enterprise can determine the standard of living of tens of thousands of American retirees. Salaried employees in Europe can no longer be considered part of the non-fund-holding "working class"; they are linked to global capitalism through the stocks and bonds that they hold, which are worth hundreds of billions of dollars. Thus they have a vested interest, for without the success of global capitalism, their savings could evaporate.

Given these realities, the part of the world that was once seen as "abroad" is today neither the source of cheap resources it was in the age of colonization nor the stable export market it was before the age of turboglobalization; instead, it is the country where suppliers and subcontractors of our own companies are established and where our own citizens have important private assets. Power, property, and influence are no longer the black-and-white concepts that they used to be for centuries. It is in this complicated environment that international competition is increasing, and grasping the interrelationships within this system of references is a difficult intellectual task. This is partly the reason for the misunderstandings and misconceptions about turboglobalization.

For Europe, the key question is what chances does the continent have as an economic and political entity in this worldwide competitive struggle. With my differentiated approach to competition, I do not mean to suggest that there is no answer to this question. I simply want to indicate that we must be careful when trying to find the answer; we must reevaluate several factors to be able to update the concepts of competition and competitiveness for the age of turboglobalization.

In recent decades, globalization has increased the interdependence of large regions. As new powers (e.g., China) emerge, Europe keeps losing its competitiveness and potential for growth, despite its favorable conditions in many areas. In an age when the world market is expanding dynamically and transnationalization is accelerating, a country or region can only be successful if it is able to become integrated into the mainstream of international trends. Naturally, this requires the reevaluation of a number of traditional concepts—such as national sovereignty—and poses scores of new questions and dilemmas. In a swiftly changing world, international economic and financial institutions must also undergo reform. Solutions must be found to spread the benefits of globalization and technological revolution to the entire world and to keep the negative effects in check. The future of the new economic world order is unclear. Although the international economy has never changed so fast before, we can see a blurred silhouette of things to come, if not a clear contour. Market fluctuations happening at unprecedented speed, the world's "flattening," China's emergence, desperate attempts by the EU to close the gap with the United States, the first significant monetary union in history, the introduction of a new global currency, the reform of the international institutional framework and deeper social developments such as the loud antiglobalization hysteria (the bloody outcomes of protests against the WTO in Seattle and Genoa) all point toward the same unavoidable fact: We have come to a turning point.

Today, there is competition everywhere: among states, regions, currencies, enterprises, financial institutions, and socioeconomic models. The pace is being set by transnational corporations, regional financial centers and stock exchanges, and research centers and innovation clusters, and thus governments can only try—and sometimes fail—to keep up with it. The global competition between cultures and civilizations is not as serious as the media would like to have one believe. Muslim extremists may be waging a religious war, but the rest of the world does not give it much thought. There is a widespread public consensus favoring today's world order based on free market principles, trade, and nonconfrontational but increasingly fierce (market) competition. Of course, there are also very different models—just think of the American and the Chinese models. Yet China is also a WTO member, and it is getting richer from trading with other countries, not from conquering and pillaging them.

When considering international competition, one tends to get lost in the details and forget about the key level of competition, which is difficult to measure and analyze statistically: the competition between socioeconomic models in a world built on market (i.e., nonviolent) competition. Due to this international competition and globalization, the various American, European, Asian models are approximating each other. Even so, with respect to China, I would not venture as far as Mark Leonard, who argues that China will have to opt for a European model when the time comes for choosing one.[24] It is indeed an interesting question whether China will go for the American hawk or the European pigeon. Casting aside doubts that the question oversimplifies the two Western models, the answer is: neither. As the emerging power of the third millennium, China is too strong and too different to follow either of the two Western models. China will find its own way—which the West will discover and explore, and to which it will adapt. Thus, a more important question is what model Europe will follow. The key task is for European businesses to remain competitive, perform successfully on the international stage, and ensure that the citizens of the continent's nations can enter the next phase of globalization without suffering a major setback in their standard of living.

Positions

When my previous book on the European Union's economy was published, I was asked at the press conference to briefly summarize what it was about. I said to look at the first illustration in my book: a coordinate system with some round blots and five large circles. These dots and circles symbolize the populations of countries; the bigger the circle, the larger the population. The position of the circle in the coordinate system is also important—the richer the country, the higher the circle is placed; and the richer its citizens, the more to the right the circle is positioned. In the top right corner, there are three small circles—none of them bigger than a ten-cent piece—symbolizing the United States, the European Union, and Japan. In the bottom left corner, there are two big circles—each the size of a €2 coin—symbolizing China and India. The development of the world economy in the coming years will be about the two large circles moving toward the top right corner, where two of the three smaller circles will be shrinking.

Unsurprisingly, today's economic powers have all made boosting competitiveness the centerpiece of their economic policies. Different regional blocs face different problems: the United States has no problems with growth, employment or productivity but the ticking time-bomb of its huge twin deficit (a concurrent wavering of its external and internal macroeconomic balance) casts a dark shadow over future prospects, not only on the

American continent but globally too. If the U.S. economy runs into trouble, the whole world will feel the impact.

The uncertainties surrounding the stability of the U.S. economy have already plunged the dollar's exchange rate versus the euro to historic lows, which has had disastrous consequences for the export-driven European economy. A currency's revaluation (in the EU's case, the euro) against another currency (the dollar) means that the sum received for the goods sold in the given export market (the United States) will be worth less at home (in the EU). The costs arise in the revalued currency (the euro), while the income is realized in the devalued currency (the dollar). Since 2002, when it was at parity with the euro, the dollar has lost a quarter of its value, which has meant a 25 percent net loss of revenue for European exporters. Exchange rates make a big difference for Europe, the world's biggest trading bloc, and especially Germany, the world's biggest exporter.

Unlike the situation of the U.S. economy, which is based on domestic consumption, the growth of the European economy hinges on exports. No exports, no growth—this has been the story of the last five years or so. The Japanese economy, which back in the 1980s was feared by all, has been paralyzed and is unable to climb out of this sustained paralysis. Japan seems to be unable to decide whether the fire-breathing dragon at its coasts—a China that it had defeated and humiliated time and again—is a danger or an opportunity for climbing out of the current inertia. For China, conversely, the greatest challenge is how to keep its breakneck speed of growth under control. Year after year, growth figures exceed the desired optimum level. The other Chinese issue that has an impact on the world economy is the yuan and its artificially low exchange rate. China may be a favorite with investors and a key engine of world economic growth, but it is still a Communist-led regime, which will disregard the rules of international economic cooperation without thinking twice, as soon as those rules do not suit it. The yuan's exchange rate is well below what free market conditions would justify. How can one best describe in a nutshell how the world operates these days? America consumes (buys) what China produces (sells). What does the yuan's exchange rate, kept artificially low by the Communist government, mean for China? It means just the opposite of what the strong euro means for Europe. The weak yuan generates colossal extra profits for Chinese exporters as they convert the dollars received in return for their exported goods. After paying their costs, incurred in yuan, they have difficulties investing all the money they are left with.

In addition, Chinese companies have mastered the art of squeezing European competitors out of the market, creating a huge imbalance in the world economy, which—many believe—could trigger a major global crisis. Let the rest of the world deal with that problem, China says. But China also has its own problems; blinded by Shanghai's skyscraper-filled skyline and deafened by the boom of the economy's brutal growth, we tend to forget about the nation's hundreds of millions of workers and peasants living in desperate poverty. Disparities and tensions are growing in Chinese society. Despite its modern approach to governance and economic liberalism, the time will come when the Communist Party can no longer blatantly violate fundamental rights and resist social liberalism. This will not be a venture without risks and dangers.

Moreover, drawing parallels between the weak dollar and the weak yuan is a dangerous exercise. There is a huge difference between the two. The dollar is kept weak by the markets' concern about instability in the U.S. economy, whereas the yuan is kept weak artificially by politicians who could not care less about market rules and who dread the thought of losing China's competitiveness. It would be foolish to believe that the United States is not concerned about losing its competitiveness; America does care, but it compares itself to China and not Europe and tries to minimize the risks linked to China's emergence as an economic powerhouse. In early 2006, President George W. Bush announced a $136 billion competitiveness program, which includes training 70,000 science and mathematics teachers in five years. Who will lead the world is what is at stake, it is said. The American Competitiveness Initiative, also launched in 2006, puts innovation and training at its heart, which is not far from the philosophy of the EU's Lisbon Strategy. Meanwhile, of course, China and India have been sending divisions of science graduates, mathematicians, and software developers into the marketplace battlefield.

Which economic power will emerge as a winner? It is impossible to give a straight answer to this question, but one thing is certain: Europe's chances —especially considering the demographic trends—are not too rosy. The European Union is still the most important economic bloc, the biggest global trader with the biggest GDP (one-third of the world's GDP). However, the importance of these indicators is waning as turboglobalization causes priorities to be reevaluated. What good is it that Europe is the world's biggest trader if it is unable to manage the course of WTO negotiations according to its own multilateral approach? What good is it that the EU is the world's largest single market if that market is far from truly single? What good is it that the EU has the world's biggest GDP if its per capita GDP is well below the U.S. GDP and if this gap keeps widening with new EU enlargements? These questions are provocative for a good reason: Finding answers to them can help us see the difference between reality and communication, and to discern what European integration can and cannot do for its participating states.

I will discuss these matters in detail below. Here, I can say that according to the traditional definition of global competition—a competition among regions to have the biggest GDP, population, or trade volume—Europe does not stand a chance. But changing global conditions have redefined the concept of competition, which may give Europe a new gleam of hope. Even though twice as many people speak Mandarin Chinese as English, there is no doubt as to which is the more important language—in which more contracts are concluded, more books are published, and more software is developed. Occasionally, it is worth peeping behind statistics, not because—as Mark Twain suggested—they are the biggest lies in the world, but because we may be looking for the answer to the wrong question. As a South African teacher told me years ago: "Broken English is the most spoken language of the world."

Containers

While we are sunbathing on the beach, sitting in a theater watching a movie, or lying in our bed fast asleep, millions of freight containers are being shipped all around the world. Millions and millions of containers are moving around the world around the clock, as befits these slaves of international trade. There are more of them in Europe every year. The goods turnover of Hamburg's port doubled between 2000 and 2006, and it will double again by 2015. The world is "going large"; containers used to be 20 feet long, but today they are 45 feet long (and eight out of ten are manufactured in China). Ships have also grown out of all proportion; the days of the PanMax standard (i.e., the dimensions of the largest vessel that can sail through the Panama Canal) are long gone, and the post-PanMax age has also ended; today's freighters are of a super-post-PanMax size. In 2007, there were about 4,000 container ships afloat, and another 1,300 had been ordered. The biggest of them was the *Emma Maersk,* which started its operation in 2006 carrying toys from China to Europe before Christmas. It can carry 5,500 40-foot containers in its 400-meter hull. A train carrying that load would be 71 kilometers long.

The European Union plays a leading role in world trade. Though its twenty-seven member states make up only 7 percent of the world's population, they account for 20 percent of world trade (the United States accounts for 18 percent) and have an even bigger share of the services market, with 27 percent. The EU accounts for 43 percent of foreign direct investment—with the United States accounting for 32 percent and China for 1 percent—and is also the number one destination for foreign direct investment, with 31 percent—with the United States having 20 percent and China 13 percent.[25] Fostering trade has been a key objective from the beginning of European integration; it brought about the creation of the customs union with the dismantling of internal customs borders and a common commercial policy among its members vis-à-vis third countries. Since then, the European Community has evolved into a commercial superpower and the world's largest single market. The significance of Europe's export industry is demonstrated by the fact that it employs more than 12 million people. EU trade can be divided into two distinct categories, intra-Community trade between its member states and external trade with third countries, with the former accounting for 60 percent and the latter for 40 percent of all Community trade. And despite the relatively common trade disputes between the economic powers on the two sides of the Atlantic—which can escalate into trade wars but affect only a marginal part of bilateral trade—the United States is still the EU's number one trading partner.

A new kind of international division of labor is developing, which is reflected in international trade. In the mid-1990s, 90 percent of all goods sold on the U.S. market were produced domestically. In fifteen years, this ratio has fallen to 75 percent. Over the course of the last decade, Europe has become much more open; for example, the share of exports to other European countries has fallen from 80 to 65 percent in Belgium and from 65 to 50 percent in Germany. Accordingly, the share of intra-European trade in all world trade has fallen from 30 to 20 percent. China became Europe's largest supplier of processed industrial products in 2006, stealing the top position from the United States, which had always been number one.

As things stand now, the situation is not bad; the EU is a world leader both in trade and international capital investment. Yet the trends give rise to concern: Europe is weaker in markets, mostly in the Far East, that are likely to record the quickest growth in coming years, both geographically and sectorally. China, whose fame is still larger than its might, keeps rising in the ranks of world powers, feeding the voracious America. European exports are not concentrated in the right sectors and geographic regions, and Europe is having difficulties redirecting them to the right areas, something that Japan and the United States have managed to do successfully. The recent upsurge in Japan's development is largely due to its exports to China. Despite its seemingly favorable position, there is a danger that Europe could become marginalized in world trade in the long run, unless it is able to re-focus its exports on the most dynamic regions and high-technology sectors. The same can be concluded for attracting foreign direct investment.

This conclusion poses two questions. First, can Europe maintain its lead-ing position in top-of-the-line products, such as those manufactured using biotechnology. This is not only a question of having the technological ad-vantage; the quality, image, and services related to such products are also decisive factors in determining how many customers are willing to fork out good money for a given product. The ability to innovate will remain as im-portant as ever, perhaps even more so. Second, will Europe benefit from the growth of developing countries by penetrating their markets? The nature of Europe's trade with these countries is in question—whether trade in differ-ent products will dominate, which is more or less the way things are now; or whether trade in similar commodities will dominate, which is character-istic of trade within Europe. The second alternative is clearly the more at-tractive one, but it does not preclude some kind of specialization. Trade re-lations between Europe and China are showing signs of change; similar goods of a very different quality already account for 10 percent of trade.

To what extent will the EU be able to use its commercial policy to its own advantage? Trade policy is a "Brussels thing"; it is the job of the Eu-ropean Commission to implement and—to a large extent—shape the EU's common commercial policy, which entails lengthy negotiations, compro-mises, and sometimes trade wars. Every now and then, when these trade wars break out, they tend to be overrated due to the media attention they at-tract, even though they only affect a negligible part of all trade to and from the EU. Trade wars used to be typically American-European affairs, but China is getting involved more and more often. One can recall the disputes concerning genetically modified organisms and hormone-treated beef, when the EU introduced a continent-wide import ban and the United States . retaliated by imposing a 100 percent punitive duty on French cheese, which in turn triggered a boycott against McDonald's fast food in France.

Farm subsidies are another transatlantic bone of contention. Washington keeps demanding that Brussels phases out export subsidies on agrifood pro-duce and support to farmers. The European Commission's counterargument is that the 2 million American farmers receive $60 billion worth of farm aid, while their 7 million European counterparts have to make do with just $40 billion. We live in the age of transnational companies, and therefore Euro-pean trade sanctions affect not only American firms but also European con-sumers and enterprises that directly depend on U.S. exports.

Just the possibility of trade wars can make life more difficult for businesses in a globalized world. American subsidiaries of European companies generated €66 billion in revenue in 2004, which was a fourfold increase from 2001. Three-quarters of all foreign direct investment in the United States comes from Europe; the three biggest industrial Länder in Germany (Hessen, Baden-Würtenberg, and Nord-Rhein Westphalia) invest more in the United States than in the EU. It is easy to see that the two continents have a vested interest in keeping economic and trade relations undisturbed. China is quite a different matter; it is not yet organically integrated into the tissue of the global economy. The failure of the latest Doha Round of WTO negotiations is forcing governments to review their approach. Thus, multilateralism could give way to a bilateral approach, whereby countries and trading regions would engage in one-to-one talks, giving the stronger party more leverage because the weaker one would have fewer potential allies and tactical leeway. According to Pascal Lamy, a former EU commissioner and now the WTO's director-general, bilateral trade agreements are more popular because they give politicians hundreds of opportunities to "make the news," whereas a multilateral agreement gives them a single burst of media coverage.[26]

A good example of the "new regionalism" was then–Russian president Vladimir Putin's announcement in September 2006 that Russia, Belarus, and Kazakhstan wanted to form a customs union, which other former Soviet states were also considering joining. Another example comes from closer to home. A few weeks after the collapse of the Doha Round, the EU opened bilateral negotiations with India. German chancellor Angela Merkel even floated the idea of an EU–United States free trade zone, but the EU commissioner holding the relevant portfolio remained more cautious, saying that such a move could frighten and alienate the rest of the world.

Whatever the case with such negotiations and agreements, the world has changed so much that international trade policy must be refocused on intellectual property rights and the modern plague of fraud and counterfeiting. Bilateral negotiations do offer an advantage; the EU can strike deals with its partners in areas for which the WTO framework proves to be ill fitted—for example, services, public procurement, and the protection of intellectual property rights. However, bilateral agreements also complicate world trade with their maze of special safeguard clauses.

The European Union is the world's number one exporter, at least for the time being. But it must give more thought to competitiveness and to which markets it should target. The Doha Round negotiations aimed at liberalizing world trade collapsed under the pressure of protectionism. Now it would be disastrous if protectionists were to gather around Doha's corpse during the burial ceremony and decide what the world's—and the EU's—trade policy will look like in the coming years.

Currencies and Floors

The dollar, euro, yen, and yuan—they are more than merely a means of financial settlement for international trade and transactions. In the global money market, billions of dollars change hands every day; the grand total of global financial transactions per day adds up to roughly $2 billion, 95 percent of which is purely financial, where money and not goods or services are traded. As we have seen, exchange rates have a huge impact on the competitiveness and prosperity of a country or region. Currencies and securities in countless different forms circulate in financial hubs, stock exchange floors, and large international banking houses—just as containers and goods do.

In the salons of the Western, globalized world, currency exchange rates are determined on the market floors. Meanwhile, below the service stairs, in China, they are still decided by politicians in dark, smoke-filled rooms. This causes considerable anxiety and concern in "white-tie country."

The U.S. economy dominates the world economy, setting its growth and many of its trends. Over the course of the last few decades, the U.S. economy has produced growth figures and productivity gains that even developing countries find hard to emulate. Accordingly, corporate America was at the top of investors' lists, and money flowed to the U.S. states. The strong dollar was the token of excellent economic performance, but since its nosedive in 2002, American economic trends have had a smaller impact on the world economy and the United States has ceased being able to pull out of downturns or crises single-handedly. A stable currency is incompatible with a sustained current account deficit—even for the United States, which is no exception to this rule, even if it is the favorite destination of foreign investment and the main driving force behind the global economic and financial system.

There is a limit to everything, and the United States would need an inflow of $3 billion to stop the dollar from further weakening. Yet as we have seen, the dollar began losing value against the euro despite the impressive financial inflow. The American global economic hegemony of the late 1990s and the turn of the millennium has lost much of its shine, almost as if the turboglobalized economy would be too big a morsel to chew, even for the United States. In the meantime, by 2008 China's dollar reserves reached

$1.3 trillion (that is right—more than 1 trillion greenbacks). That is how much the United States—as the issuer of the global currency—virtually owes to China. The weak dollar poses a serious challenge for the world economy. Devaluation could foreshadow the beginning of the end of America's economic hegemony, and it could also underscore the fact that the United States' domestic, demand-based growth is no longer sufficient to ensure balance in the world economy, which became evident during the 2008–9 global financial and economic crisis.

Consequently, a reshuffling of international currency exchange rates is unavoidable. But it is doubtful whether this can be done without a great international financial crisis. Some see little hope for American-European coordination, and therefore they advocate enhanced cooperation between the euro and the yen. The American deficit is financed by Europe, China, Japan, and the other smaller countries of Southeast Asia; while America's household savings have dropped to rock bottom, Europeans tend to save too much money. The general trend of strengthening Asian currencies was mainly due to investors' willingness to pour any amount of money into Asian capital markets in order to tap into China's incredible growth.

How can this anomaly be handled? For starters, American households should spend less and save more. However, this is unlikely to happen, because investing in securities still offers bigger yields than bank savings due to the low interest rates. In addition, falling American demand would hit European exports, which are the basis for the old continent's modest growth. If American demand falls, European demand would need to rise to reduce the twin deficits by curbing American consumption. The key step, however, must be taken by China. The United States keeps demanding a more flexible Chinese exchange-rate policy, but a sudden and total liberation of exchange rates would probably trigger another Asian currency crisis. Let us face it: China's successful integration into the global economy has been mainly thanks to the stable and undervalued yuan. Though all attention seems to focus on the dollar's exchange rates, we should not forget that 25 percent of Chinese exports go to Europe and 10 percent of imports come from Europe, whereas this ratio is, respectively, only 20 percent and 8 percent for trade with the United States, and only a quarter of the American trade deficit is vis-à-vis China. Why is the dollar still so important? It is important simply because all the Asian countries are strongly linked to it, using it as the universally accepted currency of their regional trade, which is more significant than their trade with Europe or America. As a result, a more flexible dollar exchange rate could destabilize Asia's regional economy.

Nonetheless, China's crawling peg policy, liberalizing and devaluing the yuan in tiny little steps, is very damaging for the Western world. Better coordination and mutual understanding between the economic powers on the two sides of the Atlantic would facilitate a solution. Stopping the dollar's depreciation would serve both Europe's and Japan's interests, which raises the possibility of coordinated intervention policy between the European Central Bank and the Japanese Central Bank, while China could peg the yuan to a currency basket giving the euro and the yen more weight. In 2007, the so-called subprime mortgage crisis—that is, the financial turmoil caused by the massive failure of American households to repay their mortgage debts, many incurred through questionable lending practices—clearly showed the instability of the system. It seems that the consequences of the unsustainable indebtedness in the United States are here to stay.

According to Jacques Attali, the former president of the European Bank for Reconstruction and Development, a crisis as deep as the one in 1929 could occur if the financial operators start to panic, causing a loss of 10 percent of global GDP ($4 trillion). In times of trouble, a significant redistribution of global wealth can take place in a relatively short period—as has been shown by the recent rise of the so-called sovereign wealth funds. These funds are state-controlled investment vehicles financed with foreign exchange assets, and, traditionally, they were the preserve of oil-rich countries and were invested in neutral assets, like U.S. state bonds. However, these funds have started to serve the major strategic and political interests of countries such as China and Russia by buying up American and European companies. These funds now control assets worth about an astounding $2.5 trillion. These funds also come into play when giant global financial institutions must be saved from the consequences of the financial crisis. The biggest banks—such as UBS, Morgan Stanley, Merrill Lynch, and Citigroup—all received money from sovereign wealth funds to help them try to overcome the turmoil.

The introduction of the single European currency, the euro, has boosted Europe's international financial might and improved its negotiating position vis-à-vis global financial issues but has also put more responsibility on its shoulders. As the euro is becoming more widely used in international financial settlements, the dollar is beginning to lose its absolute dominance as the reserve currency of choice—although its primacy remains unquestionable, for the time being. The appearance of the euro has also increased the world's interdependence; thus, developments in the euro zone influence the U.S. economy to a much greater extent than before its introduction. Admittedly, European markets respond to American trends much more vigorously than the other way around.

There are rumors that the Asian tigers—Hong Kong, Singapore, South Korea, and Taiwan—are contemplating the idea of following the European model and forming a monetary union. This is in the lap of the gods, but one can safely say that China's entry into the global game has also increased international interdependence; the world increasingly depends on the yuan's exchange rate, while China is more and more dependent on global—especially American—consumption. These trends will only be amplified when India bursts onto the international economic and financial scene in a few years' time and with the oil price fluctuations caused by falling oil reserves.

With respect to the international financial exchanges, Europe is dwarfed by the United States, the true Goliath, and China is microscopic. The New York Stock Exchange (NYSE) is by far the world's biggest, with a fourfold advantage over the runner-up, Tokyo's Nikkei, in the value of the securities traded on its floor. Europe's largest exchange, the London Stock Exchange (LSE), comes in fourth, just ahead of Nasdaq in the United States. America also dominates the banking sector, as home to the world's biggest banks. European capital markets and the stock market sector are fragmented; thirty European exchanges trade less in value than the half dozen American ones. The integration of financial markets is not just another fad; it does have serious implications for economic growth. The efficiency gains brought by concentration through the mergers of financial entities could add more than 1 percent to Europe's growth rate, making it that much easier to have access to capital for investment in development and job creation. For years, this has been in the air; if a stock exchange does not merge with another one, it will end up being acquired itself. Due to the combined competitive squeeze of regulatory liberalization, the electronic revolution, globalization, and the introduction of the euro, the European exchanges, the NYSE, and Nasdaq have all toyed with the idea of merging, and thus news of planned mergers and alliances is aired monthly.

The three biggest European stock exchanges—the LSE, Paris-Amsterdam's Euronext, and Frankfurt's Deutsche Börse (DB)—have been making amicable or hostile approaches to each other for almost ten years, with their aim being integration, as the only means of survival in the face of international competition. In July 1998, the LSE and the DB announced their strategic alliance to establish a common electronic trading system, but in the end they could not agree on principles and technical specifications, the LSE backed out, and the plan fell through. Europe's second-largest and first pan-European exchange, Euronext, was created in September 2000 through the merger of the Paris, Amsterdam, and Brussels bourses, with 60, 32, and 8 percent shares, respectively. The Lisbon Stock Exchange later joined the Euronext alliance. Nasdaq has also appeared on the scene wanting to cooperate with the iX exchange, the would-be end product of the failed London-Frankfurt merger. In the end, Nasdaq acquired majority ownership of Easdaq, which was renamed Nasdaq Europe. Nasdaq also engaged in talks with three other exchanges (LSE, DB, and Euronext) and in the spring of 2002, a Nasdaq-LSE merger seemed to be within grasp. It would have created the world's biggest stock exchange in terms of turnover, exceeding even the NYSE, but the plan was never realized.

In April 2002, two years after their stillborn alliance, the DB made a takeover bid for the LSE, which was rejected. In December 2004, Euronext also joined the bidding war for the LSE. In the meantime, Euronext had acquired one of the world's biggest options exchanges, the London International Financial Futures and Options Exchange. Having been turned down several times, the DB approached Euronext-Paris with a merger offer and negotiations began, albeit without much enthusiasm. All this time, the integration of the clearinghouses, which are the second pillar of the stock market system, has only existed on paper, adding hundreds of millions of euros to the cost of trading both for investors and companies, and making access to capital more expensive.

Recognizing the opportunity in a fragmented European stock market sector where stakeholders were not showing much willingness to compromise, American players burst onto the scene. Nasdaq was the first to make the jump across the Atlantic, quietly acquiring a 25 percent share of the LSE, which it hopes to increase in the future. The NYSE came second, announcing its intention to buy Euronext. This announcement gave politicians a good scare; both the French president and the German chancellor actively lobbied against an American takeover of this stock exchange that symbolizes pan-European cooperation. The destiny of Euronext, the cradle of European capital market integration, was not to end up in the hands of American competitors, especially not before it could realize its potential and blossom into a full-fledged, globally acknowledged bourse. Panic-induced political consultations began between heads of state and governments, with the large euro zone countries throwing all their political weight behind their attempt to protect Euronext. This is an excellent example of how markets have no consideration for noble political intentions. Do not get me wrong; this was not a shotgun marriage, because the NYSE's owners did not hold a gun to the head of their counterparts in Paris to sell Euronext. They were simply a more desirable partner, or, in other words, they made a better offer.

If Europe means what it says about integrating the European stock exchanges—which keep its economic blood flowing—while maintaining them under European control, it must go beyond political protests. Naturally, I am not suggesting introducing protectionist measures and banning foreign competitors from the continent altogether, but rather creating the right environment for European exchanges while observing free market rules. This may be even easier in the aftermath of the global financial turmoil, when new codebooks have to be written. It is not surprising that the DB renewed its efforts in 2009. Of course, all this would have been much smoother without those five years of mud wrestling. There is a lesson to be learned: Being European is not a value in itself. Some compare the stock exchange saga to the case of Airbus, the flagship pan-European airplane-manufacturing project based on Franco-German cooperation. The cream of Europe's political elite shared the spotlight at the lavish ceremony when the prototype of the new Airbus A380 superjumbo plane was unveiled. A few months later came news of delivery delays due to production problems, sending the share prices of EADS, Airbus's parent company, way down. Competition knows no borders, but it also knows no mercy—as governments know all too well, and the corporate world knows even better.

Corporations

Traders ship goods, and banks and stock exchanges finance the investment needed to produce those goods, but someone actually has to make them: corporate America. We have heard a lot about it, and we all know what it means: the world's most formidable economy, the home of the world's leading companies. These are telling facts. Has anyone ever heard about corporate Europe? I do not think so, but household names such as Philips, Shell, or Unilever have a nice ring to them wherever you go. In 2006, the *Fortune* 500, *Fortune* magazine's annual ranking of the top 500 American public corporations, as measured by gross revenue, were led by these 5 companies: Exxon, Wal-Mart, General Motors, Chevron, and Ford. According to a 2004 *Financial Times* Global Survey, of the world's 500 largest companies, 247 were American, and only 156 were European (and 92 Asian), with 15 of the top 20 based in the United States. In 2007, for the first time ever, a Chinese firm—the state-owned oil company—qualified as the biggest company in the world, and by 2009 several Chinese firms are positioned in the top 20.

In themselves, these firm rankings should give no reason for Europeans to panic, because a company's competitiveness and ability to renew itself are more important in the long term than its market rank. The U.S. market is the world's biggest and freest market, with the most formidable political power in human history behind it. No wonder the biggest transnational companies all have their roots in America. The average company size is bigger in the United States and Japan than in Europe; to compete in this field would be impossible and useless. The problem is not company size but competitiveness. Europe's high-technology sector accounts for 14 percent of its industrial output, just over half of the sector's 23 percent of the U.S. industrial output on the other side of the Atlantic.

The lack of entrepreneurial spirit in Western Europe is an even bigger problem; there, unlike in the United States and Eastern Europe, start-up companies are few and far between. Even so, the productivity of Europe's industry keeps improving. In the years since 1995, industrial production has increased by 15 percent, while employment has dropped by 10 percent. Many of the workers who lost their jobs in the industrial sector were hired by the quickly growing services sector. (The services, industrial, and agricultural sectors generate 71, 27, and 2 percent of Europe's GDP, respectively.[27])

The development of large economic blocs has varied greatly in the years since World War II. In 1950, Germany, France, and Italy, the three big continental European countries, along with Japan, stood at 35 percent of America's level of development; but by 1991, they had worked their way up to 80 percent, only to fall back to their 1973 level of 70 percent by 2004.[28] There are several reasons for this. One is that both continental Europe (especially Germany) and Japan had strong, traditional industries and cultures, and thus when the service sector revolution took place, they had a powerful, embedded industrial basis to set them in motion. By the end of the 1980s, it had become apparent that the times when economic strategies were based on national industrial champions were long gone, especially as these champions—benefiting from globalization—moved their production to regions offering cheaper labor. In these same countries, the service sector could only blossom slowly because its development was hampered by rigid national economic traditions and rules. The nations of the Anglo-Saxon world, conversely, found it much easier to reorient their economies toward services (especially the information technology, or IT, sector), and their financial systems also proved better at channeling savings toward consumption and investment.

Europe has accumulated a significant competitive disadvantage, but it still remains competitive—or a world leader—in a number of sectors, such as semiconductors, mobile telephony, medical instruments, and environmental technology. At the same time, it is quite weak in areas such as IT and biotechnology. Interestingly, Europe's IT sector can almost match its American counterpart in productivity but is only half the size. Accordingly, its weight in total productivity gains is relatively lower (40 percent, compared with 60 percent in the United States). We should not disregard the fact that IT is an explosive, changeable sector, which—until recently—has played a key role in the growth of the entire economy, but which requires above-average flexibility. This flexibility applies to the whole economic environment, from the regulatory framework through institutions to employment rules. Costly bankruptcy or layoff procedures can easily deter such a hyperactive and mobile sector. Investment in research and development (R&D) in Europe is well below its competitors': 1.9 percent of GDP in the fifteen pre–2004 enlargement members of the EU, compared with 2.6 percent in the United States and 3.2 percent in Japan.[29] Even though Europe is slowly getting the better of America in nanotechnology—an increasingly important sector—in terms of research, it has a hard time putting those research results into practice and converting them into business. The United States spends $100 billion more on R&D every year, and the number of U.S. patents per person registered annually is four times the European figure. (The latter may be partly attributable to the fact that it costs four times more to register a patent in Europe than it does in the United States.)

Nonetheless, there are also positive trends. Spain has managed to reduce the time needed to start up a company from two months to two days. France is holding its ground against trade union protests sparked by the annulment of the law on the 35-hour workweek. In countries where governments are dragging their feet, the corporate world moves in to take control of things: German companies are carrying out massive layoffs, and German car and chemical industries are among the best in the world. The world has an "Exportweltmeister" not an "export world champion"; Germany exports more than the enormous United States.

It may be commonplace to say so, but it is true that companies are founded and run by people. Thus, entrepreneurial spirit is the sine qua non for growth and development. Undoubtedly, America is far ahead of Europe in this respect.

The fundamental question for Europe is how it can catch up with its competitors and convert its competitive disadvantage into an advantage. There is one huge obstacle in the way: Europe's fragmentation, which shackles progress in competitiveness. Instead of creating national champions through subsidies and protectionist laws, Europe should create a level playing field for European enterprises where they can realize their full potential.

Here, mention needs to be made of China's corporate sector—as the future competitor. Chinese corporations have begun shopping around for American companies as part of their global expansion. In early 2005, Lenovo acquired IBM's personal computing division for $1.75 billion, and there are several other examples of the Chinese shopping spree in telecommunications, engineering, and even the automobile industry. Chinese cars will soon be marketed in the United States, no doubt giving Detroit quite a headache.

Venture capital firms also merit a few words. They invest in enterprises with a risky but promising and potentially lucrative project, often some kind of technological innovation. Venture capital tends to focus on research-oriented businesses with a high added value. No wonder that many in Europe see venture capital as the key to catching up with the United States. American companies that raised funds through venture capitalists created 10 million new jobs in the last thirty years, which represents close to 10 percent of America's private labor market. Venture capital–financed enterprises generated a turnover of $1,800 billion, roughly 10 percent of corporate America's total turnover.

Venture capital firms are often backed by gigantic pension funds as their main investors. As a result of unavoidable reforms, private pension funds will also become stronger in Europe, and this will encourage the development of the European venture capital sector, which at present plays a minor role despite the grand Lisbon objective of the EU spending 3 percent of its GDP on R&D by 2010. According to plans, two-thirds of R&D spending should come from the private sector, necessitating a much livelier European venture capital market. The total volume of venture capital investment in Europe hardly exceeded €1 billion in 2004, mostly going to biotechnology and pharmaceuticals, medical instruments and devices, telecommunications, and computer software. On the global market, the United States maintains its advantage due to its more business-friendly environment and several market-related and administrative factors (e.g., bigger and more advanced stock exchanges, and more favorable taxation rules). Access to finance and free market conditions are prerequisites for progress and international competitiveness, but without the brains to carry out innovation and R&D, even the best conditions will not help much.

Brains

Despite popular belief to the contrary—shaped by China's domination of the world market—the European Union is still the world's biggest trader of goods, the United States leads the pack by a mile in financial services, and the United States–European Union–Japan trio dominates global competition in technological innovation, each being the strongest in particular sectors. However, in this age of turboglobalization, there are no guaranteed places on the podium. If a given region falls behind in the intellectual race of researchers and development engineers, it will not be able to maintain its leading position in the long run.

Thus, the "brains market" is the most important market of the future. However frightening it may sound, this is the field where Europe and the rest of the West will have to face the toughest competition. The law of large numbers and the teaching of Confucius that learning is the greatest good in the world, mixed with the rules of the free market, give the good people of China a lethal weapon: out of the quarter billion primary school pupils in China, 5 million make it to a university. About a million engineers graduate in India and China every year, while the combined figure for the United States and Europe is a measly 170,000. But this is only half the story. The payroll costs for one American engineer will buy you five in China and eleven in India. No wonder that leading companies have opened R&D centers in India or China, including Google, General Electric, Dell, and SAP.[30]

And there is even more to the story. China has the most students studying abroad of any country in the world. In the last twenty years, there have been 600,000 Chinese studying in the United States alone. About 160,000 of them returned home, but most of those who stayed have built important business or research links with their homeland.[31] Four years after acquiring their doctoral degrees in the United States, 90 percent of Chinese and 80 percent of Indian students are still working in the United States. Grand plans are not foreign to China; a plan was adopted in 1993 to establish a hundred top-notch universities that would become the best institutions of higher education in the twenty-first century.

Development is far less intensive in the West. America used to thrive on attracting foreign scientists, but the brain drain came to an almost complete halt due to the visa and immigration restrictions introduced in the wake of 9/11. Europe is clearly a loser through the brain drain; thousands of researchers leave the old continent behind every year for better opportunities on the other side of the Atlantic. And the brain drain is by no means a modern phenomenon; the first documented exodus of scientists occurred after the collapse of the Byzantine Empire, when they found a new home in Italy. Currently, there are about half a million European engineers living in the United States, and—according to a European Commission survey—only one in four wants to return home.[32] Although the brain drain hits developing countries the worst, this is precious little consolation to Europe. Though Western European researchers must compete with an army of Asian science graduates, and finding such American jobs is becoming ever more difficult, they enjoy far superior conditions in the United States than in European countries. The brain drain is more than just a loss of scientific capacity; it entails the loss of potential development, patents, industrial applications, and jobs.

At the turn of the century, the United States was spending €290 billion on R&D, about €120 billion more than the EU. No wonder that the number of high-technology patents per capita was almost double the European figure. In addition to its lagging IT sector, Europe's other major weakness is the low level of investment in human resources. One-third of the American population has a tertiary degree of some kind, whereas only one in five Europeans can boast the same. With a few exceptions, such as Cambridge, university research in Europe is outdated, which hampers turning research results into practical development. Europe does not have the R&D clusters that bring together researchers, industry, and venture capitalists to help convert scientific inventions into practical solutions and products. As a result, European companies tend to invest in research on well-prepared American ground; thus, European firms invest three times more in American research than vice versa.

What should be done? Learn, educate, and invest. Learn from the good examples: Asia's voluntarism (directing more students toward engineering and technological science) and America's commitment to quality (creating a highly developed institutional framework and technological clusters). Educate European citizens; implement a comprehensive training program to raise the average level of knowledge and to retrain workers that lack the skills needed by the labor market. Finally, invest in retaining researchers and in R&D. The way out for Europe is the way of creativity. What Europe needs is a research and innovation policy based on creativity, a European specialty. But this is easier said than done. First, concerned Europeans must decide which is the more dangerous adversary for the rapid response European team: the American elite commando, or Asia with its millions of foot soldiers.

Socioeconomic Models

Which global region's socioeconomic model will become dominant in the future? Which models will become examples to follow, and which ones will be lost in the turmoil of globalization? This competition is not a deliberate one; the European social model does not compete, in the traditional sense of the word, with the American liberal model or the special Asian model. Nonetheless, not only countries but also regions, firms, and entrepreneurs compete; ultimately, the most viable model will emerge as the dominant one.

Europe's international position, in the present and in the future, cannot be understood without knowing the features of its peculiar socioeconomic model, with all its advantages and drawbacks. A key dilemma Europe faces is how its much-beloved model, which evolved in the postwar years of prosperity, became an obstacle to being able to compete successfully on the international scene. I would like to make it clear that there is no centrally designed, Brussels-driven model in Europe, only a meshwork of national models that evolved over the centuries and are more or less similar. This European model mix can only be considered a single model typical of the continent when it is compared with the American and Asian models.

Two aspects of socioeconomic models are worth looking at more closely: how a given region's economic model finances its economy, and how it finances society. Fundamentally, two different models for financing the economy—that is, companies—have evolved in the capitalist world: through banks and through the stock exchange. The first one is mostly used in continental Europe and Japan, the second in the United Kingdom and the United States. European continental financial systems are typically based on funds channeled through banks. In the American and British financial systems, securities and stock exchanges play a much bigger role. Accordingly, the euro zone bond and share markets are considerably smaller than their American counterparts.

The United States' economic superiority, observable since the 1990s, is often attributed to its market-based financial system. It is a widely held belief that the American system is superior, although the Japanese upswing of the 1980s did temporarily contradict this view. The U.S. market-based system is usually more effective at handling economic uncertainties. The more participants with independent views on the future there are, the likelier it is that their aggregate view will reflect the correct probability distribution. For example, a market-based system can better aggregate views on new technologies. In other words, it tends to work well in an age of virulent turboglobalization. Bank financing is usually more efficient for longer-term, more predictable projects.

The differences between financial systems basically stem from the differences between traditional corporate governance and financing solutions.

Two types of corporate governance systems—external and internal—are distinguished according to their decisionmaking, ownership, and financing. An external system has a single-level structure of governance, with members from the actual management as well as nonmanagement members representing shareholders' interests. It is characterized by fragmented ownership in the hands of many small shareholders, who will sell their shares if dissatisfied, which can send share prices into a nosedive and therefore open the way to a hostile takeover—that is, one that is against the will of the management. An external system presupposes an information and accounting framework that enables external investors to assess a firm's performance. Stock exchange assessment (i.e., share price) is the basis for management remuneration. Countries that traditionally have an external system include the United States and the United Kingdom.

The internal system of corporate governance is typical in continental Europe and Japan. Control is mainly in the hands of a strong, dominant leadership with an internal interest, but other groups also have some degree of control. The latter are called stakeholders, who do not always have ownership in formal terms and may be employees, banks lending to the company, local communities, the government, and customers (buyers or sellers). Securities markets do not play an important role in either control or financing. Management has to fulfill expectations going beyond a high share price (all the more so because the stock exchange often does not function properly). Hostile takeovers are virtually unknown. The typical way of raising funds is through bank loans, which enable family or private owners to maintain control of the company. This is typical of German medium-sized enterprises (*Mittelstand*), which are reluctant to give up their exclusive control over company affairs. In this system, shares are considered not as a financing instrument or financial investment but as a means of ownership. The world, and within it also Europe, is slowly moving toward the market-based model, which is increasing the role of securities and exchanges and is reducing the significance of the internal system. Over the last decade, Europe has shifted toward the American model for financing the economy.

Let us now look at models for financing society. Two major socioeconomic models can be distinguished in the developed world: the Anglo-Saxon model based on free market competition, and the continental European model based on social cohesion. The fundamental institutions of these two systems show a great deal of similarity; their differences lie in nuances of values. Both models are built on a competition-driven market economy, private property, and the rule of law; where they differ is how they see the role of state intervention.

The Anglo-Saxon model worships individualism, free market competition, a small state, and no significant formalized institutions or mechanisms of social dialogue. The European "social" model, which has German roots and was shaped under French influence, relies on the welfare state (the "nanny state"), which takes care of its citizens; solidarity is more important than efficiency, and state intervention in the processes of the market and society are a common phenomenon. As we will see in chapter 3, there are several variations of the European social model, such as the increasingly popular Scandinavian model.

The Chinese model differs fundamentally from the Western models, and it cannot even be mentioned in the same breath as the Asian capitalist, mercantilist models such as the Japanese one. The Chinese model is a peculiar version of state socialism, which is approaching Western economic standards with giant strides and slowly adopting Western social norms. China's socioeconomic model is undergoing swift transformation, which is fueling its annual growth of 8 to 10 percent. Yet Chinese society has many major unsolved problems, which will be discussed below. China's emergence as a power with which to reckon poses a serious challenge not only to the West but also to Asia, especially wealthy countries like Japan, Taiwan, and South Korea. All these countries owe their growth and prosperity to exports, and as China comes of age economically, they are finding that they have a huge global exporter for a competitor. Because China can now produce high-value-added products, it has no need to import such products from the Asian tigers.

China's growth in strength has suddenly exposed the vulnerability of the Asian capitalist model based on national champions and service monopolies, intense state intervention, loans from politically influenced banks, and neglected capital markets. This model works fine in good times, riding the waves of the high seas like a huge ocean liner, but as soon as a storm breaks loose and conditions change, it has difficulty adjusting its course and maneuvering into the shallow waters of a safe harbor. Thus, like the European social model, the Asian mercantilist model faces painful reforms. India, for example, must carry on with the 1991 reforms of its self-sufficient, socialist model if it is to avoid falling behind its formidable neighbor, China.

The most important trend in the last several decades has been the competition and convergence between the Anglo-Saxon and continental socioeconomic models in Europe, bringing the social model closer to the market-based model. The European economic and social mentality has undoubtedly become Americanized, gathering strength before the next era of globalization—China's true emergence.

Dragons and Tigers

China and India are on the rise. The much-discussed phenomenon of the "Asian century" could soon be a reality—at least that is what global economic shifts and geopolitical forecasts suggest. This section delineates the strengths and weaknesses of the two emerging Asian giants, China and India. It also endeavors to assess the impact of their emergence on the future of the Western world, especially Europe.

China: Enter the Dragon

During his contribution to the debate on the approval of the Barroso Commission in late 2004, a member of the European Parliament raised a small EU flag—which he had bought in the EP paper shop the day before—and said: "Do you know what the label on this flag says? Made in China!"

About a year later, I was leafing through some books in one of the bookshops on the Rond-Point Schuman in the heart of the EU quarter in Brussels, when I came across Paul Magnette's excellent work *What Is the European Union? Nature and Prospects.*[33] As I was reading the blurb, a strange line of type caught my eyes: Printed in China. The fact that it was printed in China does not detract from the value of this excellent book, but it does symbolize what we have heard so much about: the arrival of the dragon.

The dragon means something very different to Europeans than it does to the Chinese. For the Europeans, it is a dreadful monster; for the Chinese, it is a national symbol. And since 2006, the dragon has also been a symbol of wealth. It was in 2006 that forty-nine-year-old Zhang Yin became China's wealthiest person. She is the owner of Nine Dragons Paper, who has accumulated a fortune of $3.4 billion by recycling mountains of wastepaper generated in the United States. She is higher on the list of the world's richest people than J. K. Rowling, the author of the Harry Potter novels. The pace of growth of Nine Dragons demonstrates the pace of change in China; every year, it is becoming more and more difficult to make one's way onto the China Rich List compiled by the business magazine *Hurun Report.* In 1998, it took $6 million to make the top 50, but only eight years later, a private fortune of $100 million was needed to make the top 500.

It is not only dragons that the Europeans and Chinese view differently. They also see history very differently. Let us try to look at history from a Chinese perspective. What we see is an enormous, refined, and highly developed civilization that was ahead of its time economically and intellectually for millennia. It invented porcelain, paper, the compass, gunpowder, steelmaking, and the printing press. It managed to defend itself against barbarian hordes for centuries. It needed no one else, and thus it became an "introvert," closing out the rest of the world for long centuries. Then, one day, dog-faced strangers began to arrive from Europe in the far west, more and more of them coming on big ships with menacing weapons.

In the age of globalization, China has been given a second opportunity, and it has recognized that it can best beat the West with a Western weapon: trade. China will not make the same mistake twice, closing its doors to the outside world and allowing the barbarians to get the better of it. Deng Xiaoping announced the policy of Four Modernizations in 1978, covering industry, agriculture, defense, and innovation, after which market principles started creeping into economic governance. By the beginning of 2006, China's GDP had exceeded that of the United Kingdom or France, making it the world's fourth-biggest economic power. China became the world's biggest exporter of technology items in 2005, surpassing the United States. Forecasts predict that China will become the second-largest economy by 2020, and the number one economic powerhouse by 2050, but surely the biggest exporter as soon as by 2010. The EU is China's biggest trading partner, whereas China is the EU's second (right after the United States). Bilateral trade has increased forty times since the 1978 reforms, exceeding €174 billion in 2004.[34]

Twenty years ago, China's share of world trade was below 1 percent, while today it is seven times that. Foreign direct investment in China totaled more than $60 billion in 2004, making it the second-biggest capital destination after the United States. China has accounted for a quarter of global economic growth every year since 2000, helping to maintain the 4 percent global growth figure. China's involvement in the global economy was completed by its WTO membership, and it has added 800 million workers to the international labor market. Western economies and the Western political elite are riding the wave of this shock. In 2005, China was responsible for a fifth of the raw steel, a third of the rice and cotton, and half of the cement produced in the world. It surpassed Germany for fifth place in the number of patent applications in 2004. Its automobile industry churned out 2.6 million cars in 2005, up from 300,000 in 1995, making it the first year when sales within China of domestically manufactured cars exceeded sales of Japanese models. By 2015, the Chinese car industry could surpass Japan and the United States, the current leaders of the sector.[35]

China will have become the world's biggest computer hardware maker within ten years. And an IT industry shutdown of just a few days could already trigger a global shock today. New subscribers of China Mobile number more than 65 million, twice the growth in mobile phone subscribers in all Western Europe. Every second camera, every third television set, and every fourth washing machine and refrigerator are already made in China. When the Industrial and Commercial Bank of China decided to become listed on the stock exchanges in autumn 2006, it was the world's biggest initial public offering to date, with a total share value of $20 billion floated in Shanghai and Hong Kong. The previous record holder was NTT Mobile Communications Network of Japan, with $18 billion worth of shares offered to investors. China replaced the United States as Japan's key trading partner in 2004. An American study in early 2005 revealed that China had also surpassed the United States in the consumption of basic agricultural produce and industrial products. The number of personal computers doubles every twenty-eight months in this vast land. The United States still consumes more crude oil than China, and Americans owned ten times as many cars as the Chinese in 2004, but China is far ahead of the United States in domestic sales of television sets, mobile telephones, and refrigerators. Even so, the Chinese are only responsible for about 3 percent of global consumption, but this ratio will rise to 10.5 percent by 2014, a Credit Suisse First Boston study suggests. As a result, Chinese brands will become stronger, and China may even be able to dictate global standards in some areas.[36]

Western retail chains are largely supplied from China. Millions of manual laborers are losing their jobs in the West, which is not surprising if we compare the average German hourly wage of $24.00 with the Chinese average of $0.60 (2002 figures). In addition, the Chinese labor market has vast untapped potentials in rural areas, which will not be exhausted in twenty years, even if today's impressive growth trends continue. The entry of Chinese and Indian workers into the international labor market has reduced the global capital-to-workforce ratio by 55 to 60 percent.[37]

Just glance at a business magazine and you will see plenty of evidence that of the world's 500 largest firms, 400 have established their own R&D centers in China, which should come as no surprise. A key element of

China's economic strategy is acquiring foreign know-how—by blackmail, if all else fails; thus, a precondition for access to the world's biggest market for any company is handing over its technological secrets and procedures. Chinese capitalism differs greatly from the British and American models, where their own inventions and innovations propelled progress. China, conversely, borrows ready-made solutions from more developed countries. Chinese corporations use Western technology and know-how to squeeze Western firms out of the huge domestic Chinese market. For the time being, there are few—to be more precise, fifteen—Chinese names on the *Fortune* 500 list, but surely there will be more and more, just as happened with Japanese and South Korean businesses. And when China's currently wasteful financial system—it is at present unable to rechannel its huge savings into the economy—becomes strong enough, thanks to allowing in foreign banks and abolishing financial restrictions, China can also become a major international financial power.

In the meantime, American and European companies are relocating to China. Wal-Mart, America's and the world's largest retailer, is expanding its operations to China through the acquisition of a Taiwanese chain of 100 supermarkets in China for $1 billion. Wal-Mart beat its key competitor, Carrefour of France, to the deal. Philips has moved its mobile telephone production completely to China, Avon recruited 114,000 people in the summer of 2006 alone, and Citibank and Morgan Stanley have embarked on billion-dollar acquisitions in the financial services market. Mercedes opened its first Chinese factory in 2006, investing €1.5 billion, and it will make 300,000 cars annually in a few years' time. The European champion manufacturer Airbus signed a framework agreement in October 2006 to establish its first plant outside Europe, in China, where four aircraft will be assembled monthly starting in 2009. And in November 2007, PetroChina overtook ExxonMobil as the world's top company in market value.[38]

But the story is no longer just about getting a slice of the Chinese market or about exporting mass-produced, low-quality Chinese products. China accounted for $4 billion worth of foreign direct investment around the world in 2004, and it has begun developing high-value-added products specifically tailored to Western markets. Chinese companies have started shopping around in corporate America and have embarked upon global expansion. As mentioned above, the computer maker Lenovo recently bought IBM's personal computing division, but there are also other examples in the telecommunications and engineering sectors. China's leading automotive group, Geely, announced in the autumn of 2006 that it had developed a medium-sized model for the European and American markets. Initially, production will be 1 million cars a year, but Geely hopes to extend its annual capacity to 2 million by 2015.[39]

The list of similar examples is almost endless, but the few I have enumerated demonstrate sufficiently how the Chinese giant has turned things upside down since it burst onto the global scene. Chinese society is also undergoing rapid change, as is Chinese self-awareness. A survey conducted by the Chicago Council on Global Affairs in 2006 showed that the Chinese believe their homeland will become as influential as the United States within ten years. The majority of American, Chinese, Indian, and South Korean respondents were of the opinion that, eventually, China would edge ahead of the United States in global competition.[40] China's middle class is growing fast, and the wealthy few are becoming the wealthy many. At the turn of the century, China absorbed a mere 2 percent of the world's luxury items, but this proportion had risen to 13 percent in 2006 according to media reports, and it is predicted that, by 2010, every fourth such item will be sold to a Chinese customer.

The Chinese are willing and able to adapt to the expectations of Western civilization. For example, the China National Tourist Office sent out questionnaires worldwide in 2006, wanting to know how Chinese tourists were seen in different parts of the world. The 30,000 responses revealed some interesting facts. The most common complaint about Chinese tourists was that they clear their throat and spit all the time; this is considered a healthy habit in China but disgusts foreigners. The Chinese also litter and smoke in undesignated places. In view of the mass criticism, the Moral Culture Committee of the Communist Party of China decided to hand out a concise code of conduct with all airline tickets to Chinese citizens traveling abroad. In the meantime, the world has started learning Chinese; 2,500 universities in more than 100 countries now offer Chinese, and an estimated 30 million people are actively learning the language.[41]

At the start of this chapter, I pointed out that an uncritical projection of present trends into the future may easily lead to false predictions. This is no different in the case of China. It is not the size of the Chinese economy that really impresses us but its double-digit rate of growth. In terms of its size and its role in the international economy, China's economy lags way behind both Europe's and America's, even if the pace at which it is growing is truly awe inspiring. In a sense, rather than focusing on China's astounding growth rate, it would be more correct to think of China's return; before 1820, it accounted for almost a third of the world's GDP, a proportion that today of course remains out of reach, despite its rapid growth in recent decades. Nonetheless, China has come a long way since 1978, when its share of the global economy hovered at around half a percent.

The strength of the Chinese economy is surrounded by many myths. An open question is whether China is really the world's workshop or whether it is closer to the truth to call it the world's assembly plant. Considering that the average import content of Chinese products is 60 percent, "world's assembly plant" seems more precise. China's high-technology export market is misleading because it mostly consists of goods such as DVD players, which are in fact low technology.[42] Following an initial surge, China is now behind the former Soviet countries, Brazil, and Mexico in market reforms and privatization, not to mention democratic institution building. The Chinese government also faces a huge domestic dilemma: If it continues to pursue its current growth policy, its domestic disparities will grow, and the gap between rural and urban areas will widen to a point of no return, which may thrust the country into a deep crisis. The question is whether China will embark on its special "New Deal" to reduce regional and social disparities and to improve the education of the rural masses. In the previous pages, I have tried to show the flip side of the China coin, to present another face of this vast country that is often disregarded in the heat of today's China craze. We should not take everything at face value and should remember that not all that glitters is gold. China is not unstoppable, but we do need to prepare for its arrival.

There is a Chinese story about a man who was obsessed with dragons. All he did all day was paint images of dragons. One day a real dragon appeared in his workshop to express its appreciation for his work. When he saw the dragon, he was scared out of his wits and made a run for it. This is where the story ends. I will let you decide what to read into it.

India: The World's Biggest . . . What?

"India is the world's quickest-growing free market democracy, characterised by entrepreneurial spirit, a vast market, a skilled English-speaking workforce, an improving standard of living, and a population with a falling average age." So reads a condensed quotation from an advertisement published in a leading Indian business daily in the autumn of 2006. It is impressive and true in many ways, but it is also distorted and oversimplified in some—the tiger about to jump off the pages seems a bit idealized.

Years before India became independent, Mahatma Gandhi was asked whether he wanted India to become as developed as its colonizing power,

Great Britain. He said no, explaining that if Britain had to loot half the world for its wealth, India would have to pillage the whole world and still not have enough. This argument reflects the sentiments of a country sick and tired of its colonial life. Many things have since changed; India has become a key venue and symbol of globalization, its economy is growing almost as fast as China's, and one hears more and more about the international successes of Indian IT firms.[43]

India's culture, like China's, goes back to ancient times, when it had one of the most advanced industrial infrastructures in the world and maintained close ties with Egypt and the Roman Empire. From the birth of Christ until the emergence of the Mongol Empire, for a good millennium and a half, India had the largest economy in the world, producing a quarter to a third of the "GDP" of the time. During British colonization, much of India's traditional handicraft industry was wiped out and replaced with British manufacturing.

When it won its independence in 1947, India decided to follow the policy of "never again foreign interference," sealed off its doors to the outside world, and made arrangements for self-sufficiency. A special version of a socialist planned economy was introduced, which did not completely do away with private ownership in business but limited it considerably, just as it restricted acquisitions by foreign investors. By the 1980s, it had become clear that the road chosen had led nowhere but to failure and bankruptcy, which was only made more apparent by the success of neighboring China, which had opted for market reforms in the 1970s.

A shift toward capitalism by India was unavoidable, and it came finally in 1991, when restrictions on foreign investment were eased, foreign trade liberalization commenced, and the private sector was given new opportunities. The economy went boom, growing at an average of 7.5 percent annually between 1994 and 1997. But India's time has really come with turboglobalization—and particularly with the cost-driven outsourcing of IT and services from the United States and Europe. Seizing this opportunity, India's IT and service sectors, especially its customer service telephone call centers, have performed an economic miracle, putting it on the map of global powers overnight. Bangalore has become Asia's Silicone Valley. India is far from rich in natural resources, and its obsolete infrastructure is in dire need of investment. Thus, providing virtual services was a perfect opportunity because it only required computers, telephones, an optical cable network, and well-trained, English-speaking workers willing to do the same jobs for a fraction of Western salaries. Responding to these advantages, thousands of American and European businesses have relocated their back office services to India. Deutsche Bank, for example, announced at the beginning of 2006 that it would relocate half its commercial and sales positions to India, and on top of that hire hundreds of Indians for its extended research center. JP Morgan Chase has also announced plans to recruit about 4,500 employees in India, where it has relocated much of its back office business.

India also has advantages for a novel, private form of outsourcing: online private tutoring. British parents would normally have to pay about £20 to £30 an hour for private tutoring in mathematics but, with the help of the Internet, Indian teachers can do the same work for a fraction of the cost.

Industrial corporations are following in the footsteps of service companies that have moved operations to India. BMW, Suzuki, Ford, and Volvo are pushing and shoving to get a slice of the Indian market. The reason is simple: The automotive market is expected to expand by about 1.5 million units a year until 2010, and there is no shortage of cheap labor to produce those cars. A poor farmer may not be suitable for call center work, but— with some training—he can do the job required on a production line.

However, India is doing much more than just provide a highly trained workforce to transnational companies. It now also has its own multinationals. Ranbaxy, India's largest pharmaceutical company, generates roughly 80 percent of its revenue from sales abroad, and it has aspirations to become one of the top five makers of generic drugs in the world by 2012 and increase its income fivefold. In order to realize this objective, it has been making acquisitions in Spain, Belgium, Romania, and Italy. It took Infosys, an IT firm often considered a symbol of the new Indian economy, only twenty-three years to reach the $1 billion threshold in sales, and merely another twenty-three months to exceed the $2 billion mark. In the *Fortune* 500 list of America's largest companies, 125 already have R&D centers in India, and 380 have outsourced their software development activities to India.

Sensex, India's most important stock exchange index, surpassed the magic 10,000-point threshold in early 2006. Sensex stood at 1,000 points in 1990, and it took a decade for it to climb to 6,000. Then, in 2005, it shot up by 3,000 points in twelve months. Venture capital investments, essential for promising small and medium-sized enterprises, also show great potential; experts forecast that they will treble between 2006 and 2010. A number of commodity exchanges have sprouted, starting from scratch and making their way

up to the global average in just a few years' time. The extremely low level
of bad loans (2 percent, a fraction of the Chinese figure) indicates the maturity of India's banking and financial sector.

India's "new age" economic model is a peculiar one. Contrary to the
strategy of the Asian tigers, India's growth is driven by domestic consumption rather than by exports or investment, and its main exports are services
and high-value-added products rather than labor-intensive, cheap products
of the processing industry. Over the course of the last quarter century, this
model has led to a fourfold increase in the size of its middle class, which
now numbers 250 million.

Turboglobalization has given India a huge opportunity for economic recovery—as well as a fierce competitor in the shape of neighboring China.
But on the flip side of the coin, things look gloomier, as we will see in the
next subsection.

All Is Well, All Is Fine?

Is all well, is all fine? Not really—far from it. Both China and India have
several serious problems. Both are key actors and winners of turboglobalization. But, to have a clear view, one must always also look behind the
scenes. We should not think for a second that today's changes are only fast
moving for the West. Together, China and India, these two giant developing nations—let us call them Chindia—must bridge much wider gaps to
catch up with the West, which has spent centuries preparing for the brave
new world of turboglobalization. Their national economies have benefited
greatly from fast-changing globalization, but their huge economic and social problems hidden backstage are almost incomprehensible to a European
mind, and these overwhelming challenges cast a dark shadow over the
myths about those wonderful dragons and tigers.

We first turn to China's challenges. Many believe that China is walking
on a razor's edge, trying to lunge ahead to escape from its huge troubles,
but a general crisis appears unavoidable. Hundreds of millions of elderly
people could be left without care and miners protesting against their working conditions could spark local civil wars, while hundreds of millions of
peasants live at or below the subsistence level and banks are in debt up to
their eyeballs; the transition to a market economy and especially to a democratic society is still waiting to happen, and it is unclear what social catastrophes it will spark off when it does happen. The most serious challenge
is care for the elderly. Due to the official one-child-only policy and the clos-

ing down of former state-owned enterprises (which used to provide care for their retired workers), more and more elderly Chinese retirees are finding themselves left without any kind of care or provision. One-tenth of the population (131 million people) was over the age of sixty years in 2000, and this proportion is expected to rise to 12.5 percent by 2010, 17 percent by 2020, and 29 percent by 2050, when the number of those over sixty will have swollen to 438 million.[44]

To make matters worse, China's traditional social care system is falling apart, and the family ties that used to ensure that the elderly were not abandoned have already been ripped asunder. More and more people in China live in nuclear families or migrate to cities on the East Coast to earn a living, leaving the elderly and the sick behind in depopulated villages. The state-owned firms that used to provide for their former employees have long disappeared. The current crop of thirty-somethings and forty-somethings cannot expect much from their employers when it comes to their retirement, and what is more, there are hardly any savings options for them to guarantee a decent standard of living for their retirement years.[45]

China is a country of vast social disparities, and the gaps are getting wider, leading to thousands of local peasant revolts and armed conflicts every year. In 2004, according to official statistics, there were 74,000 larger riots nationwide involving a terrifying 4 million people. Instead of privatization, land is being expropriated. However horrific it may sound, the fact is that there are 70 million landless peasants and close to 200 million migrant casual workers wandering the vast countryside. It could well be the success of Chinese industry that leads the country to starvation. In November 2007, the Chinese minister for land and resources acknowledged that the illegal land acquisitions by factories (which means that they simply drive peasants away from the land) reached a level that endangers the country's food supply (with the demand rising steeply year by year). Thus, it is not surprising that the price of pork increased by 60 percent in 2007.[46]

Moving to the economic realm, if we peep behind the scenes of China's breathtaking competitiveness, it turns out that not all is rosy. China's share of world trade was just over 6 percent in 2004, but it slightly exceeded 8 percent the following year, which is an impressive feat indeed. However, Chinese trade is generated by a handful of industries, such as electronics, electric appliances, household goods, housewares, textiles, and shoes. These are the sectors attracting the bulk of foreign investment. In many areas, China is but a downstream assembly plant; many of the components built into Chinese export products come from Japan, South Korea, Taiwan, and other Southeast Asian countries. As a result, while accumulating a considerable trade surplus vis-à-vis the United States and European countries, China has incurred a trade deficit with its Southeast Asian component suppliers. Another conspicuous fact is that, despite the long boom, only a few internationally acknowledged Chinese corporations have proved to be competitive in the long run, although their number is rising slowly and steadily. China's economy remains built on massive monopolies. The three largest players have a 100 percent share in mobile telephony, landline telecommunications, and the aluminum and oil industries; a 90 percent share in the insurance sector; a 60 percent share in the agrifood sector (dairy) and in banking; and a more than 50 percent share in television and personal computer manufacturing. And protectionism flourishes in China; influential firms often turn to the government for shelter against foreign competitors and other measures to defend their domestic markets.[47]

Today, a company is more than just production lines and offices; it is also an empire of qualified and creative businesspeople—at least in an ideal world. China is desperately short of creative managers; its management culture is still light-years behind that of the West. A widely held view among Western businessmen is that, for its size, China has an insufficient number of qualified, young business managers. The emphasis is on qualified; China is producing young graduates by the thousands but, due to the ethos of its education system, they lack creativity and are merely human "robots," good only for executing instructions precisely. Their lack of linguistic skills only aggravates the problem; only one in ten young business graduates or engineers speaks English well enough to hold a job at an international firm.

And despite China's industrial might, the Chinese method of production is actually wasteful. Maintaining the nation's pace of growth requires staggering investment; it costs China $5 in investment to produce $1 of value added in the final product, which is much worse than the Western average, and which puts China behind even India. Fundamentally, China is a planned economy, where banks' lending policies disregard the most basic economic principles, granting loans according to political influence. As a result, Chinese banks held bad loans (i.e., loans that will probably never be paid by the debtors) valued at close to $1 trillion, roughly the same as the China's gigantic currency reserve. China's growth is rooted in reinvesting corporate profits but, generally speaking, little thought is given to these reinvestments and there is insufficient control. Corporate managers are not really responsible or answerable to the market, investors, or lenders, as they would be under normal circumstances in a capitalist economy; their only concern is fulfilling bureaucratically set medium-term production plans.

The chokehold of bureaucracy and corruption are strangling China. The best part of Chinese national holdings is in the state's hands; state-owned enterprises enjoy a monopoly in key sectors such as banking, telecommunications, energy, the steel industry, the automotive industry, and foreign trade. Investment suffers from rampant cronyism; the main concern of top managers at state companies is how to fill their own pockets, and—of course, for the right price—state officials are more than happy to lend a helping hand.

China and India are in close competition for the title of the world's most corrupt state, but as long as the cake keeps getting bigger, the millions of ants stealing the crumbs do not cause too much damage to the bakery. The lay observer might consider anticorruption legislation and sanctions too strict, but in reality most cases of corruption are never investigated or prosecuted. Corruption not only costs China billions of dollars but also undermines Chinese society's moral fabric. Disrespecting civil liberties and stifling the freedom of the press reinforces corruption and sends out the message to those involved that they can escape justice. For instance, in the world's second-biggest online market, the censorship of Google (called GooGe, Chinese for "harvest song") hinders the use of social resources but —contrary to the Communist Party's hopes—does not suppress the democratic process, simply because it is impossible to gag a global communication and information network.

The state of the environment in China also gives rise to concern; the Chinese economic miracle is endangering the global natural environment. Two-thirds of China's 600 large cities experience water shortages regularly; the air is so polluted that inhabitants inhale the equivalent of two packs of cigarettes in pollutants every day. More than 1,000 new cars are registered each day in Beijing alone. Sixteen of the world's twenty most polluted cities are Chinese. Almost half of China's vast wood imports come from illegal logging, particularly in poor Asian countries. About 22 percent of the world's population lives in China, but it only has 8 percent of the Earth's water reserves and, to add insult to injury, 60 percent of that water is now contaminated and thus nonpotable. Air pollution causes acid rain, which makes farmland uncultivable; one-third of arable land in China now has acidic soil, which is especially worrying in light of the fact that per capita farmland is 600 square meters, roughly one and a half times the size of a basketball court. Fortunately, China is beginning to recognize the gravity of the pollution problem, and environmental issues are no longer just swept under the carpet. There have been some original projects, such as the eco-city of Dongtan near Shanghai, in the Yangtze River Delta. This eco-city will be home to no more than half a million people, will use only renewable energy, and will be environmentally friendly, with a minimal ecological footprint. But we should have no illusions; it will merely be a drop in the ocean.

In fact, China has no place to go but forward. As long as it keeps up its breathtaking pace of growth, it can successfully keep a lid on the social tensions boiling beneath the surface. But what will happen when the economy slows down?

Let us now turn our attention to India. Here, too, we can see two very different faces of the same country: the glass palaces of Bangalore, the city of software development and services, and the slums of Calcutta, where millions live in deep poverty, barely surviving on less than a dollar a day. A quarter of a billion people are malnourished, but soon they will not only be underfed but thirsty too, as India's water reserves are slowly depleted. Road conditions are catastrophic, power cuts are a daily occurrence, and medical care is a luxury in rural areas. Healthcare workers miss almost every second day at work, and teachers often do not show up at school either. Child labor is not uncommon; according to the International Labor Office, there could be some 44 million child workers in the country, the biggest number in any nation in the world.[48] Masses of people are hopelessly trapped in the caste system and bogged down in despair, which paralyzes growth.

As in China, public life in India is poisoned by corruption; even the $23 billion IT and outsourcing sectors are not immune to it. A report by a British television channel in the autumn of 2006 triggered quite an uproar when it came to light that confidential data—such as credit card numbers—of American and European clients had been mishandled by Indian telephone call centers and used for fraud on an industrial scale. In addition, the government itself occasionally adopts measures that delivered serious blows to the sector responsible for the nation's competitiveness. One such measure came in 2006 when the authorities of Karnataka State, which includes the capital city of Bangalore, banned teaching at its primary schools in all languages except the indigenous Dravidian. The ban gave a headache to both the hundreds of thousands of English-speaking IT experts who had moved to the capital and the 2,000 schools using English as the language of instruction, which had to close down.[49] However, it will be Karnataka itself and ultimately the whole of India that will suffer the consequences if Bangalore—home to 1,500 world-class IT firms and a third of all the state's export capacity—goes into decline. Indian politicians hostile to globalization are trying to sail against the wind, but they will lose out eventually. Years ago, when West Bengal introduced its "no English, only Bengali" policy, it sent the local economy downhill, forcing its politicians to backtrack and reverse their decision.

India's financial system, together with its banking and insurance sectors, is screaming out for reform. Foreign holdings in financial institutions are still limited, and investors may have to fly for up to four hours before they can find a decent stock exchange that trades globally. The global financial crisis hit the Indian banking sector, but, more important, reinforced the antireform and anti-Western sentiment in the country. Badly needed reforms of the financial industry were therefore frozen. India's important companies are still listed on exchanges in Singapore or Hong Kong, partly because commercial and financial conditions are not fully liberalized at home and the rupee is not convertible. Apart from New Delhi, Dubai and Bahrain also long to become the bridge between the stock exchanges of New York, London, and Hong Kong, so India had better get its act together. The Indian economy has demonstrated before that reform pays off and that removing the rules shackling the economy can release huge positive forces. The Indian government faces zillions of problems and seems unable to shake off the nation's huge deficit and to spend its money intelligently and effectively by investing in infrastructure. By liberalizing its economy, India could hope to emulate the Chinese miracle.

The Dragon and the Tiger: Friends or Foes?

During the 1970 May Day celebrations in Tiananmen Square, Mao Zedong turned to Brajesh Mishra, the Indian diplomat sitting beside him in the box of honor, and said: "India is a great country, and the Indian people are a great people." So what is the big deal?—one might ask. Well, relations between these neighboring countries were extremely tense after World War II, and thus for Mao to come out with such a statement was a big deal indeed.

Years later, in December 1988, Rajiv Gandhi's visit to China was a turning point in Sino-India relations, as was shown by the prolonged handshake between him and Deng Xiaoping. It was the first visit by an Indian prime minister to China after a gap of twenty-eight years. High-level talks were resumed; and working groups were formed to deal with border disputes, bilateral trade, cultural ties, and research cooperation. As a result, cross-border trade has been expanding steadily since the 1990s at an ever-increasing pace. The relationship between the two countries has not always been so ideal; following their fruitful cooperation in the 1950s, political ties disintegrated in 1962, when border disputes resulted in a short war. In the Bangladesh War of Independence, China and India found themselves on opposing sides yet again; while India declared war on Pakistan, China supported the occupying forces of Pakistan and later actively assisted the Pakistani nuclear weapons program. India's policy on Tibet was also a constant thorn in China's side.

The ties between China and India are deeply rooted in history and can be traced back thousands of years. Yet these ties were never really close or deep, due to the vast differences in mentality between the two societies. Their different mentalities were also manifest in the way they shook off the yoke of colonialism—China with an armed fight, military force, and militant ideology; India peacefully, with quiet resistance and negotiation. Many Indians believe—exactly because of the militant Chinese mentality—that China will be its biggest strategic threat in the future. Even so, prospects for cooperation between the two countries have never looked brighter, which naturally does not preclude peaceful competition.

China and India have a lot to learn from each other's mistakes and successes. In GDP per capita, India ($2,500) is well behind its Communist neighbor ($4,600), but if it manages to accelerate market reforms, it could close the gap within twenty years. At present, however, the differences are conspicuous. In China, there are hardly any urban slums, whereas in India tens of millions live in subhuman conditions on the edges of cities and towns. Their relationship is not one of equal partners; India is weaker in many respects, which makes it anxious. China's neighbors watch the rise of the Chinese dragon in awe, as they begin to resemble a planetary system revolving around the Red Star of China, shaped by its economic and diplomatic forces. This satellite group includes Pakistan, Vietnam, Taiwan, and Myanmar, but the orbits of South Korea, Japan, and even Australia are increasingly affected by China's gravitational pull. The pincers are tightening around India, which has realized that, with a 3 percent growth rate, the gap with China will only widen.

What India needs are reforms and then more reforms. It must improve its decrepit infrastructure and render its labor market more flexible. It cannot continue to provide the kind of protection it does to workers when the majority of the population has not the slightest chance of finding a job. Every enterprise employing more than a hundred people needs the government's approval for any layoffs, whereas in some sectors it is impossible to operate above a certain company size. The number of working-age people will rise by 71 million between 2006 and 2010, many of whom will join the ranks of the tens of millions officially considered unemployed and the masses of unregistered jobless people. We should not be misled by the news about India's world-beating IT sector with which we are constantly bombarded; the IT industry only employs 1 percent of the population.[50]

On top of all its other priorities, India must also boost its industrial capacity. India missed the boat when the first wave of outsourcing swept through the global economy and the mass production of simple, low-value-added goods was relocated to Asia. India has only benefited from the outsourcing of services, and missing such a golden opportunity to strengthen its manufacturing sector is a luxury it cannot afford a second time. Once again, this is easier said than done. Apart from telecommunications networks, in India infrastructure and electricity are twice as expensive as in China; to transport freight by rail costs three times as much as in its northeastern neighbor. To make things worse, China invests considerably more (in 2003, seven times more) in infrastructure development. The problem Indian governments face is not only the lower income and higher spending of the budget; a political system based on free elections will often force the administration to opt for projects that yield quick and tangible improvements in voters' standards of living.

China, with its reform totalitarianism, must pay little attention to public opinion and thus can afford to build motorways—which absorb vast sums of public funds and are only paid off in decades, but are crucial to modernization—instead of schools in rural villages. India lags behind China not only in its public roads; its industries—more reminiscent of those in poor developing countries than in an emerging market economy—are much less developed than China's, where leading companies abound. The "made in India" label is becoming more attractive, however; for instance, car making and the manufacture of mobile technology are advancing in giant strides, which is no wonder when mobile telephone subscription figures are galloping at 2 million new users a month, unmatched anywhere else in the world. There were 50 million mobile phone subscriptions at the end of 2005, which—if current trends continue—will mean more than 300 million users by 2009, attracting the biggest makers of handsets, who will then supply the entire globe from India.[51] In other words, the same basic process will unfold in India as in China ten or fifteen years ago.

Despite the shared success stories, however, the differences between the two countries are still vast. In 2004, China attracted six times as much foreign direct investment as India ($6 billion). The Indian government, and especially the nation's industrial lobby, has a completely different view of foreign direct investment than China, considering it a threat to their own market positions and privileges. Oddly, the Indian government seems to take orthodox economic principles less seriously than the officially Communist politicians of China.

Nonetheless, India has some advantages over China, which it could use to its benefit. Its demographic prospects are more promising; according to UN forecasts, the ratio of those who are active in the workforce to those who are inactive (roughly, the ratio of workers to retirees) will have sunk below China's by 2030. In spite of corruption and political uncertainties, India's institutions are superior in many aspects—its legal and financial systems are more developed, it has the world's largest working democracy, its private sector is relatively stronger, and people's knowledge of English is much better (along with Hindi, it is somewhat of a lingua franca among the country's many indigenous languages). The economy has revved up in recent years, spurred mainly by efficiency gains and not by investment in new factories, as in China's case. India's growth potential is based on services, medical technology, and the IT sector, which is more future oriented than China's, and business schools are also more numerous and provide a better education. As India pushes through the necessary reforms, the shortcomings of the Chinese miracle are beginning to come to light. The race between the dragon and the tiger is far from over, but this time it will be fought out on center court with the whole world watching, and not on a practice court in a far corner of the sports complex.

This race between China and India, particularly boosting industrial output, requires an awful lot of energy. Chindia is lining up at the global gas station with huge cans. Chinese factories have a ravenous appetite, and the old adage that appetite comes with eating could not be truer than in their case; their need for energy has exploded. We should also remember that motorization has just begun in both countries. Per capita oil consumption is fifteen times lower in China and thirty times lower in India than in gas-guzzling-obsessed America. But if consumption went up to half of the American level in both countries, it would mean 100 million barrels of fuel burned every single day; by comparison, today's daily total global consumption is 85 million barrels.

Twenty years ago, China was self-sufficient in oil, but now it imports more than the industrial powerhouse Japan. Oil is the lifeblood of up-and-coming superpowers, therefore they will do whatever it takes to ensure their security of supply. A World Bank report talked about the rebirth of the ancient Silk Road connecting the Roman Empire with China and India, but this time it would link Chindia with Africa and carry oil.[52] The two Asian giants will go to extraordinary lengths to lay their hands on Africa's black gold, often turning a blind eye to many a ruthless regime. Economic and political relations between Asia and Africa are flourishing; more than a quarter of the African continent's exports end up in Asia, up from one-sixth at the turn of the millennium. Exports from Africa to China have been growing by 50 percent annually since 2000, now making China the number one importer, ahead of Japan. China is happy to lend to African nations, whose debts have been canceled by the West. The first Confucius Institute opened its doors in Nairobi in 2005, hoping to imitate the example of the goodwill fostered by the British Council and the Institut Français, both of which have information offices and libraries in major cities around the world. China is behaving in Africa like an old-time colonial power, exploiting natural resources and making mutually beneficial deals with the local elite. India is also extremely active in African markets—it is the destination of 13 percent of the continent's export and the origin of 9 percent of its imports. Although their interests often clash, China and India sometimes join hands in their search for oil, as they did in 2005 to acquire a minority share in Syria's market-leading oil firm, Al Furat Production Company (the deal involved the China National Petroleum Corporation and India's Oil Corporation). This business maneuver carried an important political message: China and India are willing to cooperate to ensure the security of their energy supply.

China is particularly worried about the security of its oil sources and the tankers transporting that oil. The maritime routes concerned are currently patrolled by the U.S. Navy, so no wonder China is developing its military capabilities as fast as it can. When one recalls that the last potential tipping point of this magnitude, Japan's inability to safeguard its oil shipments to Southeast Asia, led to Pearl Harbor, it sends a chill down one's spine.

The relationship of these two immense emerging powers, the undemocratic but increasingly capitalist China and the democratic but far-from-capitalist India, will have a decisive impact on the century ahead of us. Goldman Sachs forecasts that, by 2050, China will be the world's largest economic power and India will be its third largest, with the weakening United States wedged between them.[53]

The two Asian giants must find the model that will enable them to modernize their societies and improve their populations' standards of living without trashing the Earth's natural environment or stirring military conflicts with the West or each other. This recognition is reflected in the idea of a "third way," which would be—in essence—a peculiar "Chindian" model, skipping some of the stages of traditional Western development, and superseding the technological, political, and cultural framework of the West. "Third way" projects have rarely been successful, but the appearance of these two giant actors on the world stage is a force majeure in the world's history, and unusual circumstances need unusual solutions. In 2005, twenty-seven years after Deng Xiaoping's Four Modernizations program, the Chinese government named the nation's eleventh five-year plan "Five Balances": promoting a balance between rural and urban development, between interior and coastal development, between economic and social development, between people and nature, and between domestic and international development—the emphasis always being on the first element. In November 2006, Hu Jintao visited India's prime minister, Manmohan Singh, and they described their countries as "two major countries in the emerging multipolar world order." They also added that there is enough space for them to grow together. The next century could easily be about the global spread of a new, modern, Asian socioeconomic-cultural-political model.

Chindia is now home to 40 percent of the Earth's population, equaling the combined population of the next twenty most populous countries. Many compare the significance of Chindia's rise to economic and political power with that of the end of the Cold War or the birth of the Roman Empire. Although such comparisons may be slightly exaggerated, there should be no doubt that a new world order is being born.

Triads and Pentads

The West's most tormenting problem is that it has no idea what China really wants. The West would love to know how this Asian giant wants to use its growing muscles. The late Communist Party leader Deng Xiaoping is still quoted in the Pentagon with respect to the Chinese military strategy: "Conceal our capacities and prepare for when our time comes." The conclusions of a 2005 Pentagon report and of the renowned London-based International Institute for Strategic Studies are almost identical on China's military potential: The People's Liberation Army is developing and modernizing its capabilities with surprising speed, especially when it comes to its nuclear capacity.[54] It needs to be noted, however, that in 2003 China's defense spending totaled $40 billion, roughly 2.7 percent of its GDP, about one-tenth of the U.S. defense expenditure of $460 billion for the same year.

The West is really worried about two things concerning China. First, China's real defense spending is suspected to exceed official figures by a wide margin. Second, the People's Liberation Army is focusing on weapons that can engage the U.S. Air Force in a contingent conflict with Taiwan. As China starts to show its power, one remembers the satellite incident, when it shot down one of its obsolete satellites with precision weapons, and the Costa Rica affair, when it used its mighty reserve funds to convince San José to sever ties with Taipei and establish closer relations with Beijing.

Sino-American relations will be the key geostrategic relationship of the coming decades, and perhaps even of the entire century ahead. The United States is undoubtedly the world's leading—and only global—power, but China's rise will certainly rearrange the world order. The destiny of the world —and of Europe—will depend on whether this rearrangement is peaceful or brings military conflict, and whether the new world order is built on a delicate balance between the two superpowers or on a multilateral consensus based on compromises and international institutions. In the first scenario, Europe will unavoidably play second fiddle to the dominant America-China pair and reluctantly side with America. In the second scenario, Europe could have a bigger role, although still be a supporting actor to the two main stars.

Bilateral and multilateral relations between the main players of the new world order—the United States, China, the European Union, India, Japan, and Russia—could take many different shapes. Relations between the United States and Communist China, which set the stage for the whole multilateral framework, have never been untroubled, and have been marked by numerous critical moments, such as the Tiananmen Square massacre in 1989, the Taiwan crisis in 1996, and the bombing of the Chinese Embassy in Belgrade in 1999. Both countries are big on national pride, but they differ in almost every other aspect. America is the individualistic child of the Enlightenment and liberalism, cherishing liberty and constitutional order. In contrast, China is the successor of an ancient, fundamentally agricultural empire, oozing tradition and respect for authority, with stability as its core value. In spite of their obvious differences and China's formidable economic growth, recently the two have been working hard on mending ties, especially since 9/11.

In a Huntingtonian world, the creation of a new world order and the emergence of new superpowers inevitably leads to a crisis, or—in the worst case— a world war. This is what happened in the twentieth century, when four new powers—the United States, Japan, Germany, and Russia—appeared on the international political scene. The balance was broken, and world wars followed. In a bizarre twist of fate, the rise of the Soviet Empire to the rank of a global power did not lead to war because the arms race between the two superpowers led to a stalemate, which was rather convenient to both parties. Armed to their teeth, Russia and America realized that a nuclear war could be disastrous. The picture is much more positive in the case of China and the United States. They may not be the closest of friends, but they have no territorial disputes, do not wish to export their ideologies, and have nothing to gain from a conflict. There are some hot issues, such as Taiwan and energy, but all the stakeholders know too well that a global armed clash could be potentially more dangerous today than during the Cold War. However, peace should not be taken for granted; every important global player must actively seek to maintain it by pursuing better international relations.

China is still in the dressing room, trying to decide what to wear for the new show, in which it will play the part of superpower on the stage of the new turboglobalized world order. Knowing that the United States will continue to top the bill for some time to come and that it will need to bide its time as number two for now, China is willing to accept a multilateral model, in which Europe and perhaps even its strategic competitors, Japan and India, will have roles. This is good news for the world, and music to Europe's ears. China has fourteen neighbors and, like every giant, it can expect these terrified neighbors to join forces against it. That is why China is so keen on maintaining the regional peace and balance in its Asian hinterland. The United States has no such headaches, being a continent in its own right, with friendly neighbors to the north and south. Japan-China relations remain tense, and Taiwan is a powder keg, but due to its special geographic location, China instinctively pursues a consensual policy. Again, this is good news for the world and for Europe. China is undergoing a dramatic transformation; it only needs time to get to know the global scene better so that it can choose cooperation over aggression. Otherwise, if it feels cornered, it may not respond well, which could spell disaster for the entire world. The issue of energy and natural resources has cropped up a few times before. As one of the biggest consumers of raw materials, China demanded in the autumn of 2006 that it be allowed to use political means to push down the world prices of natural resources. Such aspirations demonstrate a total lack of knowledge of how markets work; it is China's growing demand that generates price hikes. Like it or not, that is how markets work.

Lately the world was in an anti-American mood (though this is being replaced with Obama-induced goodwill), but it expected the United States to guarantee global stability, even if it is in denial about it. In a new world order, China could have similar tasks. For the time being, it is difficult to imagine that China would be entrusted with such a task. First it needs to prove that it can rise to the occasion. It is a positive sign that China condemned North Korea with harsh words when it publicly announced having carried out nuclear tests in the autumn of 2006. When the United States became independent two and a half centuries ago, China was a hundred times bigger than the young America in population; today, the difference is only four times, and the gap will continue decreasing as a result of demographic trends and immigration.

In other words, the West's fear of the dragon is overly simplistic. If China can steer clear of great social shocks during its eventually possible, yet not at all guaranteed, democratizing process and thus avoid the fate of Russia—which was not ready for democracy, and instead has ended up with part authoritarianism and part anarchy—the West has no reason to fear the end of the world. It will be possible to build a world order based on cooperation with a more-or-less democratic, socially stable China. It will only require concerted efforts to focus on common projects in areas where conflict could arise in the absence of cooperation. One such area is energy. Europe, America, and China must join forces to promote the worldwide use of energy-efficient technologies and renewable energy sources. Other areas for international cooperation include the environment, combating Muslim fundamentalism, and the fight against terrorism. The U.S. administration has recognized the need to cooperate and has set up a standing Chinese-American working group, cochaired by Prime Minister Wu Yi and Secretary of the Treasury Timothy Geithner, which is collecting dozens of experts around a table. The purview of this strategic working group covers globalization, environmental protection, innovation, and the energy supply, while diplomatically excluding those issues that are inconvenient for China, such as trade policy, armaments, and intellectual property rights (it is common knowledge that at least half of all counterfeit goods originate in China).

As China continues its rapid rise and the United States adjusts, what role can Europe hope to play? In any case, Europe will need to play second fiddle to the America-China pair, but what score it must play from, who plays the other instruments, and the number of solo violinists all will make a big difference. Europe is interested in building a consensual, multilateral world order, where it can be player number three behind the America-China duo. Europe's relations with China are in essence trouble free, apart from occasional dumping allegations. However, this idyllic situation is slightly misleading, because it is mainly due to the fact that Europe can dodge the conflicts as long as the more dominant United States does the dirty work. On the downside, as a result, China now considers the EU a lightweight power. The economic ties between Europe and China are significant (trade increased eightfold between 1990 and 2003), but China—justifiably—does not look upon Europe as a political or military player to be reckoned with. This puts Europe at a disadvantage in the competition for engagement with China, because European companies are locked in a battle with corporate America for the juicy bits of the Chinese market. Apart from its political divisions, Europe is also handicapped by its universities' inability to attract more than a few thousand students, while the vast majority of China's business, political, and scientific elite is educated at American universities. When these leaders and researchers return home, they will all have assimilated American knowledge and attitudes, will foster closer ties with America through their networks, and will probably be sentimentally attached to the United States for the rest of their lives. The United States continues to have the upper hand in the field of global technological and IT standards, which clearly favor American companies.

Europe would like to build a multiplayer world order, which would give it a more important role but is also more likely to guarantee global stability. A multipolar system could also accord a role to India, which was and is closely linked to Europe. The EU is India's largest trading partner, with a 22 percent share, and the volume of trade is growing at 10 percent annually; at this rate, its value will exceed €150 billion by 2012.[55] Most of India's foreign direct investment also comes from Europe. Negotiations on an EU-India free trade agreement began in late 2006, aimed at expanding bilateral trade. This seems necessary, because China exports five times as much to the EU as India does. Relations between Europe and India are predominantly economic; political links remain largely bilateral, at the level of EU member states. Europe should pay more attention to India, which is a potential key strategic partner, especially because a United States–China–European Union equilateral triangle as the basis for the new international system seems out of the question. The European Union is too weak geostrategically and too fragmented to be able to join the other two powers in a triad. I also believe that it is unrealistic to predict, as Mark Leonard does, that Europe will serve as an example for China, which would thus build a new world order based on European values and institutional solutions as the dominance of the United States fades.[56]

Europe must help the United States find the right tone with China and find the right institutional setup to guarantee the stability of the new world order. Europeans have a vested interest here. It was only yesterday that the post–World War II international system was created, and it looks as if it is already about to be replaced with a new one. Europe must be vigilant, and not commit any strategic mistakes. It must not shrug off the risk of China's emergence driving a wedge between Europe and America; that would be the worst possible outcome of a global power reshuffle. The United States has much more to lose with China's rise to power, which could cost America its global dominance. Europe, conversely, could view China's entry onto the international political scene as an opportunity to make the international situation more balanced. The Chinese policy of peaceful development is attractive, but caution is advisable.

There is some truth in the American criticism that Europe, having no strategic interests in the region and a relatively smaller responsibility for global security than the United States, likes to take a free ride on the China express. The United States was not happy—to put it mildly—to learn that the EU had opened up the Galileo space project (a planned satellite navigation system that would compete with America's own global positioning system) to China, and America was seriously considering lifting its weapons embargo against China in retaliation. This incident demonstrated the divergence of Europe's China policy; the large EU member states have a range of differing interests and goals shaping their attitudes toward the Asian giant. But it is in Europe's strategic interest to avoid a situation whereby its China policy leads to a clash with its traditional stalwart ally, the United States. Europe must, therefore, develop a coordinated China policy. It was in recognition of this necessity that the European Commission adopted its new China strategy at the end of 2006.

China is an ever-more-important factor in American and European foreign policies, but it is also becoming a domestic issue for the EU member states and for the EU as a whole. The rise of the Asian dragon is already one of the key elements of the debate on what Europe should do to maintain—or regain—its competitiveness and reform the new uncompetitive European social model.

* * *

Further Reading

For the global picture, see Nicole Gnesotto and Giovanni Grevi, *The New Global Puzzle: What World for the EU in 2025?* (Paris: Institute for Security Studies, 2006). Another similar publication is by the U.S. National Intelligence Council, *Global Trends 2025: A Transformed World* (Washington, D.C.: U.S. Government Printing Office, 2008). This latter one focuses more on geopolitical issues. For climate change, a principal source of information is Nicholas Stern, *The Economics of Climate Change* (London: Her Majesty's Stationery Office, 2006); though not the first economic report on climate change, this is significant as the largest and most widely known and discussed report of its kind.

As far as the topic of globalization is concerned, for one of the most substantiated works available, I recommend Martin Wolf, *Why Globalization Works* (New Haven, Conn.: Yale University Press, 2005). A thought-provoking analysis of the relationship between economics and democracy, which adds to the debate on globalization, is given by Daren Acemoglu and James A. Robinson, *The Economic Origins of Dictatorship and Democracy* (Cambridge: Cambridge University Press, 2006).

As far as geopolitical issues are concerned, among other volumes, I consulted Fareed Zakaria, *The Post-American World* (New York: W. W. Norton, 2008); and Samuel P. Huntington, *The Clash of Civilizations and the Remaking of World Order* (New York: Simon & Schuster, 1996). Today, both are widely used basic books.

On Europe's international economic stance, I recommend André Sapir, ed., *Fragmented Power: Europe and the Global Economy* (Brussels: Bruegel, 2007). On the rise of China, literally thousands of books and articles are available, one of them is Ted C. Fishman, *China Inc.* (New York: Scribner, 2005), which gives vivid and genuinely business point of view. On EU–United States economic relations and interconnections, excellent sources are Daniel S. Hamilton and Joseph P. Quinlan, *Deep Integration: How Transatlantic Markets Are Leading Globalisation* (Washington and Brussels: Center for Transatlantic Relations and Centre for European Policy Studies, 2005); and Daniel S. Hamilton and Joseph P. Quinlan, *The Transatlantic Economy 2009* (Washington, D.C.: Brookings Institution Press, 2009).

Chapter 3

Pan-European Problems:
The Intermediate Layer

Europe's demographic trends are some of the most worrying in the world, and therefore its generous welfare state model is under serious pressure, which is amplified by the forces of globalization. Competitiveness and sustainability thus are now and will remain the key policy issues for the continent, which at the same time will need to find a way to handle immigration and energy supply scarcity.

The Illness of the European Social Model

After two world wars, the Western European countries realized that the stabilization of their societies was literally a question of life or death. These formerly viciously competing nations achieved this stability by integrating themselves into a close alliance to make war impossible and by building the most generous welfare system in history to avoid any public unrest. This welfare state model was successful for decades, bringing about the most prosperous years Western Europe ever lived, including Germany's miraculous economic rise. Nevertheless, in the era of globalization, with the rise of new competitors on the global scene, this generous model seems unsustainable.

Indigestion

One of the two "children" of European liberalism, Welfare, has not been feeling too well lately. Fortunately, its twin sibling, Democracy, is as strong as an ox. Welfare is not suffering from an incurable disease, only indigestion; it had too many sweets, and it is feeling rather sick and weak at the moment. Clearly, it needs medical help, but the doctors gathered around its sickbed cannot agree either on how serious its case is or what treatment it needs. I am one of those who believe that Welfare's illness should not be treated lightly—symptomatic treatment will not do. The patient must go on a strict diet, and its immune system needs to get stronger again.

It is often argued in defense of the social model that liberals—nowadays called *neo*liberals (and the prefix makes even me have a sneaking suspicion)—only want to use European integration to guarantee free markets and open the gates of Europe to the troops of globalization. As a consequence, European societies and the forces representing Europe's real values should counter such intentions and defend what is most precious—social welfare and justice—or in other words, the European social model. I would not like to engage in an ideological dispute, but those who think that guaranteeing free markets and letting globalization run wild in Europe is the *aim* of neoliberals obviously have blurred vision. These are merely the (best) means of achieving the aims considered essential by all in the mainstream of European politics—lasting democracy, welfare, and social equity—and then of preserving them in the long run.

Another common opinion claims that the rejection of the European Constitution was "Europeans'" way of saying: "We have had enough of market-driven integration! We want care and protection from globalization!" The defeat of the Constitution was simply the rejection of a European integration built on the economy and market freedoms, which had already proved a fiasco as it failed to guarantee prosperity and job security. What then is the solution? The political and social facets of integration should be reinforced, which will bring both popularity and recovery. Adam Smith's invisible hand has failed to deliver; Europe needs a strong, visible hand: the hand of politics. Those with these views, however, are constantly on the defensive as developments in Europe and worldwide make it increasingly difficult to justify prescribing more chocolate for indigestion.

I have already mentioned earlier in the book that one of Europe's key unsolved puzzles is how and why its social model, the welfare state built on the rapid growth and prosperity of the postwar years, hampers its international competitiveness. Or perhaps those who say that this model could help Europe compete more successfully are right. The debate on the destiny of the social model goes way beyond the issue of international competitiveness. For many people, the welfare state is an important value in itself, the survival of which is crucial to preserving European identity. There is a lot of truth in their position. However, others reckon that the necessity of maintaining the social model justifies European federalism, or at least the creation of a closer political union. Some go even further and suggest that concerted European action in foreign policy—a truly common European foreign policy—would be needed to put more weight behind the European social model in international relations. In other words, they want to make Europe an example for the rest of the world to follow and thus stem the spread of the American and Asian wild capitalist models—the unscrupulous forces of globalization. Although I do not completely share these widely held views, I thought it would be worthwhile to give a taste of them to illustrate that the debate currently raging in Europe is not about increasing the retirement age, or cutting the unemployment benefit eligibility period, but about Europe's self-identity, values, institutions, and future destiny.

What Is the European Social Model?

There are two significant socioeconomic models in the developed Western world: the Anglo-Saxon one, based on market competition, and the (continental) European one, based on social cohesion. The European model was not shaped in Brussels; more or less similar models of the welfare state evolved in the European Union's member states over the decades. According to Anthony Giddens, one of the fathers of the "third way" of the reformed left in Britain epitomized by former prime minister Tony Blair, a social model presupposes the existence of five criteria: (1) a developed and interventionist state, where the taxes collected represent a significant part of the national income; (2) a strong welfare system, which serves all citizens, especially the needy; (3) a system guaranteeing the reduction of economic or other disparities; (4) social partners and trade unions, which play a key role in operating the welfare system and protecting workers' rights; and (5) increased welfare and employment as a key element of all political initiatives. Europe's social policy systems have played an important part in shaping the continent's economy and its unique social model, which has gone through several shifts in emphasis over the decades.[1]

The German concept of a "social market economy" and the European social model are cognate ideas. The former sets out to guarantee freedoms, fair competition, and protection of the weak through the division of power, acts of legislation, and institutional regulation. It is thus the task of the state to create the framework for an economic order that eliminates unjustified privileges and promotes social equality. In 1949, the Christian Democratic Union of Germany's three—occupied—western zones set itself the task of creating a "social market economy," which was based on rejecting a planned economy, defending private property, fair and free competition, prices suitable for the market, the independent control of monopolies, ensuring the social security of the vulnerable, and negotiated wage agreements. These Christian Democrats were opposed to the social command economy as well as the ultraliberal state's withdrawal from the economy. Justice, the state, traditions and morals, and firm standards and values are the foundations for this type of social market economy, but the model—in order to control economic policy, social policy, and market conditions— tries to reconcile interests and "protect the weak, restrain the immoderate, cut down excesses, limit power, set rules of the game and guard their observance. The market economy is a necessary but insufficient condition of a free, happy, just and orderly society," Wilhelm Röpke, the economist, wrote more than a half century ago.[2] The concept of the social model has undergone several modifications and has been interpreted in various ways.

In a wider interpretation, the European social model goes beyond social protection (pensions, health care) and includes areas such as benefits, social dialogue, lifelong learning, and other active employment policy instruments, as well as the fight against poverty and discrimination. The model acknowledges the role of social dialogue, particularly in areas such as combating unemployment, linking work and training, and introducing new methods for organizing work. In Europe, the state lays down the fundamental rules of employment, and expectations for social protection have come to be deeply embedded in people's minds. The realization that economic development is a necessary but insufficient precondition for society's development and its citizens' welfare is much more embedded in European than in American thinking. Accordingly, the welfare index—which measures economic development as well as the quality of life—is higher in most European countries than in America, which is an eloquent testimony to the advantages of the European model.

The easiest way to understand the European model is to compare it with the American or Asian models. If we focus on a comparison with America, the fundamental institutions are very similar on the two sides of the Atlantic; the differences lie in values. Both rest on private property, a competition-driven market economy, and the rule of law, but they interpret the role of state intervention differently.

The Anglo-Saxon or liberal model started out as an *English* model, and it was later perfected in the United States to reach its final form as an *American* model. Subsequently, it served as the basis for a global market competition-centered model. As I have mentioned above, this model is about competition, market freedom, individualism, and huge income gaps. It is characterized by deregulation, liberalization, prices and wages shaped by markets, weak trade unions, a weak state presence, and wide tolerance for social inequalities. In contrast, the European social model—of German origin, as described above—centers on the idea of the welfare state and has as its key features social cohesion, the coexistence of competition and interest reconciliation, solidarity, and strong state regulation.

To give a simplified comparison, the differences between the social (European) model and the liberal (Anglo-Saxon) model are as follows. The European model gives preference to equality, while the Anglo-Saxon model tolerates inequalities to a large extent. The European model puts the emphasis on job security, while the Anglo-Saxon model stresses labor flexibility and efficiency. In the liberal model, state social security systems and redistribution by the state play a smaller role, and the two models differ considerably in their corporate governance (anonymous shareholders vs. stakeholders), corporate financing (stock exchange vs. bank), and corporate management cultures.

EU countries are characterized by a large state sector, disposing of roughly half of all goods produced, the two extremes being Ireland (35 percent) and Sweden (60 percent). The weight of the state and its gross domestic product (GDP) disposition rate was increasing in Europe until the mid-1990s, partly due to the evolution of the social model (and primarily its redistributive policies, e.g., health care, education, and unemployment benefits) and partly due to other macroeconomic trends (e.g., the obligation to repay state debt accumulated as an aftermath of the 1973 oil shock, or the anticyclical policies necessitated by the recessions of the 1980s and the 1990s). Taxes collected totaled 42 percent of GDP in the EU in 2003, compared with 26 percent in Japan and the United States and 17 percent in China and India. The average EU member state spends 27 percent of its GDP on social policy, while Japan and the United States, respectively, devote 17 and 15 percent of state revenues to such purposes. These figures should shed some light on the differences between the two models.[3]

Many are preoccupied with answering the question of what the EU could do in the area of social policy. This is not a European Community competence, and—as we have seen—there exists a British (and Irish) model, which is markedly different from that of the continent. Because the EU member states have been unable to agree on the harmonization of social policies, the answer to the question is: not much. The impasse is well illustrated by the inability of ministers of employment to come to an agreement at their fourth consecutive summit on whether member states should be allowed to deviate from the European ceiling of the 48-hour workweek. Every third British employment contract includes a clause enabling the employer to exceed the 48-hour maximum; therefore, the United Kingdom would like to set the ceiling at 65 working hours a week. France, conversely, introduced the 35-hour workweek only a few years ago.

At the European Union level, there is no single definition of the European social model. Building a "European Social Area" through common standards and harmonizing national social policies was a novelty of the 1990s, although the Union's social policy aspirations have been growing more and more ambitious since its creation. In 1957, the Treaty of Rome only set the objective of improving workers' living and working conditions to help create what would become the Common Market; today, the objectives range from full employment and a high standard of social protection through gender equality to solidarity between the EU's member states. Even though social policy largely remains a national competence, there is a certain degree of coordination at the Community level. The open method of coordination, which was introduced gradually, starting in the late 1990s, is based on voluntary cooperation by the member states without any binding rules or trespassing of national competences. The open method rests on soft law mechanisms such as guidelines and indicators, benchmarking, and sharing best practices. Broad common strategic goals are agreed on, which are translated into national action plans, the implementation of which is monitored and evaluated in comparative reports. Community social policy has taboo areas that it avoids, which typically include wages, salaries, social redistribution, and related issues. Community social policy is quite limited in its scope; it mostly applies to specific groups and situations and tends to set minimum requirements.

The EU has declared that a key priority for its policies is to maintain the balance between the liberal market economy and social security, or—in other words—between competitiveness and solidarity. Although market liberalization is a fundamental principle of the EU's Founding Treaties, the Union has precious little competence in social policy. This is one of the underlying contradictions of the debate on the future of Europe. Many have had enough of a liberal Europe and see social Europe as the panacea.

However, the reality is that a main trend in recent years has been the strengthening of the Anglo-Saxon model, with the social model and the market-based model becoming more and more alike. One must wait and see what comes next after the global financial and economic crisis of 2008–9. By the way, the British liberal model has also moved toward the continental social model, at least as far as welfare spending and taxes are concerned; the general tax burden has shot up by 10 percent in the last thirty-five years. Nonetheless, the differences between the two models remain striking.

The social model based on strong state control is unavoidably retreating, despite the fact that the state's redistributive budgetary role has been expanding in recent decades. The world keeps changing; governments' role in shaping the international economic framework is becoming less important and is being taken over by economic actors in the private sector. This process began well before the dawn of "turboglobalization" in the 1990s (see chapter 2 for a full description of turboglobalization). In the blooming international economic order of the 1950s and 1960s, states had an important role to play in fostering sectors with a comparative advantage. Until the 1970s and 1980s, the state was not only a regulator but also a large owner of enterprises in Western European economies. Significant state ownership was not only beneficial to competitiveness but also contributed to strengthening the social model; the state could promote its social policy through its enterprises, which had a trickle-down effect on the private sector. But as the world began to open up and competition grew fiercer, the ability to adapt to changes became a valued asset. And adaptability was something of which the state was incapable, which led to the widespread privatization of state-owned enterprises all over Europe. Over and beyond the loss of its large enterprises and national champions, the state's influence was further trimmed back by the new trend of international rules being set by the market instead of governments.

Is There a Single European Model?

The European socioeconomic model rests on fundamental Western values such as democracy, the rule of law, respect for human rights, and national self-determination. According to its self-identity, the European model's economic philosophy is "more social" than the American or Asian models; the place of social equality is more emphatic, and economic performance is viewed as necessary to pursue together with other goals such as social cohesion, environmental protection, and the general welfare of citizens. Accordingly, the state plays a stronger role than in other models. Still, critics say that the European social model is not really a model, is not particularly social, and is not truly European. The EU's economy functions through the cooperation of different cultures and languages, and we can hardly talk about a European society or European culture, only about the sum of European peoples and cultures. Employment, welfare, health, and pension policies vary greatly from one country to another, and these differences only grow with each enlargement. For most people, mention of the European social model brings to mind social justice and solidarity, but—as we have seen—the European social model is often invoked to stress the differences between EU and U.S. social policy.

It is a difficult task to define the European social model. In truth, it is as much a political as a technical concept. The EU's member states pursue different social policies. The EU may issue guidelines and set targets (e.g., the 70 percent employment of the age group of fifteen to sixty-four years by 2010), but jobs are not created in Brussels. The welfare, health care, and pension systems also vary enormously from one country to another. Even though we cannot precisely define the model, the concept does carry important indications as to what is meant. In other words, just like terms like "European Union" and "Common Foreign and Security Policy," it suggests convergence, in this case of employment and social policies.

The conclusions of the 2000 Lisbon EU summit referred not only to the rivalry with the United States but also to full employment and a finely knit social safety net as objectives to be achieved by 2010. Common goals yield convergence. The European social model is as much European as the Common Foreign and Security Policy is common. In this case, "European" refers to a process of convergence of the views, goals, and instruments needed to achieve these goals. Obviously, there is no such thing as a single European minimum wage or an EU health care system. The former would be absurd; the latter—although it would be very useful, indeed—does not even exist on the drawing boards of Europe's social architects.

When referring to the European social model, the adjective "European" has another dimension: an institutional one. Common values and principles may be important, but they are of little use without common rules and institutions. As I have already stated above, the EU is rather weak in this sense. One can safely say that the Treaty of Amsterdam in 1997 was a turning point in European cooperation in the fields of employment and social policy. In addition to the open method of coordination, the EU's member states entrusted the European Commission with the responsibility to make proposals for legislation combating discrimination in and outside the workplace. The Constitutional Treaty could have been a real breakthrough, because it would have incorporated the Charter of Fundamental Rights—

which only had the status of a political declaration—into the Founding Treaties, which in turn would have enabled the European Court of Justice to use its rulings to force the member states to harmonize their legislation, even in the absence of specific European legal acts.

Even though we cannot define precisely what is meant by the "European social model," and though the boundaries of the concept are rather blurred, there is a kind of European model, or model family. When talking about the European social model, it should be remembered that the concept covers a wide spectrum of social systems. There are major differences between the welfare, fiscal, and transfer systems of the various EU member states, which are worth a closer look. Before the EU's last rounds of Central and Eastern European enlargement, it had four distinct models for the welfare system: the Nordic (or Scandinavian), the liberal Anglo-Saxon, the continental, and the Mediterranean. Then, in 2004, the EU's new members brought in their heterogeneous hodgepodge of models, which were typically market friendly with little attention devoted to welfare aspects, making it all the more difficult to establish a single social image of Europe. But it is useful to briefly examine the four previously distinct welfare systems.[4]

The *Nordic model* for the welfare system, which has lately become an example to follow, is characterized by guaranteeing—widely interpreted—social rights and high redistribution rates. The funding to maintain the high standard of social protection comes from high taxes. Employment does not appear to be a problem; registered unemployment rates are low, and both the public and private sectors play their part in achieving these low rates (in some parts of Scandinavia, the public sector employs 30 percent of the workforce). There is active state intervention in the labor market, with training programs and job placement schemes. The trade unions are the strongest in the world. An average 60 percent of workers are trade union members, but in Scandinavia and Denmark, this figure exceeds 75 percent. Society is consensus based; 82 percent of employment contracts are protected by collective agreements. As a result, income disparities are small, and the whole of society enjoys generous social care. The Nordic model is an ideal example of the welfare state and egalitarian society.

The *Anglo-Saxon* model for the welfare system is selective in providing care to its citizens; social care is not an inherent right. Accordingly, the level of redistribution is low, and the state is of moderate size. Systems following this model have managed to cut back public spending through comprehensive reforms, which has led to an increase in the number of low-income families and in social inequalities. The reforms have included the privatization of the pension system and trimming unemployment benefits, which is a guarantee of long-term sustainability. This model is an example of the self-provision approach.

The *continental* model for the welfare system, which is found in most continental European countries, is a unique mixture of state interventions and family traditions, with a high level of social protection funded by payroll taxes. The system is characterized by high redistribution rates and inequalities in fiscal burdens. In this model, the focus is on creating new jobs in the public or private sector. Despite all the efforts, this policy has yielded modest results due to high labor costs and the budgetary burden of unemployment benefits to the many jobless people. The state plays a central role, has a protectionist mentality, and provides for its citizens instead of creating the right conditions for self-advancement, which makes this model expensive and unsustainable in the long run. This depressing conclusion is supported by the fact that taxes on gross wages were 4 percent higher in Scandinavia than in continental Europe in 1979, but 6 percent lower in 2006. This is the prototype of the European social model, cherished by countries providing the bulk of Europe's GDP (Germany and France, among others), which has been the target of much criticism for its inoperability.[5]

The *Mediterranean* model for the welfare system is similar to the continental one in many aspects, but differs in others. The pension system has a more central role, while the family takes over some of the functions of the social safety net. This model results in striking inequalities in social benefits and blatant discrimination, which divide both workers and the jobless (typically women and young people). Women are disadvantaged in these countries because they find their professional career and family life incompatible. The system is wasteful and often encourages early retirement instead of self-training and job seeking. One of Europe's biggest headaches is that those EU member states accounting for two-thirds of the EU's total GDP have opted for the two most wasteful and unsustainable models.

Although there seems to be a consensus on the fundamentals of the European social model, the systems of European countries show great differences and have also gone through transformation in the EU's new member states in recent years. The state's role is important everywhere, but it has a more direct role in some countries than in others. One extreme is direct state provision; the other is a state that only regulates private-sector service providers. The situation varies considerably in terms of the role of social dialogue, sectoral rules, and corporations in protecting workers and shaping social benefits.

To be able to choose a model for the future, it is important to have a thorough understanding of how the Nordic social democratic and the Anglo-Saxon liberal models differ. The Nordic model is a mixture of the continental and the Anglo-Saxon models. The relationship between the government and the economy is a liberal one; the body politic has a noninterventionist approach toward markets (goods, services, and labor alike), but the state's size and redistributive role are comparable to the continental model. In the Anglo-Saxon model, the approach to markets is clearly liberal, and social provision is not of paramount importance. In the continental model, social provision is an important principle, mainly because of its interventionist attitude toward markets. If—for the sake of illustration—we identify the Anglo-Saxon model with Ireland and the United Kingdom, and the continental model with France and Germany, we can see that taxes account for 34 percent of GDP in the first group, 44 percent in the second group, and 48 percent in the Nordic countries. The flexible labor market rules of Anglo-Saxon countries are reflected in the unemployment figures in these three groups—respectively, 4.6 percent, 9.6 percent, and 7 percent.[6]

The British and Irish models are European, geographically speaking. But being more liberal than social, they are closer to the American model in many ways. They show some similarities with the Nordic model, but even more differences. The British model rests on liberalism as its cornerstone; the Nordic model is built on socialism. What does this mean, precisely? The Anglo-Saxon model revolves around the economy, and its social policy serves to rectify the shortcomings of the economy's operation. The Scandinavian model, conversely, subordinates all policies—including economic policy—to social justice. Nevertheless, the Nordic model has adopted a market-based approach; the rights of active workers are much stronger than those of the inactive labor force. The Scandinavian model increasingly makes employability (individual responsibility) its focus, as opposed to the old attitude, which put the political burden of providing access to work on the shoulders of the state. In the Anglo-Saxon model, there is more room for weighing social justice against economic rationality. The British philosophy encourages people to work and tries to make them understand that active employment is in their best interest, on the basis that, unless they make every reasonable effort to find work, they cannot expect social protection, or protection of only a minimum standard. As the U.K. prime minister, Gordon Brown, has said, there is no security without change; the Swedes say that there is no change without security. According to the

Anglo-Saxon approach—contrary to the Swedish one—security and the lack of change are an obstacle to the necessary reforms, progress, opportunities.

Apparently, the single European socioeconomic model is a collective term. There are major differences from one EU member state to another, which is especially true since its enlargement with twelve new countries. Still, in comparison with the rest of the world, the contours of a European model seem to emerge, especially if we treat the British Isles separately.

What Do the Believers Say?

There is an assumption that the European social model—particularly its continental version—is what gives Europe its distinct identity. The continental model is sharply opposed to the Anglo-Saxon one, which, according to the continental model's advocates, is doomed to fail and disappear once and for all—just think of the gigantic American deficit, the British property bubble, or the social stratification in both these countries almost resembling a caste system.[7] European identity covers much more than just a single market: It needs a strong political image based on social solidarity; politics should always come before the economy. Economic integration—advocates of a social Europe argue—has never been the main common goal of European states, only a means of establishing peace and prosperity.

According to the continental model's advocates, the single market does not mean protection for Europe's citizens; on the contrary, it fills them with the fear of increased competition. European integration brought peace to the continent as well as the integration of national economies. Now it is time to start institutionalizing social Europe to ensure the welfare of European citizens. A fair distribution of the windfall profits of companies benefiting from an obstacle-free market should be the task of politicians and should be done on a European level. This would require European institutions, procedures, and competences that can guarantee social justice throughout Europe. Europe must withstand the threats of globalization, for which it must speak with one voice and have a common foreign policy. Chasing competitiveness at all costs and engaging in fiscal competition that undermines social achievements is a road that leads to Europe's downfall.

The continental model's advocates also maintain that what this continent really needs is higher pan-European taxes, or at least minimum tax rates, and —if necessary—sanctions against countries slashing taxes. Consequently, the EU needs extended regulatory competences and not a larger budget. Europeans can all feel the erosion of social achievements every day; public opinion is turning away from the European project, and riots have erupted in the *banlieues* of Paris. The key mission of this "imaginary" social EU is to eliminate the disparities, which contradicts the idea of unlimited enlargement; with limited resources, the EU's ability to absorb new members is restricted. And the accession of more poor countries would cause social tensions in the more prosperous states. Companies' relocations to poorer countries has caused enough headaches for workers in the "old" EU member states; the freezing of structural funding to the "new" Eastern member states may become justified at one point. European identity is best shaped and reinforced through political decisions and actions, which should focus on preserving the social model and protecting it from the dangers of globalization. Following World War II, Europe's peoples built welfare states with jobs for life, often in state-owned companies, with high-quality education and health care and, in many cases, almost free housing.

Finally, for the continental model's advocates, it seems the golden years have ended, but Europeans should not acquiesce—European politics must open new horizons and improve the social model. French politicians have said that the failed European Constitution should be replaced by a "social treaty," which would "counterbalance the Union's economic pillar" and provide a political framework for protecting citizens by the harmonization of fiscal and social rules, the creation of large industrial firms, namely, European champions, and stronger political control of the European Central Bank.

So it goes for the old fashioned continental model's advocates. I will not attempt to refute all the above statements in detail, although it would probably not be a demanding assignment. But I will come back to them later in the book, in a wider context.

Naturally, there are more sophisticated views arguing for the introduction of the Nordic model throughout the continent, and for the model's reform. The buzzword, also borrowed from the Nordic model, is "flexicurity"—flexibility and security in labor and social policy. The Nordic model is a prime example of how high social spending and competitiveness are not mutually exclusive. Finland and Sweden have the most expensive social policies and are still considered two of the world's most competitive economies. In the case of Portugal and Greece, the opposite is true. It is beginning to dawn on people that the continental social model is facing a gargantuan challenge.[8]

Turboglobalization has two main winners: the Western world's investors, who have benefited immensely from the staggering growth of the world economy; and Asian workers, whom globalization has plugged into the international division of labor. Chinese society is going through a process similar to what British society experienced during the Industrial Revolution—children lived twice as well as their parents, and four times as well as their grandparents. At the other end of the scale, we find a big group, Western European and American blue-collar workers, who see globalization as a menace and whose standard of living has been deteriorating. The expansion of the world economy to the vast Asian labor market is the main reason why the productivity gains of U.S. firms exceed the average American's income growth. The argument that trade development increases global prosperity does little to reassure Western workers worried about their social prerogatives. A new social class has developed in the West: the worriers. Social gaps are widening in both the East and the West. Between 1997 and 2001, the top-earning 10 percent pocketed half of all income, and the top-earning 1 percent a quarter. In 1973, the average top executive earned 27 times more than John Doe; in 2000, a chief executive's pay slip was 300 times the average salary. Naturally, the difference between the haves and have-nots is even bigger in terms of income from capital assets, which is typically the privilege of the richer classes. The same trends are observable in Europe and Japan, albeit on a smaller scale.

Social problems do exist in Europe. Belligerent defenders of the social model have made it their mission to protect welfare systems established over the decades through political conflicts or street fights. The question is whether they are picking the right means for their undoubtedly laudable end—preserving European welfare and solidarity—or are playing with fire, risking further aggravating the situation. The answer is clear.

What Has Gone Wrong?

The classic European social model is unsustainable and does not serve the interests of citizens, at least not in the long run. The symptoms have been observable for a while now; Europe has been the world's slowest-growing region since 1980. Thus, between 1980 and 2000, with its 2.4 percent average growth rate, Europe ranked behind China, with its rate close to 10 percent; the United States, with 3.5 percent; and even Africa, with 2.5 percent.[9] Undeniably, economic growth is a minimum precondition for financing welfare systems, especially in a rapidly aging society.

Just to highlight the scale of progress, let me share a curious fact: Two hundred years ago, the average European enjoyed 90 percent of the present standard of living in Africa. Progress was driven by only one thing: stable and almost undisturbed economic growth. In 2006, there were 20 million Europeans without a job, unemployment stood close to 20 percent among the young, and the economy was growing at just over 0.5 percent a year. Europe's productivity is dropping, it is falling increasingly behind Japan and the United States in research and development (R&D), and its population is aging at an alarming rate. European economies are paralyzed by rigid rules, as shown by the inability of many EU member states to address the persistent problem of high unemployment. As was stated by an influential report from the Organization for Economic Cooperation Development, as of 1994, unemployment had hardly increased in the United States since 1970, while it had grown to and was hovering at 9 to 10 percent in Europe.[10] Germany, the cradle of social market economy, had 1 million jobless people in 1970 and 5 million in 2005, with more and more qualified professionals among them. European employment was above America's until the mid-1970s (64 vs. 62 percent) but, by the turn of the millennium, things had changed dramatically; employment fell to 61 percent in Europe, while it shot up to 74 percent on the other side of the Atlantic. An EU–United States employment gap appeared, meaning 34 million "missing European jobs" in 1997. The gap was the widest for three groups: young people (fifteen to twenty-four years of age), the elderly (fifty-five to sixty-four), and middle-aged women (twenty-five to fifty-four).

These, then, are the symptoms. But what about the disease itself? The traditional European social model—the continental one—is unsustainable from a budgetary point of view. It awards mediocrity and provides only average-quality services, such as free health care with long waiting lists and low-standard education ill suited to market needs. It does not encourage work, especially not effective work; on the contrary, it stimulates the avoidance of work, early retirement, and excessive sick leave. These phenomena are present in even those countries following the most efficient Nordic model. Europeans work shorter hours and less productively than their American counterparts, which hampers Europe's economic catch-up.

There are divergent views as to whether Europeans—following the doctrine of "postproductivism"—just prefer spare time over money (work) or whether the system discourages or does not cater for more work. Whichever the case, in the long run the continental model distorts people's attitudes toward work, and the strict rules guaranteeing job security force employers to think twice before recruiting new staff. All these factors contribute to a rigid, self-absorbed mentality, a Europe closing itself off from the world and suspicious of change, which is the seedbed of protectionism. Such a system repels investors with its steep taxes and deters researchers and businesses with its jungle of red tape. It is incapable of responding to frequent changes flexibly, managing immigration successfully, or dealing with aging and the role of the family in a new world. Elevated minimum wages guaranteed by law or by trade unions yield high unemployment among the members of the low-skilled workforce, who are often first- or second-generation immigrants. It does not take much imagination to see the connection with the Paris *banlieue* riots. The nanny state, for many mothers, is a substitute—at least financially—for a caring father; the nanny state, for many fathers, takes over the burden of caring for their families, which could lead to looser family ties.

Social rights carved in stone and rigid labor market rules are fundamentally changing the face of continental European societies. Thus, Germany has seen the emergence of a class of "atypical" workers, who are part of the state, but not of the welfare state. A 2003 labor law amendment aimed at addressing high unemployment has transformed the German labor market into a two-tier one—in the upper tier, we find "welfare workers" enjoying traditional full social protection, who are almost impossible to lay off; in the lower tier is the growing army of part-time and temporary workers with few social rights, who are easy to lay off and earn a fraction of what their "welfare" counterparts do, strictly without bonuses and often without paid leave. They are the European "globalized" brothers and sisters of the software developers of Bangalore, who have fallen through the loosely woven social protective net but at least have a job. They are competing with Indian and Chinese workers in the virtual global labor market without any social protection. And fewer than half of German workers are now in the first tier.

Between 2002 and 2006, more than 1 million "welfare jobs" disappeared in Germany while the same number of "globalized jobs" were created. And when I say workers, I do not only mean unskilled ones; they include many highly skilled, qualified employees, even college and university graduates. "Intolerable!" you may say, but "What is to blame, globalization or protectionism?" I ask. What does this two-tier labor market—in other words, domestic outsourcing—really reflect? Does it mean the Chinese and American devastation of European society or the healthy survival instinct of European societies, which are trying to adapt to the new rules of the new age? The current solution cannot be the ultimate one; it preserves most labor market deficiencies, causing uncompetitiveness, and it lacks solidarity, demonstrated by the glaring gap between the two tiers and the immobility between them. Further reforms are needed in a country where most mothers do not work, where most people have a 35-hour or shorter workweek, where it is almost impossible for employers to lay off staff, and where trade unions have a de facto monopoly in setting wages. Reforms are needed badly, both in Germany and Europe-wide.

Nevertheless, the welfare system was one of Europe's finest achievements while there was enough money to fund it and until its negative consequences started to make themselves felt. Europeans should not discard the welfare system; they should adapt it to the new global conditions and make it more rational and affordable. But to be able to do that, they must first come to understand its negative impact.

What are the key challenges facing the European social model? There are at least three. The first is Europe's own protectionism and the reflexes that prevent spontaneous rejuvenation. It was turboglobalization that brought the model's weaknesses to the surface, even aggravating its problems. Europe found it difficult to reinvent itself as a modern, service-oriented region, because it was more industrialized than the United States (the service sector employs 79 percent of all workers in the United States, and 69 percent in Europe). The leading sectors today are R&D and information technology. Both require a very flexible socioeconomic environment, which is hard to find in continental Europe, whose model is rigid and incapable of responding to changes quickly. A second key challenge is the problem of aging; the average male spent eleven years of his life in retirement in 1970, and eighteen years in 2005. Aging, along with its many other economic and social implications, makes costly welfare systems impossible to finance in the long run and holds back growth by about 0.5 percent annually. What we have is the classic catch-22.

A third key challenge that one should not disregard is the fact that the entry of China and India into the global economy has brought billions of new workers into the global labor market, which has cut the global capital to workforce ratio in half. This dramatic development is causing fundamental social shifts, in the East and West alike. The European Union is trying to ride too many incompatible horses at the same time: social security and solidarity, boosting competitiveness and liberalization, getting the better of the United States and maintaining balance. Europe needs change, because the days of the current continental model are numbered—even if, in the wake of the collapse of the American financial system, a triumphalist wave is gathering momentum in Europe. "We told you so," say some people in Europe, pointing fingers at the staggering American economic system. But it is not at all that simple.

France: The Weary Rooster

France is important—and not only to the French, but to all Europeans. It is the world's sixth-largest economy, a permanent member of the UN Security Council, a founding EU member, a key driving force and intellectual pillar of European integration, and a symbol and transmitter of European culture. Thus, France's fate cannot be a French-only affair. What happens in France has an impact on the future of the European community. Thus, Europe must be vigilant when French right-of-center political leaders depict liberalism as more evil than communism and see the market as a jungle full of savages that they have to fight in the name of civilization, and when the left-wing manifesto in the presidential elections talks about renationalizing energy firms, expanding the 35-hour workweek to small and medium-sized enterprises, reversing pension and labor market reforms, and imposing hefty fines on companies "guilty" of relocation. France is often a model followed Europe-wide; therefore, the example it sets and the standards it exports can make a big difference to the European Union. At the same time, France must be careful to avoid becoming irrelevant on the European stage.

It has become somewhat of a commonplace that France is in big trouble, and the French have a premonition of doom.[11] They are afraid of globalization, change, and the future. One of the victims of this fear is liberalism, of which most French people take a dim view and which is therefore a perfect candidate for the role of the scapegoat. Despite some undoubtedly positive results and trends, such as high productivity, successful French multinationals, and a high birthrate, the country is troubled by huge economic and mental ailments. Unemployment is high at 2.4 million, every fifth youngster is jobless, 3.7 million people live below the poverty line, and the *banlieues* have become lawless, poverty-stricken suburban zones. Employment rules make it almost impossible to fire employees, which—as in Germany—contributes to consistently high unemployment and the evolution of a two-tier labor market (see above); more than half of all new employment contracts concluded in 2006 were of the second type. The Labor Code runs 2,700 pages, and the collective agreement for bakers runs 500 pages. With the new millennium, the standard workweek was cut from 39 to 35 hours, which also meant more absenteeism due to hard-to-control work arrangements.[12] By an odd twist of fate, at the end of 2006, the Conseil d'État (Council of State), the supreme legislative body, annulled the provision granting the 1.5 million workers in the hotel, restaurant, and catering sector an exemption from the 35-hour ceiling, although this sector requires flexible working times. The consequences have been dire; according to a survey by the French Business Confederation (Mouvement des Entreprises de France, MEDEF), a French company employs just 7 percent more people one year after start-up than initially; this figure is 30 percent in Germany and 130 percent in the United States. Less work is detrimental not only to the economy but also to workers; net average wages went up by a measly 1 percent in real value between 2000 and 2004. Even though social security contributions weigh heavily on both employers and employees, budgetary balance has yet to be achieved, and state debt keeps piling up.

French society is lamenting the loss of its *gloire* and the stagnation of its living standards, resulting in navel-gazing. And it is not only the future that looks bleak; the past also keeps haunting France, as is indicated by a 2005 law instructing schools and course book editors to emphasize the positive side of France's past as a colonial power. This law, like so many things these days, triggered a violent response among the general public as well as leading public figures. Many are contemplating the idea of emigrating, and many are becoming radical. There does not seem to be a light at the end of the tunnel, leaving no other alternative than finding a scapegoat in capitalism, liberalism, globalization, competition, and so on.

The French should realize that there is nothing they can do about global phenomena, like China's emergence, but they can put their own house in order by updating their laws and social model. Of course, this is a lot easier said than done, especially when it comes to market reforms; the French have problems with both reforms (these days, meaning austerity measures) and markets. In a survey by the pollster Globescan, of those responding, 71 percent of Americans, 66 percent of the British, and 65 percent of the Germans, but only 36 percent of the French, believed that a free market economy is the best possible system.[13] As a case in point, a 2005 government bill proposing the slightest of shifts toward labor market flexibility drew fierce opposition from young people, ultimately erupting in violent riots. The so-called CPE (*contrat première embauche,* first job contract) bill would have enabled companies to hire staff members younger than twenty-six years with fixed-term contracts leading to indefinite employment after the first two years of probation. This arrangement, the theory went, would have encouraged firms to take on young workers, so many of whom are without a job.

The street violence during the stand-off between the government and youth prompted Dominique Moisi, senior adviser at the French Institute for International Relations, to talk of a "clash of archaisms," with a high-handed government attempting to impose measures long overdue without proper consultation on one side, and a reactionary force of students on a Marxist platform yearning for the return of the good old days on the other. This was like the riots of 1968 in reverse playback—youth demonstrations and revolts against reforms and modernization and in favor of maintaining privileges from the past that hamper progress. The student riots soon attracted another social group, declassed young people of African origin from the *banlieues*. Their problem was not flexible employment contracts but a lack of hope for any employment.[14] The quagmire finally ended with youths from the *banlieues* going on a rampage, burning and looting cars and shops, their anger directed at anyone who had a job or business, even other neighbors of immigrant origin.

A good part of the French intelligentsia fell into a state of shock and disbelief when faced with the results of a poll revealing that for 75 percent of young people, their dream in life was "to become a civil servant." Today's young French lack confidence in the future and a spirit of adventure; they wish to be protected from life, which makes them extremely defensive, and this thinking is reinforced by their education. In a similar survey in China, the overwhelming majority of respondents said they wanted "to become a millionaire." China suffers from rampant corruption at all levels; the economy is driven from the top down instead of the bottom up. And most of the politically motivated top-down initiatives fail the test of the new globalized world. In the last twenty years, the Chinese civil service has swollen to 5 million, adding 1 million new officials. (And all this has happened at a time when state administrations are being streamlined worldwide.) The number of staff members at the French Ministry of Agriculture, which manages the affairs of a rapidly shrinking agrarian population, was augmented by 8 percent, even while agricultural policy is run more from Brussels than from Paris. The French National Bank employs 14,000 people, while—France being a euro zone member—monetary policy is made in Frankfurt and not in Paris. Just for comparison, the Bank of England, which does run its own monetary policy, has fewer than 2,000 staff. The strength of the central government is important to the French mentality; a weaker state seems to weaken the French public's sense of security. The centuries-old French traditions of mercantilism and dirigisme might have survived as gut instincts but do not work in the age of turboglobalization—even concrete walls will not protect markets today.

French firms raise their voices against red tape and "Kafkaesque" rules. Many of these firms do well internationally. The biggest French corporations generate four-fifths of their profits abroad; even the traditionally anti-market energy companies—bulwarks of trade unionism—are becoming integrated into the international economy by being floated on exchanges and providing cross-border services. Protecting the corporate sector has always been an important element of French economic policy, but protectionism now only serves to conserve the socioeconomic order of the 1960s, which is detrimental to future success and a hopeless venture. Against all the odds, the government announced in early 2006 that it wished to prevent hostile takeovers of French companies by increasing employee share using the services of the Caisse des Depots et Consignations, a state-owned financial institution performing public interest missions on behalf of the government. The state intervened in acquisitions on a number of occasions (Gaz de France, Arcelor) and fell out with Germany over providing financial help to EADS, the European aerospace consortium that is the owner of Airbus. The Germans were reluctant to reach into their pockets to balance EADS' books, arguing that it was the job of markets and not of governments. Some attach special significance to this clash between the two countries, which—supposedly—symbolizes the divergence of their economic policies, or models.

France lives in fear of the future, in uncertainty and in division. Solving problems starts with facing them, but if one searches in the wrong place for the reasons causing the problem, failure is guaranteed. Unless French society recognizes that the source of its problems is not globalization but the unsuitability of its own model, it will go astray, irrespective of what kind of political leadership it elects. The road it chooses could well decide its future. With the election of Nicolas Sarkozy as president in 2007, France turned toward a more liberal, market-friendly policy mix. In his 2007 book, *Testimony: France, Europe and the World in the Twenty-first Century,* he writes: "France has been discouraging initiative and punishing success for the past twenty-five years and the main consequence of preventing the most dynamic members of society from getting rich is to make everyone poor. It is precisely because we refuse to address our problems head-on that our flame is diminishing in the eyes of others. It is why other nations' respect for France is declining."[15]

Sarkozy has advocated reforms on many fronts: the labor market, tax policy, public administration, and better universities. A 2007 report—with policy recommendations for the French government, signed by Jacques Attali—clearly takes a stance favoring the market-friendly camp, and inevitable reforms in several layers of the French economic and social net have been initiated.[16] As the new president (he is often described as a liberal Colbertist), he started to reform the labor market and to restrict pension benefits. This latter reform triggered long strikes and bitter opposition; nevertheless, the government went on with it. A set of rules have also been introduced to also circumvent the crippling 35-working-hours rule. In the summer of 2008 came a new wave of reforms, such as deregulating the retail industry, establishing an independent competition authority, and cutting back army staff (denounced by the socialist opposition as draconian restructuring that would jeopardize the country's military independence). Economists nevertheless have broadly welcomed the reform package. France seems to have started moving. Views on the achievements and attitudes of the French government vary, but nevertheless it is a novelty that France is seen more and more as a proreform country.

How to Proceed from Here?

We have seen that—not considering the European Union's new member states and their rapidly changing social models—four basic models have evolved in Europe: the Anglo-Saxon, the Nordic, the continental, and the Mediterranean. Let us now look at how they work. Anthony Giddens and his associates call France, Italy, and Germany "blocked societies," where the need for change is evident but opposing interests and conservatism are blocking change.[17] Conversely, the Nordic and Anglo-Saxon countries and the Netherlands have been able to carry out the necessary reforms to their welfare systems and labor markets. In these "success countries," two-thirds of new jobs are created in new sectors of the economy, female employment is well above the European average, the labor market is vibrant, and people change jobs easily and frequently.

According to André Sapir, the Brussels-based economist, the Anglo-Saxon model (in the United Kingdom and Ireland) and the Nordic model (in Denmark, Sweden, Finland, and the Netherlands) work well, but the continental model (in Austria, Belgium, France, Germany, and Luxembourg) and the Mediterranean model (in Greece, Italy, Portugal, and Spain) work badly.[18] Analyzing this finding from two basic aspects—and really simplifying things—it can be concluded that the Anglo-Saxon and Nordic models are more successful in attaining high employment, and the other two less so. Combating poverty, however, seems to be a forte of the Nordic and continental models and a weak point of the other two. The Anglo-Saxon model fails on this count primarily because of a low standard of education and not because of insufficient benefits. If we also factor in economic growth, the Nordic and Anglo-Saxon models again emerge victorious. Labor market reforms in the countries following the continental and Mediterranean models should be aimed at abandoning the idea of direct job protection and abolishing rules that make it practically impossible to fire workers and thereby shackle the economy.

After the global financial and economic crisis of 2008–9 that originated in America, the new consensus, especially on the left, will probably bury the American model. Though it is true that in many ways (better regulation of financial instruments, wider social security coverage for the society, etc.) it must be revisited, it would be a wrong judgment in the long run. The United States has suffered an incredible blow, basically because of its mismanaged financial services industry, which resulted in colossal job losses in 2008 (unemployment hit a five-year high, and hundreds of thousands of jobs were lost within a few months). Uncertainty is everywhere, and drastic measures and a radical shift in policy were necessary, but we will not see the dismissal of the model as such. In the short run, I even doubt that the world will see the end of Anglo-American financial supremacy, as some of the European politicians claim. After the crisis, with new rules and new enforcement structures, companies will come back to raise funds, and banks will recover and start to lend money. With huge government interventions and enforcement efforts, the situation will stabilize in the financial sector. And then will come this question: How can the real economy react? How fit will companies, the labor force, and labor markets be in America and in Europe?

Welfare and labor market reforms are progressing slowly but surely in continental Europe, usually drawing sharp opposition from society. The German grand coalition and its reform program attract the most attention. Plans to restructure the health care sector, which absorbs €150 billion each year, by introducing market-based operational principles were strongly opposed by the profession. And then Angela Merkel's to-do list also includes labor market reforms, fiscal simplification, and commodities market deregulation. The vast majority of German society is hoping that these painful measures can be avoided, which makes the government's task of convincing the electorate of the necessity of modernization awfully difficult.

The silver lining in this cloud is that corporate Germany is not that naive; it knows that the choice is between reform or failure. Legislative and policy reforms have launched a market-driven process, which translates labor market liberalization into contractual relations. An increasing number of German firms, including smaller family enterprises, strike deals with their employees on exemptions from the strict labor regulations, while politicians keep complaining about the slow pace of reforms. Many of the companies that had already decided to relocate to countries offering cheaper labor are giving their workers a last chance; if they are willing to work for less, accept fewer rights and privileges, or work more for the same money, the company will stay after all. Such horse-trading has become a regular phenomenon, and the most puzzling thing is that the powerful trade unions, whose membership has fallen by half in the last fifteen years, are usually in favor of an agreement, recognizing the new reality and accepting a reduction in their members' wages. A similar process took place in the United States in the 1980s, when the first wave of competitors from the Far East forced American companies to shed costs. Large corporations also resort to the same method; in 2006, Volkswagen, Europe's leading carmaker, announced plans to lengthen its workweek by 6 hours without a pay increase. Volkswagen also threatened to slash 20,000 jobs and to oblige its remaining workers to undertake to assemble a certain number of vehicles and correct their mistakes in unpaid overtime.[19]

The winds of change are blowing more strongly, even if politics cannot keep pace with market developments. Still, there are many recipes and views on what course Europe should take, and which model it should choose.

Because I have already described above the thinking of advocates of the traditional European social model, I will only briefly outline it here. Although they admit that the model needs some reforming, they believe that Europe's main problem is that it is not social enough and the feeling of solidarity is not strong enough. Therefore, the model should be rationalized, but mostly it should be protected and diffused. This will require concerted political action at the European level, a common European industrial and economic policy, and stronger political control of monetary policy shaped in Frankfurt. The last will mean closer political oversight of the European Central Bank, which should give more consideration to economic growth and job creation in implementing its monetary policy. Eurogroup, the informal group of euro zone finance ministers, should be formally institutionalized (as approved lately by the Reform Treaty) and be given wider competences in representing the euro zone internationally. The overly strict Stability and Growth Pact, which inhibits growth in the EU's member states, should be made more growth-friendly by allowing member states to exclude certain budgetary items—such as research funding, which needs to be increased anyway—from the calculations of their budget deficits. The senseless fiscal competition must end, and member states must be prevented from bidding against each other in lowering corporate tax rates, while large European champions must be set up, which can compete successfully on the world scene.

The other proposed remedy is the adoption of the Nordic, especially the Swedish, social model, Europe-wide. This "magic" third way (not to be confused with the U.K. Labour Party's reform ideology) marries social protection with market principles, and solidarity with competitiveness. For many, this is the tamed version of capitalism with a human face. Thus, in Sweden, only 5 percent of people live below the poverty line, compared with 13 percent in the United Kingdom and 17 percent in the United States.[20] The Swedish economy is open (trade accounts for almost half of GDP), Swedish society is open and highly skilled, and Swedish companies perform well in international comparisons. It is a pleasure to do business in Sweden; there is hardly any corruption, almost no red tape, and—apart from the eye-wateringly high taxes—all conditions are ideal, including flexible labor rules. As a result of high taxes and a responsible economic policy, the budget consistently shows a surplus.

What should Europe do if it wants to adopt this Nordic model? First of all, it should exercise budgetary rigor, strengthen state and community institutions, and make their operation more efficient. Social benefits should be extended to all citizens, but on certain conditions, such as being actively employed. The social system should be service oriented and not just focus on handing out financial support. Taxes should be increased to finance the costly welfare system, but corporate tax rates should be maintained low to retain competitiveness and foster growth. With high wages but no job security, jobless people should be given all the help and training they need to find new employment. State institutions should be complemented by private organizations in delivering social services to citizens. Part-time employment should be encouraged, rather than banned. Investment in technology and development as well as education should be encouraged through incentives. Protecting the environment and combating poverty should be placed high on the political agenda. Social partners should have a key role to play in setting wages and setting the broad economic policy guidelines.

Not everyone shares this unconditional enthusiasm, however. According to a study by Timbro, a liberal Swedish research institute, Americans have 30 percent more to spend than Luxembourgers, the richest people in Europe, and twice as much as the citizens of the poorest of the fifteen "old" (pre–2004 enlargement) EU member states.[21] A 2005 KPMG study showed Europe, and especially its Nordic part, in an even less favorable light.[22] A comparison of incomes and prices revealed that, on purchasing power parity, Scandinavians are relatively poorer than Southern Europeans. In other words, in Europe the average monthly salary was worth the least in Denmark, Sweden, and Norway and worth the most in Spain. Of course, Americans were also the best off in this comparison. This is partly due to the fact that, while economic output has doubled in the United States in the last twenty-five years, in Europe it has only improved by 50 percent.

Yet even the welfare model is not as flawless as one would think. When they feel secure, people tend to become lazy, as is indicated by the fact that one in five people in Sweden does not work. Unemployment data are distorted; the official 7 to 8 percent figure disregards those taking part in labor market programs, in early retirement, or on sick leave. If we count them all, we arrive at a figure closer to 20 percent. Every fifth young person is without a job, even according to official statistics. The welfare state is often wasteful; 75 percent of Finns—including many high-earning ones—are entitled to housing subsidies when buying property. Such generosity can only be financed with sky-high taxes. Ironically, the Swedish tax authority produced its first television advertisement, encouraging taxpayers to pay up on time, in low-cost Estonia in a bid to escape high Swedish taxes, which can go up to 60 percent of taxable income.[23] A main source of rapid growth was large-scale immigration, which compelled a previously homogeneous society to find solutions for the smooth integration of newcomers. Looking back to the past, one can see that generous handouts had already once plunged Sweden into economic depression, which propelled the Liberals to an election victory in the 1990s, after the nation had been governed for fifty years by the Social Democrats. (The Liberal government then introduced austerity measures and tax cuts.) These critical remarks are necessary to give a full and objective picture of the Nordic model, which—for all its shortcomings—works infinitely better than does the continental one.

Let us now briefly look at the model that those adhering to liberal Anglo-Saxon beliefs suggest that Europe follow. According to these adherents, Europe, having established its internal market, should now turn its attention to the rest of the world, the global marketplace offering countless opportunities. It is time to build a "Global Europe." The EU, this integrated region, has demonstrated the benefits of cooperation, but the internal market carries with it a risk of self-absorption, which could be suicidal at a time when

China has emerged as a global economic power. The volume of world trade doubles every decade, but Europe's share is dropping as its competitors grow in strength. Contrary to common belief, China and India are not pushing competition down with their dumping prices; as they churn out technologically more advanced and better-quality products, they push competition up.

Unfortunately, Europe is ill prepared for these challenges with its uncompetitive continental socioeconomic model. The EU average unemployment rate has been significantly and continuously higher than that in the United States. This difference came with the global financial and economic crisis of 2008–9, but it probably would be a mistake to predict that this trendlike difference will disappear once the crisis is over. Europe is lagging behind America and Asia in skills and qualifications. In 2002, half as many patents were registered in Europe as in the United States or Japan, and the gap is widening in terms of investment in R&D. The entrepreneurial spirit is stronger in both the United States and—rather humiliatingly—China.

Thus, the only solution for Europe is to transform itself into a reformed, more flexible and open continent that is turning its attention to the globalized world. Both commodity and labor markets should be liberalized, to make them flexible and truly market-like. Flexibility should not be seen as a threat to social solidarity but as a means of achieving efficiency and thereby long-term social prosperity. The state must withdraw from markets and eliminate rules hampering efficiency. This does not imply that fairness and equal opportunities are not to be ensured in the labor market. But the key aim is not to guarantee a job for life but to create the right environment for employability through flexible rules and high-quality education and training. In the modern world, everyone must be prepared for rapid changes; companies rise and fall, and old qualifications lose their value while new ones become sought after. The majority of new jobs—about eight out of ten—will be created in the high-technology, high-value-added sectors, which highlights the necessity for a highly qualified and skilled workforce.

Consequently, urgent and fundamental reforms are needed to labor market rules and to people's mentality. Everyone must learn to accept flexibility —governments, trade unions, economic operators, and workers alike. Active policies such as training are needed, instead of giving generous state subsidies to those without jobs. Taxation rules should be remodeled to make it worthwhile to seek work. There is no point in imposing a single European model on all countries, but member states should share and adopt best practices, such as "flexicurity." The buzzwords for Europe should be productivity and competitiveness, which can guarantee economic growth and ultimately social welfare. Nevertheless, we must be aware that flexicurity is a complex and expensive labor market model. Denmark, for instance, spends about 4.5 percent of its GDP for flexicurity policies, of which one-third goes into active labor market measures (e.g., training). Still, it sounds much wiser than guaranteeing job security at any cost.[24]

The common denominator in contemporary public discourse is the need for reform. But—as we have seen—that can be interpreted in many different ways. Decisionmakers must not confuse tactical measures introduced for the sole purpose of reducing expenditures with real reforms. A reform package announced with loud fanfares may easily fail to bring the desired results. Unfortunately, in terms of achieving results, reforms are much like freshly hatched baby turtles trying to make their way to the sea—few succeed. There can be several reasons for the low success rate; sometimes the plans are ill conceived and unrealistic in the first place, sometimes they are watered down by political deals to the extent that they do not bear the slightest resemblance to the original blueprint, and sometimes grand plans are just plain impossible to put into practice. There are principles and elements of reform more or less accepted as right and to be followed by all, apart from the unconditional believers in the traditional social model. Clearly, the welfare state must not jeopardize budgetary stability and should be efficient and flexible. Instruments focused on promoting employability, such as training subsidies, will go much further than a guaranteed right to a job. Welfare services must be service oriented rather than benefit oriented, and should favor those with a job. And certain segments of society should have more access to work, among them young people.

Will There Ever Be a Single European Model?

Europe is in a crisis, but there is no single solution to everyone's problems. Reforms are being implemented, though not too hastily, while fundamental changes are taking place daily in the market and in society. Increasing public anxiety is forcing the heads of Europe's governments to face the question of how to ensure the long-term financial sustainability of the European social model in areas such as pensions, health care, medical care for the permanently ill, education, and employment policy. Europe's welfare systems are facing the same challenges (globalization, an economy based on services, the appearance of new competitors, an aging population, new technologies, and new family models), but they typically are coming up with different solutions, shaped by their national peculiarities (history, institutions, and culture). Models do not become homogeneous overnight, but they are beginning to grow alike.

This does not, however, mean that all of Europe will play by the same identical rulebook. Differences in rules for the labor market and welfare services will remain with us for some time, just as it is unlikely that Brussels will have a decisive role to play in social policy anytime soon. Nevertheless, "Brussels" has not abandoned the idea of giving teeth to the EU's social policy. A new social policy package was proposed in 2008, although without too many obligatory rules, but certainly with the aim of responding to the new mood in favor of greater social justice and protection. These are rather delicate objectives, as we have already seen. But one thing is true: The convergence between the social policy models of EU member states in the last decade has helped to set guiding principles at the EU level.

Despite its international rise during the last decades, the Anglo-Saxon model will not be accepted in continental Europe, not even in the long run (especially after the global crisis, for which this model as such is often blamed). It is safe to rule out a scenario whereby the continental model would spread further, because its reform is one of Europe's most pressing tasks. Unless countries following this model take radical reform steps, their economies could collapse before the demographic time bomb goes off in a few years' time. The Nordic model, which is a well-functioning and—in many aspects—desirable one, would be almost impossible to introduce in a populous country with such strong continental traditions as France. For countries cursed with persistently high unemployment, adopting the Nordic model would mean an unbearable financial burden in the short run, with all its costly unemployment benefits and active employability measures. For continental model states, the most optimistic but still practicable solution is the German one—reform and market opening, which will never be equivalent to that of the truly liberal model, due to traditions and trade unions. Whether reforms will come soon enough and be deep enough, and what will happen to France, are open questions. It may well be that, at some point, France and some other continental EU member states will opt for a two-speed Europe held together by a common social model based on common minimum wages, common tax and contribution rules, and common working hour standards. (I will come back to this scenario later in the book.)

I do not see the need for a uniform, pan-European socioeconomic model, and exporting the continental model to other parts of Europe would be expressly detrimental. How could such a heterogeneous club—with members ranging from Sweden to Romania—even dream about a single model? It is much more important that the EU member states find the solutions best for them and for Europe. Conversely, the principles and values on which these solutions are based do matter. Reminiscing about the welfare state of the past is the number one obstacle to welfare state reforms.

Europe is facing one of the most important decisions it has ever had to make. It must choose a set of values to go with its socioeconomic model in the age of turboglobalization. The choice is basically between turning its back on the rest of the world or taking up the gauntlet and modernizing. It should be clear—it is to me—which is the right choice. The global financial meltdown could easily have an accelerating effect in this respect; the fitter the model, the bigger the chance to withstand economic troubles. In any case, Europe must hurry, because there is another menace ahead, even bigger than China: Aging is its name.

Aging and the Pension Time Bomb

Along with Japan, Europe is one of the most rapidly aging parts of the world. For the European Union, this worrying phenomenon calls for a rapid and comprehensive policy response at both the member state and EU levels.

Worrying Facts

Robert McNamara, when president of the World Bank, compared the uncontrollable explosion of the world's population to the peril of a nuclear war. This problem is a persistent one, which continues to haunt certain parts of the world, mainly Africa and Asia, but the last decade has brought a brand-new danger: depopulation and, as a consequence, aging. The United Nations calculates that the population of as many as fifty countries will have dwindled by 2050. Growing prosperity and falling fertility are to be blamed. The population of Japan began shrinking in 2005, and China is expected to face the same scenario starting in 2030. Much to the delight of India, China will age before it can become rich.[25]

The pace of scientific progress is unpredictable; giant leaps could happen any day. Therefore, we cannot rule out the possibility of average life expectancy increasing by as much as decades within generations, thanks to breakthroughs in medical science and genetic engineering. Advocates of the increasingly popular "transhumanism" theory believe that science will soon rid humanity of the nuisances of diseases and aging; implants and genetic manipulations will create a more viable, if partly artificial, species. But let us leave the field of science fiction and return to reality.

Europe must face demographic changes unprecedented in their magnitude and significance. Its natural population growth rate is at a historic low, hovering just above zero; in several countries, immigration is the main or only means of preventing population loss. Fertility has dropped below the replacement level (2.1 children per person) continent-wide, and to 1.5 in a few EU member states. Oddly, the supposedly family-oriented Mediterranean countries (Italy, Greece, and Spain) are at the bottom of the list, with figures as low as 1.3.[26] This does not mean that modern parents do not love their children; the fewer, the dearer. Modern parents are willing to spend astronomical sums on their children's education or clothing. Kids used to do their bit around the house, even physical work, and were happy with the leftovers from the pater familias; today they have a say in family decisions, such as what car to buy and where to go on vacation.

Thanks to immigration, the European Union's population will increase —if ever so slightly—until 2025, and begin to fall afterward. The projected figures are 458 million in 2005, 469.5 million in 2025 (potential EU enlargements excluded), and 468.7 million in 2030. The weight of Europe in the world's population will drop from 12 percent in 2000 to 6 percent in 2030. In terms of the working-age population (people between the age of fifteen and sixty-four years), the prospects are even bleaker; their number will decline by 21 million in the same three decades.[27]

The average life expectancy will continue to rise as a result of improved health care and quality of life; Europeans can expect to live longer and healthier lives. At the same time, the gap between male and female life expectancy will shrink and the number of births will remain low. Baby boomers had fewer children than the generations before them. Low birthrates are attributable to a number of factors: incompatibility between professional and private life, housing shortages, high property prices, late parenting, and changing attitudes toward education, career, and family life. The European Union has lost its demographic driving force; its member states not facing a population decline until 2050 represent a minor part of it. Of the five most populous states, only France and the United Kingdom will see their population swell between 2005 and 2050 (by 8 and 9.6 percent, respectively). For some member states, this decline could begin before 2015 and exceed 10 or even 15 percent by 2050. Immigration has mitigated the effects of depopulation in a number of countries but has brought other major social problems instead. The two newest EU entrants, Bulgaria and Romania, have reinforced negative population trends, with an estimated drop of, respectively, 21 and 11 percent until 2030—just as the EU candidate country Croatia will, upon its eventual accession (–19 percent). Turkey's population, conversely, will expand by 25 percent (19 million) between 2005 and 2030.[28]

The real problem lies not in the predicted fall in the EU's population from the current 457 million to 454 million in 2050, but in the age structure of that population. In the forty years starting in 2010, the working-age population (those from fifteen to sixty-four years of age) is forecast to shrink by 48 million (16 percent), while the number of people over the age of sixty-five will shoot up by 77 percent, making up 51 percent of the population by 2050.[29] Not counting non-working-age youth, this is an astounding trend, which could have a catastrophic impact on the economy as well as society. The active worker-to-retiree ratio is now four to one, but it will have dropped to two to one by 2050. In other words, the "support ratio" will double by the middle of the century.

There are advantages in a falling population. With fewer people, the scramble for food and resources is less vicious. An aging population also means that people are living longer and healthier lives. Depopulation is a consequence of prosperity and the social changes it has induced. Prosperity implies much more than just a high standard of living. Today's "Everything is possible, so I want it all" Western society is trapped by its own advance stage of development. Many women decide not to have children to be able to focus on their professional careers, but looser family ties and the "general sentiment" of turboglobalization all contribute to the dropping number of children. Fewer people living longer is a simple way to describe Europe's aging societies.

Worrying Consequences

An aging population is a multifaceted problem, which can lead to difficulties in various ways. First, it weakens the economy—both its performance and growth potential. Second, it entails huge costs for the state in pension and health spending, jeopardizing the ability to finance the national economy. Third, it rearranges the social structure and thereby may create tensions between the generations as fewer young people support more elderly ones.

How can Europe handle demographic changes happening on such a vast scale? By the middle of the twenty-first century, its population decline will be so dramatic that even increasing immigration will only partly counterbalance the aging process. A waning population is an aging one, and an aging population means falling growth potential. Due to the increasing ratio of retirees to workers, GDP growth could decelerate from the current 2 to 2.25 percent to as low as 1.25 percent by 2040,[30] which would make Europe's marginalization inevitable. When global competitors grow at many times the European pace, the gap Europe hopes to close will only widen and will do so faster and faster.

It is becoming clear to most that Europe's aging population could put public finances at risk in most EU member states. We still fail to devote enough attention to the economic impact of aging. The average EU employment rate is predicted to rise from 63 percent in 2003 to 67 percent in 2010 and reach the Lisbon objective of 70 percent in 2020. This improvement will be generated by the growing participation of women in the labor market (from 55 to 65 percent). Whereas four out of ten people between the age of fifty-five and sixty-four are actively employed today, it will be one in two by 2025. These are positive trends, which—however—also contribute to falling European growth potential. The annual potential growth rate of the fifteen pre–2004 enlargement EU member states will drop from 2.3 percent of GDP to 1.8 percent between 2010 and 2030, and to 1.3 percent by 2050. The negative trends will be even stronger in the new member states: 4.3 percent today, 3 percent in 2011–30, and 0.9 percent in 2031–50.[31] These forecasts foreshadow major economic and social challenges for the EU.

Immigration will be the number one means of supplementing the population, but it will be of lesser importance in terms of labor supply, because unemployment is generally higher among immigrants. As a consequence, in addition to social tensions, immigration will also mean a financial burden for the national governments. Women's increasing involvement in the employment market is another potential source of workforce supply; the EU's working-age population will start shrinking as early as 2010, while employment will continue to rise until 2017, which will be primarily due to women entering the labor market.[32] In this context, Europe needs to figure out how to make work more compatible with family life so as not to deter more women from having children. Due to changes in lifestyles, women are having children at an older age, often waiting too late with the decision. Having children is the focus of fewer and fewer relationships. About 90,000 children are not born a year in the United Kingdom alone because mothers —who would otherwise want to have more children—decide not to so that they can devote themselves to their careers, mainly for financial reasons.

One in three British mothers in their early twenties find worse-paying jobs on their return to work than they had before pregnancy. A woman giving birth to a child at the age of twenty-four will suffer an estimated financial loss of £560,000 during her life compared with a childless woman of similar qualifications.

The EU must understand that young people are an underrated treasure. In December 2004, unemployment in the EU stood at 17.9 percent among people under twenty-five years of age and 7.7 percent among people over twenty-five. The young are particularly vulnerable to poverty (earning below 60 percent of average incomes). In the age group of sixteen to twenty-four, 19 percent are living in poverty, quite above the 12 percent who are poor in the age group of twenty-five to sixty-four, and higher even than the 17 percent of the elderly who are poor (sixty-five and older).[33]

The social problem of growing tensions between the generations should not be underestimated. The baby boomers (people born between 1946 and the end of the 1950s) grew up to witness unprecedented economic growth, won the revolution of 1968, and have generous pension payments to look forward to. They are the generation of Europe's golden age, who—too busy enjoying their prosperity—"forgot" to have enough children. As a result, the post–baby boomer generation faces the burden of fewer active workers providing for more retirees, who were better off in the first place. Uneven income transfers are only one source of tension; today's middle-class is also annoyed by the older generation blocking its upward social mobility. The conflicts between the generations are gravest in France, where twenty- to forty-year-olds are the first generation in history to have to accept a standard of living below their parents'. Only one in fifteen young graduates was jobless in 1973; in 2008, every fourth one was.[34] Salaries have failed to keep up with escalating property prices, which have doubled or trebled over the last two decades, making it difficult for young first-time buyers to climb onto the property ladder. These factors lead to dwindling prosperity, an ossified social order, frozen generational mobility, and growing desperation among the young generation. Denis Jeambar, the renowned French social analyst and a baby boomer himself, was ruthlessly outspoken when he admitted that "our children will hate us."

Aging means added health and social care costs, putting not only national budgets under strain but also corporate pension funds and life insurers. Pension funds and insurance companies have contracts with vast financial obligations to their clients, and thus demographic changes can hit them severely. When BAE, a British defense and aerospace company, reassessed the prospects of its pension fund in 2005, it was forced to increase its pension liabilities forecast by £2.1 billion (€3.7 billion). Rentokil Initial, the office services specialist, was the first FTSE 100 firm to close its final salary pension scheme to new employees in an effort to plug a £500 million pensions "black hole." Deloitte & Touche's actuaries estimate that the total deficit for the salary pension plans of Britain's FTSE 100 companies stands at more than £100 billion.[35]

Despite worsening demographic trends, employment can be kept high enough in the coming ten years for Europe to avoid a lethal blow to its economy. One precondition is that unemployment trends be reversed and reforms be launched in time. Because of its shrinking workforce, Europe's only chance of maintaining growth is to improve its economy's efficiency and competitiveness. Aging will cut European growth potential by half in a few decades, with Central and Eastern European countries faring the worst, because their growth rate will nose-dive from the current 4.5 percent to below 1 percent in 2030.[36] The biggest economic risk that aging poses is the unsustainability of pensions systems, making their reform a top priority for the near future.

The Pension Time Bomb

There are two types of pensions. One type accumulates equity, paying interest on members' savings; the other, the traditional state pension, relies on taxes, or rather the contributions of the employees and employers. In the traditional model, the state levies taxes on work to be able to fund pensions to retirees. As the number of retirees grows, either the money available to them decreases or the contributions of active workers increases, or sometimes both. If contributions are too low, poverty strikes; if they are too high, social costs become unbearable.

However, we would be mistaken in believing that funded pensions—that is, our savings, kept in a personal account and invested by our pension fund —are left untouched by aging. As the number of active earners drops, so does the number of buyers of assets invested by pension funds (securities embodying retirees' pensions) that could increase the value of such an investment. The cake is getting smaller in both cases, although accumulative pensions are more immune to aging. But there is one more factor to consider: The countries facing the biggest pension problems happen to be the high-income states, which cannot afford to raise taxes or pension contributions any higher because of their competitors. Slowly but surely, it is becoming clear that the solution must be on the other side of the equation: The pensionable retirement age must be raised.

Europe is sitting on a ticking pension time bomb. According to demographic data, Europe's pension systems are not sustainable. The number of people eligible for pension coverage is multiplying, especially among the oldest (posing quite a challenge to insurance firms and private pension funds). There are several reasons for this; the postwar baby boomers are nearing retirement, while the continent's population growth has been going downhill steeply and average life expectancy keeps climbing due to better health care. As a result, the ratio of supported retirees to active workers will double by 2050 (from 24 to 50 percent).[37]

The rapid aging of Europe's population could have disastrous consequences for state spending unless the EU's member states overhaul their welfare systems. Aging will mean an additional 3 to 7 percent of GDP in public costs by 2050. The lion's share of this increase in public spending will come from pensions. Without comprehensive reforms, the budgetary burden of supporting an aging population could weigh so heavily on the shoulders of industrial countries that, in a few decades, their credit ratings could sink from the current investor-grade "AAA" and the like to a speculative band, according to a 2005 Standard & Poor's report. The rating agency's calculations—which extrapolate the current trends of rising costs and presuppose no substantive reforms in pension financing—show that, by 2050, national debt will have spiraled from the current level of 65 percent of GDP to 239 percent in the United States, from 66 to 235 percent in France, and from 68 to 221 percent in Germany. If that does happen, the leading industrial powers will see their credit rating downgraded from AAA to below BBB before 2035.

In the five biggest EU member states (France, Germany, Italy, Spain, and the United Kingdom), a quarter of the population will be older than sixty-five years by 2030. In Germany, for example, pension costs will absorb 18.5 percent of GDP in 2035, when roughly 36 percent of the population will be above the age of sixty.[38] This recognition had led those European countries that had not already done so to set up market-based pension plans. The German federal government attempted to deactivate the pension time bomb by lowering the guaranteed level of state pension benefits and introducing a nonvoluntary funded pension fund pillar.

The situation of the European Union's decisionmakers is further complicated by the Stability and Growth Pact, which caps public deficits at 3 percent of GDP, which in turn restricts how much pension systems can go into the red. The root of the problem is that EU member states' pension systems are mainly based on state-sponsored pay-as-you-go schemes. The United Kingdom and the Netherlands are the only two member states with an adequately developed private pension sector. British pension funds have been happy to invest in securities for a long time, while their Dutch counterparts have only moved away from the more secure bonds recently. (Yet the share of stocks in their investment portfolios was 40 percent in 2003.[39]) These two countries support further liberalization of private pension fund investments at the EU level, but the spectacular bursting of the stock market bubble at the turn of the millennium was a timely warning that it is advisable to proceed with caution.

The EU must understand that unless its influential member states carry out radical reforms, it could find itself in deep trouble. Germany embarked on the reform of the continent's oldest pension system, the foundations of which were laid by Otto von Bismarck 130 years ago, but gloomy demographic forecasts (showing the proportion of people over eighty rising from 4 to 12 percent by 2050[40]) make these initial measures look insufficient. Recent pension reforms have stirred opposition of an elemental force in both France and Austria. With current demographic trends, the sustainability of traditional schemes can be ensured by raising contributions, slashing benefits, or adding a few years to the retirement age. There are no simple or popular solutions. Another thorny issue is how to counterbalance the potential shortfall in the workforce. Following the EU's enlargement in 2004, almost all the "old" EU member states closed their labor markets to workers from the new member states. Obviously, political solutions catering to present needs are not compatible with strategic plans based on an analysis of long-term demographic trends. However, the gravity of the problem has forced national administrations to launch reforms, even if halfheartedly.

In the United Kingdom, and all over Europe, the baby boom generation is nearing retirement. In 1950, there were five working-age adults for every retiree, but in 2050 there will only be two active earners for every retiree. As a result, despite its developed market-based pension pillar, the pension time bomb is the United Kingdom's biggest socioeconomic problem. There has been no shortage of reform ideas, but they have come and gone. The U.K. Pensions Commission, an independent body consisting of acknowledged experts, published its much-awaited report in 2005, with recommendations to raise the pensionable age from the present sixty-five (for men) and sixty (for women) to sixty-six in 2030 and sixty-eight in 2050 for both sexes.[41] The new proposal demonstrates more social sensitivity, because it aims at introducing the basic state pension as an automatic entitlement. Even though this will mean an extra financial burden for the Treasury, pension-related costs (8 percent of GDP in 2050) will still only be half of what continental social market economies (e.g., Germany) will have to muster for the same purpose.

In terms of pension and health care expenditures, the United Kingdom is among the most tightfisted countries in the world, along with the United States and Mexico. This lack of generosity (British social provision is more modest than on the continent), and the developed private pensions market, will be the watchword for budgetary sustainability. Corporate pension plans and private pension funds face serious difficulties in financing; their dependence on stock markets means that they will be badly hit if their portfolio performs poorly. Employer pension schemes have accumulated vast deficits and have thus been forced to break their promises to members. The membership of defined-benefit corporate pension schemes fell from 5 million in 1995 to 2 million in 2005.[42]

German society faces similar problems. According to current trends, every third German will be a retiree in 2030. Major generational conflicts can be expected because most of the sacrifices required by social reforms will need to be made by young people, who will have to tighten their belts. The Christian Democratic–Social Democratic grand coalition is raising the pension age from sixty-five to sixty-seven years, which will first affect those born after 1970. Pension benefits will be frozen, and contributions will go up by 0.5 percent, which should temporarily ease the pressure on the federal pension fund, which oversees the enormous sum of €230 billion. Germany's pension problems were further aggravated after reunification, when western Germans had to fill up the empty coffers of the former East Germany's national pension scheme. The pension system inherited from Bismarck has seen modifications recently; its last substantive reform was the introduction of the multipillar system in 2001. The pillar of mandatory contributions remains the centerpiece of the system, but there is a complementary funded pillar based on contributions from the worker and the state— dubbed "Riester pension," after the German labor minister who piloted a reform of the country's pension system through parliament—as well as a private pension fund pillar receiving generous tax breaks.

Angry demonstrators filled the streets of Paris in the spring of 2003, protesting the planned pension reforms. In the end, the reform was carried out, raising the pensionable age and encouraging self-provision. The pension reform law follows French traditions and guarantees a minimum pension to all retirees. Salaried workers, agricultural workers, skilled crafts-people, and commercial employees receive no less than €534 a month, provided that they can prove forty years of service. Similarly, civil servants and public employees are guaranteed a minimum pension benefit. Senior officials, private-sector employees, entrepreneurs, and business managers are entitled to at least €945 after twenty-five years of work. The pension law links minimum pensions to minimum wages, stipulating that from 2008 on, every retiree should receive at least 85 percent of the applicable minimum wage. The retirement age will change to sixty-five years, but early retirement will be possible for anyone with more than forty years of labor. France's pension system is also a multipillar one, allowing voluntary contributions (not exceeding 50 percent of the person's income) in the hope of a higher pension in the future. FRR, the huge pension reserve fund in the state's hands, which was launched with great acclaim in 1999 to prop up the rickety pay-as-you-go scheme, could only collect half of the foreseen €150 billion in assets. The fund is beefed up by state subsidies coming from taxes and privatization revenues. The initial failure to secure sufficient funding for FRR is a painful reminder of the fact that the pie is getting smaller, and simply renaming resources will not bring in new funding.

In Italy, one-quarter of the population will be over the age of sixty-five years by 2015, and average life expectancy will exceed eighty for both men and women. The need for reform is thus unquestionable in Italy. The reforms introduced in 2008 allow a retirement age of sixty-five for forty years of service, but those deciding to work longer will see their net income grow by as much as 32 percent. Reforms are badly needed, because the Italian pension funds are on the edge of collapse and the country's budgetary prospects are far from rosy. Still, the elderly are not poor; in fact, people in their sixties and seventies are the best off in society. Unlike today's youth, they had a safe job, could buy a house and still put money aside, and then receive a stable and lavish pension after the dolce vita of the 1970s and 1980s.

In the spring of 2006, the Portuguese government adopted deep pension reforms unparalleled in Europe, under which families with fewer than two children pay higher pension contributions in the spirit of intergenerational solidarity. Workers can decide whether they wish to work longer or pay higher contributions. The new system also includes a "sustainability coefficient," which allows for changing pension benefits, reducing pensions in line with life expectancy. If, for example, average life expectancy increases by one year in the next decade, then the pension of those retiring in ten years' time will be 5 percent lower. There was an acute need for reform, because the pension system would have collapsed by 2015 due to its generosity (indicated by the example of some people receiving pensions higher than their end-of-career salary). We should also take into consideration the drastic drop (35 percent) in the number of children born in the last thirty years, along with the growing proportion of senior citizens (which currently stands at 7 percent; but by 2050, every third person in Portugal will be above the age of sixty-five).[43]

There are people who deny the existence of a pension time bomb and who do not see the aging population as a problem. A study by the English research outfit Tomorrow's Company claims that improving productivity counterbalances the negative effects of the aging of society.[44] The study suggests that, instead of comparing the number of those over sixty-five with workers, we should look at active versus inactive citizens, which would yield more profound conclusions. Although I acknowledge that there is some truth in the methodology suggested, I consider such an optimistic approach false and dangerous. Governments should take the problem of aging very seriously, and they should implement profound reforms to their pension schemes and other social provision systems.

Of course, Europe is not the only continent with such headaches. In Asia, China is also doing its best to reinforce its embryonic pension system. The traditional pension scheme administered by the state and built on employers has disintegrated, and a suitable alternative has yet to emerge. The old pay-as-you-go system functioned without real contributions from future retirees; this is being replaced by a pay-as-you-earn funded system. Personal pension accounts are being opened, in the hope of attracting the self-employed, migrant workers, and farmers; but most reform plans remain on the drawing board. And the Japanese system is also undergoing significant changes; defined-contribution private pension funds modeled on the U.S. example were introduced in 2001, and the membership of these funds exceeded 1.5 million at the end of the fourth year.

Is There a Way Out?

The European Union's member states must face the challenges of aging. Governments must improve their budgetary positions, reduce state debt, and embark on an overhaul of pension and health insurance schemes. Also, reforms of the labor market must factor in increased life expectancy (from a European average of 61.5 years in 2000 to 62.4 in 2050) and abandon the static retirement age in favor of a dynamic limit of how long workers should stay active.[45] Naturally, this will require combating ageism, reviewing wage and tax policy, as well as promoting lifelong learning.

People over the age of fifty-five years will play an increasingly important role in the labor market; companies will need to rely more on the elderly, which will mean retaining and training them. Aging will also shape corporate innovation strategies, in the transportation, tourism, and financial services sectors. Aging will bring about changes in consumption patterns, benefiting certain types of products and services. One of the key goals must be to enable the elderly to stay at work longer or to have a part-time job after retirement, as American trends indicate. According to 2003 figures, only 5.6 percent of people between the age of sixty-five and seventy-four in the EU were still active professionally, which is less than one-third of the 18.5 percent boasted by the United States.[46]

Flexibility must be the key word for labor reforms for young people as well, who may want to spend more time with their children early in their careers and spend more time at work at a later stage. This can only be done through more flexible employment conditions and work organization, especially because education is taking up more and more years of early life. Nevertheless, the key task is encouraging employment among the fifty-five-plus group by improving labor market conditions. This will require member states to make employment a more attractive option than early retirement, by adjusting their taxation, training, and remuneration policies and tailoring rules to the needs of an aging workforce. Health services must also be upgraded to improve the physical and mental health of senior workers, and the creation of a true single European market in health care could be one of the best ways of doing this. In a single health care market, patients could turn to any national system for treatment, in the same way as Europeans have been buying foreign goods and services for decades. The pensionable age limit must be raised by a few years, and the fixed limit will probably have to be replaced by a flexible one pegged to average life expectancy.

The reform to the pension system should keep in mind the centuries-old tradition of children taking care of their parents in their twilight years. Younger generations used to channel resources back to their inactive parents; modern pay-as-you-go schemes fundamentally rely on the same principle, with the important difference that family ties have ceased to play a role. Still, one fact remains unchanged: The more young members the system has, the more money is available to pension beneficiaries. Returning to the old ways of a family-based intergenerational transfer would be nonsensical, but taking into consideration the number of children when calculating someone's pension eligibility is not a bad idea. Portugal did, indeed, factor children into its new system.

Private pension funds should move away from defined-benefit solutions to defined-contribution plans, because it will become impossible to guarantee a fixed pension for a retirement of so many years. The relevance of corporate pension plans should also be questioned in a fast-changing world where few people spend their working life in the service of a single company, and the majority change jobs many times during their career. The concept of the employer providing for its retired workers is an outdated one, and cases like the Enron scandal are a painful warning that employees' pensions may not be in the best hands with their bosses.

Europe does not have an easy task; it must improve its reproductive rates, find the social balance between generations while remaining fair, and find the resources for financing the escalating costs of pension and health care provision. Rising costs must not lead to budgetary overspending, for that would jeopardize the common European currency as well as the stability of national economies and therefore social peace. Europe must grit its teeth and do what needs to be done: encourage couples to have more children, boost productivity, keep people at work longer by revising employment and linked rules, and—last but not least—complete the reform of the pension system. A new, horizontal population policy is needed that takes into consideration aging as well as dropping birthrates. Countries hit by negative demographic trends have tried different solutions to alleviate the situation; Japan hopes to encourage marriages by sponsoring dating and other services for singles, and France announced in 2005 that mothers would receive a "premium" for having a third child. Scandinavian countries have opted for a somewhat more sophisticated policy, focusing on developing child care and parental leave rules. In some countries, population policy reforms are more difficult to implement; in Spain it is the Franco heritage, while in Germany the Nazi past casts a dark shadow over these policies. The United Kingdom also has its fair share of problems; state intervention in private life is a centuries-old taboo.

Immigration from outside the European continent might counterbalance falling population trends until 2025, although that is not a panacea and cannot replace economic reforms. Immigration will prevent the depopulation of Europe in the coming decades, but it will also mean a Muslim minority of 70 to 80 million by 2050. Finding the recipe for peaceful coexistence will not be easy. Encouraging participation in the labor market is a means of ensuring economic growth without creating social tensions. According to calculations, the economic benefits of a 7 percent boost in employment would equal the positive impact of the arrival of 1.3 million immigrants.[47] Europe must come up with ways of integrating these immigrants and find the right balance between the rights and obligations of the immigrant community and of the society welcoming them.

Immigration

There are about 200 million immigrants around the world today. Immigration is not a new phenomenon in Europe; just like emigration, it has been going on for centuries. More prosperous European states with a labor shortage, that are politically more stable, or that are more liberal in areas such as freedom of religion have been receiving immigrants for a long time. There are two types of immigration—legal and illegal. But there can be enormous variations even within those categories. A rich German plastic surgeon moving his practice to another EU member state to escape Germany's high income tax is just as much an emigrant as the Swedish retiree choosing Portugal as her new home for its pleasant climate. Some people are forced to leave their homes behind due to political persecution (they are called political refugees). Naturally, here I focus on "traditional" migration, when people decide to resettle in another country in search of a job or better quality of life. The money migrants send home while working abroad (globally, $400 billion in 2005) far outstrips development aid from the West. Conversely, traffickers and smugglers can earn as much as €30,000 per person from illegal immigrants. According to the International Labor Organization, there are 2.5 million people suffering at the hands of traffickers around the world. The United Nations predicts that the number of people migrating will continue to increase by 40 percent in the next forty years.[48]

France is an apposite case. Immigrants have always provided a significant part of France's population. The number of foreign-born French residents was above a million as early as 1881; today, the number of first-generation immigrants exceeds 4 million, or 7 percent of the population.[49] One out of five French people has at least one foreign-born grandparent. In the nineteenth century, France attracted low-paid, unskilled workers mainly from—what are today—Belgium, Spain, Italy, and Switzerland. It is not surprising that xenophobia erupted in times of economic recession. Immigrant colonies, which included second- and third-generation descendants, continued to evolve. In 1931, the biggest immigrant community was Italian (800,000), and the second-biggest was Polish (500,000). In France, historical (Italian, Polish, German, and Spanish) immigrant minorities had completely blended in by the 1950s and 1960s.

After World War II, more and more Western European countries became destinations for a large number of immigrants. The continent's booming heavy industries absorbed hundreds of thousands of foreign workers, many non-European, primarily from Africa and Turkey. Germany, which had been abandoned by many of its people, invented the concept of "guest worker" as it became an importer of labor and recipient of political refugees. This dynamic trend was broken by the 1973 oil shock. In picturesque France, vast shantytowns mushroomed and temporary hostels were built by the hundreds to accommodate foreign workers. French workers disappeared from the construction industry completely in the space of a few years as their jobs were taken by Portuguese and Algerian laborers (altogether, about three quarters of a million). The social acceptance of Portuguese and Algerian blue-collar workers showed a marked difference. The Portuguese were considered "guest workers," and the Algerians were "immigrants," evoking fear and rejection among the French, especially because the Algerians had been considered "enemies" since the French-Algerian war of 1954–62. They were excluded from promotions, and there were attempts to restrict their further immigration, which were unsuccessful due to another process: family reunification (whereby the worker's relatives in North Africa joined the head of the family in Europe).

Immigration also gradually acquired a new aspect, a religious one. The question is no longer the same as that in the early nineteenth century—how to handle the social tensions created by the arrival of migrant workers—but how Western countries can integrate the native-born descendants of immigrant workers into society. Foreigners from *outside,* who were endangering natives' jobs, used to be the scapegoats. But today the object of fears and prejudices is *inside,* endangering social peace and therefore living in social exclusion. Thus the "proletariat" of the twenty-first century, as Dominique Moisi puts it,[50] is born—predominantly Muslim, young, angry, disillusioned, and excluded, with an immigrant background.

The British member of Parliament Enoch Powell predicted in 1985 that, by 2000, 8 percent of the United Kingdom's population would be black or brown, and immigrants would account for a third of the residents of many important British cities. The result would be a disintegrating nation and perpetual violence. Nobody took him seriously, but it turns out that—at least as far as statistical forecasts go—his predictions were right. He was only mistaken about violence; most of the violent incidents take place between different groups of immigrants, not between natives and immigrants. This is partly due to the fact that the natives have moved to suburbia, away from the areas that are now inner-city ghettos, by the hundreds of thousands. More than two decades later, Rowan Williams—the archbishop of Canterbury, head of the Church of England, and leader of the worldwide Anglican Communion—made a statement that stirred controversy in the whole of British society. He said that the adoption of certain aspects of Islamic Sharia law in the United Kingdom was unavoidable. He thought it would mirror societal reality.

Illegal immigration into the EU through the Balkans is a growing cause of concern. Masses of migrants from Iraq, Iran, Pakistan, and Central Asia enter the EU across land and sea borders from Turkey. In Greece alone, 100,000 illegal immigrants were held in 2006, 40 percent more than in 2005. Net immigration to the EU was 1.7 million people in 2005, roughly three times what it was in the early 1990s.[51] And there is no shortage of supply; while Europe's population is falling, in the neighboring regions populations are growing rapidly. All Western European countries—with the exception of Finland and Ireland—have significant new immigrant minorities. The countries of origin vary from one nation to another: Iraq and Iran in Sweden; Pakistan in Norway; Turkey in Denmark; Morocco and Turkey in Belgium; the Netherlands, Morocco, and Latin America in Spain; India, Pakistan, and Bangladesh in the United Kingdom; North Africa in France and Italy; and Turkey in Germany. The successful social integration of all these diverse immigrants is essential for the future of Europe.

Eurabia?

The very idea of "Eurabia" was based on an extremist conspiracy theory, according to which Europe and the Arab states would join forces to make life impossible for Israel and Islamize the old continent, thrusting it into total Muslim servitude. The central concept of this rather ridiculous theory, concocted by the Israeli-born Bat Ye'or, has come to be used differently in public discourse. Instead of a conscious conspiracy theory, social analysts —especially in the United States—understand the idea of Eurabia as an evolving demographic process leading to the unavoidable "Islamization" of Europe, albeit one that is not politically guided.

The overseas version of Eurabia is known as Amexica—the "Hispanization" of the United States by Mexican immigrants. Fear of foreigners is not a newfangled idea in America; Benjamin Franklin feared that immigrants would Germanize Philadelphia instead of the natives "Anglicizing" the newcomers. The estimated number of illegal immigrants living in the United States is 10 million, but some put it at 20 million, and they are joined by another million entering the territory of the United States illegally every year. The largest immigrant group is Mexicans, 4 million of whom have no official papers or documents of any kind. The GDP produced by Mexican Americans would do a smaller country proud; their annual remittances total $50 billion. American policy is two-sided; they want to legalize the status of foreigners already working in the United States (the economy badly needs them for the worst paid physical work), but they also wish to put an end to the uncontrolled inflow of illegal immigrants, partly by building a 3-meter-high wall along the 1,100-kilometer U.S.-Mexican border, which would come complete with infrared cameras and robot planes. Undoubtedly, the latest Hispanic arrivals tend to live in closed communities, much more than any other ethnic minority. There are 33 million foreign-born U.S. residents—a third of whom have become naturalized citizens, a third of whom hold work permits, and a third of whom are living on U.S. soil illegally. These figures demonstrate how enormous a challenge immigration poses for America. Strictly, statistically speaking, Europe has it easier (the ratio of foreigners to natives is only 6.4 percent[52]), but it is sometimes worth taking a closer look at—and behind—the dry figures.

Those who seek to frighten Europeans with the threat of the Islamization of Europe's societies argue that the Muslim community already accounts for 2 to 8 percent of the population in Western European countries (France heads the list with 10 percent).[53] In some places, Muslim children account for 15 to 20 percent of youngsters, and in some cities—such as Amsterdam or Brussels—Mohamed is the most common given name. This is not surprising, considering the non-Muslim majority's subreplacement fertility. There have been some shockingly symbolic events confirming the theory. One was the France-Algeria football match at the Stade de France in Paris a few weeks after the September 11, 2001, terrorist attacks. At the match, fans of North African origin (most of them living in the neighboring suburb of Saint-Denis) booed the French anthem, and when France scored the first goal, angry spectators invaded the field, ending the match prematurely. (It is an interesting parallel that a very similar incident took place at a Mexico–United States match.)

Other often-cited examples in the press of the failure of social integration and the clash of cultures were the murders of the Dutch right-wing politician Pim Fortuyn, who campaigned for more stringent immigration rules and the integration of Muslims, and of the film director Theo van Gogh, who had made a documentary about the mistreatment of Islamic women. Fortuyn was assassinated in broad daylight by an extremist animal rights activist opposed to the radicalization of Dutch political life; van Gogh was shot and stabbed by a Muslim extremist while cycling through Amsterdam. The publication of twelve editorial cartoons depicting the Islamic prophet Muhammad in the Danish newspaper *Jyllands-Posten* sparked unexpected aggression in Muslim countries worldwide, and Pope Benedict XVI also had to eat humble pie and explain his words after quoting excerpts from a 600-year-old manuscript critical of Islam. Protests in Muslim countries against specific incidents are usually transformed into demonstrations against Western civilization and a general rejection of all Western values. These phenomena pose serious questions concerning fundamental rights such as freedom of speech, and to what extent intolerance can be tolerated.

Another illuminating story is that of a Somali refugee, Ayaan Hirsi Ali. Trying to escape a forced marriage, she sought and obtained political asylum in the Netherlands in 1992. Later she became a critic of Islam, a leading civil rights activist, and a member of the Dutch Parliament, where she campaigned against Muslim extremism. When she admitted to making false statements in her application for asylum, the Dutch government decided to expel her and strip her of Dutch citizenship and passport. A conservative think tank, the American Enterprise Institute, immediately offered Hirsi Ali a fellowship in Washington. The incident caused widespread indignation, aroused a public uproar, and led to her resignation from Parliament and, indirectly, to the fall of the government.

In parallel with these widely reported events, a much less spectacular but significant process of social change is taking place out of the spotlight and the attention of the media. Ghettos are forming in Western Europe's cities, where Muslim immigrants live in closed communities, completely separate from the rest of society. In Malmö, Sweden's third-largest city, four out of ten inhabitants are of non-Swedish origin. A report by a Dutch parliamentary committee predicts that non-Dutch residents could outnumber the natives in the Netherlands' biggest cities by 2017. This quiet "invasion" will happen through family reunification and arranged "cross-border" marriages. Such arranged marriages decided by and between the families are already a main source of immigration, and one of the reasons immigrant communities based on bonds between large families are formed. In such an environment, integration into the recipient society is not an important factor; on the contrary, maintaining cultural traditions is of the essence. Even so, Europe has both a responsibility and a vested interest—and not just an economic one—to welcome refugees and asylum seekers persecuted in their home country. That is what European values and Europe's moral obligation dictate.

Like any European, I get a cold shiver running down my spine from seeing a part of the American intellectual elite—who are no longer confined to just Christian fundamentalists—taking Europe's decline and the birth of "Eurabia" for granted, already wondering how to make it easier for Europe's intelligentsia—longing for freedom, democracy, and Western values—to resettle in the land of the free, the home of the brave. Scaremongering and misconceptions rooted in a lack of knowledge should be treated as what they are, but Europe cannot simply shrug its shoulders. Eurabia may only be a bombastic delusion, but clearly there are tensions and problems, and the concept of multiculturalism has failed. Luckily, there are also solutions.

Homework

American social analysts often state that the United States and Europe tackle the integration of immigrants completely differently. The American solution is the immigrant's true acceptance as an individual and future U.S. citizen: Americanization. Europe, conversely, grants immigrants a large degree of independence; instead of Europeanizing them, they are allowed to cultivate their cultural traditions within their own communities inside a multicultural society. There is at least one European state with an individualistic approach to immigrants; France considers every person—be it a Muslim immigrant—an independent building block of the republic, rather than a member of an ethnic or religious community. This, however, is the exception to the rule; the general European approach is based on the acceptance of cultural, ethnic, and religious communities as single entities and on the cohabitation of new immigrant communities in full equality. On the old continent, the emphasis is on the community rather than the individual.

This European approach is coming under growing criticism for its alleged inability to cope with the most important social task: integration. According to critics, it cannot deal with the problem of closed communities in society, which are impossible to break out of. Immigrants tend to live isolated from the rest of society, living their unhappy lives in ghettos without virtually any access to the labor market, surviving on benefits. Ghettos perpetuate seclusion; it is not uncommon for third-generation descendants of immigrants not to have learned the language of the country where they were born. And despite its republican approach, even France has its fair share of isolated, secluded communities, which can be explained by the failure to translate general prointegration policies into practice. In fact, some policies —such as education, housing, or social policy—reinforce segregation.

Managing immigration, and especially integration, requires major financial commitments. According to research by Jacques Bichot of Lyon University, immigration cost France about €24 billion in 2005 alone.[54] Most of the extra costs were incurred in the areas of law enforcement, the judiciary, criminal policing, social benefits, and education, primarily in relation to North African and Turkish immigrants. To put things in perspective, this sum roughly equals all the funding that Hungary will receive from the European Union between 2007 and 2013 to help it catch up to the EU average.

The needs of today's world point in the direction of a policy to promote the immigration of highly qualified people. There are many examples of this policy, the best one being Canada. Some European countries have taken the first steps toward reforming immigration policy, usually meaning more stringent rules. Denmark was among the first ones to do so, which resulted in an almost immediate drop in the number of immigrants. The key to this policy's success is encouraging the integration of immigrants into society. Europe has always needed immigrants, and it will continue to need them to keep its sluggish economy moving. Social inclusion, the acceptance of immigrants by mainstream society, and their integration into the social fabric —all are bigger challenges than political decisionmakers imagined a few decades ago.

I believe it is quite clear that Western Europe has an immigrant integration problem, not an immigration problem. It is time to do some serious thinking and come up with solutions for integrating immigrants and their descendants into society. Peaceful coexistence will no longer do as an objective. Immigrants should be looked upon as an important pillar of economic progress, something of which immigrants themselves should be conscious. Just like the elderly, immigrants should also be encouraged to work, which can be done by reforming the rules of the social care system and the labor market. It is in the common interest to make everyone—native or immigrant—an active member of society. It is not enough if natives pretend to welcome immigrants but think of them as "they" and accept that immigrants live in isolated subcultures without any real participation in the labor market or society. Today's immigrants must learn—as their forebears did through the centuries—to accept the fundamental values of their chosen homeland and make efforts to settle in. In the United States, the Catholic Church is an important facilitating agent in the social integration of Mexicans and Latin Americans. Of course, this is not a solution that Europe could emulate. Moreover, the more generous European welfare system makes the integration of immigrants more costly and their entry into the labor market more difficult.

Immigration and social integration is a pan-European issue, which the European Union must have a role in solving, because cooperation between its members is essential. The EU's member states will not be able to stem the tide of immigrants on their own, as was demonstrated in 2006, when close to 22,000 African immigrants landed on Spain's Canary Islands in ramshackle boats, leaving the government overwhelmed. Malta, Italy, and Greece have all received similar floods of illegal immigrants—altogether 24,000 in the first eight months of 2006. There are an estimated 3 million illegal immigrants in the EU, which has no internal borders or a harmonized asylum and immigration policy.[55] Cooperation and coordination are unavoidable; good ideas need to be put into practice, and member states must step up their joint efforts to halt economic migration, handle immigration, and combat illegal immigration. For this challenge of illegal immigration, proposals for a common European marine border squad to control the EU's borders in the Mediterranean Sea surfaced at one point. Immigration policy is a cross-cutting area—part foreign policy, part development policy, and part trade policy.

By providing aid, investment, and free trade opportunities to reduce poverty in neighboring African countries, the EU could somewhat ease the pressure under which it is finding itself. In late 2008, it adopted a comprehensive immigration package that focuses on how best to exert control over migration flows, and also proposes an EU-wide ban on mass amnesties for irregular migrants and suggests that its member states introduce an integration contract for new non-European citizens to sign before entering the Union. This would commit these migrants to learning the host country's language as well as adopting European values. This commitment emerged with the dramatically worsening migration situation in the Mediterranean Sea belt area. A European Blue Card (copying the U.S. Green Card) for skilled migrants has also been recommended. In the meantime, Frontex, the EU's external border control agency, is getting a more and more prominent role, and its budget has increased exponentially every year since it became operational in 2005.[56]

While solving the problems of immigration and social integration, Europe must also dig deeper and seek to solve more far-reaching questions. In particular, it must consider its attitude toward Islam, the religion of more and more people, which many see as a danger, and whose radicalization could pose a serious threat to the daily life of European societies. A better understanding of its relationship with Islam will enable Europe to address many related social issues. Europe must stand firm and not abandon its fundamental values; it must not give in to any kind of extremist pressure but must seek reconciliation and a dialogue with sensible, moderate forces. This dialogue promises to be difficult, because it is not clear how to define the partner—is Islam a religion, a civilization, or a community of peoples? Both sides are full of prejudices and know little about each other. And many questions must be clarified concerning Europe's relationship with its immigrants from predominantly Muslim countries. There are already more than 9 million Muslims living in France, Germany, and the United Kingdom; their number has trebled over the last three decades, and the pace of growth of this population will only accelerate in the future. Treating immigrants from traditionally Muslim countries en bloc as Muslims is not only an oversimplified approach but also runs against the interests of Europe. Turkey's EU accession will surely be the touchstone for this Islam-Europe dialogue. The question is whether reconciliation between the West and the Muslim world is possible. But one way or another, due to its special situation, Europe must try its best to make it happen. This question has been haunting Europe for 1,300 years, which have been marked by enmity and wars but often also by cultural cooperation and a dialogue between cultures. Now, however, Europe has come to a turning point and, in a world of accelerating change, it can no longer put off finding a solution for cohabitation.

The time has come for Europe to face the inconvenient issues. Sweeping them under the carpet could have serious consequences, the first signs of which are showing—extremist political forces that reject the fundamental principles of democracy and liberty have been gaining strength all over the continent. Some have a gloomy view and cry "Weimar" already, prophesying social and political radicalization due to Europe's indecision. This may be an exaggerated, pessimistic vision, but if Europe is unable to face its internal social problems openly and find solutions for them, the goal of maintaining its competitiveness and international role will remain but a dream.

Energy Dependency

In the modern age, everything requires energy—more and more energy—and therefore it is not accidental that energy sector has become the biggest sector since the Industrial Revolution. Without a continuous energy supply, there can be no production, no consumption, no entertainment—a short blackout can cause a shock to society, the same as a few moments of breathlessness for a human being. Energy policy has thus become a global environmental and geostrategic issue. Energy generation and consumption contribute to global warming, and the ownership of increasingly scarce energy sources can decide the rise or fall of societies, countries, and regions.

In addition to its acute dependency on imported energy sources, Europe is also troubled by rising oil and gas prices, growing energy demand, its antiquated energy infrastructure, the failure to create a true common European energy market due to national protectionism, and the impact of burning fossil fuels for energy on global warming. As these energy-related problems became more and more pressing, the EU has begun laying the foundations for a common European energy policy.

The energy sector comprises primary production (e.g., coal mining), conversion/generation (burning coal in a power plant and transforming it into electricity), and transmission/distribution (delivering power to consumers). Transmission and distribution require special networks (pipelines and grids) in the case of natural gas and electricity, which have kept market principles out of these segments, thereby fossilizing state-regulated monopolies, whereas oil and coal have been open to competition from the very beginning. Liberalization has commenced in the gas and electricity segments, primarily in the liberal United Kingdom, where production and distribution have been separated (a process known as ownership unbundling), thus serving as a model for energy liberalization at the EU level. This arrangement puts an end to exclusive rights to network use and grants all energy producers access to energy networks, enabling them to supply end users, thereby eliminating monopolies.

Much of the energy humanity uses is nonrenewable, which means that sooner or later the Earth's reserves will be depleted. Fossil fuels such as coal, crude oil, and natural gas make up the bulk of human energy use. Coal reserves are evenly distributed around the world and are likely to last another few hundred years. Oil and gas, conversely, are concentrated in a handful of—usually politically unstable—regions of the Earth and will probably run out much sooner. Oil is now extracted from fields far from users at a high cost. Natural gas could become the key fossil energy source of the twenty-first century, especially because of its technological and environmental advantages over coal or oil. Although nuclear energy became a political hot potato after the 1986 Chernobyl disaster in the USSR—when a reactor exploded, leading to thousands of deaths from the explosion, radiation poisoning, and aftereffects such as cancer—it nonetheless accounts for one-fifth of all electricity generation. There is plenty of uranium in the Earth, and nuclear power plants are environmentally friendly, as long as there are no accidents. On the flip side, disposing of nuclear waste is a costly and unpopular task. However, without relying on nuclear power, it will be impossible to satisfy the world's growing energy demand while reducing carbon dioxide emissions from the burning of fossil fuels. Renewable energy sources (wind, water, and biomass), which are still relatively expensive, will not do the job alone.

A 2006 study by the International Energy Agency (IEA) painted a bleak picture of the future.[57] It suggested that without serious energy savings, the situation could become dramatically worse in a few decades. The IEA predicts that coal use will rise sharply (by as much as 60 percent between 2004 and 2030, when it will be around 8.9 billion tons), mainly due to growing demand in Asia. Oil consumption will also hit new highs. The IEA calculates that every \$1 invested in more efficient, energy-saving technology could yield \$2 in savings in investment in the infrastructure for power generation, transmission, and distribution. The IEA concludes that the energy sector needs to be modernized and that alternative energy sources, among them nuclear power, should be supported. Energy savings should primarily also come from reduced consumption of fuel and of electricity, because global electricity consumption will double in the coming twenty-five years. Recent disruptions in electric power supply in both the United States and Europe indicate that networks and capacities must be extended and developed. Without determined action, which includes promoting nuclear energy, the world's daily oil consumption could reach 116 million barrels by 2030.

If current trends continue, global energy use will have gone up by 60 percent by 2060. With the right energy saving measures and efficient technologies, the pace of this growth could be cut by half, to which nuclear power could contribute by as much as minus 10 percent, provided that generation capacity increases by 40 percent to 519 gigawatts in 2030, as proposed by the IEA. That could also yield a 16 percent reduction in carbon dioxide emissions, the level of the current combined emissions of the United States and Canada.[58]

Energy consumption in the twenty-five (post–2004 enlargement, pre–2007 enlargement) EU member states increased from 1.6 billion tons of oil equivalent in 1995 to 1.7 billion in 2005. With this pace of growth, Europe was below the world average; its share in global energy use (16 percent in 2005) had been falling for ten years. Petroleum is the most important element of the European energy mix, accounting for 40 percent, while natural gas is the runner-up, with 25 percent. Europe relies more heavily on oil than the rest of the world, where oil accounts for "only" 36 percent of consumption, but is less coal oriented, with 17 percent, compared with the global average of 28 percent. Renewables account for less than 7 percent in the EU. As of 2004, Europe's biggest energy consumers were Germany (20 percent), France (16 percent), the United Kingdom (13 percent), and Italy (11 percent). In the same year, the EU's primary production was 882 million tons of oil equivalent, less than half its consumption, which shows just how dependent the continent is on external supply. The EU's biggest energy producers are the United Kingdom (25 percent), Germany (15 percent), and France (15 percent). Only two EU countries have significant oil reserves: the United Kingdom (72 percent) and Denmark (15 percent). The British also lead gas production (45 percent), with the Dutch coming second (32 percent), while France leads the pack in nuclear power generation, with 46 percent, and Germany is a distant runner-up, with 17 percent.[59]

Energy efficiency has improved in Europe. In 1999, producing €1,000 of GDP required 214 kilograms of oil equivalent, whereas in 2004 this was down to only 205 kilograms. This improvement is attributable to a shift to less-energy-intensive production as well as energy-saving technologies and the spread of modern heating methods. In terms of energy efficiency, the twenty-five EU member states in 2005 showed great variation, with Germany, Ireland, Denmark, and France leading the way and Estonia and Lithuania bringing up the rear with one-fifth the efficiency rate.[60]

Improved energy efficiency does not change Europe's energy dependency, which amounted to 1.4 billion tons of oil equivalent from external sources in 2004, 16 percent higher than five years earlier. If we subtract EU exports, the remaining net import is still 900 million tons. Oil makes up about half of imported energy, gas a quarter, and coal a tenth. The biggest importers are Germany, France, Italy, and Spain. Denmark is the only net energy exporter in the EU, which explains one of Europe's biggest headaches: its growing energy dependency. As the years go by, Europe increasingly relies on third countries for its energy supply. Its energy dependency ratio (energy imported / energy consumed) was 50 percent in 2004, which means that every second drop of fuel driving Europe's cars and every second watt of electricity lighting its homes comes from abroad. In some EU member states, this ratio exceeds 90 percent, but the future looks even gloomier; global energy demand will go up by 60 percent by 2030 (driving prices through the roof) and the EU's energy dependency will be above 70 percent.[61] Amid such prospects, it is not surprising that the energy supply is increasingly considered a crucial security issue.

Security

In November 2006, the energy ministers from the then–twenty-five EU member states were debating the security of the Union's energy supply in the European Council's Justus Lipsius Building when something bizarre happened. The meeting room suddenly went dark, and the interpretation service was cut off—there was no light or sound. The meeting had to be suspended until power was restored half an hour later. This power failure, as it turned out, was caused by an accident nearby, which also injured several people. This incident illustrated what was at stake, although it was a only a minor nuisance compared with the massive power outages a week earlier, which had left swaths of Western Europe without electricity. This continent-wide disruption in the electricity supply was caused by a "grid anomaly," which is why the interrupted EU meeting was convened in the first place.

The fault causing this grid anomaly originated in northern Germany, where a high-voltage line had to be switched off on November 4, 2006, to let a ship pass underneath. This planned switch-off led to an overloading of the power lines, and it started a domino effect that, at 10:10 PM, abruptly split Germany and Austria into two unconnected areas of the electric power grid. The western part, where the frequency of the network fell to 49 hertz, stayed connected to Belgium, the Netherlands, Spain, Portugal, Italy, and Slovenia. The eastern part stayed connected to the Central European countries (Poland, the Czech Republic, Slovakia, and Hungary), Ukraine, and initially to Southeastern Europe. In the western zone, demand exceeded infeed, and this lack of power activated automatic load shedding, resulting in millions of customers being switched off and temporarily plunging millions of homes across Western Europe into darkness. In the eastern zone, electricity overgeneration caused the frequency to rise above 51 hertz, which triggered automatic load regulation systems in several power plants but proved insufficient due to cascading trippings of transmission lines toward Croatia, Serbia, and Romania, splitting the continental grid into three. Similar power outages had already struck in September 2003, when much of Italy was left cold and dark for hours. These incidents are tangible examples of the possible negative consequences of a lack of European coordination. They highlight the need to interconnect energy networks, eliminate capacity bottlenecks at national borders, and liberalize European energy markets.

Russia's Gazprom announced at the end of December 2005 that it would unilaterally raise the price at which it was supplying gas at to Ukraine from $50 to $230 per 1,000 cubic meters, which Ukraine considered unacceptable. The skirmish did not remain a row between the two of them; the EU's member states were also affected. While Russia threatened to turn off the taps, Ukraine decided not to relay some of the gas destined for Western Europe. Ukrainians had to get used to the cold, and several EU states introduced emergency measures and restricted consumption. This anomaly has been repeated several times since then. After many years, Europe was afraid of being cold again. The tone of media reports was unusually sharp: "Russia Using Gas as a Political Weapon in a New Cold War" (*The Times*), "Europe Held Hostage by Russia's Gas War" (*La Tribune*), "Ukraine Today, Western Europe Tomorrow?" (*Die Welt*). Russia is the EU's key supplier of natural gas and crude oil, delivering half of all imported gas, and accounting for a quarter of gas consumption. Russia supplies one-third of the EU's imported crude oil and other petroleum products (i.e., a quarter of oil consumption). The stakes were high, but a deal was finally struck, which improved the security of the supply and solved the temporary crisis. This agreement distinguishes between gas for use in Ukraine and gas sent across Ukrainian territory but destined for the EU. Plans call for the building by 2010 of a pipeline between Russia and Germany that will bypass Ukraine, and that will be eventually extended to France and the United Kingdom. The gas price conflict was only one in a long line of events pressing the EU toward forging a common energy policy.

Energy security means several things: the security of the energy supply; the safe operation of power plants, especially nuclear power stations; and the integrity of networks and pipelines. Both large European energy operators and economic analysts consider the sorry state of Russian and Ukrainian transmission infrastructure a serious danger. Putting off investment in modernizing extraction and transmission capacities brings short-term benefits to producing countries; not only do they save money but technological weaknesses also naturally limit production, and the stagnating supply keeps prices elevated. This strategy, however, is dangerous in the long run.

Half of Russia's pipelines are over thirty years old and poorly maintained, which makes them prone to accidents and waste.[62]

The issue of energy security should be seen in a wider context than just gas supply shortages and power disruptions. Greenhouse gas emissions contribute to global warming, which can drastically change the climatic conditions of certain regions. As a result of droughts or frequent torrential rains and floods, economic migrants and political asylum seekers will be joined by climatic refugees from such regions. Thus, Europe can begin preparing for a new type of immigration: the arrival of masses of people fleeing their homes due to the disrupted climate.

The most wide-reaching dimension of energy security is geostrategic. Therefore, what needs to be done to ensure access to energy resources, how to compete for them, how to handle other regions competing for the same resources, and how to deal with groups of countries holding such resources and thus growing stronger geostrategically?

Foreign Affairs

"Europe Has Nothing to Fear from Russia's Aspirations." So read the title of a 2006 comment in the *Financial Times,* penned by Russia's Vladimir Putin himself, in the form of an open letter.[63] This choice of title was not coincidental; there is growing fear in Europe that Russia will play the energy card and turn off the taps if it does not like Europe's behavior. In his open letter, Putin stressed the significance of cooperation, common values, and shared interests. However, a few weeks earlier, the spokesperson for Gazprom, Russia's huge state-controlled energy firm, had demonstrated less tact on the pages of the same newspaper when openly threatening the European Union with redirecting gas supplies to other markets. Gazprom would like to make European countries understand that it has other alternatives for selling its gas, he said. The Chinese market is expanding rapidly, and liquefied natural gas can always find a market in the United States. Thus, he added, if the EU wants Russian gas, it must have regard for Gazprom's interests.

This crossing of verbal swords between Gazprom and Britain came in response to Downing Street's negative reaction to Gazprom's investment aspirations. The U.K. government wished to obstruct Gazprom's acquisition of Centrica—a key actor in the British wholesale energy sector and owner of British Gas—by amending the national merger regulations. It is worth marking the words of Gazprom, because it is the world's largest gas company, is responsible for one-fifth of global gas production, and sits on 16 percent of the Earth's known natural gas reserves. Two-thirds of its revenues—$40 billion in 2005—come from foreign trade, primarily to Europe. However stunning this may sound at first, Gazprom supplies one-third of all gas consumed in Europe. A few days after the Gazprom statement, the head of Transneft—a state-owned enterprise holding a monopoly on Russian pipelines—announced that as soon as its pipeline to Asia was completed, oil supplies to Europe would be reduced and prices would be raised.[64] Energy policy has become a key pillar of foreign policy, and it will only become more important in the future. The emergence of the two Asian giants, India and China, is a threat to Europe and America, but a huge business opportunity for Russia and oil-rich countries. The Russian Treasury has probably never been as full as today, when a barrel of oil sells above $70, sometimes close to $100. No wonder that Russia is paying off its debts, often before maturity.

Kind words and open threats are a daily occurrence in international energy policy relations. China builds complimentary palaces for African dictators in the hope of being awarded lucrative energy deals. Then–U.S. vice president Dick Cheney, on his visit to Vilnius, accuses the Russian government of using energy to blackmail its partners; in response, the Putin administration cries cold war and compares Cheney's speech to Churchill's famous Fulton address, in which the term "Iron Curtain" was first used. Russia announces that it will redirect a third of its gas and oil exports from Europe to Asia within a decade. In response, Europe hastens to reinforce its ties with the Mediterranean countries and concludes a partnership agreement with Azerbaijan to bolster its security of energy supply. In this agreement, the Azerbaijani government undertakes to pattern its energy market rules on European norms. Ukraine announces that it will stop importing Russian oil in 2007 and instead buy oil more cheaply from countries in Central Asia. Germany and Russia strike a €5 billion deal to build a pipeline under the Baltic Sea, carrying gas from the Yuzhno-Russkoye field in Western Siberia. The United States and Poland protest the Nord Stream pipeline; the former due to geostrategic misgivings, and the latter due to lost transit fees. Other EU member states accuse Germany of pursuing its own interests and undermining Europe's collective clout. A confidential NATO study, leaked to the press in late 2006, informs ambassadors of Russia's secret plan to set up a gas equivalent of the Organization of the Petroleum Exporting Countries, an international price-setting cartel, which would help Moscow boost its political influence over Europe and its other neighbors. This organization, experts suggest, would include Algeria, Qatar, Libya, the countries of Central Asia, and perhaps Iran. Naturally, Moscow vehemently denies the speculations.

Concerns about Europe's dependence on Russian energy supply date back to the Cold War, when U.S. president Ronald Reagan tried to stop the Soviet Union from increasing its gas exports to Western Europe in order to curb its potential influence. The United States blocked exports of gas production and transportation equipment to the Soviets and tried to limit its Western European allies' gas purchases to 30 percent of their total consumption. In the long run this obstructionist strategy did not work, and it would be a hard task even today. The demand for gas in Europe is likely to rise for another decade, at least partly because the EU's emissions trading scheme will reward relatively cleaner, gas-fired methods of generating energy in the coming years. Moreover, Europe's own gas production is declining steeply; at the current rate, by 2020 it will be half its 2006 level.[65]

More important, oil and gas have enabled Russia to gain economic as well as political muscle. Its energy potential has enabled it to realize its aspiration to again rise to the ranks of the most powerful nations. Reality, however, is more nuanced. Even if we disregard far-reaching social issues, the situation is not quite as bright as it seems at first, even in the energy sector. The corporate sector of Russia, the world's biggest gas-producing country, suffers from chronic gas shortages; and the oil sector of the world's second-biggest oil-producing country, also Russia, is showing little development. Russia is in dire need of capital, investment, and technology, while Europe undoubtedly needs Russian energy and a Russia it can consider a reliable partner.

Relations between the EU and Russia will certainly become closer, but problem-free cooperation will require political will on both sides. This will include Russia's ratification of the Energy Charter, which forty-nine countries have already signed, laying down the basic principles for European energy, trade, and transportation. Russia's signing of the charter would open the way for the convergence of Russian and European energy market standards. Russia's economy and society face numerous problems that Europe could help solve, as long as cooperation and relations are extended. Life has demonstrated on many occasions that oil is more of a curse than a blessing if the windfall profits it brings in are not spent in the right way. Nevertheless, it would be foolish to blame Russia for redirecting its gas and oil to Asia. Why should it not do so? Asia is clearly the economic hub of the future, where turboglobalization will come into its own. Asia is where America is relocating its call centers, Europe is moving its production capacities, and Russia is taking what it has: energy. Europe had better secure its alternative energy sources, whether supply sources (e.g., North Africa), transportation routes (the Nabucco Pipeline planned to transport natural gas from Turkey to Austria, via Bulgaria, Romania, and Hungary; or the liquefied natural gas sea depot in Croatia), or new energy sources (biogas). Europe must take concerted action in energy foreign policy, because this is the only way to fend off the political pressure it is feeling.

Some accuse Europe of energy paranoia, arguing that the continent becomes hysterical about any threat to its energy supply and thereby falls prey to energy-producing countries. I say, better safe than sorry. Like it or not, energy policy has become a geopolitical issue.

What Can Europe Do?

The draft European Constitution called for a common European energy policy, but it was never adopted. The current legislative framework does not include such a policy, and therefore whether Europe will have a common energy policy will depend on the political will and promises of the EU member states. With or without a legal base, solutions to the energy problem can be found if they are needed badly enough. The member states are beginning to recognize that things are done more easily together. The European Union's energy policy must have six priorities: improving efficiency; finding alternative supply markets, through geographic diversification; making use of alternative energy resources, through resource allocation; building a single European energy market, through market liberalization; forging a common energy foreign policy, by talking with partners with a single voice; and introducing into public thinking and political culture the concept of dealing with energy policy in a complex manner, through an understanding that energy policy must increasingly include aspects of environmental policy, climate policy, geopolitics, and even national security policy.

The best of all remedies for the energy problem would be to increase energy efficiency. This should be the bedrock of all reforms, as the most forward-looking, most innovative policy bringing the most synergies and benefits. Better efficiency not only yields savings but can also reduce emissions and dependence on exporters without holding back economic growth. European countries are wasteful in their use of energy; calculations suggest that as much as 20 percent of all energy is wasted. The EU's plans call for 20 percent energy savings by 2020, which would equal almost 400 million tons of oil equivalent. To achieve that goal, the EU will need to improve its energy efficiency by 3.3 percent annually, which will require a massive investment and intensive research.[66]

In the coming years, we should see technology using less energy, more advanced buildings and heating solutions, and more economical cars—and not only in Europe but also in all parts of the world. The United States, which is responsible for a quarter of global oil consumption, has only recently begun to update its fuel consumption standards for new cars after not doing so for sixteen years—not to mention the abysmal standards in China and India, which have led to horrific urban air pollution. And efficiency should be improved in both use and production. Germany, France, and the United Kingdom paid almost 10 percent more for Brent-grade crude oil in 2006 than the United States, which, according to IEA data, added $7 billion to the cost of oil imports annually. What is the reason for this? European refineries cannot process lower-quality oil, but American ones can.

Europe must not be held hostage by another country or a region, and thus it must try to diversify its alternative sources of supply, especially because its own reserves are being depleted at an alarming rate. European oil, gas, and coal production will fall to a quarter, third, and 60 percent of the current level, respectively, by 2030. Europe's oil dependency will rise to a staggering 94 percent.[67] For this oil, the continent will mainly depend on Russia, which is why alternative sources of supply to the south are so important. In the previous chapter, I described North Africa as a kind of danger; in energy policy, it offers an opportunity that Europe cannot miss. Algeria, in spite of its political instability, has remained Europe's third-largest gas supplier (behind Russia and Norway), but there is quite a bit of room for improvement in using its potential to the full. In addition, contrary to protectionist Russia, Algeria welcomes European companies seeking to establish and invest there. There are plans for the 4,300-kilometer Trans-Sahara Pipeline from Nigeria to Europe, which would bring enough natural gas to meet all the needs of Austria, Slovakia, and Greece. There are other ideas, such as the Nabucco Pipeline mentioned above and the liquefied natural gas terminals off the Adriatic coast. The aim is to establish a pan-European energy community, which would include Ukraine, Turkey, the nations in the Caspian Sea region, and the nations in the wider Mediterranean region.

The diversification of Europe's energy supply does not imply only geographical diversification but also the inclusion of new and sustainable energy sources in the continent's energy mix. One of Europe's main problems is its reliance on fossil fuels; today it stands at 80 percent, but without the necessary reforms it could go even higher, which would be harmful to the environment and increase Europe's dependence on oil- and gas-exporting countries. There are numerous alternative energy resources, but they are usually very expensive. The technologies enabling the use of biomass (an area where Europe's achievements are modest), hydrogen, and other energy sources need to be refined, which will require massive investments in research. Renewable energy sources—solar power, wind power, hydropower (hydroelectricity, tidal power, wave power), geothermal heat, biomass, and biogas—play a minor role in European energy generation (accounting for less than 7 percent), even though Europe is at the forefront of application and technology. Renewables are most important in Austria (where hydroelectric plants supply a considerable part of the power consumed domestically) and Scandinavia.[68]

Nonetheless, we should not expect miracles from renewable energy; its volume will be insufficient to replace traditional energy sources in the foreseeable future. Global energy demand will double by 2050, that is certain. If fossil-fuel-based and nuclear power production were frozen at current levels, renewable energy production would need to increase seventyfold to cover the world's needs. To satisfy half of the power accounted for by global electricity consumption, we would need 100 million wind turbines. The growth potential of biomass is also limited because humanity needs more space, animals and plants need their habitats, farming occupies more and more land, and there is only so much space on Earth. Solar power only gives 0.04 percent of all electricity generation for a good reason: Photovoltaics is a complicated and expensive technology. Despite these limitations, renewable and green sources of energy will become more important, as suggested by the fact that even the traditionally hard-line George W. Bush administration's announced an "energy independence" program in 2006, which was to involve promoting biofuels made from plant waste.

In addition to renewables, a reasonable compromise may be the so-called clean coal technology, which uses advanced technology to reduce carbon emissions from coal-fired power stations by as much as 90 percent. The increased use of coal seems a safe bet; the IEA reckons that it will grow by 1.5 percent annually until 2030.[69] Most of the extra coal will be burned in China, where coal contains a lot of sulfur, which does not prevent the People's Republic from opening a new coal-fired power plant at the astounding pace of every four days. The widespread use of clean coal technology could become very important from an environmental point of view.

The other alternative is nuclear power, which has always attracted the strongest social resistance, as explained above. In 2006, the IEA proposed a wider use of nuclear power for the first time in its thirty-two years of existence.[70] And British prime minister Tony Blair took a 180-degree turn toward the end of his term as prime minister, announcing a new nuclear energy program entailing plans to build a dozen nuclear power plants by 2018. The trends are clear: More and more countries are recognizing that they cannot avoid enhancing the role of nuclear power in their energy mix. Finland recently decided to open Europe's first new nuclear power station in ten years, and many other nations—such as Belgium, the Netherlands, and Sweden —will probably break their promise to decommission existing ones. The United States is planning to add twenty new commercial nuclear reactors, and Australia has set up a commission to look into the issue. At the time of writing this book, there were twenty nuclear power plants under construction worldwide, and enthusiasm for nuclear energy will only grow in the coming years. The thorniest question of all has yet to be answered, however: How to dispose of the nuclear waste that keeps piling up?

The really pioneering idea was not using nuclear fission to produce energy but to replace it with a fusion reactor. This idea itself is not brand new; the project known today as ITER (the International Thermonuclear Experimental Reactor) was first proposed by Ronald Reagan and Mikhail Gorbachev in 1985. An agreement on the €10 billion project was finally signed in 2006 in Paris. The reactor, to be built in the South of France, will serve experimental purposes and will not produce electricity. According to experts, electricity produced by fusion will power households starting in 2045 at the earliest.[71]

The area where the European Union has a key—and probably increasingly important—role to play is the realization of its longtime goal of creating a single, liberalized gas and electricity market. The objective is to put an end to the current situation—in which national frontiers cut the European energy space into small fragmented markets, large energy operators enjoy monopolies in domestic markets and keep prices elevated, energy producers are also owners of transportation networks, and politically motivated government interference can prevent foreign companies from entering national markets or acquiring a share in national incumbents. The European energy market is fragmented both in a technical and legal sense. Technical fragmentation means the lack of proper interconnection between national markets. As we have seen, this can prevent networks from sending sufficient electricity from one country to another when there is a problem, which in turn can lead to blackouts across the continent. Legal fragmentation means that every country is trying to safeguard its national energy champion's monopoly, doing its best to protect it from foreign acquisition. There have been many examples of such government interference recently, always with the pretext of guaranteeing security of supply.

It is hard to see how a fragmented energy market could be safer than a single one, but it is easy to see that prices are higher in a monopoly than in a fully functioning market. The first step toward a single European market for energy must be unbundling; thus, the large monopoly companies need to split up (unbundle) the production and transmission and transportation sides of their business and have them operated by legally separate entities. Imagine the energy market as consisting of a pizza oven (power plant), the pizza delivery boy (energy provider), the road he uses (transmission network), and yourself (the consumer). Obviously, the pizza represents energy itself. Now imagine a situation in which the pizza delivery boy owns the road network, and where only he can use it, and no others may deliver pizza on it. That would probably mean one hell of an expensive pizza. Fortunately, electricity—unlike pizza—is a homogeneous product, so in the case of energy, the delivery boy cannot say he only delivers pepperoni topping, which you do not like. It is easy to see how you, as the consumer, can only benefit from having a greater choice of pizza delivery services.

The next steps toward building a single European market for energy could be the establishment of a European energy network and the setting up of a pan-European energy regulatory authority. Luckily, market processes have begun to evolve on their own in the meantime; the EU's first multinational energy exchange, Belpex, opened its doors in October 2006, trading electricity at the same price on the French, Belgian, and Dutch markets. The appearance of Belpex is a symbolic step toward the creation of a single energy market without frontiers, even though it currently only covers 5 to 10 percent of daily electricity trading. According to plans floated in the press, trading will be extended to Scandinavia in 2008, when the submarine pipeline with Norway is completed, and the inclusion of Germany is also foreseen.

In 2008, the EU adopted a comprehensive energy and climate package aiming at achieving a competitive energy market, accelerating the shift to a low-carbon economy, and boosting energy efficiency. It sets out three targets: first, a 20 percent cut in greenhouse emissions by 2020 (compared with 1990 levels), with the promise of a 30 percent cut if other countries joined in; second, obtaining 20 percent of energy from renewable sources; and third, raising the share of biofuels in energy production to 10 percent by the same date. However, this third target could drive up fuel prices and lead to massive deforestation in poor countries. The global drive is evident; even the Bush administration bowed to pressure on climate matters and agreed for the first time in July 2008 to a long-term target for cutting greenhouse gas emissions in more concrete terms, proposing to halve them by 2050. With Barack Obama as president, this process is certainly accelerating. And rightly so, because the United States is responsible for 21 percent of the world's carbon dioxide emissions (China is in the lead, with 25 percent; and Western Europe accounts for only 12 percent).[72]

I have mentioned above how important it is, with respect to energy, for Europe to speak with one voice on the international scene. The European Union is the world's second-biggest energy market; therefore, its negotiating position vis-à-vis suppliers is far superior to that of individual EU member states. The mentality that energy security and sustainability are too important to put into the hands of "Brussels" is mistaken and misses the point. Competition for available energy will become increasingly fierce, as China and India grow more energy hungry (their demand will double by 2030[73]). Europe must understand that it cannot afford to be disunited. It should also be crystal clear that energy policy must be put into a wider context and become part of a policy mix, which includes environmental policy, traditional foreign policy, neighborhood policy (Ukraine and the Mediterranean), enlargement policy (Turkey), security policy, and R&D policy.

Is European Competitiveness Impossible?

At the 2006 Innovation Day in Brussels, Bill Gates shared the following story with his audience. He receives calls from influential decisionmakers and businesspeople almost weekly asking when Microsoft will establish an R&D center in their country. His answer is always the same: when your country's population reaches a billion. No wonder that outside the United States and Europe—the two bulwarks of Western civilization enjoy an exception to this billion-people rule—Microsoft only operates global R&D centers in China and India.

Countries compete to attract R&D capacities, but R&D firms pick and choose their headquarters according to market size. Both attitudes are rational and have become somewhat commonplace in our understanding of global competitiveness. However, public views are often mistaken. It is sufficient to look back upon the last thirty years and see how fast our view of the world's economy has changed and how easily we believe that a country or region is going downhill while others shoot ahead. We are also easily persuaded that we are witnessing a paradigm shift when stock indexes soar or that a country's economy is growing at breakneck speed when house prices shoot through the roof over the course of a few years. Economists, stockbrokers, politicians, business columnists, and academics have been collectively deceived this way many a time in recent decades.

In the early 1990s, everybody accepted it as a fact that Japan had once and for all surpassed the United States, which had started slipping back and whose companies would eventually all be acquired by Japanese firms out on a shopping spree. Germany, with its highly developed industry and social care system, was considered the other prodigy. The end of America would signal the dawn of a new era: the age of the socialist German and the mercantilist "planned economy" Japanese models—at least according to the general opinion of the time. Then came the new millennium, and with it a new mantra: the "new economy." There was much truth in the predicted dawn of the "new economy," but global economic trends were largely simplified in public discourse, which becomes apparent when we analyze the bursting of the dot-com bubble in 2001 and the overoptimistic economic policies of the time.

But why am I saying all this? One could argue that twenty years ago, the mercantilist model was in vogue and that people who were predicting the end of the Anglo-Saxon model turned out to be charlatans. Today, it is fashionable to lash out at the European model and, in a few years' time, we will see that those burying the social model were fooled by appearances and could not have been more wrong. However, this is not going to happen—for two reasons.

The first reason is that—contrary to what some say—the economic model based on economic freedoms, competition, creativity, and individual (or corporate) prosperity is the most effective one ever invented. A mercantilist, capitalist planned economy might yield impressive results in the short run, but it cannot guarantee the driving force of all progress: creativity. That was one of the key reasons for Japan's economic setback. A high degree of redistribution can create a happy and just society, but it has two faults: It only works in times of boom, and it cannot sustain the other driving force of development—people's *motivation* to work, compete, and fight.

The second reason is more pragmatic than theoretical. In an age of turboglobalization, isolationism is not an option. International competition will get fiercer and fiercer. China and India are vast, cheap, and full of diligent people. Americans are not only a hard-working people but also creative. It would be an illusion to believe that concerns about Europe's competitiveness are nothing more than the usual scaremongering. Unfortunately, everything is telling us that these concerns must be taken seriously. We are only fooling ourselves if we attach too much significance to studies like the World Economic Forum's *Global Competitiveness Report,* according to which the United States has slipped down five places on the global competitiveness list and was bettered by Finland, Sweden, and Denmark in 2006, although on the 2009–10 list it climbed up again to second position behind Switzerland.[74] Such reports are not completely unfounded, but one must see the forest for the trees: Long-term trends and annual changes are two very different things.

Google, Intel, Yahoo, Sun Microsystems, and eBay: What do they have in common, in addition to being five of the world's most successful—and perhaps most significant—companies? They were all founded or cofounded by immigrants. The world has become an open place; capital goes where its finds the best conditions, and creative minds do the same.

There were times when Americans turned to Europe for lessons in economic policy—in the early 1990s—in other words, a long time ago. Comparing the economic performance of Anglo-Saxon countries, of euro zone member states, and of Japan, it becomes clear that a dramatic realignment has taken place during the last fifteen years. GDP growth in the large Anglo-Saxon countries (Australia, Canada, the United Kingdom, and the United States) since 1990 has been well above that of France, Germany, Italy, and Japan. Average growth in the first group has been about 30 percent, while the second group can boast only half that figure. GDP per capita was 3 percent higher in the reunited Germany than in the United Kingdom in 1991, but this had changed to 11 percent in favor of the British by 2004. Italy has seen a similar trend; it fell 9 percent behind Britain from an initial 2 percent lead.[75] And the Scandinavian countries and the Netherlands have done really well compared with Europe's big players.

The sixty years since the end of World War II are best described as a roller-coaster ride for Europe's economy. In the early 1950s, the level of development in Japan and the three largest European countries stood at about one-third of the United States'. By the early 1990s, they had managed to fight their way up to 80 percent, only to slide back to 70 percent (the 1973 level) in the last decade and a half, as if they had stood still in the last twenty years. There are many reasons for this relative backsliding, the difference in productivity being the key one. Another culprit is the inflexible labor market. In the 1950s and 1960s, America's jobless rate exceeded Europe's, but today the situation is just the opposite. It was not the U.S. rate that dropped but the European rate that shot up; in 2004, unemployment in the United States was at the 1960s level, while in Germany, France, and Italy, it varied between 8 and 10 percent. Return on investment also showed considerable differences; the rate of return in the Anglo-Saxon world was double the rates in continental Europe. And once again, it was not the English-speaking world that improved considerably but rather Europe and Japan where indicators declined. (In Japan's case, the deterioration was dramatic; the implicit incremental capital output ratio, or ICOR, indicator, which measures the inefficiency with which capital is used—the higher the ICOR, the lower the productivity of capital—skyrocketed from 3 in the mid-1970s to 20 in 2004.)[76]

One explanation for these trends is that, after World War II, Europe's continental economies had a lot of catching up to do with the United States in terms of productivity; this was a one-time, historic challenge and opportunity, which Europe seized. The real problem came when Europe was unable to follow up the first dynamic wave with the hard slog of restructuring required to live up to global challenges. The heyday of the 1960s and 1970s reinforced the continental model based on redistribution, high taxes, and a generous welfare system. This model paralyzed flexibility, the energies of renewal, and the adaptability of economic actors, which in turn led to weaker competitiveness and rising unemployment (although the latter clearly ran counter to the model's aims). Another important phenomenon of the time was that, while the continental societies became richer and richer, the available workforce dwindled, which meant diminishing domestic demand; in other words, a chronically high level of savings was accompanied by a chronically low level of domestic demand.

Strangely enough, at the dawn of the postmodern age, having a highly developed industrial sector and a complex system of social dialogue proved to be a disadvantage for continental Europe, especially Germany. Industry was the flagship of the economy, and corporate (shareholder-based) management was the basis for running it. After the boom of the services sector, and particularly of information and communication technology, large and cumbersome industrial and business management systems needed to be overhauled and tailored to the requirements of the new age. As I have already indicated in chapter 2, efforts to do so brought little success; by the late 1980s, it was obvious that the economic strategy based on the global success of big national industrial corporations could no longer work. The services sector found it much more difficult to develop in countries with strong industrial traditions, with their "old ways" and inflexible rules.

In the age of the "new economy," information and communication technology is the key to success or failure, depending on whether a country is capable of making progress in this field. And apart from equity, information and communication technology wants one other thing—flexibility—and if does not get it, it moves on before you can say Jack Robinson. Flexibility in this case applies to the entire business environment, including flexible economic framework rules, flexible institutions, flexible labor regulations, and a flexible bankruptcy procedure. Today, services play an astonishingly important role in production, the extent of which is sometimes overlooked even by executives of industrial firms. According to the McKinsey Global Institute, shipping, wholesale, and retail services make up one-third of the retail price of a consumer product, while other ancillary services such as accounting, banking, legal counseling, and business consulting make up another fourth. Against this backdrop, it is easy to see why the services sector accounts for 70 to 75 percent of a modern national economy.[77]

An overly strict monetary policy and an inflexible economic policy, along with excessive export dependency due to insufficient domestic demand, have often been cited as possible roots of the euro zone's problems (which are discussed in more detail later in the book). Oddly, despite relatively weak internal demand, euro inflation rates remained persistently above 2 percent, indicating the inadequate functioning of market forces. The Anglo-Saxon countries managed to reorient their economies toward services and information technology with relative ease and considerable speed. Their financial systems proved more effective in funneling savings into consumption and investment, and their business management systems were better suited to ensure survival in an accelerating world. Their cheaper and more flexible social policy cushioned the blow of the emerging Asian giants.

Nothing lasts forever, of course; the course of fortune changes like the wind. The United States, for example, in spite of its convincing economic performance in the past, had to live with the looming danger of its vast twin deficits, and in 2007 its financial sector suffered a devastating blow, and its real economy followed, soon taking Europe with it to recession.

The landslide global financial and economic crisis of 2008 turned many things in the United States upside down, which position is true to the economy and to the way Americans see the world and themselves. In the middle of uncertainty in September 2008, a hilarious article by Bill Saporito, titled "How We Became the United States of France," was published in

Time. Forget factual correctness; it is the general sentiment shining through the article that is so telling:

> Admit it, mes amis, the rugged individualism and cutthroat capitalism that made America the land of unlimited opportunity has been shrink-wrapped by half a dozen short sellers. We're now no different from any of those Western European semisocialist welfare states that we love to deride. You just know the Frogs have only increased their disdain for us, if that is indeed possible. And why shouldn't they? The average American is working two and a half jobs, gets two weeks off and has all the employment security of a one-armed trapeze artist. The Bush Administration has preached the "ownership society" to America: own your house, own your retirement account; you don't need the government in your way. So Americans mortgaged themselves to the hilt to buy over-priced houses they can no longer afford. Now our laissez-faire regulation-averse Administration has made France's only Socialist President, François Mitterrand, look like Adam Smith by comparison. All Mitterrand did was nationalize France's big banks and insurance companies in 1982; he didn't have to deal with bankers who didn't want to lend money. . . . Mitterrand tried to create both job growth and wage growth by nationalizing huge swaths of the economy, including some big industries—automaker Renault, for instance. You haven't driven a Renault lately because Renault couldn't sell them here. Imagine that: an auto company that couldn't compete with a Dodge Colt. But the Renault takeover ultimately proved successful, and Renault became a private company again in 1996, although the government retains about 15 percent of its shares. Now the U.S. is faced with the same prospect in the auto industry. GM and Ford need money to develop greener cars that can compete with Toyota and Honda. And they're looking to Uncle Sam for investment—an investment that could have been avoided had Washington imposed more stringent mileage standards years earlier. But we don't want to interfere with market forces like the French do—until we do.[78]

To be correct, one must add that many analysts think that the collapse of the big American car factories was the consequence of their too-friendly relationship with the American administrations that have always been ready to offer a protective umbrella to these giants in times of trouble. Furthermore, the powerful but inefficient trade unions representing these companies' workers also did not facilitate competitiveness.

Coming back to Europe, we see that the EU is competitive in a number of sectors. But even when it betters America in research, it falls behind in putting theory into practice, that is, in development and innovation. Moreover, when it comes to action, European leaders regularly falter or get cold feet (just think of the Services Directive, which was supposed to complete the internal market in a sector providing 70 percent of Europe's GDP but was finally watered down due to pressure by some member states).[79] As we have seen, when governments are slow to act, the corporate sector moves in and takes things into its own hands; thus, German companies are carrying out massive layoffs. European businesses must become stronger; Europe has some companies that are considered major players even on the global scale, but it has too few of them.

Some analysts say that America's steady growth (averaging between 2 and 3 percent in the last fifteen years) is thanks to its faster population growth of 1.2 percent, compared with Europe's 0.4 percent. This, however, is not the real reason. America has become richer and its economy has been growing faster due to the more effective use of resources by society. One hundred and fifty years ago, America was light-years behind Europe in development and now—astonishingly—it is almost impossible to find a European country richer than the poorest U.S. state. What is behind this? Stable and sustained growth, which ensures that individual purchasing power and the states' redistribution capacity keeps growing. According to calculations by the Swedish Timbro Institute, at current rates, only in 2022 will Portugal, Italy, Sweden, and Finland reach the United States' 2000 level of development. Growth is the key to success—at least in the long run. From 1995 to 2005, the world grew by almost 50 percent, the United States by 40 percent, the EU by 25 percent, and the biggest European economy by only 15 percent. Faster growth brings more wealth and consumption. Americans consume 30 percent more than Luxembourgers, who live in Europe's richest nation. But if we compare the United States to the whole of Europe, the difference is almost 80 percent. Improving living standards helps reduce poverty, even in the United States, where the welfare system is not quite as generous as in Europe. If the pie is bigger, a thinner slice can feed more people. Of course, it also works the other way around; 40 percent of Swedish households would be considered low-income families in the United States. Research by the Luxembourg Income Studies reveals that, in terms of gross income, a smaller ratio of the American population falls below the subsistence line than in Europe, meaning that the economy itself generates less poverty than on this side of the Atlantic.[80]

But the picture becomes very different if we look at social redistribution. When government transfers are included, in most European countries fewer people live in poverty than in the United States. This, however, has little to do with the economy; it is thanks to social policy, which puts the model's sustainability in question. European governments have a bigger slice of a smaller pie to redistribute to the needy, which can often mean an enormous fiscal burden for society. After paying all taxes, contributions, fees, and duties, an American service provider can keep roughly half of his or her net income, while his Irish and Belgian counterparts can, respectively, pocket only 25 percent and an eye-watering 10 percent.[81]

Europe keeps comparing itself to the United States, trying to keep up with its transatlantic partner. The United States gives little thought to "good old Europe"; it is too busy trying to maintain its advantage over its new rivals, such as China. Europe needs to close the gap between itself and the world's leading economies, but the real challenge is that the train it is trying to catch is moving faster and faster.

The difference in per capita GDP between the two sides of the Atlantic is attributable to three main factors: lower productivity, shorter working hours, and a lower employment rate. Europe began to fall behind in productivity in the 1990s due to less investment, less competition, and less innovation. The productivity gap is not too wide; in 2004, the fifteen pre–2004 enlargement EU member states stood at 92 percent and the twenty-five post–2004 enlargement EU member states at 83 percent of the American level, and some member states (Luxembourg, France, Belgium, Ireland, and the Netherlands) even exceeded it. It is important to remember, however, that higher unemployment yields statistically higher productivity because, for calculating average productivity, jobless workers are disregarded.[82] (A bizarre and rather detrimental European paradox is that while unemployment rates are high, there is a painful shortage of skilled labor armed with the latest technical know-how.) Another factor is shorter working hours, which have held steady in the United States but have been falling in Europe since the 1970s, which may simply reflect differing mentalities: Europeans want more free time, even if that means a loss of income. But whichever way we look at it, the key objective indicator of success is productivity.

Productivity & Company

Productivity is neither a sexy nor a sublime concept. In plain words, it means hard work or smart work. Still, what this dull concept covers can decide whether a region, society, or country "makes it" in the world or not. Productivity is the basis for growth as well as prosperity and competitiveness. Productivity's unrecognized work in the sweltering heat of the ship's hold enables the much-appreciated Miss Social Justice to stand on the main deck and admire the endless waves of the ocean while holding the hands of her bow-tied partner, Mr. Consumer Society. In the more mundane words of a 2006 Eurobarometer survey: "It gives rise to concern that European citizens fail to recognize the connection between quality of life and economic performance."[83]

Political decisionmakers set productivity as a key objective, just as corporate players do, because it is closely related to profitability. The differences in per capita GDP figures (i.e., in wealth) between various countries fundamentally reflect differences in productivity. In other words, the more productive a country's economy, the faster it grows and the sooner it becomes rich. The U.S. economy is the most productive in the world, with the exception of a few sectors (the car industry, consumer electronics), where Japan or Europe excels. The American retail sector is twice as productive as Japan's, and U.S. telecommunications services are twice as productive as Europe's. This means that, in the United States, half the work is needed to produce the same value (service). According to popular—Luddite—misbelief, productivity gains cost jobs, the argument being that improved productivity means fewer people are needed to produce the same quantities. This logic is fundamentally flawed, because it considers the pie—the economy—to be constant in size. In reality, higher productivity may create temporary unemployment in certain sectors (although this is less likely in the age of globalization), but basically what it does is increase the size of the pie and thus ensure economic growth—not to mention that it is also often the engine of technical and managerial improvements. In addition, productivity tends to determine a country's development and standard of living in the long run.

For instance, with respect to productivity, the Japanese economy is characterized by a unique duality: Flagship companies in certain sectors (car industry, robotics, consumer electronics) have become unbeatable thanks to vast government subsidies, mostly invested in research; but productivity in other sectors primarily producing for the domestic market stands at a half or third of that of the United States. Europe also has its fair share of productivity problems. Its biggest problem is not that it lags behind the United States but that Europeans work fewer hours, are more frequently jobless, and are aging more quickly; thus, even an American level of productivity could not stop the gap from growing. Due to its structural problems, Europe would need to be more productive than the United States just to maintain its international position. Something happened to Europe in the 1980s; following the golden postwar decades, the old continent stalled in its development and for thirty years its standard of living has been stagnating at the level of the 1970s in the United States. Oddly, Europe began falling behind the United States at the peak of European integration and at the time of the creation of the single market. So now, here stands Europe, at the beginning of the third millennium, exposed to the gusts of turboglobalization. What exactly has happened?

Today, it can take as little as a few years for a production or management process to become "traditional" and be replaced with a newer, more modern, and more productive one. The age of mass production has ended and given way to intelligent and flexible production solutions, whereby outsourcing and internationalized business relations make productivity and adaptability the most valuable virtues. The economy is no longer about manufacturing products but about identifying and servicing (and shaping, if necessary) consumer demand. In this new industrial climate, Europe's industry remains structurally inflexible and keeps falling behind in productivity. Europe's information and communication technology sector is weaker than its U.S. counterpart, and the gap also keeps growing in the area of research. Western European investment in software development per capita does not exceed four-fifths of the average in the United States, where three times as many software developers are employed, and, at the same time, the European information and communication technology sector's productivity is a quarter below that of the United States.[84] A well-oiled, cheap, and fast patent system and an intellectual property rights framework are key prerequisites for investment in R&D, because exclusive rights to the results of innovation are guaranteed and enforced. If the process of registering a patent is complicated and takes years, inventors and innovative companies leave and take their good ideas with them.

The best way to boost productivity is to promote creativity, research, training, and new, more-efficient production processes. Another economically equivalent option is to induce people to work more for the same wages. There are a number of examples of this latter solution, and a Western Europe terrified by Chinese competition will probably opt for it increasingly often. The advantage of the "working more for the same money" solution is that it produces instant results. But there is a drawback: It does not contribute to economic progress and unavoidably leads to social tensions. The other alternative is innovation and development, which requires more time, an enterprise-friendly environment, and—not least—creative people as well as good managers. It is somewhat of a commonplace to note that companies are founded and run by people, and thus nurturing an enterprising spirit is a sine qua non of development. Another commonplace is that the United States is far ahead of Europe in this respect.

The Management Culture

In the autumn of 2006, I visited Tampere, the capital of the Nokia Empire, where I met two young Nokia employees in Bar Europe—a place made to look like a British pub. I told them I was writing a book about the European model and the old continent's competitiveness. One of them, who was wearing a jacket and a tie and looked like a middle manager, explained to me with quite some enthusiasm and a sparkle in his eyes the secret of Nokia's success: a healthy balance between efficiency and business with a human face. Nokia employs the best experts, he said, demanding a lot but never refusing special vacation or flexible working time for those who need it. Software developers are incredibly independent, which requires tremendous trust on the part of management. The other fellow, an information technology specialist with a long, braided beard and a Pearl Jam T-shirt, smiled, but when his colleague asked whether he had ever had any request refused by his superiors, he answered no. He admitted to having a lot of independence and feeling on a daily basis that his employer took him seriously and took care of him.

Both these Nokia employees saw their firm's culture as the essence of the European model and the key to Europe's competitiveness. For them, it was natural to equate the Scandinavian model with the European one, as opposed to that of the Far East or India. They said they would never be able to work efficiently in an "Eastern" command-driven business model, which is based on obeying direct orders and not on creativity. At this point, we were joined by the leader of a major new software development project, who explained that the creative part of the work was done almost exclusively by European experts (mainly Russians, Hungarians, and other Eastern Europeans), while routine tasks were assigned to Indian employees.

Is this mentality typical of the whole of Europe? My short and disappointing answer is NO. At the end of 2005, a leading international human resources firm surveyed 200 European business leaders about their management practices. In this survey reported by the business press, most of the people involved were chief executives of large multinational companies, who—one would suppose—think and act alike, according to a standardized global set of values. Surprisingly, the survey revealed that the chief executive mentality varied according to nationality; the British were meritocrats, the Germans were democrats, and the French were autocrats. British executives do not mind if their decisions are questioned, Germans put the emphasis on modesty, and the French enjoy the power of making decisions without asking their colleagues. Two-thirds of French, half of German, and only a third of British top managers consider having the power to make decisions single-handedly and without any restrictions as one of their key competences. In the United Kingdom, two out of three, in Germany every second, and in France only one in ten corporate leaders listed nurturing talent within the company as one of their top three tasks. For French respondents, possessing power was three and eight times as important, respectively, as for their British and German counterparts. Every third French company head considered social recognition as one of the three most important aspects of their job, while only every sixth German and fiftieth Briton did. The biggest fear of German executives was failure, while Britons considered failure part of the learning process. The most common fear of French company heads was—not surprisingly—tensions within the company due to clashes of egos.

Nationality is a major factor in European management culture. Another survey in 2005 of 450 large European companies showed appalling results. Out of the 75 Italian companies in the survey, only one was headed by a foreigner (a Frenchman), and the trends were similar elsewhere—2 out of 75 in France, 3 out of 75 in Spain, and 4 out of 75 in Scandinavia. Only in Germany and the United Kingdom were the results slightly different (12 and 26, respectively), which shows that, in these countries, individual abilities and performance were more important considerations than nationality. Out of the 75 directors of French firms, 33 came from the elite universities, the École Polytechnique or École des Hautes Études Commerciales.[85] When it comes to choosing Europe's top business leaders, neither the decades-old institution of the Common Market nor the more recent phenomenon of globalization seem to play a role; nationality and a prestigious diploma cut more ice. This is a typically European phenomenon. The teaching of entrepreneurial and management skills is very specialized and almost exclusively confined to business schools and universities of economics. Therefore, having the right kind of diploma goes a long way toward paving the way to one's success in business life—much more so than in the United States.

If you type the name "Sergey Brin" into Google, the Web search engine he cofounded, you will find that the Russian emigrant quit his doctoral studies at Stanford University. Not to mention that Bill Gates dropped out of Harvard to devote all his time to Microsoft. "Don't get a business degree—get angry," said Anita Roddick, the late multimillionaire founder of the Body Shop.[86] European entrepreneurs and executives have a lot to learn and to get used to in the tough world of turboglobalization. German firms using bank loans to develop must get used to hostile takeovers, or the complicated reporting and transparency rules that companies must abide by if their stock is traded on the exchanges. European companies must also come to terms with the fact that their traditional corporate structures—based on cross-ownership between large firms and their suppliers; and on maintaining good relations with state-owned banks, the state itself, and local authorities—are antiquated and will soon disappear. Finland's economy has already gone through this transformation, which was critical for the Finnish economic miracle. Until such a transformation takes place, the line between business and state intervention remains blurred, and we will keep hearing European heads of state announce grandiose projects, such as the Franco-German co-produced Quaero Internet search engine devised to break the monopoly of Google. These sweeping plans may be respectable, but they miss the basic point: Political plans cannot replace the entrepreneurial spirit. The job of policymakers is to create the right environment for the spirit of enterprise to fly freely and develop. If businesses are hampered by obstacles, they cannot thrive; and if foreign companies are surrounded by walls of protectionism, they cannot prosper—not in the age of globalization. In mid-December 2006, some months after Quaero's launch was announced, I searched for it —but in vain. It was nowhere to be found.

If Europe has much to learn in encouraging the entrepreneurial climate, then Japan has a hundred times more to do. It once had a formidable weapon with its economic policy designed in minute detail by the state and its intricate web of large conglomerates called *keiretsu.* But now they have become obsolete, just as the Japanese development policy of adapting and perfecting others' ideas no longer works. Imitation must give way to innovation. Japan can boast of impressive R&D results, and it remains unbeatable in robotics, but the Japanese economic model seems to be in a dead-end street, while China's emergence just adds extra pressure to the equation. Yet the greatest opponent that Japan must overcome is not China but its own shortage of creative managers able to think out of the box and willing to take risks. The machinery of the Japanese economy keeps working (however perfectly) only as long as it can stick to its old ways without the need for a shift or readjustment. But when the time comes for such a readjustment, the system will be paralyzed because there will be no one to keep it going. In the age of turboglobalization, the straight stretches of the road are getting shorter and the turns are getting sharper.

The Magic Triangle

In late November 2006, I was invited to speak at the Czech Academy of Sciences in Prague. In my lecture, I spoke about how to use fiscal instruments to support R&D, something that Europe badly needs because it is falling increasingly behind its competitors. My fellow lecturers—mostly representing senior academic circles—did not conceal their anxiety over the fact that the R&D centers of European companies were relocating to Asia, while researchers were moving to the United States. Jerzy Buzek, the former Polish premier who is currently the president of the European Parliament, went further and said that American researchers were packing up and moving to Shanghai.

Of course, the picture is rarely black and white. During lunch, a top European academic told me about returning from a one-year stint in Japan with mixed impressions. During the twelve months he spent at a leading Japanese molecular chemistry research institute, he worked in a group where there were almost as many foreign researchers as Japanese, the language of communication was English, and foreigners were paid twice as much as the project leader. The Japanese, a smart lot themselves, understood that they needed the knowledge and especially the creativity of foreign brains. Everyone got what they wanted, and the disciplined locals kept polishing their ideas. After the first two years, however, foreign researchers would have their salary cut to one-third—if they wanted to stay on, that is. Japan needs European and American creativity, not more Japanese who do not even speak the language, the professor concluded with a smile. Experience has shown that after spending two years in the country, foreign scientists lose their most precious asset—their creativity and fresh perspective—and thus there is no point in holding on to them any longer.

That night I went sightseeing; I was standing on Charles Bridge, one of the chakra points of Europe. On my left were the imposing Castle, the lean towers of Saint Vitus Cathedral, and the dome of Saint Michael's Church; on my right were the Gothic Old Town Bridge Tower and the beautiful facade of the Rudolfinum. It was like watching a "best of Europe" promotional video.

Beside me was a young girl also trying to absorb the view. I asked her where she was from, and we started talking. She told me that she was a student, studying electrical engineering in Vienna. I asked Yoko (what else could have her name been?) what she thought about the city at our feet and Europe in general. Her answer astonished me: "For me Prague—and generally all picturesque historical town centers in Europe—seem unreal. For me this is not a real world, more like a bizarre Disneyland where I feel foreign and lost." It was not just the strange architecture that looked alien; the European mentality was a bit of a culture shock for her. There were too few rules, there was too much freedom—and nobody was holding her hand. Although she had been living in Europe for years and was much more open than your average Japanese person, she could hardly wait to return to Japan, where she could feel safe again.

The first time I ever heard about the magic triangle was at a lecture in Brussels, where they spoke about the trinity of education, R&D, and innovation. Successful high-technology firms built on the pioneering results of highly educated researchers to create jobs, break into new markets, own international patents, and sometimes create global standards. A brave new world—the only problem is that this is exactly what the United States is doing and what China is dreaming about.

The European Union has decided to copy the example of the Massachusetts Institute of Technology—the world's leading knowledge factory—and set up a European version, the European Institute of Technology, a knowledge center with a looser institutional framework, whose mission is to build a magic triangle (also known as the knowledge-technology triangle) by providing a common platform for education, R&D, and innovation centers and thus put research into practice. These knowledge centers—consisting of professors, researchers, and high-technology entrepreneurs—will form the building blocks of Europe's knowledge-R&D-innovation triangle. The idea, which received mixed responses in academic circles, will take a few years to implement. Naturally, such a project, however big its symbolic value, is only a drop in the ocean; it is Europe's mentality that needs changing. It must learn to connect education, research, and innovation.

Although there are several excellent European business schools, the area of business education is also dominated by America; the Economist Intelligence Unit's 2005 list of top ten universities featured only two European ones, and the 2006 ranking by the *Financial Times* showed the same trend. Today, young people in Western Europe must have it explained to them that the aim of education is not to receive a diploma at the end entitling them to a safe job in public administration for life. They had better believe it, or they will need to learn it the hard way—with globalization, millions of Chinese and Indian engineers will be flooding the European labor markets. Disillusionment will follow, and disillusionment is a bad counselor. If, instead, these European youth would look at education as a tool to enable them to succeed in the rat race, it would save them a lot of frustration. This is the mentality that politicians must advocate.

Along with this outmoded mentality, obsolete institutions are also to blame. Europe's higher education system is fragmented; there are many good universities but hardly any outstanding ones (again, only two in the top ten). Acquiring the skills and knowledge is not the problem—the standard of education is high in mathematics and the natural sciences. The problem is with the next step. Therefore, university reform to promote market-based financing through the generation of revenues is under way in several European countries. Finland, for example, carried out a comprehensive overhaul of university finances, enabling state institutions to run a more business-oriented budget and build closer ties with the private sector.

Great economic processes often unfold in very small steps over a long period; the U.S.-Japanese economic superiority already began to show two decades ago. In the late 1980s, high-technology products accounted for half of Japanese and two-thirds of American exports but barely a quarter of European Community exports. It became clear that small European countries, which spend a much smaller proportion of their GDP on research and innovation than their overseas competitors, are unable to live up to the challenges of global competition. Fragmented national R&D programs had too many unnecessary overlaps. So Europe got down to the task of elaborating a common R&D policy. The task of this policy is to coordinate the research sector and help it work cooperatively with economic actors. Thus it must put more emphasis on disseminating the latest scientific achievements, subsidizing market-friendly research, creating communications channels and interfaces between research institutes and the business sector, and supporting spin-off enterprises.

According to Europe's political objective, the EU's member states should spend an average of 3 percent of their GDP on R&D. In 2006, they were far from meeting this target, clocking a measly 1.9 percent, far behind Japan (3.1 percent) and the United States (2.6 percent). The world is not waiting for Europe to get its act together; global R&D is soaring. Companies worldwide are spending more and more on research; in 2006, the 1,250 biggest companies on average spent 7 percent more on R&D than a year earlier. The really shocking fact is the breakdown of this figure: American corporations increase their R&D efforts by 15 percent, European companies by 5 percent, and German firms by only 2 percent (hardly living up to the fame of German engineering). Looking at global figures, the United States accounts for 41 percent of all R&D activities and is home to 6 of the 10 biggest research companies (mostly in technology, pharmaceuticals, and the car industry).[87] There are only 3 European companies in the same top 10 (DaimlerChrysler, Siemens, and GlaxoSmithKline). What is more, this is not a temporary trend or a one-time fallback; the 500 biggest European corporations reduced their R&D budget by 2 percent in 2003, while in the same year, outside Europe, R&D expenses went up by 4 percent. As a result, the gap between Europe and the United States widened further, despite all the ambitious political declarations.[88]

In 2006, China surpassed Japan as the world number two in terms of R&D. China earned the runner-up position by raising investment in R&D by 20 percent that year. Nevertheless, its R&D budget of $136 billion is still dwarfed by the $330 billion of the United States. China not only invests in state-of-the-art facilities and equipment at science departments in its universities but also tries its best to attract foreign companies and their research centers. In a few years' time, this will mean that China spends more on research in relation to its GDP than Europe. But the really new element is that China puts increasing emphasis on basic or fundamental research.

The sum a country forks out on R&D has a significant—albeit not exclusive—impact on scientific progress and also on the development of the whole economy. Temporary cuts in research funding for short periods do not lead to a deterioration of the research environment, capacities, and human resources, but a longer stagnation in R&D investment can cause serious setbacks in economic development, which are then difficult to reverse. Every emerging economy without exception demonstrates that sustained economic growth can only be attained if sufficient attention—and resources —are devoted to education, R&D, and innovation.

Innovation means converting ideas and the results of research into patents, products, or services. It requires an intimate cooperative relationship between universities, researchers, and businesses. Unfortunately, this is proving to be one of Europe's biggest weaknesses. As a report by Esko Aho, a former Finnish prime minister, puts it, a paradigm shift is needed in Europe. An innovation-friendly economic and political environment must be created with improvements in many specific fields, such as the regulatory framework for intellectual property rights and venture capital markets, to mention just two examples. Society must learn to accept the fact that the world is changing at an increasing speed and that it is better to lead the change than try to defend yourself against it. If Europe does not produce results in research, others will, and thereby dictate the terms in international markets by setting the standards. Europe is well placed to compete successfully in some sectors, such as renewable energy and environmental technology.[89] This is an opportunity that Europe must not waste, because with global climate change, these areas of technology could play the same role in the 2010s and 2020s as information and communication technology did at the turn of the millennium. And for innovation to really boom, a lot more is needed, such as carefully devised tax breaks and leading players of science and business organized in clusters.

Europe does not really have a common industrial policy, and its innovation policy is still in its infancy. One could say that the United States has no industrial policy either, apart from Nasdaq and the New York Stock Exchange. But that is only partly true, because the state plays a key role in promoting innovation in three different ways: as regulator, as customer, and as facilitator. State intervention means much more than setting up support schemes, even though they can be important, as the success of the EU's research framework program shows. The state can also serve as a customer in the market for innovative products. The state has an obligation to guarantee intellectual property rights, patent rights, and the smooth operation of public procurement. But the state should also create the right environment so that innovative companies want to stay and not move on.

The Lisbon Agenda—and Others

It is common knowledge that a public figure cannot be considered really famous until one of his wisecracks has become globally used as part of universal culture. Economic concepts are similar; they cannot be considered really important until economists have published at least one theory about them. In this respect, the concept of competitiveness has no reason to complain, because it has proven to be fertile soil for theories approaching the issue from the aspects of trade policy, economic policy, and productivity or by offering analysis at the microeconomic, macroeconomic, or regional level.

In trade policy, the theory of competitiveness looks at how the sector of a national economy can perform on the international scene, which is best measured and expressed in terms of the sector's share of exports in the world market. The economic policy approach focuses on corporate competitiveness, which plays a serious role in the international division of labor and is a good indication of a national economy's degree of competitiveness. The productivity approach is based on productivity measured by unit labor cost as a competitive edge. The regional competitiveness approach amalgamates elements of economic policy and economic geography and has physical regions at the forefront of its attention. Those regions have a competitive advantage where the structure of the economy is healthy (a low share of the primary sector), qualifications and employment are above the national average, the geographical location is favorable for the movement of goods and workers, and the ratio of applied patents is relatively high.

So much for theory. Let us now examine the practice. Europe knows all too well that it has a competitiveness problem. A famous 2003 report by André Sapir emphasized the need to dynamite the single market, to invest in knowledge, to reinforce the rules of the Monetary Union and to reform the EU's budget and decisionmaking in order to restore competitiveness in Europe. The Organization for Economic Cooperation Development (OECD) and Eurochambers (a powerful body representing industry in Brussels) were rather critical of the implementation of the Lisbon Agenda, stating that growth had remained sluggish in Europe and Japan compared with the United States. Per capita GDP in France, Germany, and Italy was then 30 percent below that in the United States, and the gap was getting wider. The OECD made several suggestions to the European countries: Make better use of the available workforce, especially of people over the age of fifty-five years, who should be encouraged to stay active longer; cut red tape and ease the administrative burden on economic actors; liberalize postal services and the railway sector; improve public procurement rules; intensify competition in the network industry, where incumbents continue to enjoy a de facto monopoly; trim subsidies to farmers; and last but not least, improve labor mobility by increasing the portability of pension rights. The OECD report reckoned that 60 percent of the difference in employment is attributable to anomalies in national regulatory frameworks. In the age group of twenty-five to fifty-five, employment figures are similar on the two sides of the Atlantic; the problem is with young people and the elderly. Europe has a long way to go in liberalizing its labor markets, which will entail painful political decisions—cuts to minimum wages, increases in working hours, and curbing social rights.[90]

According to Eurochambers, in terms of competitiveness, in 2005 Europe stood where the United States was in the 1970s; the last time America had an employment rate of 64 percent was in 1978, and Europe spent as much on R&D as the United States did in 1979. Europe will only catch up to the United States in productivity by 2056, and then only if its annual productivity gains remain 0.5 percent above that of the United States. Interestingly, the productivity of Europe's information technology sector is comparable to its overseas counterpart but is only half its size. As a result, its weight in productivity gains is smaller (40 percent, compared with 60 percent in the United States). In addition, R&D investment in much lower in Europe, accounting for a mere 1.9 percent of GDP in the five "oldest" EU member states, as opposed to 2.6 percent in America. The fault lies mainly with the private sector and member state authorities. An additional disadvantage is the lower ratio of people with college or university degrees; one in five in Europe versus one in three in the United States. This is coupled with the fact that university research is more developed in the United States, which explains why it is the number one "brain drain" destination—although to a smaller extent in the aftermath of 9/11.[91]

It needs to be noted that the detailed data discussed above are now a few years old—they reflect the situation when this book was first published in Budapest. Moreover, the 2008–9 global financial and economic crisis shook both the United States and Europe, bringing criticism of American laissez-faire economic policies during the last decade. Nevertheless, I find that I still today cannot question either the existence of the underlying weaknesses of the EU's economy or the necessity for economic reform.

The single most important document pertaining to competitiveness dates from March 2000 and comes from Lisbon,[92] where European heads of government decided to transform Europe into the world's most competitive economy by 2010. The year 2000 was the highpoint of the "new economy," a time of global optimism and grand plans among both political and corporate leaders. The markets were all bullish in New York, London, and Frankfurt, with the Dow Jones, FTSE, and DAX indexes all hitting historic highs. The economy looked robust and growth was unstoppable. World-shaking plans were born, companies borrowed billions in loans, politicians spoke in superlatives. Still, the Lisbon Program drew up several important and sensible priorities. What is more, it adopted a very modernist approach; it placed the knowledge-based economy and information technology at the center of its attention. (What else to expect at the peak of the dot-com bubble?) Then the cracks began to show, the problems began to appear—and Lisbon was reinterpreted again and again. In Brussels, the expression "Christmas tree" stands for something very different from the pine tree decorated for the holidays. It means an EU initiative dressed up during the negotiations, consultations, and political deals, when everybody adds their own ideas and pet projects. The Lisbon Program became a real Christmas tree, and everybody put another decoration on it. Or rather, it was a hodgepodge, to which everybody added their favorite ingredient—a bit of environment, a drop of competitiveness, a taste of market reform, a pinch of social care, and so on. It was about everything, so it was about nothing; it wanted to speak to everybody, and thus it spoke to nobody. A reformulation was unavoidable, not because it was obscure and impossible to communicate but rather because all its targets proved to be unrealistic (70 percent employment rate, 3 percent of GDP spent on R&D). By halftime, not only had Europe not caught up to the United States but it had fallen even further behind, while China had appeared on the radar screen. The 2005 midterm review reduced the number of objectives and called for more EU member state involvement in the program's implementation.

The three new key objectives for the Lisbon Program were European competitiveness, economic growth, and job creation. Europe abandoned the dream of becoming the world's most competitive economy, and rightly so. Not because it was not a noble idea, but because it was an unrealistic one. Europe has enough on its plate already. In 2006, European companies had to spend an estimated €600 billion on complying with Community legislation, which is double what analysts predicted. This expenditure is partly necessary and justified, but some EU rules cost a lot of money without bringing any benefits to society. The process of weeding out unnecessary rules and streamlining legislation has begun in recent years. A new European innovation policy is being outlined, which includes an overhaul of the patent system and intellectual property rights, a reform of public procurement rules, and reinforced support to R&D clusters.[93]

The reality of domestic politics can overwrite reform plans; bills on youth employment were swiftly revoked after the violent demonstrations in Paris. French society is not in any mood for reforms; it wants scapegoats, not changes. Nonetheless, reforms are taking place, if ever so slowly—two steps forward, one step back. The task is clear; education must be modernized, the labor market must be liberalized, and the pension system must be tightened. Perhaps the EU's member states will recognize that they need "Brussels" badly to convince their disillusioned citizens of the necessity of painful reform. And not just one or two countries need reform in Europe. Germany finally understood that it was more expedient to cut its own corporate tax rates than to complain about unfair fiscal competition in new member states. The new member states of Central and Eastern Europe have many painful structural reforms ahead of them; once they have balanced their budgets, they must take the necessary steps to guarantee the long-term sustainability of their public finances with a view to an aging population. The question is: How can the EU add real significance to coordination and guidelines and ensure that its member states respect their commitments? This is a difficult question, but sooner or later the time will come when sweeping the issue of real economic policy coordination under the carpet will no longer be an option.

The most important achievement of European integration—apart from the euro—is the creation of the single market. When the idea of the Common Market emerged, it meant the adoption of hundreds of European economic rules, but in the early days the EU's member states could veto such legal acts. Then along came Jacques Delors (who was to become probably the most successful of the European Commission's presidents), and he said what nobody had said publicly before him: As long as the member states have a right of veto and can obstruct any piece of European legislation they do not fancy, the nice plans for a single European market will remain just plans. So the system of qualified majority voting was introduced and—lo and behold—the single European market became a reality.

Today the political climate is very different from two decades ago; "Brussels" now has a different meaning. The time will come when Europe must decide what is more important: national interests or European competitiveness. There are good examples in some EU member states, where e-government (whereby citizens can manage their administrative affairs online without having to visit the authorities in person) is developing in giant strides; equally, more and more countries are encouraging R&D by offering tax breaks to the private sector. And the employment of the elderly is on the rise Europe-wide.

Some are hostile to "Lisbon" because they see it as the Trojan horse of Americanizing Europe and as a product of Europe's inferiority complex. I believe these views are exaggerated; perhaps such critics of the Lisbon Action Plan suffer from an America complex themselves, which is why they are so stubbornly opposed to the idea of learning from the United States. Many also believe that people voted against the European Constitution to indicate that they do not want an American model. These people are crying out loud for a political approach instead of actions to step up economic competitiveness. My question to them is: How many more times does it have to be proved that political visions are doomed to failure without the proper economic foundations? European companies do not seem to share the same sentiments as European politicians; they are actively involved in and benefit from globalization, as was demonstrated by the 60 percent growth in their profits in 2004. Political leaders should learn from their corporate counterparts.

The problem with programs originating from Brussels is that implementation is often left to the will and pleasure of the EU's member states; and Brussels has no means of enforcement at its disposal. Naturally, no one would want a head teacher directing and instructing the member states from Brussels, but in a fast-paced world and an increasingly heterogeneous European Union, coordination is essential—not for Brussels but for the member states. To explain this to the person on the street is an almost impossible task. One of the reasons behind the failure of the original Lisbon Program was—as with so many initiatives—that people have not the faintest idea what "Europe" really wants, and "Europe" does not know what its citizens think either. When Eurobarometer (the official EU pollster) asked people about the economic problems and policies of their respective countries, they demonstrated a sound knowledge of the national situation but knew very little about Europe's global position and economic policy initiatives at the European level.

Europe—by which I mean both "Brussels" and the European Union's member states—is in a difficult situation. It must present an economic policy package containing more and more unpopular measures to an increasingly skeptical public amid growing international competition. And it must do this while a good proportion of public figures, opinion leaders, and politicians question its basic premise: that it is in Europe's best interest to regain its competitiveness. Europe's real magic triangle is liberty, creativity, and motivation—guaranteeing political liberties and economic freedoms, nurturing creativity, and motivating people to work and companies to invest.

*   *   *

Further Reading

On competitiveness and productivity, I recommend William W. Lewis, *The Power of Productivity: Wealth, Poverty, and the Threat to Global Stability* (Chicago: University of Chicago Press / McKinsey & Company, 2004). Numerous discussion papers are available on European competitiveness as well as other key issues such as energy dependency by Brussels-based think tanks.

On societal models and the necessary reform of the European welfare state, good insights are given about the dilemma of the European left by Anthony Giddens, Patrick Diamond, and Roger Liddle, *Global Europe, Social Europe* (Cambridge: Polity Press, 2006). Similar to this is Mike Dixon and Howard Reed, "Tony Blair's Opportunity: An Anglo-Social European Model," Open Democracy Ltd., July 27, 2005. http://www.opendemocracy .net/democracy-europefuture/society_2705.jsp. Nevertheless, the most comprehensive analysis of the different types of the European welfare models comes from André Sapir; see André Sapir et al., *An Agenda for a Growing Europe: The Sapir Report* (Oxford: Oxford University Press, 2004). On France's reforms, an interesting take comes from the current French president; see Nicolas Sarkozy, *Testimony: France, Europe and the World in the Twenty-first Century* (New York: Pantheon Books, 2007).

EU energy policy and energy diplomacy is becoming one of the most á la mode topics these years, and the available literature is indeed vast. I could recommend Centre for European Policy Studies, "Energy Policy for Europe: Identifying the European Added Value," 2008, http://shop.ceps.eu/ BookDetail.php?item_id=1623.

Chapter 4

The European Union's Deficiencies: The Internal Layer

The future of the European nation-states is closely linked to the future of their unprecedented alliance—the European Union. It is likely that most European countries can only remain successful in the foreseeable future if the EU is successful, and vice versa. The EU, however, needs to tackle some very important challenges in the years ahead.

How Does the European Citizen Feel?

A feeling of European identity is an almost nonexistent among European people, except when they define themselves in a negative way—claiming that they are not Americans. This lack of adherence to the pan-European ethos hinders the furthering of the "European project." What can one expect on this front in the future?

Herr Müller, Madame DuPont, Mr. Smith, and Many Others

My secretary speaks six languages fluently, and she can make herself understood in another four. Since she started working for me, she has also begun learning Hungarian. Her father is a German Protestant born in a town that now belongs to Poland, and her mother is a nonpracticing German Jew. She was born in Switzerland and spent her childhood in Italy. The family moved to Brussels in the late 1970s, and then on to Dutch-speaking Flanders. She holds a German passport, although she has never lived in Germany, but she pops over to Cologne or Aachen once a month to buy German sausages, bread, and Haribo candy. Her first name is Norwegian as a result of her parents' fondness for Ibsen, and she is crazy about English humor. German is her mother tongue, but she counts and dreams in English, and when she is angry, the words often come out in Italian. When she is caught speeding in her car, she opts for German as the official language of proceedings—an option offered by Belgian law—not because she speaks it better than French or Flemish, but because she wants the Brussels police to be at a strategic disadvantage. During the last football World Cup tournament, she supported the German team, which was a difficult decision, not least due to the Italian players' good looks. When I asked her what she really considered herself, she answered without hesitation "European." She does indeed feel European, but what about the rest of the continent's population?

Is there such a thing as a European identity? Not really, at least not for the average European. A European identity is the privilege of a few select minorities and national elites. It is certainly not part of the thoughts, feelings, and everyday actions of most Europeans. Common values—such as liberty, equality before the law, and the rule of law—do not distinguish between national identities. Those independent, pan-European ideas or reflexes that are observable in daily life have yet to develop. National identity is much more important than European-ness. The European Union is a community of nations, and not a unified nation of federal territorial units (or states, with some exaggeration) like the United States. But will the EU ever become one? I do not think it will. In fact, European integration itself is not quite sure what it is, and therefore it is not surprising that the citizens of Europe's nations do not know what they are either. The evolution of Europeans' identity can be facilitated by a negative self-definition—delineating what they are *not*. The most critical distinction is the comparison with the United States, the other bulwark of Western civilization. Europeans could look at America the same way as the gigantic but "uncivilized" Roman Empire was perceived by the ancient Greeks—who were fragmented into city-states, and yet considered themselves the cradle of all culture.

However, we should resist temptingly convenient historical analogies, which are dangerous and would make Europeans look like a might-have-been artist lamenting over not being understood by his contemporaries. The world was very different two millennia ago; take the emergence of China, for example. In the eyes of many, the United States is eating up European culture. Europeans watch American movies, listen to American music, and speak English with an American accent; no other culture affects Europe's as much as America's does. The average German absorbs and enjoys more

American culture than he or she does Danish, Italian, or French culture. And the same could be said for the citizens of most European countries.

European integration—or, in other words, a unifying Europe—is a political venture, which inevitably bears the mark of elitism. Accordingly, the bottom-up mental unification of European citizens, the spontaneous evolution of a common European identity, has yet to take place. Europe has not become rooted in people's daily routines, habits, value choices, and thinking. Modern Europe was created to put an end to Franco-German belligerency once and for all. It became clear that the only way to prevent war was to make it economically unprofitable (and impracticable). But guaranteeing peace is a far cry from making people feel European. European identity will not be stimulated all by itself; all traditions begin somewhere, but a tradition only survives if the common experiences, principles, and myths that can build it—and ultimately create identity—come from the person in the street. Political leaders will still have to shoulder a huge responsibility in shaping a European identity. I got my hands on two copies of the first-ever joint French-German history textbook in late 2006, one copy in German and one in French. Students now learn history from the same book in both countries. This is a good start.

Europe is extremely heterogeneous, and it is becoming more so with each enlargement of the European Union. Its history is one of bloody wars and endless enmity. It does not have a single common language; it uses English—the language of America, the global cultural steamroller—as its lingua franca. Thus, Europe's common language with China, Mozambique, or Venezuela is American English, which is hardly a European achievement. Europe, unlike individual member states, does not have notable figures, and the workings of its institutions are too complicated for ordinary people to understand. The European Commission, European Council, and European Parliament are not anything like national institutions. Given all this, the evolution of a European identity will be a painfully slow process. There have been many attempts at unifying Europe—from Charlemagne to Napoleon to Hitler. None of them had plans to build a common European identity, only to spread a central ideology. Charles de Gaulle's vision of Europe—"from the Atlantic to the Urals"—was also political, and in his case was fundamentally based on the nineteenth-century principles of co-operation between nation-states.

In 2006, A Eurobarometer survey asked European citizens what would make them feel more European.[1] Not surprisingly, one-third of the respondents said that the best way would be to elevate welfare policy to the European level. The survey also showed a big difference between the fifteen "old" and twelve "new" EU member states in this respect. For the citizens of the poorer twelve new EU member states—for which membership is considered an act of righting a historical wrong—more than half the population, and for those of the richer fifteen old EU member states less than a third, expressed their belief that making social welfare a European Community competence would be the key "Europeanizing" measure. A remarkable 27 percent of respondents said that a European Constitution and another 16 percent said that a directly elected European president would strengthen their feeling of European-ness. Conspicuously, the latter two suggestions were more political than citizen friendly. And finally, only one in twenty thought it is important to have a common European Olympic team.

Europeans tend to take little part in "European activities," according to the Eurobarometer survey. On average, only 43 percent maintain relations with citizens of other member states, but these figures vary significantly, from 75 percent in the Netherlands to 20 percent in Hungary. Only one in three Europeans traveled abroad in 2005, which is hard to believe but true. More encouragingly, almost one-fourth of respondents read books or magazines in a foreign language. As one would suspect, the Irish and British came in last (the exception to the rule that Nordic people are good at foreign languages), which is only natural considering that, as native speakers of English, they are most likely to get by around the continent without any additional linguistic skills. Non–English speakers rely on English—or rather American English—as their lingua franca. Young, urban, Internet-user graduates live the most European-centric lives and are the most enthusiastic about European integration. The same cannot be said for everybody. According to the survey, two-thirds of the population is interested in domestic politics but less than half in European affairs. The general level of knowledge about European issues is very low. When Eurobarometer asked people three simple yes-or-no questions (Does the EU have fifteen member states? Are members of the European Parliament directly elected? Does your country have a commissioner?), only one in five could answer all three correctly.

Symbols also play an important role in building a common European identity, but their impact is limited, apart from the euro. The European flag and anthem are not alternatives to national symbols, which remain far more important. It speaks volumes about European identity that euro notes, one of its key symbols, carry indistinct bridges and buildings. Extraordinarily, euro notes do not depict famous buildings, famous historical figures, or typical animals. It is easy to guess why—Leonardo da Vinci is considered Italian, Marie Curie is a Polish-born Frenchwoman, and Wolfgang Amadeus Mozart is identified as Austrian; none of them is "European." Engraving the image of a famous figure from any EU member state on a euro note would only lead to diplomatic complications, which—as we know—are best avoided in Europe.

The year 2005 was an awful one for both Europe and the European idea. The Constitutional Treaty was rejected, the bitter debate on the EU budget (totaling a mere 1 percent of Europe's gross domestic product, or GDP) dragged on endlessly, and fears of globalization and of the social and security effects of EU enlargement intensified, while the first signs of failure in the Doha Round of World Trade Organization talks appeared. The European idea faded; Europe fell into depression. There had been scores of new developments in the previous two decades—the single market, the single currency, Europe's reunification, the enlargement of the EU with twelve relatively poor member states, and the launching of EU accession negotiations with Turkey. All these were just too much to digest for Europeans; they became hesitant, and they were forced to reevaluate their nascent "Euro identity" and adjust it to the changing reality of a Europe in transition.

Even so, as the physical frontiers separating EU members disappeared, the economic and social links among them intensified, Europe became tangible in more and more new areas, and people's European awareness and identity became stronger. European identity is an evasive concept, which is much more difficult to grasp and measure than popular support for European integration. Building Europe has always been a top-down project with an elitist approach, about which the media has been and still is somewhat puzzled and uninterested. Even though there are more than a thousand news correspondents following events in Brussels, each looks at events through a national lens, which always gives their reports a national tint. Likewise, the campaigns before the elections to the European Parliament are dominated by domestic issues.

Watching the hysterical political talk shows on French television before the referendum on the EU Constitution, I felt as if I was on a ghost train with weasel-faced Uncle Sam's blood-curdling screams of liberalism on one side and a ruthless Polish plumber about to strike a devastating blow with his monkey wrench on the other. The political elites of member states focus on domestic issues even when communicating EU policies, and the fact that different societies are debating the same questions does not mean that there is a common European approach or even a coalescing "European" public opinion. Euroskepticism is flourishing Europe-wide, to which chauvinism, the fear of losing hard-earned prosperity, the lack of a true European identity, and the democratic deficit and incomprehensibility of the European project all contribute. Nonetheless, a majority—albeit a thin one—of Europeans have a positive opinion of the continent's integration, and the political mainstream is fundamentally pro-European in the EU member states.

Thus, one cannot speak of a European identity, European public opinion, or a European state. There is, however, a place where the EU has made it to the ranks of sovereign states: the Internet. In April 2006, the authorities introduced the ".eu" top-level domain, which enables European firms and individuals to replace their ".com," ".uk," or ".hu" URL endings with a ".eu" domain if they want—and by the looks of things, they do. The European Commission had expected roughly 1.5 million ".eu" applications in the first year, but it received almost that many on the first day.

The European project is similar to the film *Bicentennial Man,* in which Robin Williams plays a robot that is sui generis—although he has a metal heart in his manufactured chest, he also has human emotions. In his quest to become more human, the robot has a real heart transplanted into his metal chest. Believing himself to have human qualities unknown to any other robots, he goes to the World Congress and asks it to pass a bill declaring that he is human. At first, his wish is denied. But finally, after a hundred years, he is recognized as a human, as one of them. The European project is similar; it has the metal heart of European Community legislation—the *acquis communautaire,* the EU's total legislative achievements—and the single market beating in its chest, and there is nothing it wants more than to be accepted by the continent's people and one day to be considered as one of their own.

It is true that one of the reasons for the failed referenda on the EU Constitution in France, Ireland, and the Netherlands was the lack of connection between these nations' citizens and the EU. There is still no European nationalistic feeling. Europe lacks symbols, though it does have a flag—twelve gold stars in a circle on a dark blue field—that is known all over the world and is probably more recognized than most individual European national flags. Europe also has an anthem, the "Ode to Joy" by Beethoven, but it is much less powerful than the flag. It is thought by some to be too sterile, and besides it is never heard or sung in official EU circles—its lyrics are simply not known. And of course, there is no common or at least officially declared lead working language. The official EU policy is for the citizens of its member states to learn two foreign languages from a very early stage. This sounds good, but nevertheless it is not that easy to put in practice; learning a third language is more than most people can handle. Even "multilingual" countries are not really multilingual—for instance, only about 18 percent of Canadians know both English and French, and try to put a question to a French-speaking Belgian in Dutch. But more important, this EU policy of encouraging multilingualism does not opt for a single dominant language (which logically would be English) to facilitate communication across borders. This is not only expensive but also hinders the evolution of European residents' sense of belonging together. Strangely enough, most of the time, when people from Europe declare themselves to be "Europeans" (in English), it is when they are in America.

How Is Today's European Union Viewed?

The Eurobarometer survey also asked people what were the first adjectives that came to mind when they heard the term "European Union."[2] Two-thirds of respondents gave *democratic* and *modern* as their answer, and half said *protective, technocratic,* and *inefficient.* According to a poll by the weekly *European Voice* published in the summer of 2006, Europeans know very little about how the EU operates, and only a third trust the Union.[3] One-third is not such a bad ratio, especially considering that only every fifth respondent trusted his or her national government. The gap is even wider in the case of new EU member states, where every second citizen trusts Brussels but only one in ten has confidence in the national government. Almost 60 percent believed that their country benefited from EU membership, but only 40 percent said that they did so at the personal level. Popular support for EU membership has fluctuated between 46 and 56 percent over the course of the last ten years, while 25 to 31 percent of the population maintains a negative opinion. Traditionally, the EU is most popular in Luxembourg, the Netherlands, Belgium, Spain, and Ireland.

The majority of survey respondents took a dim view of communication by the EU; more than four-fifths reckoned that EU institutions did not properly inform the public. As a result, two-thirds stated that they understood domestic politics, but only one-third claimed to have an understanding of the EU's workings. Views on European affairs are heavily influenced by national political moods. Polls confirm that the European population is in a very pessimistic mood, especially since the global financial and economic crisis hit the old continent. Europe is white with fear of globalization, of China, and of job losses, and polls sometimes produce extraordinary results; the majority of Europeans consider the United States a bigger threat to global security and peace than an Iran edging closer to acquiring a nuclear bomb.

The image of the EU, which has sometimes failed to respond appropriately to people's growing fears and anxiety, has also diminished in recent years. The EU projects a positive image to less than half of the populace, while every third person is unequivocally critical of its image. Remarkably, most would support a common European foreign policy (65 to 70 percent steadily poll in favor), a political union (60 percent), and even the euro, although support for the euro shows a slowly declining trend.

What do people expect the EU to do? Naturally, there have been numerous surveys conducted on this question. According to Eurobarometer, European citizens expect the European Union first and foremost to reduce unemployment, tackle poverty, safeguard peace and security on the continent, and combat organized crime and terrorism. As this lists reflects, Europeans know precious little about the EU, because Brussels has limited competences in all these areas, which remain fundamentally within the competence of the EU member states. This does not stop the electorates of countries without serious social and employment problems—such as Finland—from positively assessing the Union's employment and social policy. Conversely, France, which has had to weather a series of social storms, takes a more unfavorable view of Brussels' social policy—another example of projecting domestic conditions onto the EU. Clearly, people do not understand the Union, and therefore much uncertainty surrounds its future.

How Is Tomorrow's European Union Viewed?

As with so many other issues, Europeans tend to look at tomorrow's shape of the EU from the perspective of their wallets. A 2005 survey on the future of Europe found that half of Europeans were convinced that the key task for the future of the EU was to reduce the disparities in living standards within the Union. This conviction was shared by three-quarters of respondents in the new member states. One in four in the overall sample cited the full extension of the euro zone and the adoption of a European constitution as important tasks for the years ahead. And then there were some really curious answers—one in five respondents suggested the introduction of a common European language and the definition of the borders of the Union, and one in ten would have liked to see a common European army. More than two-thirds of those queried were of the opinion that social welfare systems should be harmonized, and half saw globalization as a threat rather than an opportunity. (Only 37 percent saw globalization as an opportunity, and it was much less hated in the new member states.) Globalization was loathed most by the French, Belgians, and Greeks; the elderly; and low-skilled workers—while left-wingers shuddered just at the thought of it. Just for comparison, in a 2003 preenlargement poll, 56 percent viewed globalization as an opportunity.[4]

The enlargement of the EU is a central issue for Europe's future, and also the source of much social angst. Enlargement and Western Europe's failure to conduct widespread public dialogue on it (in a 2006 poll, merely 29 percent claimed to be informed about it) was what sank the ship of the Constitutional Treaty, one of Europe's most ambitious political ventures. Even so, European public opinion is evenly divided about the concept of enlargement. The majority of the Austrian, Finnish, French, German, and Luxembourger publics reject it, and two-thirds of all Europeans reckon that future enlargements will create further problems in the labor market. Enlargement finds most of its support among young, highly educated people with a leftist leaning. Eurobarometer tried to gauge people's emotional attitudes toward enlargement, asking them what was the first thing that came to their mind when hearing the expression "future enlargements of the EU." *Hope* topped the list, with 30 percent; *indifference* came a distant second, at 17 percent; and *fear* following closely on its heels, at 15 percent. The other two reactions in the top five were *anxiety* and *frustration,* with 12 and 9 percent, respectively.[5] The majority of European nations' citizens seem to share the deep conviction that further EU enlargements will be more in the interest of the acceding countries than of the EU itself. And support for enlargement candidates varies enormously, from enthusiasm for Croatia to mixed feelings about Turkey. Most Europeans would not like to see Turkey inside the Union, even if it met all the accession criteria, which clearly indicates that there is a "Turkish dilemma": Can a Muslim country with 90 percent of its territory in Asia Minor be considered European?

As a colleague of mine in Brussels once said, with a bit of self-irony, at a meeting on the social acceptance of the euro: It is not certain that citizens are always wrong about everything. And indeed, when asked what they considered crucial for the success of further EU enlargements, most people replied: the existence of a distinct European political project. In plain words, we must figure out what the European Union is really about.

Does the Internal Market Exist?

Modern European integration began with the integration of the continent's markets, not with the integration of its various cultures or the political spheres of the European Union's member states. In the twenty-first century, the internal European market is still the core of the EU's integration, and therefore its performance is key to that of the whole EU.

What Is It, and How Did It Evolve?

Once I was lecturing German university students visiting Brussels on the customs union, quite a boring subject even by EU standards. I admitted that much to the students, but I added that the customs union is to the EU like air is to humans: Nobody gives it much thought as long as it is there; but without it, we would suffocate. The customs union is one of the earliest achievements of European integration, which is as much the lifeblood of the Common Market as of citizens' daily lives. If the server of the European Commission's computerized transit system were struck by lightning, exports and imports would come to a halt Europe-wide. Trucks carrying their load would come to a standstill at border crossing points, transforming Europe's roads into one giant *Stauzone* (congestion zone). The customs union, the abolition of customs duties between member states, and the introduction of a common commercial policy with third countries together also form the bedrock of Europe's most successful project: the single market. The free movement of goods was not completed with the creation of the customs union; there remained nontariff obstacles to trade between the member states (technical rules, standards, etc.), as well as taxation hurdles, physical borders, and internal border controls.

To ensure the free movement of goods, persons, services, and capital, Europe had to climb further steps of economic integration. In the first two decades of the Common Market, the operation of the "common" European economy was ensured by enforcing bans enshrined in the Founding Treaties rather than by legislative instruments. The rule of thumb was "do not violate the four freedoms." The economic recession of the 1970s made it clear that new solutions were required; the economy needed to be regulated at the European level. An increasingly European economy deserved increasingly European rules. By the mid-1980s, it was obvious that member states needed to combine forces and dismantle those internal market obstacles that were blocking economic growth. The European Commission published a

White Paper on completing the internal market—the most influential document ever to come out of Brussels—in 1985, which proposed almost 300 pieces of European Community legislation aimed at guaranteeing the EU's four freedoms.[6] In addition, the application of the principle of mutual recognition was extended, which meant that goods lawfully produced in one EU member state could not be banned from sale in the territory of another member state as long as they met common European minimum standards. Since that point, Community rules on the internal market have been adopted with a qualified majority, meaning that there is no more right of veto. This was the most ambitious economic integration program of all time, with a detailed timetable for adopting the necessary measures and ways to make decisionmaking more efficient. No wonder that the single market was born and Europe's heyday followed.

The Cecchini Report, which paved the way for the Single European Act creating the internal market, and which bore the popular title of "The Costs of Non-Europe," estimated that a truck traveling 1,200 kilometers within a single member state could complete the journey within 36 hours, but if it crossed two borders, the journey time rose to 58 hours.[7] Expert calculations put the total cost of "non-Europe" at €200 billion, which was confirmed by subsequent analyses. But the internal market is not just about abolishing internal borders; it also requires the harmonization of rules and standards. With a single directive on telephones, mobile handsets, modems, remote controls, and God knows what else, the EU harmonized 40 previous Community rules and 1,500 national technical regulations with the stroke of a pen. The new approach to harmonization appeared gradually starting in the late 1980s, replacing the excessively detailed, overly complicated European Community regulations with framework rules giving EU member states a certain degree of leeway in implementation—"approximation" of national laws became the buzzword.

Pooling vast national public procurement markets at the European level was another key task (EU member states spend roughly €1.5 billion a year on buying computers, staplers, armored vehicles, and whatnot, which comes to about €3,500 per citizen). Unsurprisingly, shutting foreign competitors out of participating in public procurement tenders under the same conditions puts domestic suppliers in a convenient situation. According to the Cecchini Report, this lack of competition cost governments €22 billion annually.[8] Opportunities for foreign suppliers have been increasing as a result of liberalization, but they still hold a much more modest share of national markets than their domestic competitors. Opening up member state markets to Europe-wide competition has slashed prices in telecommunications and transportation; prices have dropped by half in the former sector. As we saw in chapter 3, liberalization is proceeding much more slowly in the energy sector. An important reason is that, although there are no technical obstacles in telecommunications, energy networks have bottlenecks at national frontiers—for instance, the maximum throughput of the French/Spanish electricity "border" is a measly 4 percent of generation. As a result, only 8 percent of all electricity consumed in Europe comes from another member state.

The harmonization of financial services has been progressing with giant strides, which was facilitated by the global boom in banking and capital markets, revolutionary advances in information technology, and the preparation for and introduction of the euro single currency in 1999. Corporation law has undergone substantial harmonization, and the American stock market scandals provided a great stimulus for coordinating corporate governance at the European level. This phase in the completion of the internal market, which ended in 2006, focused on the modernization of banking and securities market rules, the further liberalization of network industries (energy and transportation), and the simplification of European Community rules. However, the objectives have remained unfulfilled in many areas, such as the full liberalization of services and the creation of a common European patent system.

In sum, the EU's internal market has come to cover many more areas than just the free movement of goods, persons, services, and capital. These areas include the customs union, corporation law, accounting standards, intellectual property rights, public procurement, taxation, mutual recognition of diplomas, and the like.

The European Commission published a report on the tenth anniversary of the internal market in 2002 acknowledging with satisfaction that the single market had boosted the EU's GDP by 1.8 percent (the equivalent of €165 billion) and created 2.5 million new jobs, thereby increasing Europe's wealth by close to €1 trillion.[9] The range of available products had widened and prices had fallen, especially in the telecommunications and transportation sectors. The corporate world had also benefited, because the annual 60 million customs declaration forms, along with many other forms of red tape, became a thing of the past. Before the creation of the internal market, Europe was riddled with endless lines of vehicles at national borders and a jungle of obscure national regulations for customs procedures. Today, Europe is a very different place, where traveling, working, investing abroad, or spending one's retirement years in the sunny Mediterranean is easy to do. These improvements could not have been achieved without deep reforms and a switchover from unanimity-based decisionmaking, with its protectionist vetoes, to qualified majority voting. And these ambitious steps could not have been taken without the political will and courage, strengthened by the fallout from oil shocks. Today's economic problems are far greater, even if some of them—aging, energy security—are only beginning to become apparent and will penetrate the public mind as full-blown crises in years or decades. Once again, the answer is not to hide behind a Maginot line of protectionism but to consistently pursue common European interests.

The Good, the Bad, and the Ugly: The Four Freedoms, the Twenty-seven Protectionisms, and the One Court of Justice

Above, I have mentioned several times that the EU's four freedoms constitute the foundation for the operation of European integration. The scope and interpretation of these freedoms has widened gradually over the course of the last five decades. The breakthrough Single European Act spoke of the four freedoms as the central principles of European construction. The free movement of goods was ensured relatively widely from the beginning of European integration. The milestones in this process were the customs union of 1968 and the prohibition of discriminatory national taxes (whereby EU member states cannot impose a direct or indirect tax on products from another member state higher than that applicable to similar domestic products), quantitative restrictions (quotas), and measures of an equivalent effect.

The free movement of persons covers two distinct economic freedoms: the right to take up work and the right of establishment in another EU member state. The free movement of workers has been featured among European Community rules from the very beginning. At first, it only applied to economically active workers, but it has come to also apply to families of workers and inactive persons, such as retirees and students. With the creation of the single market in 1993, it came to mean the free movement of all natural persons. The other component is the freedom of establishment, which entitles private individuals, entrepreneurs, and companies to set up business in any member state. The freedom of establishment aims to ensure the right to take part in the economic life of another member state.

Under the freedom to provide services, all restrictions on the provision of services within the EU are prohibited, which guarantees that a foreign company established in one member state providing services in another member state cannot be discriminated against by the host country. Previously, restrictions on the free movement of capital remained in force the longest. Capital movements related to exercising any of the other three freedoms (purchasing goods, buying services, and wages) were unrestricted from the beginning, but member states only embarked on liberalizing their capital markets in the late 1980s in preparation for the introduction of the single currency, the euro.

Are the EU's four freedoms truly guaranteed after fifty years of European integration? No, they are not—primarily because of the EU member states' reluctance to abandon their protectionist ways. Member states frequently relapse into protectionism, which is often welcomed by domestic society, especially in times of recession. In a 2006 survey, widely reported in the press 65 percent of the French agreed that it is the government's task to protect domestic companies from foreign takeovers. The decision of Volkswagen at the end of 2006 to close its factory in Brussels and lay off thousands of workers sparked a massive wave of protests. Workers took to the streets, carrying "Hands off my job!" signs, which illustrates the common belief that a job is a worker's acquired right and not a market situation in which the worker contributes to providing a product or service for which there is—or is not—commercial demand. Ironically, when the protesters learned about the generous severance package offered by VW, they dropped their signs and swiftly proceeded to the cash desk.

This story illustrates how governments often come under pressure from society, forcing them to opt for the easier solution—just like the VW workers, who opted for a severance pay that only lasted a few months. Protectionism is a simple and popular instrument but, in the long run, every intervention that reinforces society's false illusions is another nail in Europe's coffin. Many have raised their voices to speak out against shortsighted market restrictions. Those who would like the single market to succeed have a legitimate fear that frequent restrictions on economic freedoms by the EU's member states could jeopardize the very essence of integration.

Moreover, protectionist tendencies are strongest where attempts to shut out other European firms from a national market are the most surrealistic: in the euro zone, the select club of EU member states sharing the same currency and monetary policy. These member states hold "golden" shares in a third of the top 300 European corporations. A golden share is a special share that gives its holder—the government—privileged voting rights or the power of veto. The government can use these golden shares to exert influence in various sectors, from banking to retail to the automobile industry. A French decree passed in late 2005 identified eleven protected sectors in which the government can veto, or impose conditions on, foreign takeovers. There have been a number of such state interventions in the last few years; one example was when the government prevented the takeover of the energy giant Suez by Italy's Enel through an artificial merger with Gaz de France. Spain sabotaged the acquisition of its energy champion Endesa by Germany's E.ON, but Germany does not have a spotless track record either; it attempted to block the hostile takeover of Volkswagen with a bit of legislative magic dubbed the "VW Law."

Teeny weeny Luxembourg has also tried to flex its muscles and, with a bit of help from France, managed to prevent India's Mittal Steel from taking over its steel giant, Arcelor. When the European Commission's White Paper on completing the internal market finally did go through, Lakshmi Mittal admitted having learned a valuable lesson. He said that in America, it is just about shareholder value and profits. But it is different in Europe, where values, culture, and tradition are also important, he claimed at a press conference. The figures back him up; between 1998 and 2003, there were 480 hostile takeover bids in the United States and 280 in the United Kingdom but only 19 in France, 7 in Germany, and 3 in Japan. Even so, there is only so much politicians can do to hold back market developments in the long run, which is why we are witnessing an unprecedented wave of restructuring and takeovers in corporate Europe. Companies have come to realize that they cannot sit on their laurels if they want to perform well in the global marketplace. This recognition will slowly but surely reach the Mittelstand, that is, medium-sized German enterprises. These firms are traditionally the most conservative, even though they produce several leading products. They depend on banks rather than stock exchanges for financing, and their owners are usually the grandchildren of their founders. Nevertheless, this sector will also open its eyes to the new world sooner or later.

EU member states' protectionist practices usually increase during times of recession or social unrest, which—unfortunately—end up in a vicious downward spiral. The efficient operation of the internal market is hampered not only by political intervention in free markets but also by the nonimplementation of European rules. In 2005, more than a thousand infringement procedures were running against member states for noncompliance with European Community law. As a result, the European Court of Justice has a growing workload, perched in its redoubt on the windy Kirchberg Plateau on the outskirts of Luxembourg city, out of the European public's sight. The

Court owes its existence to the constructive mistrust of the founding EU member states, which knew that the disputes of legal interpretation and clashes of interests between sovereign states could only be settled by an independent arbitrator, a sort of European constitutional court.

As is often the case, the Court of Justice, like the legendary Golem, turned against its creators. Although its rulings are sometimes to the taste of the EU member states, the Court—as the interpreter of the letter and the guardian of the spirit of European Community law—regularly puts an end to protectionist practices by declaring national law in violation of the EU's four freedoms. Frustrated over the jurisprudence of the Court, the then–French president Valéry Giscard d'Estaing said at the 1980 Dublin summit: "Something must be done about this Court and its illegal rulings," proposing that the biggest member states nominate not one but two judges to counterbalance its integrationist majority. The judges, sitting in their spartan offices only yawned, knowing all too well that such a change would require amending the Founding Treaties, naturally by a unanimous decision. There are two important things to remember: First, EU law has supremacy over national law; and second, the Court's rulings constitute part of the body of Community law.

This should make it clear how much power the Court of Justice, this secluded "hermit institution"—ignored by politicians, the media, and the public—really has. It should also make it clear how important a role it plays in guaranteeing the EU's four freedoms and building a European Community spirit. The Court's role is greatest where there is room for interpretation—in other words, in areas without common rules, such as the directives and regulations that are adopted through political negotiations among the EU's member states. These are generally those areas of the internal market that remain under the unanimity rule, giving every member country the right of veto. Any one of them, even the smallest, can say "I do not like this proposal," stand up, and leave—and the legislative proposal is rejected.

In the case of economic issues, there are hardly any left under unanimity rules, and most of the Court of Justice's decisions are now made by a qualified majority. However, taxation is one area that remains caught in the pre–single market era decisionmaking process. Thus, it is no wonder that the Court hands down decisions with multi-billion-euro implications almost weekly. The EU's rules on taxation are few and far between, especially for corporate and personal income taxes; thus, EU member states have free rein to regulate taxation, as long as they respect the four freedoms and the principle of nondiscrimination. If a "person"—whether legal or natural—feels that a member state has violated these principles, this person can turn to the Court. If the ruling is in this person's favor and the Court finds that the fundamental principles have been violated, the national practice in question must be discontinued.

In this regard, a recent precedent was the Court of Justice's ruling in the Marks & Spencer case, which said that Britain was wrong to forbid the parent company of this giant department store chain from deducting losses reported by its subsidiaries in Belgium, France, and Germany from its taxable profits if the company could not claim the losses in those countries. Why can a resident parent company deduct losses incurred by a subsidiary in one EU member state from the profits of another subsidiary established in another country? Because national frontiers are blurred when seen from Luxembourg; they have no place in a single market. Trying to protect their sovereignty—taxation is one of the symbolic strongholds of national sovereignty, together with defense—the member states prefer not to sit down and negotiate common taxation rules, which would be quite a cumbersome task due to unanimity rules. As a result, the majority of tax rules are imposed on them from Luxembourg. Once the gavel comes down and the Court has spoken, the member states must obey the ruling.

People, Markets, Services, and Ideas: Where Are They?

The Brussels-based economic think tank Bruegel concluded in 2006 that the single European market was in many respects only a dream. Financial markets are integrated, and the single market in products has come a long way, but the overwhelming majority of Europeans work, shop, and invest in their home country. The fifteen preenlargement, "old" EU member states, which generate 95 percent of the EU's GDP, spend 86 percent of their GDP on their home territory and only 10 percent in other EU countries. In the securities market, 65 percent of investment goes into domestic shares and stocks and only 18 percent into other European financial products. To top it all, only 2 percent of Europeans work in another member state. Even though interstate trade in the United States is on a two-to-three-times-smaller scale than intrastate trade, it is still three times the volume of trade between two EU member states.[10]

The free movement of labor proved to be an extremely sensitive issue politically in the old EU member states, due to an excessive public fear of a mass influx of unemployed Eastern European workers in the wake of enlargement. To protect their labor market from the competition of cheaper workers, the fifteen pre–2004 enlargement EU members insisted on including in the Treaty of Accession of 2003 the option of restricting the free movement of labor for a transitional period. Such national measures are applicable to workers from all the new member states except Cyprus and Malta. Ireland, Sweden, and the United Kingdom liberalized access to their labor markets under national law. The United Kingdom, however, adopted a mandatory Worker's Registration Scheme. The remaining twelve old member states required work permits, often coupled with quotas. The new member states opened up their labor markets to each other, but Hungary, Poland, and Slovenia reciprocated against the fifteen pre–2004 enlargement EU member states by applying respective restrictions. Transitional arrangements were reviewed after the first two years. After the first such review in 2006, Finland, Greece, Portugal, and Spain decided to lift their restrictions on May 1, 2006, and they were joined by Italy on July 27. They were followed by the Netherlands on May 1, 2007, and Luxembourg on November 1, 2007. Belgium, Denmark, France, Italy, Luxembourg, and the Netherlands opted to maintain transitional arrangements, but they simplified their procedures or reduced restrictions in some sectors and/or professions.

The first years after the European Union's enlargement in 2004 proved fears of a mass migration wrong. A relatively small number of citizens of the ten EU members that joined in 2004—the Czech Republic, Cyprus, Estonia, Hungary, Latvia, Lithuania, Malta, Poland, Slovakia, and Slovenia— moved west in search of a job in countries not applying restrictions, where they did not create any major disturbance in the labor market. Foreign workers tend to supplement the fifteen pre–2004 enlargement EU members' labor market needs, filling important skills gaps. Immigration from outside the Union is happening on a much larger scale than mobility within it. According to 2005 statistics, in Austria and Germany, the two countries with the highest ratio of foreigners in the active population (10 percent), only a miniscule percentage of workers came from the ten EU members that joined in 2004 (1.5 percent in Austria and 0.6 percent in Germany), compared with about 7 percent from third countries.

The EU member states should think twice about maintaining these transitional arrangements, because they do not seem justified either economically or by labor market figures. The movement of workers is ultimately determined by supply and demand, and restrictive rules will only contribute to strengthening the underground economy. The influx of a new, cheaper workforce did not lead to social tensions. The situation nevertheless worsened in the wake of the 2007 accession to the EU of Bulgaria and Romania, whose workers are denied equal access to labor markets by even some of the other new member states, which had protested vehemently against the restrictions from the fifteen old EU members in 2004 but then themselves adopted a similar policy vis-à-vis the two latest newcomers three years later. It is true that there was a difference between the accession of the eight Central and Eastern European countries plus the two Mediterranean island states (Malta and Cyprus) in 2004 and that of Bulgaria and Romania in 2007. At the time of the latter accession, widespread corruption and the consequences of the weak judicial system made Brussels and the West nervous, and so did the millions of people rushing out of these new member states looking for temporary jobs or simply a better life in southwestern European countries.

At the time of the referendum on the European Constitution, a defining moment in modern French history, two bogeyman emerged: the Polish plumber; and "Frits Frankenstein," a nickname for the internal market commissioner at the time, the Dutchman Frits Bolkestein. These two emblematic bugbears symbolized the same negative concept: the liberalization of Europe's services market. Services account for 70 percent of the European economy, yet the EU still cannot talk about a single market in services—far from it.[11] Providers of cross-border services face many obstacles if they wish to do business in an EU member state other than their home country, whether they wish to establish themselves in the given country or not. Services come in all sorts of shapes and sizes—hairdressing, legal counseling, business consulting, tourism, and travel arrangements. The consulting company Copenhagen Economics collected and analyzed the data of 275,000 European service providers to forecast the impact of the EU's Services Directive, and it came to the conclusion that dismantling the remaining obstacles, increasing competition, and reducing administrative burdens would lower prices for consumers, companies, and member states. The predicted benefits would translate into a 0.6 percent boost in consumption (€37 billion) and half a million new jobs.[12]

The Services Directive, labeled "ultraliberal" by its opponents, stirred unprecedented controversy. Its most disputed provision was the country-of-origin principle, which stipulated that cross-border service providers would have to abide by the rules of their country of establishment. The French and German governments, as well as trade unions, argued that it would pave the way for social dumping, and domestic companies would find it impossible to keep up with enterprises from the EU's new member states, employing cheaper workers and thereby offering cheaper services. The two groups of

EU member countries—those that wanted faster and wider market opening, and those that dreaded social dumping around every corner—clashed over the directive afresh. French electricians went as far as to cut off power in Bolkestein's second home in France in retaliation for his procompetition statements. (He said that he would hire a Polish plumber if it meant getting the job done more quickly.) French electricians were not the only ones to make it into public discourse: the Polish plumber (*plombier polonais*) became a symbol of cheap Eastern European labor, which many saw as the archenemy of Western European social achievements.

In the end, Brussels bowed to the enormous political pressure and watered down its proposal for the Services Directive. Although removing the remaining barriers to services and trade between the EU member states remained the key objective, the amended proposal was a step back compared with the original text, which had applied to the widest possible range of services. Labor law and the posting of workers fell outside the scope of the final draft, just as did many other important types of services. In its original form, the text included the country-of-origin principle, which in the final wording was simply replaced with the freedom to provide services, thus really taking the sting out of the directive. According to the directive's watered-down version, the country where the services are provided can impose national requirements, but only if they are not discriminatory and are justified on grounds of public policy, public security, public health, or the protection of the environment.

The Services Directive brings many positive changes, among them easier rules on setting up a business in the EU; businesses will be able to complete all formalities online and through a single point of contact ("one-stop-shop"). Authorization schemes will be clearer and more transparent, while "economic needs" tests (expensive procedures requiring businesses to prove to the authorities that they will not "destabilize" local competition) will no longer be allowed. This will speed up authorization and reduce costs for businesses. The EU's member states will have to step up cooperative interstate administrative arrangements to ensure the improved and effective supervision of businesses. Yet despite all these positive developments, by removing the country-of-origin principle that should underpin a true Europe-wide market, the European Union missed an important opportunity to complete the single market in the most important sector of its economy.

Innovation requires not just the work of bright minds but also legal certainty. Inventors and innovators need to be safe and assured that their inventions and/or innovations can be patented quickly, simply, and cheaply across Europe. In an internal market that has been in existence for decades, one might take this for granted, but the single European Community patent is still only a good idea waiting to be implemented. Patents must be registered separately in every EU member state, which obviously means extra time, energy, and costs. (This is the so-called European patent system, which is not to be confused with the Community patent, a truly single patent system.) It costs $10,000 to register a patent in the United States, which is then valid in the entire American market; in the EU, it costs four to six times more. This puts a region that is falling behind in the international innovation competition at a distinct disadvantage. The idea of a Community patent is not a new one; it dates all the way back to the 1970s. Three decades later, renewed efforts within the European Union resulted in a Community Patent Regulation proposal but, in 2004, the Council of Ministers failed to agree on the details, in particular the technicalities of translation. Commissioner Bolkestein spoke out harshly against the Council: "It is a mystery to me how Ministers at the so-called Competitiveness Council can keep a straight face when they adopt conclusions for the spring European Council on making Europe more competitive and yet in the next breath backtrack on the political agreement already reached on the main principles of the Community Patent."[13]

Finally, let us look at what an integrated European money and capital market would mean for the continent. Enterprises would have access to cheaper capital through the stock exchanges, which would fuel growth and create jobs. According to calculations, the integration of financial markets would boost the EU's GDP by as much as 1.1 percent (the equivalent of €130 billion at 2002 prices), corporate investment by 6 percent, private consumption by 0.8 percent, and employment by 0.5 percent.[14] Europe is faring well in terms of foreign direct investment (cross-border investments), but there are still too many barriers hampering the integration of capital markets, among them the fragmentation of the securities clearing and settlement infrastructure and the excessive number of stock exchanges. A single European clearing and settlement infrastructure is unlikely to become reality in the near future, partly due to the rivalry between clearinghouses and partly because European capital markets and stock exchanges are far from uniform.

How to Proceed from Here?

The overall picture in the EU's 2006 Internal Market Review was positive.[15] The corporate world, various organizations representing industry, consumers, and citizens could all make their voice heard, and they spoke about the many benefits that the internal market has brought. Small businesses and consumers were among the less enthusiastic; they felt that a homogeneous market was far from realization. Small and medium-sized enterprises had found it more difficult to expand beyond national borders; and consumers had experienced discriminative restrictions applied by their home countries, which should not happen in a single market. Examples included the car registration tax regime found in several member states and the huge gaps in energy prices. The internal market is a reality for goods, but their free movement is still encumbered by the extra provisions added on to Community rules. The situation is much worse for services, as illustrated by consumer banking and the energy sector, where even the seeds of a single market are hardly visible. As we have seen, the free movement of persons is restricted in several ways, and in other cases people do not make use of the mobility offered by the EU.

The corporate world is essentially satisfied with internal market rules, often preferring them to cumbersome national regulations. However, many actors—especially small and medium-sized enterprises—complain about the excessive costs and administrative burden of European rules, which are not always easy to apply. The Brussels bureaucracy is considered slow and expensive, and only every third economic operator feels that its interests are taken into consideration in Brussels.

Despite the continuous progress of the last few decades, there are still enormous grey areas of the internal market, such as taxation, which—for historical reasons, as mentioned above—is a sacred cow and thus little harmonized or coordinated compared with competition or monetary policy. The lack of coordination is bad for all stakeholders, citizens and enterprises alike; divergent tax rules hinder the movement of persons and capital. It is equally detrimental to the EU member states, and in the present chaotic situation, the Court of Justice could find any of their tax rules incompatible with common principles. Tax harmonization extends beyond the realm of taxation, partly because it concerns the sensitive issue of sovereignty, and partly because in today's world of social tensions, Western Europe is paranoid about "unfair fiscal competition in Eastern Europe." Advocates of closer tax harmonization would like to see taxes raised, which could be a key ideological issue in the debate on the future of Europe.

Should the EU's internal market policy of the future aim to remove barriers, or should it be innovative and aim at new ideas and sectors? What regulatory techniques can best serve Europe in the future? Should Europe adopt a more traditional regulatory approach, or should it stimulate markets and competition with nonregulatory instruments, for example, by modernizing competition policy? Should the EU move toward a lighter regulatory touch and focus on better implementing and enforcing the existing rules? All these questions need to be answered. It is important to know what conditions best suit economic actors and how the benefits of the internal market can be made tangible for consumers and citizens in general. (Going back to the robot story from the film *Bicentennial Man* described at the outset, how can we give the metal-hearted single market a human face?) The internal market policy of the future must improve market dynamism and the adaptability of economic actors, which includes cutting red tape both at the national and the European levels.[16]

In any case, the EU must remain firm in enforcing common rules in its member states. Creating an innovation-friendly environment must be at the heart of its policies, whether for small and medium-sized enterprises, competition, taxation, or intellectual property rights. The Union must improve access to markets and capital and help translate innovative ideas into marketable products. Services and innovation play an increasingly important role in the world. Europe cannot afford for much longer the luxury of not having a single market in services and a smoothly operating, cheap single patent system. In the 1980s, the emphasis was on creating economies of scale by dismantling market obstacles; innovation and flexibility were not all that important. The phenomenon of relocation was virtually unheard of, and reforming labor markets and pension systems were much less pressing tasks.

New challenges require new approaches; an EU with twenty-seven members cannot legislate on everything and should not deal with every sector of the economy. It must focus on those sectors that are of key importance for its global competitiveness—energy, telecommunications, electronics, and the like—and its own wealth. This approach is outlined in the 2007 Internal Market Review, which, contrary to its ground-breaking predecessor of 1985, does not list concrete EU legislative actions.[17]

It is in the interests of the EU that its internal market rules and standards become global models. There are good examples for this, such as the Global System for Mobile Communications standard and the light-handed regulatory environment of the London Stock Exchange, which made it possible for hundreds of companies and major investors to choose this European bourse, fleeing from the rigorously regulated American exchanges. European internal market standards in anticartel, consumer protection, health, and market surveillance policy could serve as bases for global solutions. In other words, it is in Europe's interest to export the internal market.

Almost inarguably, one of the key economic sectors of the near future is climate and smart energy technology. The question is who will develop it and benefit from it. For the time being, Europe does well in this regard—in some areas, it is even the world champion. It is imperative that Europe keep up this position—and not let the United States harness this wave, as happened with the information technology industry in the 1980s.

As the researchers at Bruegel, a leading Brussels-based think tank, put it: "To improve financing for high-growth-potential companies, policymakers should focus on the legal and regulatory environment and on market incentives, rather than on subsidies or other direct intervention."[18] Competititon among intermediaries, securities regulation, insolvency legislation, prudential rules, and taxation are the key components to facilitate the life of the companies with the highest potential in the EU. Fostering corporate growth should be an absolute priority. There are other spheres where the concept of a European internal market can offer something to its member nations' citizens, where there is still a lot to do. A typical example is patient mobility, that is, an internal market for health care services where people can use (and be reimbursed after) other member states' health care system. A comprehensive reform started in this respect in 2008, following up on a solid body of European court rulings.

Finishing the ongoing business of eliminating existing obstacles is important—and I know this sounds a bit odd—but when shaping the new internal market principles, Europe cannot think only in terms of the internal market. In the 1980s, the fundamental task was to unify the economies and markets of the EU's member states. Globalization was in its infancy, which gave Europe a grace period to build its single market. Today, however, the modernization and integration of the European economy must continue in an unprecedented international environment of intensely interrelated nations and regions and a rapidly changing global environment, which means that before submitting a legislative proposal, the EU should always ask itself: What will this mean for Europe's place and role in the world?

What Will Happen to the Euro?

If a European, or even an American, were asked to name a true symbol of Europe, he or she would probably choose the euro, the common currency for much of Europe. But the euro has much more than symbolic power. In fact, as the global financial and economic crisis of 2008–9 was unfolding, more and more people began to speculate that the euro would soon become a true rival for the dollar.

Europe's Stateless Currency

On the eve of December 31, 2001, crowds celebrating the new year in cities throughout Western Europe had to negotiate their way among long lines of people. Brussels was no exception—instead of partying, many people chose to stand in line in front of cash machines. Most were probably too busy celebrating to stop and wonder why these queuers were awaiting midnight so anxiously in this strange manner instead of joining in the fun. At 11 PM, most television channels showed pictures from Athens and Helsinki, the two capitals one time zone to the east, where people were holding the new euro notes in their hands. Those in the rest of Western Europe had to bide their time and wait another 60 minutes before they could do the same. For the first time in history, and for just a few minutes, Frankfurt, the seat of the European Central Bank (ECB), seemed like the heart of Europe, the place to be. The people in the street were probably unaware that the banknotes in their hands were the end result of a common European political project lasting more than a quarter century. Nonetheless, for these same people, Europe had become tangible for the first time—in their hands, they were holding proof that Europe was for real.

Four decades ago, in 1966, a member of the European Parliament said that Europe would become tangible for Europeans at the moment when they held a pan-European coin in their hands with the figure of a young lady riding on a bull. Although, in the end, the euro coins bear a different image—only Greece has coins with the lady on the bull—it does not diminish the symbolic value of the European Union's single currency. Some prophecies date from even earlier. The illustrious British weekly *The Economist* predicted in an op-ed piece 120 years ago that "one day Europe—but not Britain—will have a single currency." The British pound is the oldest Western currency, with a much longer history than most of its European counterparts. The pound sterling and its predecessors have been in use for 1,300 years; which explains the British public's emotional attachment to the pound and their reluctance to let go of their beloved currency and join the EU's monetary union.

Let us first clarify what we mean by "monetary union." Contrary to popular belief, this does not necessarily mean a common currency, even though the euro is the tangible result of the European monetary union. The requirements for a minimal monetary union are set exchange rates of the participating currencies (e.g., French francs are always converted to Italian lire at the same rate) and the full convertibility of the currencies (no matter how many bags of francs I put on the desk, the banker must exchange them for lire). At the other extreme, the requirements for a full monetary union are that the participating currencies disappear and be replaced with a single currency managed by a common central bank. This is the scenario currently playing out in Europe. The main advantages of a monetary union are a reduced exchange-rate risk (because companies and citizens can be certain that the exchange rates will remain unchanged) and no more exchange costs. The biggest disadvantage is that participating countries lose some of their key policy instruments for regulating their economies by delegating their right to make monetary policy and set interest rates to a central body—in this case, the ECB in Frankfurt.

Relinquishing a country's sovereignty for a monetary union is by no means a novel phenomenon; in 1867 the United Kingdom, France, and the United States—the three leading powers of the time—had already contemplated the idea of introducing a single world currency. The idea was soon abandoned as unrealistic. Monetary unions have come and gone on all continents. The four colonies of New England, on the East Coast of the current United States, established one in 1750 by recognizing each other's currencies. A more noteworthy one was the Latin Monetary Union of the late nineteenth century, created at France's initiative between Belgium, Bulgaria, France, Greece, Italy, and Switzerland. This "franc zone" (which was somewhat similar to what was, in effect, the informal "deutsche mark zone" in the 1960s and 1970s) was characterized by the dominance of one strong currency. The Latin Monetary Union had a single currency, but it lacked a common or coordinated monetary policy. Officially, it ended in 1926, but its practical significance had disappeared long before that as the Anglo-Saxon world gradually switched to the so-called gold standard system. The Scandinavian Monetary Union, founded by Denmark, Norway, and Sweden in 1873, also proved to be a short-lived experiment.

Some monetary unions evolved as nation-states emerged—for example, that of the Austro-Hungarian Monarchy, or the Prussian-dominated one created by Otto von Bismarck for the North German Confederation, and the creation of its customs union (Zollverein). Under pressure from Bismarck, and after full German unification in 1871, Germans using dozens of different currencies accepted the reich mark as their sole legal tender, even though the Reichsbank had exclusive competence to print money. Bismarck's monetary union was very stable, outliving the Great Depression and two world wars. The reason for its stability was simple: Behind the currency was an increasingly united state. Another often-forgotten monetary union, between Belgium and Luxembourg, has been in existence since 1921, and it has only been "overwritten" with the introduction of the euro.

Let us turn our attention back to the most ambitious and influential monetary union to date: the European Economic and Monetary Union. Before outlining the brief history of this union, we should remind ourselves that the euro is not only a major symbol of Europe but also a rather ambitious political project, which not only crowns internal market integration (which is, of course, far from completed, as explained elsewhere) but has also managed to breathe new life into the idea of a political union—a United States of Europe.

In 1969, Pierre Werner, the prime minister and finance minister of Luxembourg, was appointed chair of a committee entrusted with the task of elaborating the details of creating a European economic and monetary union. In 1971, the then–European Community's member states unanimously endorsed the Werner Plan, with the target date of 1980 for setting up the Economic and Monetary Union. However, the crisis of the Bretton Woods global financial system in May 1971 brought differences of interests among the member states to the surface, making it obvious that the new monetary cooperation initiative rested on weak foundations. Some countries, including Germany and the Netherlands, temporarily suspended the pegging of their currency to the dollar, floating them freely and withdrawing from the cooperative European exchange-rate system.

In April 1972, Belgium, France, Germany, Italy, Luxembourg, and the Netherlands signed the Basel Agreement, which introduced the "currency snake" to reduce exchange-rate fluctuations. These signatories agreed to keep exchange rates vis-à-vis each other's currencies within a narrow band. This arrangement was commonly known as the "snake in the tunnel," because the currencies of the participating countries allowed serpentine undulations (the "snake") within a narrow band, which in turn was within the wider band of the exchange rate against the dollar (the "tunnel").

After the collapse of the Bretton Woods exchange-rate system in 1973, the then–European Community's member states abandoned their peg to the dollar and allowed the exchange rates of their currencies to float freely against the dollar, just like those outside the currency snake. Ultimately, the currency snake failed to live up to the hopes for it and proved rather unstable. A few key participating countries left the system from time to time, and the medium rates needed adjustment quite frequently. It became obvious that a system of fixed exchange rates could only be operable if the economies and economic policies of the participating countries were sufficiently aligned (i.e., monetary convergence). Consequently, at the time of the review of the first phase of the Werner Plan in 1973, the European Commission admitted the failure of the plan. A harmonization of economic policies would have been necessary, but because the member states found that unacceptable, the first plan for European monetary union was aborted.

In 1979, the European Union's member states decided to have a second go at a monetary union and set up the European Monetary System. This system's mechanism allowed only a minor fluctuation of exchange rates. Due to the nature of the system, if participating countries wanted to keep their currencies within the set band, they had to follow the monetary actions of Germany, the country with the strongest currency. Thus, in reality the system entailed quasi–fixed exchange rates based on the quite successful monetary policy of the Bundesbank, the German central bank. So it was only natural that the idea of a monetary union surfaced again.

The legendary Jacques Delors, the European Commission's president at the time, launched the idea of the single currency, the introduction of which would require the full convertibility of the participating countries' currencies, the full abolition of capital restrictions, and a final and irreversible fixing of exchange cross-rates. As mentioned above, the creation of a monetary union does not presuppose but—to a certain extent—is crowned by the introduction of a single currency, which goes hand in hand with a common, supranational monetary policy; the United States' Founding Fathers—rightly—understood that coordinating national monetary policies would not suffice, for reasons of credibility. They understood this without knowing that, decades later, Greece would cook the books and furnish manipulated economic figures when submitting its application to join the euro zone, and that every second EU member state would exceed its budgetary deficit requirement just five years after the single currency was introduced.

A common monetary policy requires a proper institutional structure, in this case a European central bank taking over and extending the role of the Bundesbank and safeguarding the value of the single currency. It also requires rules, which—when observed—guarantee that applicant states are prepared and ready to adopt the euro and do not jeopardize its stability. These rules became known as the Maastricht convergence criteria, which certain European governments still find difficult to meet today. The Maastricht criteria are often blamed by governments for their election defeats, and they—along with Brussels—are usually cited as justification when austerity measures need to be adopted. It is enough to point fingers at the Brussels-Maastricht axis, and people know what you mean—or do they? Perhaps the Maastricht criteria are not to be blamed. The fault may lie with national governments prone to overspending and eating up the future of their quickly aging societies.

This is one of the most pressing issues of today's European economy. The euro's stability and credibility are serious matters—of which, fortunately, national governments are aware. They may drag their feet, but in the end they follow the rules. Even so, warnings and disciplinary action by Brussels, as well as Frankfurt's adamant insistence on remaining free from member state influence, frequently stir controversy and cause uproars. The introduction of the euro was primarily politically motivated, symbolic of the spirit of European unity, with some finer considerations in the background; by pooling their monetary policy competences in a common bank, France and the Netherlands increased their independence from the German Bundesbank, which used to dictate European monetary policy (not by force but rather by following market realities). Conversely, by relinquishing the Bundesbank's hegemony in monetary policy, Germany made a beau geste toward European countries anxious about its reunification. The symbolic move of giving up the deutsche mark, one of the most successful currencies of all time, served to demonstrate Germany's European-ness.

Even though there is no single European market or a single country behind the euro, so far it has been a success story—it is a stable currency that new EU member states wish to adopt, it has brought along significant drops in inflation rates and budgetary deficits in participating countries, it has made life much easier for companies that do business within the euro zone, it has boosted intra-EU trade, it has freed travelers from the burden of having to exchange national currencies, and it has accelerated the integration of financial markets and thus reduced investment costs. But what can be said about the euro's role on the global scene? Decades before the introduction of the euro, John Connally, secretary of the Treasury in the Richard Nixon administration, told his European counterparts: "The dollar is our currency, but your problem." Have things changed since? Can the euro break the global dominance of the dollar?

The World's Currency?

In considering the euro's likely future, allow me to quote a 1998 observation by the Canadian Nobel laureate economist Robert Mundell: "The euro will probably challenge the dominant position of the dollar, making it the single most important development in the international monetary system since World War I, when the dollar took over the pound's role as the leading reserve currency."[19] Will his prophecy come true?

Since the euro was introduced, the world economy has undergone major changes, and the trends suggest that the unipolar global monetary system based on the dollar's absolute hegemony is shifting toward a bipolar system. To put it in plain language: The euro has appeared as a competitor to the dollar. When it was introduced, the euro became the number two reserve currency overnight, and it has gradually been gaining in strength as such. All this time, the U.S. economy has accumulated vast debts vis-à-vis the rest of the world (particularly China) and has thus weakened astonishingly. The U.S. current account deficit is double (6 percent) the historic high recorded during the years of the arms race under Ronald Reagan in the 1980s. The United States has turned from the world's biggest lender to the world's biggest debtor, which shaved off about half the dollar's value (against the euro) in just a few years.

Moreover, many believe that this decline of the dollar is only the beginning. They argue that, due to the United States' accumulated global imbalances, the collapse of the dollar cannot be ruled out. In such circumstances, global capital starts looking for escape routes and finds them in the euro zone. Others, however, foresee a less dramatic future and consider a collapse of the dollar unlikely, arguing that the growing U.S. debt is mainly attributable not to increased foreign purchases by Americans but to factors beyond American control—namely, the unshakeable confidence in U.S. bonds fueling a buying spree, which has led to American indebtedness and an erosion of the dollar's value.

Whatever the case, the dollar is becoming weaker and weaker, and the euro is growing stronger and stronger (the yuan's peg being rock solid), eroding Europe's export competitiveness. This puts things in a different perspective by disproving the common misconception that a strong euro is beneficial for Europe. As far as exports are concerned, the opposite is true. The dollar's depreciation is by no means a rare occurrence; it has happened in almost every decade since the first oil shock. The novelty lies in the fact that this is the first time that after such a depreciation, the dollar finds itself facing a rival currency that may actually stand a chance as a global competitor. The introduction of the euro marked the end of the dollar's global hegemony.

Undoubtedly, a strong currency is one in which capital markets have confidence, and it is therefore used as a reserve or settlement currency. This is precisely what is happening at the moment; in late 2006, a senior official of the Central Bank of China—which sits on its billion-dollar reserve—hinted at the possibility of converting some of that huge pile of dollars into euros, exactly because the dollar was getting weaker. Of course, such a move would have made an even bigger dent in the value of the dollar. At about the same time, Russia and the Organization of the Petroleum Exporting Countries also announced that they would increase their euro reserves to the detriment of the dollar. This news followed in the wake of the announcement by the United Arab Emirates that it would increase the share of the euro in its portfolio of $25 billion from 2 to 50 percent. The club of reserve currencies is an exclusive one with only a few select members; 90 percent of the world's currency reserves are held in just four currencies: the dollar, euro, yen, and pound. The dollar is hanging on to its position with a share of roughly 60 percent, with the euro a distant second with 20 percent. Nonetheless, every third currency in the world is now pegged to the euro or to a currency basket featuring the euro.

The international clout of a currency is determined not solely by its role as a reserve currency. A clear indication of the euro's worldwide acceptance is its share in the international bond market (i.e., in the market for nonbank loans), where it already stole the show in early 1999 when—for a brief period—most bonds were issued in euros and not dollars. In the years before the euro's introduction, the situation was just the opposite: European currencies struggled to maintain their position, naturally competing against each other, while the dollar gained ground to the detriment of the yen. Since the introduction of the euro, the dollar has had a new competitor to face, one that has been advancing with giant strides. For non–euro zone issuers, the rule of thumb, however, remains: When the target investors are European, the bonds are issued in euros; when it is a global issue, including Europe, the dollar is preferred. This rule has been changing slowly but surely. The key questions that experts and market actors were trying to predict in the run-up to the creation of the euro zone were (1) whether the euro's role in currency markets would be bigger (and if so, by how much) than the combined role of participating currencies before its introduction; and (2) whether it would outperform the late deutsche mark. The years since have shown that the answer is "not really"—the weight of the euro in currency markets is similar to what the deutsche mark used to have.

Countries with close trading or institutional ties with the euro zone generally use the euro as their key currency for influencing exchange rates, invoicing, and payments (in addition to their own currencies, of course). Lebanon, Egypt, and Israel have all opted for euro-based loans in the international money market. Nevertheless, on the international scene, the euro still only plays a fundamentally regional role. It serves as a secondary currency in Central and Southeastern Europe and in parts of the Balkans and the Mediterranean, which is only logical because the deutsche mark, and to a lesser extent the Austrian schilling and the French franc, used to play the same role.

The Iraqi crisis provided further evidence of the euro's growing international role. Essentially, the euro became stronger at the time because the markets looked for what they believed was a stable currency. The euro has become an important stability factor in the world economy, and it enjoys a strong regional role. Slowly but surely, it is also becoming a more and more important money of account and reserve currency, while the eurobond market has established itself as a force to reckon with on a global scale, though it is admittedly still a second-grade currency compared with the dollar. The dollar has twice the share of the euro in currency transactions, and it maintains its role as the currency of choice for invoicing in international trade, especially in the oil business. In EU–United States trade relations, the dollar is used for settling accounts in 80 percent of bilateral trade.

Experts are divided over whether the euro will ever be on a par with the dollar or even take over its place as the world's leading currency. Some— including the economist Fred Bergsten—say that such a scenario is not an unlikely one, reminding us that currencies may outlive their age precisely because opinions change slowly.[20] A prime example of this is the British pound, whose hegemony only ended with World War I, even though in terms of GDP the United States had surpassed the United Kingdom much earlier. The euro does indeed possess certain characteristics that make it destined to become a global currency. One such feature is its low risk factor—that is, its stability—which is guaranteed by the strict anti-inflationary policy of the ECB, which sets the acceptable rate of inflation at 2 percent.

The economic potential behind the euro is huge, comparable to that of the United States, and in addition the euro is the currency of an internationally active region, with the world's largest foreign trade volume. Yet, as explained elsewhere in this book, Europe is of course far from being unified, either culturally or economically. Europe's markets are not uniform, which impairs its international clout. But this is not the main obstacle preventing the euro from becoming the world's leading currency. The real stumbling block is that it is a currency without a country. I agree with André Sapir, who argues that politics are just as important as economics—if not more important—in positioning a currency on the global scene.[21] Euro zone members are yet to sing from the same hymnal internationally, especially such at forums as the meetings of the Group of Seven and the International Monetary Fund.

The euro is a currency created by politicians but lacking a political image. The Convention on the Future of Europe, entrusted with the task of drafting a European Constitutional Treaty, had a working group devoted to economic issues. The key problem on which the group focused—as I witnessed during the several meetings I attended as an observer—was how to build an image for the euro zone by encouraging participating countries to speak with one voice when talking with the rest of the world. Along with the EU's Constitution, this initiative was fated to remain in the drawer.

The question remains: How do Europeans see the euro? Do they see it as an economic initiative completing the single internal market and boosting Europe's competitiveness, or do they see it as an initiative strengthening Europe's international role and laying the foundations for a future political union? Does the euro have a newfound chance to prevail in light of the turmoil in the American financial markets? I would prefer not to answer these questions hastily but rather keep you in suspense until later in the book. But I can already say this much: Whichever approach prevails, Europe would be making a big mistake if it did not try to use the euro not only for economic purposes but also to reinforce its international role in a world characterized by increasingly fierce competition from a growing number of new competitors.

By 2008, the international credit crisis had become a danger to the whole global economic system, and in the long run even to the geopolitical status quo. When pointing to the dollar's predicament, more and more people started to evoke the fall of the British pound sterling, which used to be the leading currency until World War II. Then, because of the collapse of the British economy and the evaporation of Britain's imperial might, sterling lost its pole position. This could also happen with the dollar—American economists say—and not only because of the hardships of the American economy but also because, for the first time in history, the dollar has a true and strong competitor: the euro. If the euro were to displace the dollar, this would create a vicious circle for America; once the dollar lost its global supremacy, the United States would face a seriously reduced economic and geopolitical influence. For the time being, this scenario is not very probable. But the primacy of the greenback is no longer to be taken for granted. We have entered a multicurrency era.

The Two Jean-Claudes and the Two Geniuses

Just take a look at euro notes! They bear *my* signature!—So the ECB's president, Jean-Claude Trichet, fumed at a press conference a few days after the euro zone finance ministers elected the prime minister and finance minister of Luxembourg to chair their Eurogroup for a second term. His irritation was directed not at the journalists but at his namesake, Jean-Claude Juncker, the freshly reelected "Mr. Euro" sitting beside him. (It is curious that Luxembourgers should play such an important role in European monetary integration.)

Of course, this was not a duel of egos that journalists witnessed. President Trichet's quip hinted at a serious dispute over principles: stability versus growth. The debate—in plain terms—rages over whether central banks alone can dictate the terms of monetary policy or whether governments should continue to have a say. On a broader scale, the dilemma is whether the economy needs market liberalization and low inflation or active state intervention. While central bankers and finance ministers engage in this power struggle, the geniuses behind the two main schools of thought in modern economics, Milton Friedman and John Maynard Keynes, watch from above the clouds. As the crossing of swords becomes more and more frequent, we see that the ECB in Frankfurt is to finance ministers what the Court of Justice in Luxembourg is to heads of governments.

The "growth versus balance" question is not unique to Europe; the United States faces the same dilemma. In a 2005 essay, Daniel Griswold, a research fellow at the Cato Institute, went as far as to argue that, in the light of historic experience, the U.S. current account imbalance was a precondition for the growth of the U.S. economy. He analyzed economic figures from the past two and a half decades and concluded that the growing deficit regularly yielded increased growth and employment. In comparison with the record U.S. deficit of $620 billion, in 2004 Germany accumulated a global surplus of $200 million, but with an unemployment rate of more than 11 percent.[22] (The last time the United States saw such a high unemployment rate was in 1982, when it had a negligible $5 billion deficit.)

The United States, as the world's strongest economic power and the holder of the number one global currency, is in many respects in a different position from Europe, especially because Europe is troubled by the peculiar situation of its two arms of economic policy moving to different beats. Monetary policy—the setting of interest rates, with a direct impact on economic growth and unemployment—is made in Frankfurt by the ECB, with the governments having no say whatsoever. The strings moving the other arm of economic policy, budgetary policy (i.e., what the state spends money on) are in the hands of the EU's twenty-seven member governments. Brussels, or to be more precise the European Commission, is caught in between, trying to coordinate and orient national budgetary policies by sanctioning member states that overspend and allow their budgetary deficit to exceed 3 percent of GDP. This is a colossal task but, fortunately, the rules are cast in stone, laid down in the EU Founding Treaties.

Even so, the ECB is constantly under attack from the twenty-seven capitals, accusing Frankfurt that, as an institution without political legitimacy (i.e., per the attackers, not elected) or political responsibility (not replaceable when economic recession strikes), it acts in a voluntarist manner and disregards the interests of the economy (the member states). In turn, the European Commission accuses the member states of ignoring budgetary rules despite their commitments. The member states—and sometimes also the Commission presidents—criticize the rules as simply stupid. The EU member states' citizens accuse their national politicians of incompetence and impotence, for failing to generate growth and create jobs. And finally, when introducing austerity measures, the politicians put the blame on Brussels. This seems to work like a well-oiled system, which is holding out for the moment, but there are tensions building below the surface and serious dangers loom ahead.

Many have looked to the euro to accelerate economic growth. This should come as no surprise; it is a rational expectation—especially because the introduction of the single currency came at a time of "hooray" optimism at the dawn of the new millennium. The growth, however, never came. Instead came agonizing stagnation, for which many have blamed the euro—the monetary policy of the ECB. What is behind such criticisms? The ECB does not encourage economic growth by keeping official interest rates too high, which diverts capital and family savings from investment and consumption to bank accounts, where deposits yield a high return. Those who are not well versed in economics may ask: *Why, then, does the ECB pursue such a policy? Does it not mean well? Are central bankers fools?*

Of course not. The aim of keeping interest rates high is to keep inflation low, which—according to the EU's Founding Treaties—is the ECB's key task. The EU's member states, conversely, believe that the ECB puts too much emphasis on keeping inflation low and not enough on stimulating the economy. In economists' slang, such banks are called hawks, which is how the ECB is commonly referred to in the European capitals. The ECB is criticized for its pronouncements, sometimes for being too predictable and sometimes for the opposite. Yet we should remember that a central banker's every word translates into billions of dollars in international financial markets. If he raises an eyebrow, it is interpreted that he may be worried about recession and could announce a quarter of a percent cut in interest rates in the coming days. For instance, in America the capital movements from the money markets to Nasdaq triggered by the raised eyebrow can be on the order of the GDP of a medium-sized country. Legend has it that when the Fed chairman visited the Senate or the Treasury, he was followed by a herd of observers watching every detail, from the thickness of his briefcase to the bags under his eyes.

In this vein, Mr. Euro, Jean-Claude Juncker, asked for a U.S.-style tête-à-tête with Mr. Euro No. 2, ECB president Trichet. Trichet kindly declined the offer, seeing it as an attempt to influence his decisions. Some EU member states, led by France, do not deny their intention to influence the ECB. They claim that political intervention is justified not only by political legitimacy but also by the fact that the economy cannot balance itself and cannot manage self-fulfilling prophecies (e.g., private consumption falling due to fears of recession) if its fate rests solely in the hands of a central bank keeping its distance from real economic trends.

There are two schools of thought concerning the role of the central bank. The first, liberal school, is content with an independent central bank setting interest rates on its own without politicians meddling in its business. The second school argues that, because political legitimacy and responsibility lie with EU member state politicians, they should have the right to influence European monetary policy. Job creation is a national competence, but one of its key elements—interest rate policy—is now in Frankfurt's hands, creating an unjust and untenable situation. Because the member state leaders have the ultimate responsibility to their electorate for prosperity and jobs, they cannot and should not be deprived of the key instrument of interest rate policy.

The differences between these two schools of thought are rooted in a deep conceptual disagreement over whether a monetary union is sustainable in the long run without the strong political backing of a political union. Interventionists, with historical evidence partly on their side, believe that a political union is vital for success and that an important first step toward such a union would be giving politicians some say in interest rate policy. The other school maintains that the monetary union can stand on its own two feet as it is; the current level of political integration is sufficient to ensure a bright future for the single currency.

I think they are both wrong. On the one hand, the last thing the European monetary union needs is politicians having a finger in every interest rate decision. On the other hand, European integration is well below the degree that would guarantee a safe future for the euro. Political integration will surely become stronger. In what shape and size—that is, with how many EU member states participating, and in what form—is an open question. In any case, closer political integration will have a positive spillover effect on the euro, provided that economic and monetary affairs do not become over-politicized. As far as the fate of the euro is concerned, there is a more important form of integration—at least in the short run: the economic integration of the euro zone countries.

How the rules supposed to guarantee fiscal stability in the euro area can be enforced and reinforced is a critical issue. Most of the recent news coming from Brussels is about the infamous stability pact and its bodyguard, the excessive budgetary deficit procedure. This is no coincidence; at any given time, as many as a dozen EU member states—some already in the euro zone—are in violation of the budget deficit ceiling.

The rules of the Stability and Growth Pact were proposed by Germany, wary of member states with poorer economic track records. Germany had to convince its citizens that the euro would be just as hard a currency as the deutsche mark, and would not be jeopardized by other euro area countries under any circumstances. Essentially, then, the pact is a complex supervisory system to prevent crises by enabling member states to constantly keep an eye on each other, with the excessive deficit procedure acting as a deterrent. The pact was born as a compromise between Germany and France. The Germans managed to realize their pet project and have their pact adopted, but the sanctions (fines) for offenders finally agreed upon were not quite the deterrent originally envisaged. First, sanctions are not automatic but depend on the discretionary decision of ministers of finance. Second, the time until the deposit becomes a fine is so long that it hardly forces governments to make the necessary corrections. Countries afraid of being sanctioned thus have time to explain the reasons behind their deficit and avoid being fined. The sanctions foreseen in the pact have never really been applied in practice; the two big euro zone economies of France and Germany got off cheap, which largely discredited the pact. People started questioning the point of having the pact and whether its rules could be enforced.

The problems surrounding the pact are often traced back to the Maastricht convergence criteria, which—for the sake of simplicity and clarity—set objectives that disregarded real economic processes. The key shortcoming of the pact, critics say, is its inability to respond to changing economic circumstances in a flexible manner. This rigidity is most apparent during a recession or years of stagnation, when the pact leaves little room for maneuvering to stimulate the economy because such measures could temporarily increase the budget deficit. In a 2002 interview in *Le Monde,* Romano Prodi, the then European Commission president, called the pact stupid and inflexible, adding that more intelligent forms of regulation and more flexibility would be desirable. Nevertheless, the pact creates unity in the European monetary system, and allowing economic policies to diverge would be "complete madness."

Although Prodi did not question the need for a pact, he did foreshadow its reform, which was carried out recently. The rules of the pact have been revised to make them more flexible and give EU member states more time to try to cut their deficits and abide by the rules. An important element of the reform package puts the hitherto-neglected criterion of public debt back on the table, urging every country to respect the 60 percent cap, and to update its statistical systems used to calculate deficit and debt figures. The second part of the reform package—as is so often the case—was the result of a huge scandal involving Greece, which had introduced the euro years earlier without ever having fulfilled the 3 percent budget deficit condition. Such "creative" uses of statistics have not completely disappeared, as another Grecian example illustrates. In 2006, the Greek government announced that it would retroactively modify the nation's GDP figures to virtually reduce its deficit. This modification involved the inclusion of the underground economy in calculating GDP, from the incomes of prostitutes to the proceeds from tobacco smuggling.

The reform of the Stability and Growth Pact received heavy criticism for keeping one important aspect untouched: The EU member states still do not really own and share the common objective of sensible, moderate spending. The rules for imposing sanctions have not become more realistic, and the member states still do not seem to fully understand that fiscal discipline is not for the sake of Brussels or even the euro, but for their own good. The popular criticism that blames sluggish growth on the fact that governments are discouraged from spending is easy to rebut. It is enough to compare growth rates for countries that tend to overspend (Germany, France, Italy) with those for ones that exercise budgetary discipline (Finland, Ireland, Spain): Growth in the second group is well above that of any in the first one.

Despite the EU's fragile macroeconomic institutional framework, which finds it hard to cope with the downside of the economic cycle, there is a growing awareness of the importance of fiscal discipline; hopefully more and more member states will realize that economic upswings should be seen as an opportunity for painful reforms rather than a spending spree. The changing attitudes are best reflected by the proposal of German chancellor Angela Merkel to put the issue of budgetary discipline on the agenda of the Group of Eight when chaired by Germany. Together with the International Monetary Fund, Germany is proposing global guidelines to maintain the long-term budgetary balance of aging Western societies. But will this be sufficient? Obviously not, but the former French finance minister, Edmond Alphandéry, is right in saying that the Keynesian approach has become outdated. This does not mean that politicians do not try to take political control over the common monetary policy. And in times of crisis, this pressure only intensifies.

Is the Euro Here to Stay?

The euro is nothing more than a system of fixed exchange rates covered by a glossy coat of political paint. The malfunctioning rules of the euro area unite countries that would otherwise be economically incompatible and that could easily be wrecked by a handful of global hedge funds. The luck of the euro is that—for the time being—it is not in the interest of hedge funds to do so. Views like these are easy to come across in the European—especially the British—press. The euro will disappear, American financial investors say. Are all these opinions nonsensical, or is there some truth in them?

Let us brush up on our theoretical knowledge a little bit. The theory of optimum currency zones originated in the swinging 1960s and has become somewhat worn out, overtaken by life and European monetary integration. Timing was a critical issue; when is the best time (and when is it possible) to establish a currency union? The answer to this question largely depends on the extent to which the relevant regions are united economically, socially, and politically. If monetary union goes hand in hand with political union, then fiscal and budgetary transfers (and migration) can reduce or even overcome regional disparities, while the costs of managing region-specific shocks are shared. For a single-currency zone to remain operable in the long run, it must meet at least two key conditions. First, a common and independent monetary policy is required. Second, the probability of asymmetric shocks that could potentially put its operation at risk must be minimal. This is the case when the economies and industries of the member countries are homogeneous and integrated, and production factors—especially labor

—can move freely within the region. Regional shocks can be cushioned by a "federal" budget by channeling funds from prosperous regions into areas worst hit by recession. The problem in Europe was that, at the time the euro was introduced, economists did not consider it an optimal currency zone. Strictly speaking, the euro area is still not such a zone, but leave that trouble to the theoreticians. Nonetheless, we should not overlook some important warning signs just because they are based in theory.

Historical experience shows that monetary unions are successful when they have among their members at least one economic powerhouse acting as the engine. Central institutions are also needed to control and enforce the rules. The most successful ones are preceded by a political union, as in the case of the United States, the United Kingdom, or Germany. Price and wage flexibility is a fundamental criterion, so that wages can be limited in poorly performing regions, just as interregional transfers can be useful. Fixing and applying criteria on economic convergence also prove to be necessary. In the euro zone, we can hardly talk about real flexibility of labor markets, just as we cannot talk about a political union. Nor is the EU budget designed for major income transfers, because it only disposes of 1 percent of GDP. The euro zone meets all the remaining conditions. The U.S. federal budget is about €3.3 trillion, compared with the EU's "federal" budget of roughly €120 billion, a good part of which is transferred to non–euro zone countries.[23] The difference between the internal transfer capabilities of the two monetary unions is obvious. Conversely, in the absence of a European identity, it is much harder to convince a German factory worker of the benefits of financially supporting Portuguese fishermen than to explain to a Californian why it is important to help the good people of Utah. What is left to do, then? The single market should come to the rescue of the monetary union established on political grounds.

One can observe serious shortcomings in the operation of European monetary union. These have been partly caused by the imperfections of the institutional setup, and partly by the increasing disparities within the euro area in inflation, productivity, and growth rates. (The fact that Spain has accumulated a 9 percent current account deficit while Germany has a 9 percent surplus also speaks volumes.)[24] The gaps are growing, even though they should be diminishing, as we have seen. To make things worse, Europe is losing ground relative to the United States in competitiveness. Both problems can be traced back to the same roots: the unwillingness of certain EU member states to carry out the necessary reforms and push ahead with modernization. Before the introduction of the euro, governments were all for reforms because their participation in the single currency was at stake. Italians even had to pay a one-time "euro levy," and they did not take to the streets in protest. As soon as people had the euro notes in their hands, the purse strings came loose again. With the disappearance of national currencies, depreciation is no longer a monetary policy option; the only instrument governments have at their disposal is to dismantle labor market obstacles and allow competition in all sectors—in other words, to strengthen competitiveness through exposure to market forces.

Strangely, what we see is that the EU member states that have opted out of the euro—Denmark, Sweden, and the United Kingdom—have liberalized their labor markets at a much quicker pace than those that opted for the single currency. But then again, the three non-euro countries had more flexible markets to start with. Another peculiar tendency is that member states outside the euro area are better at transposing single market legislation than those inside, the poorest performers being Italy, France, and Germany. Productivity has declined radically in recent years in the euro zone, while the trend has been the opposite in the three non-euro member states and countries belonging to the Organization for Economic Cooperation and Development in general. Services, which account for 70 percent of GDP, make up only 20 percent of intra-EU cross-border trade.[25] The reason: obstacles.

Italy could be the first serious test case for the euro. Many put the blame on the ECB and the euro, instead of on the Italian government's lack of reforms and a corporate sector sitting on its laurels. Italy was in similar trouble more than a decade ago, when it devalued the lira by one-third and thereby quickly restored competitiveness. This time around, however, Italy was in for a surprise: The euro is a strong currency (just like the deutsche mark was a few years before, and German companies had learned to live with it), and depreciation is out of the question—especially not for Italy's sake.

Theoretically, Italy has another option: abandoning the single currency and leaving the euro zone. But that would have disastrous consequences for both Italy and the euro area as a whole. Naturally, the bigger the country leaving, the more dire the impact. Italian political parties and even ministers floated the idea of Italy's exit, but even that would not solve the underlying problem of a languishing economy caught in a vicious circle of high taxes and high costs.

Some studies—including a 2005 report by the large global bank HSBC —reckon that in addition to Italy, Germany and the Netherlands might also consider leaving the euro zone.[26] Such speculations are ludicrous—if not for other reasons, then just because of the analysts' failure to consider the tremendous costs that such a move would entail for the countries leaving (the loss of credit ratings would send the interest rates of their public debt skyrocketing), the diplomatic consequences of losing face, and the fact that the exit of just one euro zone member could lead to the collapse of the single currency. It is a safe bet to say that none of the participating countries will take unprepared, unilateral steps. The biggest danger the euro zone needs to fear is failure, not its members leaving.[27]

The euro area is enlarging all the time. The EU's new member states all know very well that having an independent monetary policy is much more of a minefield than not having one. So for them, euro zone membership is a no-brainer—it can only bring benefits. These small, incredibly open countries, which have weathered many storms and fought off many attacks on their weak currencies, will look to Frankfurt and the ECB for support and protection. In the film *The Bear,* a little cub is cornered by a bloodthirsty cougar and a sad end seems inevitable, when the cub—in sheer desperation—breaks out in a roar. It is in fact a modest, soft cry, but lo and behold, it is enough to scare the hungry cougar off. The cub is quite proud of his feat, when suddenly a huge figure casts a shadow over him: A huge adult bear has come to the rescue at the last moment. By analogy, a currency having the weight of Frankfurt behind it (and new entrants to the euro area have the ECB behind them as soon as they join the common exchange-rate mechanism, at least two years before entry) would be much less likely to become the target of speculators than one standing on its own. Nonetheless, the EU is doing the right thing by strictly following membership criteria and trying to ensure that its new members do not slacken off once they have cleared the last hurdle. The euro zone has seen too many disillusionments, gimmicks, and cooked books. The formal fulfillment of convergence criteria is one thing; and modernizing the economy, ensuring the stability of economic policy over the terms of office of successive governments, and raising the standard of living to a certain level are other things—they are conditions that euro zone countries can be expected to meet for the sake of preserving the euro's stability and image.

The key problems in the euro zone are low productivity, rules that hamper flexibility, barriers that still limit the potential of the internal market, and the imperfections of common macroeconomic rules. I have focused extensively on the necessary market reforms; let me now turn to how the EU's macroeconomic institutional setup and decisionmaking procedures could be improved. As mentioned above, the first priority should be a stronger member state commitment to respecting the rules. Community rules (the 3 percent ceiling, or Commission/Council recommendations for deficit reduction) are only part of the package. A novel element, proposed by many economists, would be to create an "elite team" of countries that take budgetary stability very seriously and are willing to enact the economic policy principles of stability and sustainability into national law, which every successive government would then have to respect.

At the time of the creation of the EU's monetary union, it was generally believed that the success of the euro would hinge on two things. First and foremost would be the reform of European markets—dismantling the welfare and bureaucratic rules that prevent the economy from unleashing its potential. Second would be building stronger political integration. The first is important because countries changing over to the euro lose the option of depreciating their national currency but must remain able to respond flexibly to changes in the world around them. The second is important because a successful stability-oriented economic policy requires social and political legitimacy. When preparing for the introduction of the single currency, political union was temporarily taken off the agenda—to prevent national governments from exerting political pressure—and the ECB was given full independence; no one can just walk into the Eurotower in Frankfurt to do a bit of lobbying. As a complementary measure, the Stability and Growth Pact was adopted with the aim of reining in EU member states' overspending.

As we can see, this institutional framework is built on mutual distrust: European Community institutions without political legitimacy act as the guardians of economic stability vis-à-vis the politically legitimate member states that are not to be trusted. The question is: How long can this arrangement be maintained, when will the steam blow the lid off, and who will get scalded when it does? One potential solution—call it an escape route, if you will—is to continue with political integration. But there is an even more pressing question: If political integration continues, what will it mean for managing the economies of the euro zone—stability or a spending spree? Despite all these difficulties, I believe that political integration should not be rushed only for the survival of the monetary union; the euro can wait for slower political integration, but not for slow market integration.

As the world's most powerful banker, U.S. Federal Reserve chairman Ben Bernanke, claims, we must accept the euro zone for what it is: a bold political project, which is not a textbook case of an optimum currency zone, and as such cannot be judged by solely economic aspects. As he put it, "From a purely economic point of view, the creation of the [Economic and Monetary Union] is at least partly an exogenous event. . . . An assessment of the success of the euro, indeed the entire experiment in European integration, rests not only in economic criteria, but also on the success of Europe as a political entity."[28]

The euro was created by politics—and what a good deed it was. Politics must also help preserve it, but not by taking the easy way out and exercising direct political control over exchange-rate policy; instead, the focus needs to be on completing internal market integration and agreeing to a higher degree of coordination of EU member state economic policies. As Jean Pisani-Ferry and André Sapir put it, the euro area needs fewer routine procedures and more ability to act in times of real crises.[29] The euro zone's approach to economic changes and political changes—such as enlargement—is still very legalistic, and it still has no international strategy and proper representation in institutions like the International Monetary Fund.

More profound economic coordination need not mean full harmonization, because that would impair the euro zone members' ability to conduct an economic policy best suited to their own conditions and economic cycles. And it certainly should not mean hindering the ECB's functioning, but instead coordination of structural reforms. The euro is not only an important symbol and an economic stabilizer; it should also be the stepping-stone to more coherent European action on the international scene. It is not only the driving force behind economic integration but also enhances European identity and reinforces Europe's global role. As Ottmar Issing puts it, the euro "is still an experiment whose outcome seems likely to remain uncertain for a considerable time to come."[30]

The United States of Europe?

It is hard to define the European Union. It is obviously much more than an international organization or a loose alliance of nation-states, but it is not really a political entity. However, closer political integration has been on its agenda for decades, and it is about to take important steps in this direction.

What Is Europe's Phone Number? Economic Giant, Political Dwarf?

"Who do I call if I want to call Europe?" It would be impossible to count the number of times that this rhetorical question asked by Henry Kissinger in 1972 has been quoted on both sides of the Atlantic. The question remains unanswered; Europe does not speak with a single voice, and it has no common foreign policy or political union. As a result, there are several possible numbers to call. If you dial 00.49.30.40.00, you reach the Bundeskanzler-amt, but I am not sure Paris would approve. Calling 00.33.1.42.92.81.00 will connect you to l'Élysée, but you are likely to offend people on the other side of the English Channel, who will tell you to instead try 00.44.020.72.19.60.40, the House of Commons. Maybe calling Brussels is a better idea, but do you dial 00.32.2.299.11.11 for the European Commission or 00.32.2.281.61.11 for the European Council across the street, and how would that go down in Berlin, Paris, or London?

Kissinger might very well be best remembered for this one question, at least as far as Europeans are concerned. The question still reverberates across the old continent today, and it will probably continue to do so for some time. European unity can be defined by its internal aspect, which should mean a collective identity, but which does not yet exist. Economic unity is tangible both internally—for European enterprises and citizens—and externally—for the rest of the world. However, in his question Kissinger, as the U.S. national security adviser and secretary of state, was alluding to Europe's absence of political unity.

However, the world has changed since Kissinger asked his question. Asia has arisen, and Asians have also started to look for that telephone number. They do not find it either. In 2008, Kishore Mahbubani, a professor at the National University of Singapore, called the EU a geopolitical dwarf—a huge Switzerland, where people live in a bubble of security while feeling a rising insecurity about their future. Thus, Europeans feel insecure because they are surrounded by an arc of instability, from North Africa to the Middle East, from the Balkans to the Caucasus. As Mahbubani puts it: "Given Europe's ability to dominate the world for almost five hundred years, it is remarkable how poorly it is responding to new geopolitical challenges. The paucity of European strategic thinking is stunning. Most European geopolitical gurus believe that the EU can survive well as a free-rider on U.S. power, counting on it to keep the world safe while Europe tends to its internal gardens."[31] The message could not be clearer. . . .

Europe is indeed the biggest economy, the largest capital market; its GDP exceeds America's, and so does its share of world trade: Europe is the world's number one trading power. It imposes sanctions on China for violating antidumping rules; it hands out hefty fines to American corporations for disregarding EU cartel rules. Europe is not only the cradle of modern democracy, but some of its member states also command considerable political clout on the international scene. The United Kingdom and France are permanent members of the UN Security Council, and a number of European countries have sizable armed forces and nuclear capabilities. Yet, though Europe is an economic giant and does have some political stature, it is still a political dwarf. Why is that? The answer is simple: It is united economically, but not politically or in military terms. The European public would be happy to see a more united European foreign policy or defense policy, but its governments are finding such plans a bit too much to swallow.

The European Union's foreign policy, with its intricate multilayered structure, is a concept difficult for non-Europeans to grasp. It includes the traditional foreign policies of the EU's member states, particularly those with a major international role, as well as the not-so-common EU foreign and defense policy, the latter having been kick-started by the bloody events in the former Yugoslavia. In other words, it covers all the principles and actions that are coordinated and unanimously adopted by the member states. Finally, it also comprises Brussels-run policies with an external character, such as the common EU aid policy and external trade policy.

European foreign policy, like so many other European policies, has been shaped by external events, such as the war in Afghanistan, the Falklands War, the Gulf War, crises in Southeastern Europe, and, of course, the war in Iraq. European foreign policy, which is based on the mutual interdependence of the EU's member states, plays an important role in the development of mutual trust, a common political culture, and reflexes. In the long run—which, in this case, means decades—it could contribute to strengthening European identity and reinforce the European Union's internal cohesion. A common foreign and defense policy, being one of the most painful sacrifices of national sovereignty, could be the true symbol of European unity, but the road leading there is a long one. Presently, almost all the preconditions for a real foreign policy are missing: the political will, a more efficient decisionmaking procedure (without national vetoes), the money, and the institutions. Every six months, there is a new face behind the helm, which is not the right message to send to the EU's partners, which can hardly be blamed for not taking such an interlocutor seriously. There is no real ownership of the common foreign policy from the side of the member states, which is only natural considering that the large ones pursue their own foreign affairs agendas, which are more significant than Community projects that take too long to implement due to the complicated financing rules. In an EU of twenty-seven, it would be ridiculous, although formally correct, to talk about equal diplomatic partners; the foreign policy horizon of most small member states does not stretch beyond relations with their neighbors and acute security issues, which questions their added value in deciding global issues. The biggest problem is the lack of a clear answer to two questions: Who makes the common foreign policy? Who represents Europe?

The development of the EU's "common" foreign and security policy has been painfully slow. The beginnings of so-called European political cooperation—meetings between career diplomats—date back to the early 1970s. These were replaced almost a quarter century later with the EU's common foreign policy coordination, which has the official but somewhat misleading name of the Common Foreign and Security Policy. Overall, European military cooperation is still at an embryonic stage. The grand total of European military spending is about half the U.S. defense budget of €350 billion, which is due more to the fragmentation of military forces than to weakness. The United States has almost half a million troops deployable on foreign soil, the EU fewer than 100,000. Military markets are also fragmented, and so is defense procurement, which is what the European Defense Agency was set up to improve. This agency pools EU member states' defense procurement tenders, which total €30 billion annually.[32] The birth of the European Defense Agency, which was a real breakthrough, was shadowed by a rather embarrassing incident. The British and French ministers of defense fell out at a meeting, which ended with a British veto, over the sum of €1 million (as much as the United Kingdom spends on its armed forces in 16 minutes). France was quick to return the favor, the same day vetoing an EU police mission to Afghanistan, which would have been immensely helpful to the British fighting it out on hostile Afghan turf.

France's return to the military command of NATO, however, could be an excellent occasion for French-British reconciliation and for bolstering Europe's military capabilities. And indeed, convergence is taking place; forty-four years after the announcement by Charles de Gaulle that France would leave the military cooperation of NATO, in 2009 Nicolas Sarkozy brought France back. More than a symbolic step, this move has the potential both to bring the United States and the EU closer to each other and to build a more cohesive EU military alliance. As Sarkozy put it at a press conference: "In my mind, there can only be progress in integrating France within NATO if there is prior progress in European defense."

Dampening this hopefulness, however, is the reality of intra-EU tensions over foreign policy. Such disputes between the EU's member states and between European Community institutions are not a rare phenomenon. One example of the latter occurred in November 2006, when the Commission and the Council both wanted to chair the Russia summit.

European foreign policy is evolving, slowly perhaps but surely. The EU is trying to learn from its past mistakes, as was indicated by its swift and unified response to the Lebanon crisis in the summer of 2006. But the real reason behind the weakness of the Common Foreign and Security Policy is not the lack of coordination at the EU level or cumbersome decisionmaking; these are only symptoms of a more serious, deeper-lying problem.

Suez, Srebrenica, and the Azores

In November 1956, Russian T-54 tanks rolled into Budapest, rumbled down the cobblestoned streets, and crushed the Revolution in just a few days; the Soviet empire had intervened. But the Hungarian uprising was not the only event keeping politicians anxious. Another event loomed, perhaps of more geopolitical significance: the Suez Crisis. The Egyptian government decided to nationalize the Suez Canal, which was a strategic shipping route for Europe's oil supply and had once been under British control. The United Kingdom and France intervened, Israel launched an attack on Egypt, and Russia threatened to intervene on Egypt's side. It seemed as if World War III was about to erupt. But then the United States ordered the French, British, and Israelis out; the other empire had intervened. America, the new power of the new age, reprimanded the two former colonial powers, which had to walk off with their tails between their legs.

The United Kingdom and France drew very different conclusions from the Suez Crisis. France learned from the failure that it must, first, unify Europe to counterbalance America's power; second, develop its own nuclear capabilities; and third, never trust the British again. For the United Kingdom, the crisis meant that it was time to face reality and admit that British global rule had ended once and for all. If Britain wanted to preserve some of its global status, it had to build special friendly relations with the new superpower, the United States. And even though France managed to torpedo the United Kingdom's accession to the European Community, in a Cold War situation, with American nuclear force safeguarding Europe against the Soviets, French attempts at weakening the transatlantic alliance were frivolous.

Similarly, the British realized that, unlike in the time of Winston Churchill —who was ready to let the French and Germans get on with the European project on their own while Britain kept busy managing its Commonwealth—America's friendship would not guarantee success on its own if the United Kingdom was left out of efforts toward European integration. The two ex-powers on the two sides of the English Channel have learned to accept each other, but real trust has yet to develop between them. Moreover, even though the two nations have been at loggerheads for decades, today it is obvious that the British-American special relationship is just as symbolic as France's attempts to build a Europe than can offset America's dominance on the global scene. Europe is not among the main concerns of the United States, and has not been for a while now. Unless the European powers are willing to cooperate and pursue common policies, they cannot expect the noise they make to be heard on the other side of the Atlantic.

The searing sign of this crucial need for European cooperation came in July 1995, which saw one of the worst cases of genocide in modern European history. Bosnian Serb forces overran the spa town of Srebrenica in eastern Bosnia-Herzegovina, which had previously been declared a UN-protected "safe area," where tens of thousands of civilians had taken refuge. Over a period of five days, the Bosnian Serb soldiers separated Muslim families and systematically murdered more than 7,000 innocent men and boys. The 400 lightly armed Dutch UN peacekeepers in the area looked on without as much as firing a shot. (The Serbian aggressors made sure that no UN blue helmets were harmed.) Europe, which had negotiated and struck a deal with Serbs, watched the massacre numbly in disbelief. Europe was ill prepared for these events; Europe had failed. There were a number of investigations into the Srebrenica massacre. In 2002, the entire Dutch government resigned after an inquiry blamed officials for giving the poorly armed troops the impossible task of defending the enclave. The EU began to beef up its common security policy and build up the muscle of its common defense policy, which now meant more than the kind words of diplomacy; it meant an armed force.

Then came the Iraq crisis. A crisis summit was held in the Azores in March 2003 with the participation of the U.S. president and the British, Spanish, and Portuguese prime ministers. A few days later, President George W. Bush declared war on Iraq despite the French veto in the UN Security Council. The United Kingdom, having learned its "Suez lesson," lined up behind the United States, and it was followed by many other nations. But France, Germany, and some other countries on the continent vehemently opposed military intervention in Iraq. Europe was torn into two camps. In this real international crisis, it had taken only a matter of minutes to expose Europe's foreign policy fault lines.

There is hardly a book or article on foreign policy that does not use two expressions coined by the American political scientist Joseph Nye: soft and hard power.[33] In international relations, soft power means the ability of a country or region to get what it wants by attracting and persuading others to adopt its goals. Hard power is the carrots and sticks of economic and military might (often taking the shape of bombs and tanks) to make others follow your will. The theory of soft and hard power, which became popular quickly and has a wide literature, goes further and associates Europe with the former and America with the latter. We know from Robert Kagan that Americans are from Mars and Europeans are from Venus.[34] Yet this view, which has now become deeply embedded in public thinking, suffers from historic narrow-sightedness—it disregards the fact that no other continent has been torn and scarred by as many wars as Europe (two world wars in the twentieth century alone). Many believe that Europe should abandon hard power altogether because it undermines the credibility of soft power, and that it should focus on rebuilding social order, civil society, and democratic institutions in problem countries. In other words, Europe should try to avoid American tanks blazing the trail for its values and policies. That, of course, would mean that Europe would abandon its military role, which might not be to the taste of all EU member states. And that is exactly why it has been suggested that defense policy should become an area that member states can opt into or opt out of, with hawks and doves going their separate ways on a strictly voluntary basis.

Srebrenica showed the failure of soft power and the failure of Europe. Iraq is proving a fiasco for hard power and American foreign policy. Srebrenica pushed Europe to closer cooperation; Iraq made the United States realize the importance of transatlantic cooperation. Even so, a half century after the Suez Crisis, the Channel separating the United Kingdom from France and the ocean separating Europe from the United States are as wide as ever.

Washington, Beijing, and New Delhi

In November 2003, U.S. secretary of defense Donald Rumsfeld (who lost his job over the failure of the U.S. campaign in Iraq) put Germany in the same group of problem countries as Iran and Libya. In response, the German minister of justice, Herta Daeubler-Gmelin, likened the hawkish President George W. Bush to Hitler (also costing her her job). Who would have thought, a few decades ago, that such a thing would ever happen? During the Iraq war, EU–United States relations sank to their lowest depths in a long time. Comments like "you are either with us or with the terrorists," by George W. Bush, or the use of the invidious "old Europe" / "new Europe" dichotomy by Donald Rumsfeld did not go down well on the continent.

Thus, kind and not so kind words, disguised and not-so-disguised reprisals, and sophisticated economic sanctions and discreditable statements abounded on both sides of the Atlantic. Europe responded to America's *divide et impera* policy with sharp anti-American sentiments. The two strongholds of Western civilization seemed to be drifting far apart as a supercilious United States stoked the fire of Western Europe's deeply rooted anti-Americanism. Pro-American statements by new EU member states, which had only shaken off Russian rule a few years earlier, drew rebukes from Western Europe.

With the election of Barack Obama as U.S. president in 2008, a wave of new hope spread across Europe. Everyone was certain that the wounds of the Bush era would soon be healed and U.S. foreign policy would change to become closer to the European taste. A true "Obamamania" emerged among the European public and in political elites, but analysts warned people to remain cautious because any president is to a great extent in the hands of Congress, and, moreover, the basic strategic interests of the United States have not changed with the new president.

It is useful here to bring China back into the picture. Just before I began to write this chapter, I met a former senior U.S. diplomat, who suspected that there are appalling social problems behind the Chinese success story. In China's hinterland, society is aging; hundreds of millions will receive no old-age pension whatsoever and cannot count on the support of their children, due to the breakup of the traditional family model. That is one sure recipe for disaster. America and Europe, especially the latter, have their own fair share of problems, and to make things worse, their relationship has deteriorated in recent years. Yet there is more connecting than dividing them. America and Europe must join forces and prepare for the rise—as well as the fall—of the mighty China. Whatever turn American policy takes, Europe should hope that many Americans realize the same. There is cutthroat competition for the Chinese market, just as there was fierce competition for acquiring the prairies, which in their day also represented vast new markets.

In such competitive circumstances, it is not unusual to punch below the belt, but that should not be confused with long-term strategic interests, just as the personalities of individual national leaders should not come before geostrategic considerations. Legend has it that Reagan once told Gorbachev that, if the Martians arrived, they would both put aside their differences in a second. American hegemony has weakened somewhat recently due to the Iraq war, and this trend will continue in the long run as China grows in strength. But not all is lost; Europe is not out of the race completely. Nevertheless, trying to counterbalance the United States is a hopeless venture and does little to further Europe's cause. The best approach for Europe would be to become America's trusty sidekick and build an international order to which it contributes its values and strengths. The United States will need allies as it loses relative weight and the world becomes more complex. Europe, in its own interest, should reach out and grab the hand when America finally extends it.

Let us have no illusions: America is an empire and behaves as one—first, because it can afford to; and second, because it has no other choice. And thus, today it is America's dominant status that shapes the international situation. The question is: To what extent can the United States use its imperial status for the good of the whole world, or to what extent might it abuse its dominant position. An overuse of its dominance could easily backfire, especially in our swiftly changing world. I agree with Stephen Walt that it is in the interest of every global actor—including the United States—to tame American power.[35] Europe could play an important role in this "taming," but only if it is not driven by knee-jerk reflexes.

Europe has a vested interest in building a multipolar world order, because in a bipolar world it would certainly be squeezed behind the United States–China duo. (The United States has been seen recently in Europe as more a source of global instability than of global problem solving, which could aggravate the perception of a scenario like this. Nevertheless, with the election of Obama, this image can be reversed; at least, hopes are high in Europe in this respect.) That is a likely scenario in any case, which Europe should accept without much huffing and puffing but should do its best to avoid. Exercising soft power could help Europe boost its prestige, particularly in the European sphere of influence, but will be insufficient for retaining its leading global role or molding China to a European model. Still, there is nothing wrong with the image of a smart, calm, cool, collected, and democratic Europe—at least as long as events allow it to play that role.

Some believe that the theory of soft power is nothing but a fairytale and that Europe can only preserve its geostrategic role by traditional means. In this respect, undoubtedly, India could become a strategic ally of Europe in the future; lifting India to the ranks of leading global powers could benefit the Western world and Europe in more than one way. India has a natural balancing role in Asia and can preclude a bipolar world. It also has important cultural ties and a great potential for productive cooperation with Europe. Luckily, when the Doha Round of World Trade Organization negotiations collapsed, the EU focused its attention on an EU-India economic cooperation agreement. Naturally, China will occupy more and more pages in the dossiers of foreign ministers, although mostly in relation to economic issues. Therefore, the EU will consider its rise a competitive challenge. Presently, the key issues in the China file are access to markets, dumping, counterfeiting, and increasing the competitive edge of European companies in China, in addition to the weapons embargo introduced by Europe for political and human rights reasons.

And we should not forget about Russia, even though it is going through difficult times and is not easy to cooperate with. Europe must help Russia find its place among the Western democracies. A Russia-China axis—which is not an impossible scenario, however unlikely it may seem at the moment —would be a nightmare for the West. Lately, Russia has become a serious headache for the United States and the EU. Putin's Munich speech in early 2007 was an angry, Cold War–style intervention that introduced an assertive, aggressive Russia. Whether the issue is missile defense, arms control, Kosovo, energy blackmail, or Georgia, the West has had to realize that Russia tends to turn back to its old ways. Fortunately, its strength is not at all comparable to that of the Soviet Union. And time is not playing in its favor; incredibly serious ethnic, demographic, and economic challenges await it.

Of course, many aspects of foreign policy depend on external factors. For Europe, much depends on how America will act. Will it follow a balancing and containment policy to slow down China, will it build a Fortress America, or will it encourage the building of a bipolar liberal-versus-authoritarian capitalist world? There are as yet no clear answers.

The foreign affairs agenda will nevertheless change quickly. Energy is already becoming a key issue, and immigration, drinking water, and climate change will soon line up alongside the traditional problems of armaments, terrorism, and regional military conflicts. The nightmare of nightmares would be going from a world in which failed states support terrorists to a world in which there are states controlled by terrorists (there is hardly a spy movie without a comment on how nice the Cold War years were compared with now), and only the Lord knows what else will come our way tomorrow. The question is which way Europe will decide to move in its foreign policy strategy and in restructuring its political institutions. Is there going to be a real European minister of foreign affairs representing the EU to the rest of the world? This is exactly what the EU Constitution wanted to create, together with an EU diplomatic corps, representing the Union all over the world.

The EU Constitution

At a conference I attended on further EU enlargement in the autumn of 2006, the head of France's prestigious Foreign Policy Institute asked us to raise our hands if we had read the draft EU Constitution from beginning to end. I was sitting in the first row and turned around with curiosity to see how many hands were raised; the attendants were baffled. Then he asked us—EU experts, researchers, academics, and diplomats—to raise our hands if we had *not* read the Constitution from the first page to the last. The result was surprising; many hands were raised, among them mine.

Napoleon once famously said that constitutions should be short and hazy. The rejected draft EU Constitutional Treaty met only one of le petit caporal's criteria—it was hazy all right, but way too long. I am not suggesting that we should follow Napoleon's advice two hundred years after his reign, but such a lengthy document is easy to misunderstand or misinterpret. Even so, it was not its size that killed off the Constitution; it was citizens' EU fatigue, their instinct to reject any top-down political initiative and, mostly, their revulsion at domestic political conditions.

What is this draft Constitution that stirred such intense emotions and whose rejection has plunged Europe into what many argue is a crisis? It had a misleading name, promising more than it would really deliver; it was not really a constitution for the EU, but more the codified text of the Founding Treaties of the EU, which aimed to extend EU competences in some areas. The choice of name was largely symbolic; it was baptized "constitutional" to step away from the boring medium of EU law defined by decisionmaking procedures that are distant and unclear to the member states' citizens. Many believe that its name caused its downfall: "European Constitution" had an unfortunate ring to it, which triggered the killer instinct of Euroskeptic opinion makers and raised the suspicion of the "average Jean." It was the first EU treaty preceded by wide social dialogue and lengthy consultation in the so-called Convention.

When drafting the new treaty, which followed the first constitutional proposal by Altiero Spinello twenty years earlier, three objectives were set: to make Europe more democratic, to strengthen its global role, and to bring the European project closer to the citizens. With all the EU's member states already being functioning democracies, to make Europe more democratic would have meant making EU decisionmaking and governance more democratic. Strengthening the Union's global role would have meant strengthening the Common Foreign and Security Policy, which would have entailed the abolition of the national veto in this field, which the Constitution finally shied away from. The key instrument for bringing Europe closer to its citizens was going to be the Charter of Fundamental Rights adopted in 2000, which—among other things—set out the right of each citizen to dignity, liberty, equality, solidarity, justice, and citizenship.

The constitutional process revolved around three fundamental questions of principle. Number one was the old choice of models: Should Europe maintain its social model (whatever it may be) or abandon and sacrifice it on the altar of international competitiveness? Number two pertained to the unity of an enlarged Europe: Could Europe achieve its aims in unity, or should it give up those aims and resign itself to being divided on what its future should look like? Number three: Could Europe's set of values have an impact on the rest of the world? Political questions are usually asked in a way that anticipates the answer expected, but how that answer is given should have been determined by the interpretation and application of the Constitution.

I do not see any point in speculating about this. In addition to its important ideological and symbolic value, the Constitution could have simplified an EU decisionmaking system that appears hopelessly complicated to anyone outside the legal profession. It would have also done away with the complicated system of three pillars (the internal market, foreign policy, and justice and home affairs), which perhaps looked impressive in a PowerPoint slide show presentation but made daily life awfully complicated. The Constitution would have stipulated, *expressis verbis,* the supremacy of European Community law (the long-accepted principle that rules adopted in Brussels override national legislation), and it would have introduced popular petitions, allowing a minimum of 1 million European citizens to initiate European law on issues directly affecting them. Contrary to common belief, the Constitution would have hardly extended the competences of the EU, but it would have reduced the number of areas where member states can exercise their right of veto. It is a telling fact that neither taxation nor foreign policy would have been placed under qualified majority voting. The Constitution would have brought a number of institutional changes, such as a European Council president appointed for more years (as opposed to the current practice of rotating presidencies) and the post of the European minister for foreign affairs, who would also have served as the vice president of the European Commission.

The failure of the European Constitution was not so much the rejection of a constitution as it was a fiasco undermining an important symbol: the unceasing evolution of European integration. What, then, was the problem? Why did voters decide to reject the Constitution in referenda? The original plans called for its ratification (either through a parliamentary vote or a referendum) by all EU member states by November 2006. Everyone, including the prime minister, Tony Blair himself, was afraid of what might happen in the United Kingdom, when disaster suddenly struck: The French electorate, troubled by social and economic problems, voted against this vision of Europe so badly wanted by the French political elite and prepared by a former president of the Fifth Republic. The French had thus turned down the one treaty that could have benefited them the most. The treaty closest to Europe's citizens had turned out to be the furthest from their hearts.

However, that is only how things appear. It is worth recalling the French referendum on the Maastricht Treaty on the euro, which only passed by a whisker. Even worse, the Dutch referendum produced a second and resounding NO. As I have said, the negative reaction was not about the Constitution at all; it was more about people's opinion on the situation of their own country and of Europe. Yet the majority of European politicians and public figures panicked and started talking about Europe's deepest crisis. The search for the reasons and persons responsible for the failure began. Among the explanations offered, one can find French people terrified of social uncertainty and Dutch citizens letting out the tensions created by immigration; both would preclude all future projects pointing toward globalization or integration and driven by the top brass. There was much talk of the EU's Eastern European enlargement being too much to digest and the role of the fear of further enlargements. Others sought to explain the unsuccessful Constitution referenda on the basis that people were fed up with the reforms necessitated by the single currency and accelerating global competition.

There are many more explanations, and there is probably some truth in all, but the important fact is that people had had enough of too many things happening too suddenly, bringing mostly negative changes. As soon as they were given a chance to obstruct another initiative imposed on them from above, they knew where to put the cross on the ballot. Thus, the Constitution was a good opportunity for a protest. The Constitution would have crowned the so-far triumphant march toward European unity, marked by milestones such as the customs union, the internal market, the single currency, German reunification, and the reuniting of Western and Eastern Europe. But it was rejected.

With the defeat of the Constitution, the plan to build a political European Union—at least one of twenty-seven members—had suffered a devastating blow, which everyone interpreted according to their own political affiliation and temperament. Western European Communists and many others on the left were overjoyed and celebrated the death of a Constitution beginning "His Majesty, the King of the Belgians" instead of "We the people of . . ." (strange to see extreme leftists wanting to copy something American). They celebrated the failure of a liberal plan that—they reckoned—would have brought destruction upon Europe, marked the end of European solidarity, and unleashed "Frankenstein" competition upon Western Europe. The continental political mainstream saw the defeat as an enormous loss, and Europe thus having been thrust into an identity crisis. There were those, among them myself, who believed that what had happened was not a disaster and that Europe had better things to worry about than having or not having a treaty called a Constitution. The constitutional vision had been rejected by the people, or more specifically the French, by a convincing majority—55 percent against, 45 percent for. And then there were those who blamed the failure on the injustice of referenda, arguing—and rightly so—that a referendum is a feeble approximation of democracy and can yield highly misleading results, so careful consideration should be given to the risks they pose in a Union of twenty-seven democratic nations.

Along with the assessment of failure, the search began for a way out of the deadlock. First, Europe should understand what its citizens want, but it is equally important that political leaders and the intellectual elite ask themselves and then answer these questions: What does Europe need? Does it need a successful and well-functioning economic model and a satisfied society, or a pan-European political vision, or both? If that is the case, then we must ask what kind of a Europe this pan-European political vision really means, over and beyond such issues as whether every member state should have a commissioner and who will be the boss and deputy of the European minister of foreign affairs. The average citizen is not bothered by such issues. Then politicians must think about whether they will have enough courage to explain to people that they might want a welfare-oriented Europe guarded by thick walls, but such a Europe can no longer be financed and must not be financed, for the sake of our children and grandchildren.

I agree with those who say that Europe needs a clear vision for the future—a political vision, if you like. Such common visions have proved their worth; the principles, tasks, objectives, and timetable for the construction of the internal market were all clear, and so were those for the single currency. Those successful efforts required political guidance, which is exactly what Europe needs to climb out of its current economic and institutional impasse, which has also affected its vision for the future. The views on Europe's economic and political model are extremely divergent, much more so than for economic integration or the common monetary policy. Neither the economy nor the public mood favors grand projects, and an enlarged EU is proving more heterogeneous and more difficult to manage.

However, to learn from the past, in the early 1980s the economy was also not in great shape, the second oil shock sent inflation rocketing, and societies were skeptical—yet significant pan-European projects were still carried out. That precedent should give Europeans some hope. Politicians will be forced to put the issue of a new constitutional treaty on the table again, because the current treaty framework would not allow for Croatia's accession. In fact, a new treaty was put on the table after several months of digesting the Constitution fiasco. No one dared to call this reform treaty a constitution, but in fact it quietly borrowed all the essential elements of the rejected Constitution. It would have introduced a real European president and an almost-real European foreign minister; reduced the scope of areas where member states can veto EU legislation; reinforced the Community strand in foreign, police, and military policy; given legal status to the EU itself; reinforced the status of the "Eurogroup"; and brought about many other important developments.

However, this new treaty bill, officially the Treaty of Lisbon, lacked symbolic power—on purpose, so it would not irritate the "Eurorealist" politicians and the population. Resubmitting the same Constitution to a new referendum would have made it look as if politicians were trying to shove it down people's throats—"Like it or not, you *will* have a Constitution!"—when one of the motivations for the constitutional project was to reduce the "democratic deficit." Deficit or not, the Irish (the only people who voted on the text) said no to the new treaty in 2008, putting Europe in a deep crisis by allowing the situation to drift on for a few months more.

It would also be worthwhile to give some thought to ratifying future European Founding Treaties by referenda. The current arrangement, in which people vote on treaties providing the foundation for European construction in their own states—within their own national political, economic, and social environment, completely secluded from the European context—is neither democratic nor European. The Dutch, the French, and the Spanish hear Dutch, French, and Spanish national songs from the national hymnal in the national media. Yes-or-no referenda make it impossible for people to voice their opinions, and therefore if they have the slightest reservations about something fundamentally vague and unclear to them (e.g., a European treaty running hundreds of pages), they can only make their voice heard if they put the cross next to NO on the ballot. That gives the NO camp a huge psychological advantage. Those who campaign against "more Europe"—with very few exceptions—have extreme political views or represent organizations insignificant in the sociopolitical fabric, but they still must be entitled to half the air time if we want to maintain the appearance of democracy.

There are at least two possible solutions to this problem: (1) Politicians who adopt treaties in the name of an EU member state should be directly elected before the drafting begins; or (2) a single referendum should be held in all the member states on the same day. The first solution would allow the electorate to choose the men and women whom they trust to draft a new European treaty, instead of those people being appointed by the government. In return, no referendum would be held on the final text. The second solution, a pan-European referendum, which I personally prefer, would put the issue in a truly European context, which could prevent domestic politics from hijacking the treaty and using it for parochial or provincial purposes. Yet that solution would only treat the symptoms, not the disease; Europe would still have to regain the trust of its citizens and define a pan-European vision for the future.

First of all, can one declare with full certainty that the rejection of the Constitution has thrust Europe into a crisis? Is it not the case that Europe is undergoing a common identity crisis? Andrew Moravcsik and others say that the Constitution was nothing more than a public relations strategy, which was supposed to direct public attention to the European project and provoke social dialogue about the future of Europe.[36] In a sense, it has managed to do just that, although not quite as intended. The constitutional project exploded in the face of the political elite, who were unable to make the EU attractive enough for voters to fall in love with it, even when they promised much more than an internal market—not the sexiest of things. Citizens were not touched by this project; generally, they projected their frustration with domestic problems unto the Union. The EU has not collapsed economically, politically, or institutionally; but the wound is very deep. The question is what trends the shelving of political integration will generate in the future, when Europe will need to further tighten its belt as new members join the club. A pragmatic and problem-oriented approach, whereby the Union focuses its attention on acute policy problems (e.g., terrorism, energy dependency, dismantling market obstacles, and labor market reforms) could prove to be expedient. In parallel, constitutional reforms could be slowly restarted, first by overhauling decisionmaking procedures and strengthening the EU's international profile.

Will this satisfy everyone in a European Union coming under increasing pressure? I do not think so. Nor does Joschka Fischer:

> June 12, 2008 [the day of the first Irish referendum], will have to be remembered as the day that made European history. No matter what desperate rescue efforts will be undertaken, they cannot hide the fact that the European Union has left the world stage as a serious foreign policy player for at least ten years (if not much longer). This happened at a time when the problems on the Balkans remain unresolved, America is experiencing a relative decline, Russia is regaining strength, Turkey's domestic policy is taking a wrong turn, the Near East, the EU's direct neighbor—threatens to explode, and the speed of China's and India's rise as emerging powers will define the global economy and politics of tomorrow. Poor Europe! With the Irish referendum, it has blindly and needlessly thrown itself into a political calamity.[37]

And it has also thrown itself into geopolitical irrelevance, I would add. The question, then, is how to get on. Different suggestions have emerged. Some say that the EU should simply forget this constitutional treaty, which is not even necessary for really important issues such as fighting terrorism or climate change. Some have compared the ratification procedure to a bus that stopped in Ireland but no one got on. The bus will come back once more, after twenty-six other passengers have gotten on. But if Ireland refuses to get on this next time, the bus will never come again. Moreover, the timing was extremely risky for Ireland because of the depressing effects of the global financial crisis and the "end of the golden era" sentiment spreading all over the country. The French president was crystal clear: "The Irish must vote again, and I will veto any EU enlargement as long as there are no new institutions."

It has become clear that managing the EU, with its obsolete legal basis, will be impossible in the long term, and the negotiation of another constitutional treaty would not be realistic, given that the EU's leaders have already spent a decade negotiating failed treaties. The success of the second Irish referendum on the Treaty of Lisbon in October 2009 will finally enable the EU to further its institutional and political integration. The new treaty is the necessary first step toward deeper integration, which is inevitable if the EU is to keep its international standing. Having enacted the new treaty—a watered-down Constitution—it is time to breathe life into the laws and make the best of it.

In the longer run, the creation of a European political union combined with a two-speed Europe will not be just a lunatic idea. On the contrary, more and more people will realize that it would be beneficial for the continent's development.

Options for a Political Union

Caius—let that be the name of our protagonist, a merchant—left his home in Rome about two thousand years ago to sell his goods in the far corners of the territory of the political and monetary union (The Roman Empire) in which he lived and buy products that would fetch a good price back home. His first stop was in Augusta Treverorum, today called Trier, where he had an old debt to settle with a fellow merchant. Before making his way to Lugdunum, today Lyon, he made a small detour to the northeast, which he had never visited before, to see what it was like up there. Maybe he was curious and wanted to check out new business opportunities. He found nothing but primitive villages and marshland. This was the marshland that Brussels was built on a few centuries later.

So Caius turned south toward the capital of Gallia, where he emptied his cart, filled his purse, and set off on the last leg of his journey. His final destination was Cartagenia in Iberia, where he wanted to buy a few barrels of fiery wine. During his trip, wherever he roamed, he spoke the same language, Latin; he paid with the same currency, the denarius; and he could be sure that the same law would be applied by authorities set up according to the same principles. He was a citizen of the most lasting political and monetary union in history, which had the biggest impact of all unions on humanity: the Roman Empire. Then Europe split into smaller entities, and the long and often-bloody centuries leading to the development of modern nation-states began.

The concept of a political union has been defined in many ways. In its most advanced form, it can be defined as a community of several smaller states with common political institutions and a common government. Examples include the United Arab Emirates and the United Kingdom. Naturally, there is a less radical definition of a political union; and today's European Union is in many ways much more than just a regional economic alliance. Nevertheless, the absence of a common European government, foreign policy, taxation, budget, or army, even though blueprints for them exist, makes it painfully obvious that the EU is not a political union.

Although the EU is neither a federation nor a confederation in its pure form, it does have harmonized policies—in some areas (e.g., monetary policy, cartel regulations, and foreign trade policy), its member states have almost completely given up their sovereignty—and it does have important Community institutions, including that decisionmaking duo, the ECB and the quasi-constitutional European Court of Justice. European leaders have been toying with the idea of building a political union for centuries. In a letter to his close friend the Marquis de Lafayette, George Washington predicted that one day Europe would follow the model of the United States of America. Napoleon picked up the thread of a united Europe, but his expansive, conquest-based vision quickly vanished. Still, time and again, European thinkers dust off the idea. Just a few decades after Napoleon's dreams had been shattered, Victor Hugo talked about the necessity of creating a European superstate. Then, as we know, came the age of Europe's worst civil wars, followed by the two world wars, which covered the continent with fire and blood and ended Europe's leading role in the world once and for all. World War II brought disillusionment and soul searching. A new global power from across the ocean had to come and sort things out in the old Europe, just as an adult would separate little rascals fighting in the playground. Europe was forced to admit that the only way forward was peace, which can only be guaranteed through closer ties between rival nations—in other words, through integration. Whether integration is needed or not has never been a question; the question is how far Europeans should go. Can and should they build a United States of Europe?

The term "the United States of Europe" was used by Winston Churchill in a famous speech, which he delivered at the University of Zurich in 1946, shortly after the war. But Churchill himself did not prove to be too ambitious in trying to follow up his words with deeds. Ten years later, Europe decided to shelve the idea of a political union, and to establish an economic union instead. Thus, European economic integration was born based on the customs union and the four freedoms of the Common Market. The political union was never taken off the agenda completely, and when Europe was about to make its biggest leap and introduce the euro, its single currency, the vision of a "United States of Europe" again surfaced.

Few may now know, but the baby called "euro" was meant to have a twin sibling, which was never born. The original plans had called for the birth of a political union at the same time as that of the monetary union. There had already been declarations on a political union in the 1980s, but when inter-governmental work began to prepare the ground for the euro in 1990, President François Mitterrand and Chancellor Helmut Kohl—two politicians of very different political views and backgrounds—issued a common declaration expressing their aspiration to establish a European political union. The argument was that, with a single market and a single currency in place, the next logical and desirable step would be to crown the process and create a political union to increase the EU's democratic legitimacy, to improve the efficiency of European institutions, to provide stable political foundations for economic and monetary integration, and to finally have an effective Common Foreign and Security Policy.

Therefore, the single currency and the political union were supposed to be born into this world together in January 1993. But there seems to have been a slight delay in the delivery of the latter, and with the passing of time, it is increasingly unlikely that it will ever be born. Re-reading the 1990 Franco-German joint declaration, one can see the tangible changes in the world since; back then, a president and a chancellor had the courage to use the term "political union," which is today confined to the vocabulary of ex-tremists. They even dared to set out a timetable for making that political union a reality, but those dates remained on the drawing board. Political ne-gotiations on the common currency were successfully concluded, but talks on the political union—not surprisingly—ended without any results. Many an EU member state considered the political union project premature, and the war in Yugoslavia, which had just broken out, did not help much, di-verting politicians' attention and creating tensions in Western Europe.

The conflict in Southeastern Europe divided the EU's member states as they faced the decision of whether to recognize the ex-Yugoslav republics as new states. The "United States of Europe" was a stillborn idea, but its twin sibling the euro is healthy, despite being born post-term and after a long labor. The euro almost immediately relaunched the discourse on the need to create a political union, precisely because of the need to guarantee the new currency's long-term stability. As I have already explained in the previous subsection, experts are still divided over whether the proper operation of a monetary union requires a political union. Unquestionably, the two unions would mutually reinforce each other, as long as politicians kept their hands off monetary stability issues. Nevertheless, as experience shows, the euro can do just fine without a political union, and it will probably continue to fare well in the current setup. As we have seen, technical orthodoxy—that is, the ECB's rigor and strict observance of budgetary rules (which, unfortunately, is not always the case in all member states)—helps prop up the single currency, just as the Court of Justice's orthodox interpretation of Community law shores up the single market.

Oddly, analysts predicted before the introduction of the euro that the ECB would come under political pressure, to which it could respond in two ways. Either the central bankers in Frankfurt could grit their teeth, put their feet down, and refuse to bow to the pressure; or sooner or later, the political union will become reality, which will enable the harmonization of taxation rules and economic policies in the euro zone, thereby bringing the two strands of economic governance—monetary and fiscal policy—into closer alignment.

However, it was not only the introduction of the euro that launched the idea of political union again—far from it. According to Jacques Delors, Europe has lost its vision and sense of direction. It has gotten bogged down at a point where it risks a break-up or slow regression, unless it can move out of its current impasse. Others believe that Europe must establish a political union to stand a better chance in international competition. And still others see the political union playing an important role in sending a clear message to the EU member states' citizens and bringing them closer to the European project. Some have gone as far as to say that political union is needed to avoid Europe decaying into a free trade area. They fear that, without a strong political dimension, the EU could sell its social model and debase itself to an American-style, ruthless, liberal, market-oriented region, where high-level culture and social cohesion are only a dream. They fear that if the European project is left to the "markets," without political vision and leadership, the old continent will end up thus debased. They fear that, without a political image and a common foreign policy, Europe will be condemned to the role of America's "gofer." There are a good many arguments in favor of a United States of Europe—some legitimate, some senseless, some downright harmful. I do not believe, for example, that the raison d'être of a political union should be to protect an unsustainable and uncompetitive socioeconomic model from the globalized world.

In 2000, Joschka Fischer delivered a lecture at Humboldt University, in which he spoke about the need to set up a "core Europe," an avant-garde pushing forward with the continent's integration. His words raised many eyebrows. Since 1990, when Europe was freshly reunited after the fall of the USSR, the face of Europe has changed a lot—mainly in spirit. Then, there was no fear of globalization or of the Polish plumber. The EU was an elite club of twelve relatively similar and prosperous countries. A United States of Europe then would have included all these member states. Ten years later, the scenario was quite different. And five years further on, the EU was a completely different place. Today, the Union is a heterogeneous group of twenty-seven members, a vast regional alliance. The Western European populace is suffering from an economic depression, growth is stunted, companies are relocating east as far as China, and before we can learn the name of the latest poor EU newcomer, another is about to join. Thus, it was only a question of time before the idea of a two-speed Europe emerged.

In 2005, Belgian premier Guy Verhofstadt suggested a unique model, combining the concepts of a United States of Europe and a two-speed Europe (Nicolas Sarkozy also came forward with this idea in 2008, after the failure of the first Irish referendum on the EU Constitution). Verhofstadt proposed a core of integrationist states, surrounded by a circle of states favoring a looser European construction. The core political union could lead the way and set an example for the periphery, thereby preventing a relapse from a body of nations moving toward integration to the status of a free trade zone. Core Europe could reinvigorate the EU's tired image and give something tangible to the new generations that are less receptive to the idea of Europe and take for granted peace, prosperity, and a continent without borders. The core, with the title "United States of Europe," would consist of the twelve EU states that have adopted the euro, but it would be open to further expansion through accession by those states making up the looser outer circle, which could be called the "Organization of European States." The motivations for this idea are a fear of a slowdown in integration due to the EU's growing heterogeneity and a fear of the effects of globalization. The latter covers all anxieties that, in an increasingly competitive environment, Europe, with its aging population, will be unable to keep up with its competitors and thus will be unable to maintain its welfare institutions. This model raises a large number of concerns, and it has been fiercely attacked by both EU member states and Community institutions; but it has managed to win over the hearts of some.

As long as the EU has the consensus rule—that is, member states have the veto for taxation, social policy, energy, and budget matters, and for foreign and defense policy—it cannot handle either itself or the surrounding world. Contrary to a quite popular (basically British) view, as long as the EU is irrelevant, it will stagnate and probably decline. Today the EU is irrelevant to its citizens—people do not understand it, do not like it, and do not care about it too much—and it is irrelevant to its international partners, which need a true union that speaks in a single voice. But this unity will be extremely hard to achieve given the EU's level of heterogeneity as a regional alliance of twenty-seven nations and under its current institutional umbrella.

In the long run, because of the EU's enlargements and institutional malfunctioning, Europe will likely see a major institutional reshuffling. There are two difficult questions associated with this issue: Under what conditions can a two-speed or multiple-speed Europe be formed? And where do Europe's borders really lie?

Where Do Europe's Borders Lie?

Europe has no clear boundaries, in either the geographical or political sense. Consequently, probably the most challenging dilemma for the European Union is how to manage its continuous enlargement while preserving its institutional and political stability.

The Blue Banana: Gentlemen's Club

Under Roman rule, united Europe had grown too big for its own good. As a result, politically speaking, its western part collapsed in the fifth century under the weight of its own impotent institutions and barbarian attacks from the north. Thus the Roman Empire, which had stretched from Britannia all the way to Armenia, faded into history. But the dream of unifying Europe and reviving the Roman Empire never died. As the continent fell to pieces, the kingdoms and principalities that rose from the empire's ashes became locked in constant wars. All this time, in the east, the Byzantine Empire, also known as the Eastern Roman Empire, survived for another millennium, until 1453. The Arabs conquered the Iberian Peninsula in the seventh and eighth centuries, which was the first time that Islam had reached the European continent.

The only thing that survived from the once-mighty Roman Empire was its glorious past; its institutions, military, and culture had all perished. The one exception was the Catholic Church, which came to play a key role in feudal Europe both culturally and politically. The first feudal king to make a serious attempt at reunifying Europe was Charlemagne, the king of the Franks, whom the pope crowned "European" emperor in AD 800. His empire consisted roughly of what is today France, Germany, the Benelux states, and a good part of Italy. Does that list ring a bell? Indeed, these are the same states that founded the modern European Union 1,158 years later. (Perhaps it is not a pure coincidence that the building housing the European Commission's External Relations and Enlargement directorate-generals is named after Charlemagne.)

After Charlemagne's death, the Carolingian Empire fell to pieces, but the idea lived on. Half a century later, the German Emperor Otto I founded the Holy Roman Empire (of the German Nation), which lasted in some form for many centuries. These centuries brought the Renaissance but also bloody dynastic wars. In the meantime, a common Western European culture was slowly evolving, along with a consciousness of global supremacy. European nations, normally locked in bitter conflict, joined forces briefly to fight off the Turkish menace, but the rift in Western Christianity and the ensuing Reformation served as a basis—or pretext—for more bloody wars across Europe. Modern Europe evolved by the seventeenth century, and great powers such as France, England, Spain, and Portugal consolidated their positions. The "West"—that is, Europe's western half—conquered the world; nothing and no one could stop its ships, traders, and soldiers, except for one of its own.

Napoleon also tried to reunify the continent, but his makeshift empire crumbled like a house of cards in the wake of military defeats. The Congress of Vienna in 1815 redrew Europe's map after the defeat of Napoleonic France in 1814 and the dissolution of the Holy Roman Empire in 1806. It consolidated the nearly three hundred states of the Holy Roman Empire into a much more manageable German Confederation of thirty-nine states, which was the first step toward German unification. Europe was at its peak of international power, but the social systems of its countries were unable to adapt to the challenges of a rapidly changing world, and revolutions swept across the continent.

After a few happy decades of peace, Europe witnessed World War I and World War II, the worst wars yet. It was back to square one—the European powers were at it again, up to their knees in blood, with the economy in tatters, cities bombed to ruins, and sworn enemies staring at each other from the two sides of borders. Europe's role as a global power was gone; it needed America to come to the rescue and save it from itself. The continent became divided by an Iron Curtain, after the Russians—just like the Turks four hundred years before—stopped only outside Vienna, claiming the continent's eastern half. Europe fell to pieces. Following World War II, lawyers and diplomats succeeded where generals and emperors had failed before them. They created a unified Europe with laws instead of armies and economic integration instead of conquest. Thus the "Blue Banana" club was born.

The Blue Banana was discovered by astronauts. When they looked down from space at Europe by night, they saw the image of a glimmering snake, stretching from around Birmingham in central England, through the Benelux countries, the Ruhr Basin and Bavaria in Germany, the upper Rhine in France, and then Switzerland, all the way to Milan in northern Italy. The Blue Banana, clearly visible in satellite pictures, covers cities like London, Brussels, Amsterdam, Cologne, Frankfurt, and Basel. It is one of the world's most densely populated areas, and most probably its most important economic, industrial, financial, and cultural region. It has the highest GDP per square mile in the world and is the biggest trading bloc. The Blue Banana is the backbone and quintessence of industrial Western Europe. It is a megalopolis stretching thousands of kilometers, built on the ruins and partly on the cultural foundations of the Roman Empire.

On a global scale, the Blue Banana is the size of a napkin, but there are few places on the globe where so many peoples and cultures are squeezed into the same area. It is the cradle of Europe's modern history, where postwar integration began and which has served as a point of reference for the European Union of twenty-seven members and now almost half a billion people. In the EU, one can trade freely from Cyprus to Lapland according to rules adopted around a table in Brussels.

What we might thus call the "Blue Banana Alliance," the European Community of founding member states and the United Kingdom, used to be a community of countries at roughly the same level of social and economic development—a homogeneous region of integration. But, in historical perspective, the Blue Banana has kept growing at breakneck speed. The accession of Ireland, Denmark, and the United Kingdom—which Charles de Gaulle vetoed twice in four years in the 1960s—brought a shift in the mentality of the previously strictly continental integration. Free market principles were reinforced, and a functional, economy-oriented approach appeared alongside the political approach led by France. In other words, the debate on the role of European integration surfaced, together with the dilemma of whether there should be a primacy of the free market or of political union. Enlargements of this body, serving political stability, began in the 1980s; both Greece and the Spanish-Portuguese duo were only admitted to the club because the Blue Banana countries did not wish to have dictatorships on their borders.

The fourth round of enlargement in 1995 was the only one that increased what was now the European Union's economic might instead of weakening it. Wealthy Austria, Finland, and Sweden recognized that staying outside a single market nearing completion would be a strategic mistake, even if membership would also mean financial sacrifices. The three rich newcomers on the perimeter strengthened the Western European core. Norway once again said "Thank you, but no thank you." The last enlargement of the millennium did not shock either the EU or its new members, despite the extensive and sophisticated body of European Community law that they had to take on board. After all, they were all functioning market economies and, as members of the European Free Trade Association, had adopted the bulk of Common Market regulations.

In the meantime, the Soviet empire had collapsed, and as the Central and Eastern European countries regained their independence, they placed gaining EU membership at the heart of their national strategies. This applied particularly to Austria, which was then a member of the European Free Trade Association. It would have been bizarre for this leading nation of the former Hapsburg Empire to opt out of joining the EU while the once-subjugated dominions whose poverty had been aggravated during the decades of Communist domination became members. By the 1990s, the Blue Banana Alliance bore little resemblance to its original self; it now stretched from Crete to beyond the Arctic Circle. As the Berlin Wall came crashing down, it was time for Europe to prepare itself for reunification. It seemed a daunting task in the West and a chance to fulfill centuries-old dreams in the East.

The Red Star: Political Giant, Economic Dwarf

In 2004, less than a decade after the previous round of enlargement, the European Union embarked on its biggest enlargement ever: the reunification of Europe through the accession of ten new member states in Central and Eastern Europe. The Union's population increased by 20 percent, but its GDP by only 5 percent, which meant that disparities in levels of income and development grew wider, with Luxembourg at the top, with 210 percent of the EU average for GDP per capita, and Latvia at the bottom, with 40 percent.[38] Unification with the center gave Europe's periphery a historic opportunity to catch up with the rest of the continent by sharing the same institutions and decisionmaking systems, by coming under the enforcement clout of the European Court of Justice, and by having a chance to adopt one of the world's key currencies, the euro. Also worth mentioning are the common budget and financial transfers from the EU and the adoption of the sophisticated and extensive body of European Community law. But the most important advantage of membership is that the Central and Eastern European countries have been given a break to reform and modernize themselves, to put their recent pasts behind them, and to close the historical chapter of falling within the Soviet sphere of influence.

Its May 2004 Eastern enlargement was one of the European Union's great historical events. The hope of accession helped spur the Central and Eastern European countries to make up for forty years' arrears of modernization in just fifteen years so they could meet the criteria for EU membership. Their political and economic transitions were peaceful, smooth, cheap, and fully voluntary. For these candidate countries, the EU offered security, democratic stability, and an economic upswing. In return, the hopeful applicants dismantled customs duties, privatized state-owned enterprises, restructured the banking sector, trimmed back state subsidies, opened the telecommunications and energy sectors, combated corruption, and adopted the *acquis communautaire* in full, including its costly environmental standards.

Many studies were conducted before May 2004 to forecast the economic impact of this EU enlargement. The new member states expected significant economic growth (an extra 1.5 to 2.0 percent of annual GDP growth), and the old ones also expected economic benefits. However, these economic benefits were thought to be marginal, due to the limited size of the new members' economies—a mere 5 percent of the GDP of all twenty-seven EU members.[39]

A few years down the road, we can now safely say that the expectations were well founded; the EU's Eastern enlargement has brought favorable economic changes. The new member states have carried out major reforms and now have modernized, fully functional, and dynamically developing market economies. Trade and investment flows between the fifteen "old" EU members and the twelve "new" EU members have multiplied, creating jobs in the latter and offering new investment opportunities for the former.

However, the new members were given a rather cold welcome by the old members' general public. Popular fears forced most of the old members states to apply restrictions against workers from the east, depriving them of one of the fundamental freedoms of the internal market.

The first year after accession turned out to be a critical one, as growth ground to a halt in the largest economies, the rift over Iraq was healing very slowly, and the French and Dutch electorates rejected the EU's proposed Constitution in a referendum. Although what could be seen as the EU's "Big Bang" enlargement was proving a success economically, the EU had not digested it completely. And after the accession in 2007 of two more countries, Bulgaria and Romania, the attitude toward further enlargement became very different. Western Europe was now unhappy; taxpayers were moaning and groaning about having to foot the high bill of Eastern enlargement, and workers felt that "Polish plumbers" were squeezing them out of their jobs. But the huge gap between these kinds of public sentiments and reality was well illustrated by the interesting fact that—according to media reports—at the end of 2005, there were an actual 150 Polish plumbers officially working in France, while the French plumbers' trade union reported 6,000 unfilled vacancies for plumbers nationwide. The truth was that the new EU member countries did not cause any major disturbances in any of the labor markets of Western Europe. However, after Bulgaria and Romania joined, this changed a bit at first; Italy and Spain were flooded with Romanians for a year or two, until the global financial and economic crisis put an end to the golden days.

Another popular excuse for some EU bashing was the financial support handed out to the newcomers. In reality, the figures show that, in the first few years, enlargement-related costs remained below 0.1 percent of the EU's GDP.[40]

Despite the benefits of the EU's recent enlargements, there are serious fears and unfounded myths among the populace, both at the center and on the periphery. Naturally, the political elites saw things more realistically, but they were often unable to resist the pressure generated by popular belief. The biggest fears at the center included relocation (factories packing up and moving east), unfair tax competition, the erosion of social achievements, cheap Eastern labor, waves of immigration, declining public security, and the huge financial burden of enlargement. The periphery had its own anxieties about the loss of national sovereignty and prerogatives, the prohibition of certain traditional practices, and the advent of fierce competition due to market opening. The most common positive myths on the periphery, which understandably never caught on at the center, included a rapid rise in income levels, unrestricted foreign job opportunities, and financial transfers that would make the Marshall Plan aid look like peanuts.

The mass influx of cheap Eastern European labor—which was the most sensitive political issue during accession negotiations—did not take place, partly due to the seven-year (two plus three plus two) restriction imposed by most old EU member states on the free movement of workers from the new member states. The fear of social dumping—that is, wage competition—was what drove the protesters into the streets demanding that the country-of-origin principle be removed from the Services Directive. As we saw above, in the end the demonstrators got what they wanted.[41]

The considerable wage gap between the center and the periphery has not caused Western Europe to be inundated with cheap Eastern European labor, for the simple reason that Europeans are not very mobile. The immobility of Eastern Europeans is demonstrated by the disparities in unemployment between regions within the same country; people are reluctant to move to where the jobs are. Unemployment typically stands low in and around the capitals but can be as much as 30 percent in deindustrialized or agricultural rural areas. An aging Europe needs more diligent hands, but the EU's new member states cannot become the source of extra labor in the long run because of their low birthrates and because their societies are aging faster than those in the West. The United Nations estimates that by 2050 the population will fall by a third in Latvia and Lithuania and by more than a fifth in Hungary and the Czech Republic. In the age of megaterrorism and "ghetto riots" in Western Europe, the new member states never posed an added risk to public security. Apart from the odd isolated case, Easterners landed softly and integrated smoothly into the societies of the recipient countries.

The process of relocating production to the EU's new member states—known as relocation, offshoring, or by its French name, *delocalisation*—is indeed happening, but on a much smaller scale than anticipated. The new member states are by no means the prime destination of relocation; as expected in a globalized world economy, investment goes where returns are the highest. Most foreign direct investment—53 percent, to be precise—from the fifteen "old" EU members went to another old member state, about 12 percent went to the United States, and only 4 percent went to one of the new member states. Moreover, most of the capital investment in the ten new EU member states happened through privatization. The wave of European foreign direct investment has reached all parts of the world, including China and India.[42] Western Europeans can try to keep out Eastern European workers, but they cannot stop their companies from moving East. Unit labor costs have been dropping by an average half percent annually in Western Europe since 2001, and governments are having to carry out painful structural reforms, such as relaxing rules that protect jobs and slashing welfare benefits. But it would be difficult to say to what extent wage cuts and labor market reforms are the direct consequence of the EU's Eastern enlargement. In any case, social and demographic trends observable worldwide (aging populations, the breakup of the traditional family model), European integration (the internal market, the monetary union), and global competition (with China, India, the United States, and others) would have certainly left Europe no other choice but to adapt to the changing environment.

One of the biggest fears of the EU's old member states was—and still is—that the Central and Eastern European countries would keep cutting corporate tax rates and introducing flat rate personal income tax regimes. As a result, it seems that the old member states were forced to follow suit and ease their tax burdens. Austria, for example, slashed its corporate tax rate from 34 to 25 percent. It is unclear whether this happened as a result of enlargement or was part of a wider international trend of lower direct taxes (income and profit) and higher indirect taxes (the value-added tax). I must dispel a myth: Eastern Europe is not a tax haven. Generally, tax revenues are lower in the ten new EU member states than in the fifteen old EU member states, but not by much. Corporate tax rates are indeed considerably lower in the Central and Eastern European countries than elsewhere on the continent, varying between 15 and 20 percent, compared with 34 to 38 percent in Germany, Italy, or France. However, one should also remember that tax revenues depend on two components: the tax rate and the tax base. The Western European countries offer more tax deductions than the Eastern ones, and their amortization rules are also more favorable. The actual tax burden is not lighter in the new member states, as is demonstrated by the tax revenues of national treasuries collected from the corporate sector in 2003—1.3 percent in Germany and 2.6 percent in France, considerably less than in the supposedly low-tax countries Ireland (3.8 percent), the United Kingdom (3.8 percent), Slovakia (3.6 percent), and Hungary (2.3 percent). Over the course of the last fifteen years, the new member states received a total sum of €28 billion in transfers from the EU's budget. But this seemingly hefty sum represents less than 0.1 percent of the EU countries' combined GDP, which is a more than reasonable price to pay for the reunification of Europe.[43]

What did the EU's new member states dread, and what were their hopes? Before the ten new member states' accession to the EU, it became a widespread belief among their businesses that doomsday would arrive on May 1, 2004. But even though the enterprises in the new member states are much smaller and less developed than their Western counterparts, they were not washed away by the "EU tsunami." They weathered accession without much trouble, which was mainly because they did not have to learn to play by the new rules overnight; the adoption of the *acquis communautaire* was the result of a decade of organic development, not to mention the fact that foreign investors had access to Eastern European markets well before enlargement.

Many of the ten new EU member states were afraid of losing their national sovereignty but, contrary to public belief, they have never been able to defend their interests better than now. As full members of the EU, they can participate in its decisionmaking processes and influence the final outcomes, which is a big difference compared with the times when they had to implement rules adopted by others. In a globalized world, more and more problems need international solutions—just think of the Chinese dumping of shoes and clothes. It is easy to see that a state stands a much better chance as part of the world's largest economic bloc than on its own.

When they were only EU candidate countries, alongside their fears, the Eastern European states also shared a number of myths about the EU. The biggest such myth—that as members, they would see a rapid improvement in their standard of living—proved false. The experiences of the Mediterranean countries show that income disparities do shrink, but only over the course of decades. With more than twenty years of membership behind them, Greece, Spain, and Portugal still lag behind in terms of GDP per capita, with about 72 percent of the average for the nine member states that belonged to the European Community at the time of their accession, which is a modest improvement from the 66 percent from which they started in the 1980s. It is estimated that it will take Hungary and the Czech Republic about a generation to catch up to the EU average; for Poland, it could be two generations; and for Romania, it may even be three generations.[44] And these growth paths will only be possible, of course, if these new members can maintain their current higher growth rates for the long run. As we have seen, the threat to labor markets was not quite as bad as predicted, due to a number of factors: workers' low mobility, the lack of language skills, the non-recognition of qualifications and diplomas, and, last but not least, the near recession of the Western European economy.

European reunification did not break the bank. The wealthy old EU member countries got a relatively cheap deal, but we should not underestimate the financial support that the new members will be eligible for in the 2007–13 financial perspective (an EU seven-year budget framework). If they manage to absorb all the available money and spend it intelligently, they will have a unique chance for modernization. If we were to compare the Marshall Plan aid and the EU's support for Greece, a country about the size of Hungary, the result would be shocking; during the seven years of the next financial perspective, Hungary will receive ten times what Greece received during the three years of the Marshall Plan. In the first three years of membership, net transfers to the new member states on average totaled 1 percent of gross national product, which will treble in the next period.

Within the EU, regional policy funding is surrounded by some misconceptions, mainly related to its nature rather than its scale; these funds are by no means automatically transferred from Brussels to the national treasuries. EU funding entails much paperwork, coordination, planning, and control. The only legitimate indicator of efficiency is rational absorption—the money available must be used carefully and rationally. All the time and energy devoted to a project is in vain if it does not yield results in the end, if it is not in synergy with other projects in the region, or if it turns out to be economically unjustified. The task of the EU's new member states is made more difficult by the fact that, along with planning and managing the use of these vast sums of money, they also need to build regional institutions and consolidate the idea of regionalism in people's minds. It is indeed a unique opportunity not to be missed, but success is far from guaranteed.

The new Central and Eastern European EU members have been given this historic opportunity in extremely turbulent times. Their anchor of modernization, the EU, is struggling to come to grips with many economic and social problems and is on the defensive on many fronts. It is trying to tackle its distance behind the United States, the globalization epitomized by the Chinese economic juggernaut, and people's disappointment over unavoidable reforms. The new EU members share some of these problems but also have some different ones of their own. They must make up for decades and sometimes centuries of backwardness, necessitating painful reforms; and they are thus starting their economic and social modernization from a weaker position. It is nonetheless true, however, that their political and economic actors are not being held back by ossified traditions and institutions.

For example, Estonia's lightning-speed high-technology modernization shows what they can achieve.

The new EU member states are a rather diverse group, but there is at least one common denominator: They have all traveled the road of economic modernization underpinned by foreign direct investment and social modernization based on EU membership. They are fundamentally open, small economies, which are unable to free themselves from the subsequent direct or indirect effects of international trends. The rise of China has had an impact on all EU member states, but because most of the newcomers have specialized in products similar to those China makes (e.g., textiles, electronic goods, and cars), they face a more significant threat. The Eastern European EU member states cannot compete with China in the long run; their wages might be much lower than in the fifteen pre–2004 enlargement EU member states, but they are still considerably higher than those in Asia. Consequently, they increasingly attract investment in the high-technology industries and in high-value-added services. Nokia and Siemens both operate research and development centers in Hungary, while the data-processing centers of Siemens and Lufthansa are located in the Czech Republic. Central and Eastern Europe should aim at reinforcing this trend and invest heavily in education as a precondition for building a more advanced knowledge-based economy that can compete with both the West and Asia.

It is useful here to look at Ireland's experience in the EU.[45] Despite becoming a member of the European Community in 1973, Ireland lagged far behind the rest of Europe until the 1990s. Its employment composition and standard of living were very low. Today, however, it is far above the average for the EU's twenty-five member states—the fifteen pre–2004 enlargement member states and the ten member states that joined in 2004, before Bulgaria and Romania joined in 2007—in terms of GDP per capita, and its GDP is growing faster than that of the other member states. The Irish miracle (which was seriously weakened during the 2008–9 global financial and economic crisis) was largely the result of its geographical and cultural proximity to the United States. With its relatively low wages, it attracted American companies seeking to gain a foothold in Europe. And its economy benefited greatly from the American boom of the 1990s. Its proactive economic policy successfully transformed its favorable location and size into a competitive advantage and a source of development. This economic policy included slimming down expenditures and stepping up social partnerships. A favorable economic environment coupled with low taxation made the

Emerald Isle particularly attractive for foreign direct investment as well as local enterprises. Of course, the Irish example cannot be copied completely, but many of its elements merit consideration. The new EU member states differ substantially from Ireland, and the world around them has also changed a lot since the 1990s. There are, however, universal buzz words such as stability, competitiveness, and growth.

Political stability is somewhat self-evident in the club of European democracies, but club membership can also be the guarantee of economic stability, and its key token—the introduction of the euro. The introduction of the single currency presupposes a predictable and responsible economic policy, which is characterized by credibility, long-term sustainability, and an overriding concern for budgetary stability. This last element is especially important for aging societies, like Europe's.

The problems hindering the competitiveness of the EU's new member states lie in those sectors of society and the economy that have remained untouched by market transitions and modernization, either because they are not market based or because market forces are artificially excluded. Typical examples of such sectors include health care, agriculture, and public administration.

Growth in the EU's new member states means not only growing social prosperity but also the chance of catching up with the center. Without growth, there is no stability; without competitiveness, there is no growth. Therefore, it is essential for Central and Eastern Europe that its growth be based on a modern and competitive industrial and services sectors. Otherwise, its growth will only be a temporary phenomenon. In addition, its pace of growth must exceed that of the center if it is to have any chance of closing the gap with Western Europe. The two most important tasks that the region's newcomers must accomplish in the next few years are the introduction of the euro and the effective absorption and rational use of the EU's regional policy "Marshall Aid."

The title of this subsection already alluded to the fact that May 1, 2004—the day of Eastern and Western Europe's reunification—was a political giant but an economic dwarf. What makes this day a political giant? In essence, it was the day marking the reunification of Europe, which—oddly enough—was made possible by the cowardice of the European political elite, who did not have the courage to admit only the leading group of six EU candidate countries in the first wave and postpone the accession of the remaining four.

And what makes this day an economic dwarf? First, from a pan-European perspective, the economic weight of the new EU member states in the internal market is negligible, with less than 5 percent. Second, from an Eastern European perspective, accession was a mere formality, economically speaking; liberalization, the opening of markets, the transition to capitalism, and the approximation of legislation had taken place years earlier. Yet this does not detract one bit from the merits of the acceding countries. For a long decade, they strained every sinew to modernize their economies and societies, and keep to deadlines of legal approximation timetables, consulting the corporate sector, talking with trade unions, and investing heavily in transposing rules into practice. The implementation of European environmental standards alone cost the new member states €80–100 billion, 18 to 24 percent of the GDP of the ten EU member states that joined in 2004; and the transportation *acquis communautaire* cost another € 100 billion, 22 percent of their GDP.[46] These are shocking figures even with the transitional periods and the contribution of regional policy funds in mind.

Accession crowned a lengthy period of preparation with extraordinary efforts, but the economic impact of "Big Bang enlargement" has been rather limited. The reason for that is simple: The new EU member states are much poorer than the old ones—their combined GDP is 5 percent of the EU total, their combined population of 74 million is less than Germany's, and they are a minor export market for the fifteen old EU member states. Roughly 70 percent of the new member states' exports end up in the fifteen old member states, whereas Central and Eastern Europe is the destination of only 4 percent of the exports of the old member states. Similarly, the inflow of foreign direct investment from the West is essential to the economies of Central and Eastern European Countries, but much less so for the countries of origin.

According to 2004 figures, the fifteen pre–2004 enlargement EU member states invested eleven times more in each other's economies than they did in the ten member states that joined in 2004. Considering the asymmetrical trends, it can be said that the impact of enlargement was about twenty times larger in the new member states than in the old ones. The aggregate effect of the accession of the ten new countries on the EU's GDP growth during the period 2000–2009 was somewhere between 0.5 and 0.7 percent. Naturally, the effects of enlargement vary from one country to another; those Western European countries that are adjacent to the new member states benefited the most. And the GDPs of the ten new EU member states could increase by as much as 1 to 2 percent in the coming decade as a result of their membership.[47]

One of the biggest benefits for the old EU member states is the higher growth rate of the new entrants—double what Western Europe can boast—which will provide a dynamically expanding market for the industrial and services sectors of the fifteen old EU member states. (However, it needs to be noted again that the Central and Eastern European economies represent only a small part of the EU economy.) The pace of GDP growth in the new member states is on a par with that of the world's four largest developing countries—Brazil, Russia, India, and China, also known as the BRIC countries. But this comparison is misleading because, in fifty years' time, the four BRICs will be among the six biggest economies in the world, ahead even of Germany. Clearly, in this context, Central and Eastern Europe is of marginal significance economically.

Nevertheless, the EU's 2004 enlargement has yielded some important results. It has extended the single market from 380 to 450 million consumers, the biggest in the Western world, and it has established a new division of labor. It has provided new opportunities for enterprises based in the fifteen pre–2004 enlargement EU member countries to compete successfully against Asian companies by partly relocating production to Eastern Europe, where labor costs are considerably lower (12 percent of the EU average in Latvia, and 53 percent in Slovakia).[48] And foreign direct investment was concentrated in sectors most exposed to global competition, the automotive, pharmaceutical, and electronics industries. Although the process of relocation did mean that some Westerners lost their jobs, by helping companies remain competitive, it also meant that others could keep their jobs. Overall, the EU's Eastern European enlargement has been a success politically, and relatively painless economically.

However, it would be a big mistake to end the assessment of the EU's 2004 enlargement there. This last wave has weakened the Union's cohesion and increased its heterogeneity. It is true what they say: "It is not enough to be innocent. You must also look innocent." With twenty-seven EU members sitting around the table, it is considerably harder to reconcile views and make decisions than it was with fifteen. It should also be pointed out that this was the first time that widening and deepening did not go hand in hand. Previous enlargements happened in parallel with trade, internal market, or monetary harmonization measures. But the deepening of integration that was supposed to follow this last round of enlargement—the Constitution, a step toward a political union—ended in failure. Enlargement is one of the factors to be blamed for this failure, for it contributed to the anxieties of the people of Western Europe. But these anxieties were minor compared with the sentiments stirred by the prospect of the accession to the EU by Turkey, which is already banging on the gates of Europe as a hopeful candidate.

The White Crescent: Troubled Waters

There are children's nursery rhymes and stories all over Eastern Europe that feature the Turks as wicked characters, as the enemy. The Ottoman-Turkish occupation, which lasted for centuries, has obviously left a deep mark on the once-oppressed Christian peoples. The best-selling Hungarian book of all time, and still the most widely read today, is *Eclipse of the Crescent Moon,* a historical novel set in the sixteenth century and depicting the heroic Hungarian resistance against the Turkish invasion.[49] One of the most famous sadists in history, Vlad Tepes "the Impaler," who was known for his inhuman cruelty and on whom the character of Count Dracula is based, said that he had learned his methods of torture when held captive by the Ottoman Turks. The Turks were also responsible for the official death of the first united European empire, the Roman Empire—or to be precise, its weak successor, the Byzantine Empire—when they occupied Constantinople in 1453.

Of course, these historical events have no significance whatsoever for Turkey's EU accession; but they are useful to demonstrate the prejudices that are often more difficult to overcome than the most serious political disagreements. And as long as the Western public rejects Turkey's bid for membership in the European Union, it is unlikely to happen. The French went as far as amending their Constitution to make sure that every new enlargement could be put to a referendum. The European public is not crazy about the idea of letting Turkey inside the gates of Europe. And funnily enough, the Turkish public is not so crazy about the idea either; support for EU accession nose-dived from 67 percent in 2004 to 32 percent in 2006. In some EU member states, as much as 80 percent of the population is hostile to Turkish membership. National politicians are also divided over the issue; some EU skeptics would be happy to see Turkey join, for that would dilute the Union and more or less forever rule out the possibility of a political union. It is no accident that the United Kingdom supports Turkey's aspirations so enthusiastically.[50]

Turkey does not fit the traditional picture of a candidate country in several ways. The bulk of its area lies in Asia, although the geographical borders of Europe were drawn rather arbitrarily. The overwhelming majority of its population is Muslim. It is a huge but poor country with predominantly Asian traditions, where the norms of Western societies are only partially applied. Its political culture, interpretation of democracy, and treatment of human rights differ from Europe's. Before it can become a member of the EU, many problems must be sorted out—economic, political, and cultural ones. Europe will also need to figure out how to incorporate such a vast and populous country into the EU's decisionmaking mechanisms. By the time of its prospective accession (at least ten years from now), Turkey will be the Union's most populous state, but at the moment it is difficult to imagine a scenario in which an Asian, Muslim, backward country could have the strongest vote in EU decisionmaking. The spirit of Charlemagne and of the Blue Banana would have no traces left in such a Union. Clearly, Turkey's accession to the EU will be a watershed in Europe's destiny.

As things stand today, Turkey's accession would add 17 percent to the EU's surface area and 15 percent to its population, but only 5 percent to its GDP. It would, however, bring the Union's GDP per capita down by almost 10 percent, because Turkey stands at below 30 percent of the Community average in terms of development. The EU would have to reach deep into its pockets to support Turkey—about €17–18 billion annually, under the current rules. Clearly, that is not going to happen; wealthy EU member states were already reluctant to finance the 2004 Eastern European enlargement, which was much less of a financial burden.

In the 1960s, about 80,000 Turkish "guest" workers moved west each year, mostly to Germany; even today, 50,000 leave their home country behind every year in the hope of finding better opportunities in the western part of the continent. Today, there are about 3 million Turks living in the EU, and it is predicted that another 4 million will arrive before 2030.[51] These new arrivals may ease the labor shortage of an aging Europe, but they also create anxieties, which are fueled by a fear of Islam that is amplified by terrorism and the negative experiences that Germans have with simple, uneducated immigrants coming from backwoods Anatolian villages. These immigrants are as far culturally from Germans as they are from their compatriots in Istanbul; obviously, people would have a different image of Turks if the immigrants were better educated. There can be no doubt that Turkey's EU accession would change an awful lot of things in the EU. It would necessitate an overhaul of decisionmaking, the trimming of farm subsidies and cohesion-structural funding, sustained restrictions on the free movement of persons, and even deeper changes, including the creation of a multispeed Union.

Modern Turkey has been trying to edge closer to the West and Europe ever since it was born in 1923. It was Mustafa Kemal who laid the foundations of the modern Turkish state in place of the Ottoman Empire, which had been dismembered by the great powers in the wake of World War I. Mustafa Kemal was so highly respected that in 1934 Parliament awarded him the title of Atatürk—the father of all Turks. Despite his death in 1938, his foreign policy legacy ensured that Turkey chose the right side in World War II. He also initiated what later became a close partnership with the United States, evolving into a strategic alliance during the Cold War years. Turkey's role as a key American ally reinforced the already-central national role of the military, which from the beginning has been the guardian of Atatürk's reformed, secular republic. Atatürk entrusted the army with the task of safeguarding the Constitution and the unity of the republic, for which the generals were given strong competences as well as political and institutional powers guaranteed by law.

Relations between Turkey and neighboring Greece and Cyprus were riddled with tensions throughout the twentieth century. The tensions escalated into an armed conflict, giving NATO a nasty headache, because Turkey had been a NATO member since 1952. And these tensions have also been a source of much head-scratching for the EU; Turkish-occupied northern Cyprus is a political minefield in the ongoing EU membership talks with Turkey. The powerful Turkish army is in favor of EU membership for two basic reasons: It hopes that accession would reverse the recent Islamist revival, and it fears that opting out of the Union could devalue the country's geostrategic role. The government, conversely, would like to use EU membership to trim the generals' influence and prevent the country from becoming a powder keg, a venue for the "clash of civilizations." Naturally, the corporate sector can hardly wait to be inside the Union, just like members of minorities, who are looking forward to having their rights reinforced and extended. It is "only" Turkish society at large that shows little enthusiasm, and is in fact increasingly skeptical about the whole accession process.

Turkey first applied for associated status with the European Community back in 1959. The Association Agreement was concluded in 1963, and the two parties agreed on a twenty-two-year perspective for entering into a customs union. After several delays, the customs union became a reality in 1996, but—contrary to the original idea—it only applied to goods and was not extended to cover the free movement of persons, services, or capital. Turkey submitted its application for full EU membership in 1987, but it was rejected at the time. Unlike in the case of Morocco, whose application was turned down on the grounds that it was not a European country, the fact that Turkey is part of Europe has never been questioned. The argument for the 1987 rejection was that Turkey had not fulfilled the political criteria for membership. (The fact that Turkey's "European-ness" has never been doubted is of paramount importance, because the EU Treaty stipulates that only European countries can become members of the Union.)

The next major step forward toward EU membership came in 1999, when Turkey was officially recognized as a candidate country. Accession negotiations commenced on October 4, 2005, after Turkey fulfilled the last precondition and signed a protocol to the Ankara Agreement, extending its customs union with the fifteen pre–2004 enlargement EU member states to the ten new member states, including Cyprus. (Subsequently, Turkey issued a declaration explaining that the signing of the protocol was not tantamount to a recognition of the Republic of Cyprus.) Turkey has refused to recognize Cyprus, denying Cypriot vessels entry into its ports or aircraft landing rights at its airports. It is extraordinary that Turkey refuses to recognize but occupies part of an EU member state. The Cyprus issue is further complicated by the fact that the UN has taken charge, which means that, whatever solution emerges, it will not be under the EU's aegis.[52]

The Turks are vehement, at times aggressive, negotiating partners with the EU, but sooner or later they will have to understand what all applicant countries have learned before them: They are trying to join the Union, and not the other way around. (Brussels has pointed this out to Turkish diplomats on a number of occasions, until now to no avail.) They would be committing a mistake if they overestimated their strategic significance and were unable to find the correct negotiating tone—especially because there is already enough resistance to Turkey's accession not only among the public but also among politicians. Former EU commissioner Bolkestein is one of the leading advocates of the anti-Turkey camp. He argues that Turkey has never been and will never be part of European culture, because its values differ considerably from those of the West. Bolkestein and his followers believe that Europe has no idea what it is doing when opening the gates to Turkey; once Turkey has its foot inside the threshold, the EU cannot close the door on Armenia, Belarus, Georgia, Moldova, or Ukraine. Negotiations almost froze in 2008, and in 2009 nothing spectacular happened. In 2007, the EU declined to promise Turkey membership by 2014. (One year later, the EU also declined to offer Ukraine a clear path to membership.)[53] Turkish domestic relations have worsened significantly in the meantime, as the country has drifted away from the West—with a serious constitutional court case against the ruling party and the prime minister, ultimatums by the military, and the Islamization of domestic politics—causing headaches among EU leaders.

In 2009, Angela Merkel and Nicolas Sarkozy made it clear that Turkey has no place in the EU, at least not under the current membership conditions. "The EU must stop making vain promises to Turkey and study with it the creation of a big common economic and human space," said Sarkozy. "Privileged partnership, but no full membership," added the German chancellor.

One of the main arguments made by opponents of Turkish accession to the EU is that Turkey is not a Christian country. But, ironically, one of the main arguments of supporters of Turkish accession is the same: that Turkey is not a Christian country. These advocates argue that as a Muslim country, Turkey could act as a bridge between the Muslim and the Christian worlds and could serve as an example for other Muslim countries in the region. Rejecting Turkey's bid for membership, they maintain, could send the wrong message to the Muslim world: "Europe is a Christian stronghold, and we do not wish to share it with Muslims." In their view, this would bolt the gates between the two civilizations and probably bring about a further radicalization of Islam.

However, the truth is that, from a religious point of view, Turkey does not play a leading role in the Muslim world. Nor is it particularly rich, and because Atatürk reformed it into a secular republic, Islam is not seen to play a decisive role in people's daily lives. Turkey is also a member of NATO, and it has a special relationship with the United States, which only increases the Arab's world suspicion toward it. Turkey is striving to become a credible intermediary between the Christian (developed Western) and the Muslim worlds, but inconsistent steps and statements by its senior political figures are not helping its cause, for they only add to the suspicion of the West toward it. And Turkey's bilateral relations with most of its neighbors are tense, making it a potential conflict zone on the border of Asia and Europe. Finally, it has a significant Kurdish minority with secessionist aspirations.

Nevertheless, Turkey has considerable strategic value in more ways than one. It has a geostrategic importance—lying at the meeting point of the Balkans, the Middle East, and the Caucasus—although this significance has dwindled since the end of the Cold War. Turkish EU membership would give the Union a border with Iran and Syria, the thought of which scares many Europeans. Others, including Joschka Fischer, argue that this region will determine the security of the EU in the future, and thus the Union would be better off being present there.[54] It would not be in Europe's interest, to put it mildly, if a Turkey disillusioned with Europe were to build new friendships with Russia or Iran, both of which have been anti-West for centuries. Turkey's relations with Muslim countries could also come in handy in Europe's fight against terrorism. The "Turkish connection" would link Europe with the economies of Central Asia, which could be priceless for Europe's energy security. Turkey has an unbelievably young population, a real gold mine for an aging Europe. Turkish EU accession, or even its prospect and the related strategic planning, would force Europe to complete important reforms that it has been delaying for a long time. Turkey's accession would also beef up the EU's weight on the international scene. The question is how much of a difference it would make, when the size of states and regions is becoming less important, and should Europe not be focusing instead on ensuring that the Union can prosper and function smoothly?

The prospect of EU membership has served as an important source of inspiration and motivation for reforms in Turkey, which have yielded many benefits, from social transformation to foreign policy. The latter is clearly demonstrated by Turkey's much-improved relations with Greece. These reforms would not have happened without the prospect of EU membership; maintaining and continuing them would be an important achievement in itself. Radical constitutional changes have taken place in recent years; the Turkish Constitution was amended twice in three years, and thus the death penalty has been abolished, human rights have been extended, and the army's influence and power have been trimmed back. Reforms in Turkey have always come from the top, with force if necessary. For Turkey, EU accession is a question of principle and of identity. There are serious doubts—even in Turkey—about whether Turks are Europeans; ever since Atatürk's time, the elite has been doing its best to prove that Turkey is indeed European. For Turkey, therefore, belonging to Europe is a highly emotional issue, much more so than for the British or Norwegians, whose European-ness cannot be called into question, and who thus have the luxury to be choosy and decide whether they opt in or out, depending on which suits them best.

The Turkish economy became a true, functioning market economy following the reforms of the 1980s. Until then, it had been characterized by strong state control. In the past quarter century, the Turkish economy has witnessed both ups and downs. In the new millennium, since the nation's economic crisis in 2001, it has regained its health; it has managed to apply the brakes and bring its triple-digit inflation down to a manageable level, but some persistent problems remain unsolved. Only 45 percent of working-age people are actively employed (for women, the employment rate is barely 25 percent); and the general standard of education is appalling. And regional disparities are huge; the eastern part of the country lives in feudal conditions, while the western coastal provinces are booming, attracting twice as much capital in 2005–6 as in the previous twenty years. Reforms continue, with giant strides both in the economy and society. And, as suggested above, Turkey's 73 million citizens make up Europe's youngest society—one out of four Turks is below fifteen years of age.

Turkey's potential accession to the EU, which differs from previous accession rounds, entails a great number of challenges as well as opportunities for the EU. EU-Turkey relations will be a large factor in determining the future course of European integration. It is difficult to predict what the relationship between the EU and Turkey will look like in ten or twenty years—whether opponents or advocates of Turkish EU membership will get the upper hand. Europe must be careful not to make irresponsible promises, while making sure that Turkey does not lose its drive to become part of the West. There is a huge difference between full membership and a "special partnership," the idea floated by many European politicians but yet to be defined as a clear concept. Many important decisions lie ahead, among them the eternal dilemma of the EU's "deepening" versus "widening." The question is whether Turkey will turn east or west and what impact that will have on Europe.

Boundaries and Concepts

The borders of Europe are not clearly defined; no one has ever drawn them definitively. In political terms, such borders do not exist, but Europe is also different from other continents in geographical terms. As Jacques Barzun notes in his prescient and grandiose book *From Dawn to Decadence,* "Europe is the peninsula that juts out from the great mass of Asia without a break and is ridiculously called a continent."[55] In fact, Europe is the only continent whose borders are indistinct; in the east, the artificial boundary between Europe and Asia is defined by the watershed of the Ural Mountains and the Caspian Sea. Europe is the second-smallest continent behind Australia; it only occupies about 2 percent of the Earth's landmass. The European Union is the biggest political entity on the continent; Russia, with its European territory west of the Urals, comes second. Russia, thereby, is the largest and most populous European country, with three out of four Russians living in Europe and every fourth one in Asia, east of the Urals. Does all this not sound a bit too confusing? It does to me—and I am probably not the only one.

Europe is equally difficult to define in cultural terms. Its core heritage is the cultural values of the "West," which it inherited from the Frankish and Carolingian empires; the Iberian and other formerly semiperipheral cultures only became part of mainstream Europe later on. Christianity does not define European culture perfectly either, because Enlightenment and civic values—which are now considered universal Western values—often evolved in conflict with Christian ideology. The state and society have undergone considerable secularization over the course of the centuries, on top of which non-Christian religions have grown in significance in Europe in the last few decades. Nonetheless, there exists a "Blue Banana" ethos, which can be best defined as the set of fundamental Western—or, if you like, European— values. Charles de Gaulle's veto of British EU membership was rooted in geostrategic envy rather than cultural opposition. Even though both Spain and Portugal had been ruled by fascist dictators until their accession to the EU, no one ever questioned their "European-ness." It was a similar case for both Greece, and—with some generosity—the eight new Central and Eastern European EU members, even though the former lived under Turkish occupation for long centuries and the latter had just emerged from fifty years of Soviet domination.

Europe's history is one of wars, migrations, deportations, resettlements, the mixing of peoples and cultures, and the proliferation of ideologies. European identity is an evasive concept—the closer we look, the harder it is to define Europe's cultural and spiritual frontiers. Yet they are palpable. Feeling where Europe's borders lie, however, is an insufficient ground for crucial political decisions on which nation is and which is not admissible to the EU. Clearly, the European Union has come to the point where it is stretching its own operational limits. Historical experience shows that international integration going beyond governmental cooperation has never been able to function successfully in the long term with more than ten members. Western European integration has been held together by the adhesive bond of interdependence and the "natural" cohesion that had evolved through centuries of institutional and cultural coexistence. The end of the Cold War and a rapid increase in the European Community's heterogeneity will corrode cohesion in the long run unless the Community reforms its operational model.

The history of the EU can be considered a series of enlargements; thus, its six enlargement rounds have quadrupled its number of members, trebled its area, and doubled its population. At present, there are three official candidates and five or six applicants for EU membership lined up at the gates of Europe. According to the European Union's Founding Treaties, every European state that respects democracy and the rule of law can apply for membership. But the question is whether further enlargement will dynamite, revitalize, or destabilize the Union. Will further enlargement redefine the Union, and must it redefine itself as a result of repeated enlargements? What is the real aim of further enlargement: economic prosperity or improved stability? There are many crucial questions waiting to be answered.

However, the most exciting question of them all is: Where do (will) the EU's geographic and functional borders lie? The answer to this mother of all questions will depend on the political reality of the time. With respect to the question's first aspect, geography, European citizens feel that the Union's frontiers have been extended all the way to the ends of Europe as a geographical and cultural entity. With respect to the second aspect— Where do Europe's functional borders lie? Or, in other words, what can Brussels have a say in?—the answer will largely depend on the answer to the first: How far can the EU stretch? Beyond a certain point, which is difficult to define precisely, enlargement will shape the Union. This will be a revolutionary new period compared with the previous enlargements, which have only modified the EU's functioning, credo, and institutional machinery. During the course of their accession, the new members adopted, transposed, and applied the full body of Community law, in large measure unconditionally, while the EU legal cosmos has been expanding, like the universe, at increasing speed, covering newer and newer areas with more and more rules, guidelines, and court rulings—and thus creating functional expansion.

The EU's continuous geographic expansion, however, makes many Europeans anxious, because they would dread to see the EU behave like a cosmic universe and become diluted, empty, and cold. Conversely, the EU's functional expansion is widely considered an essential and inherent feature of European integration. A popular allegory describes this integration as a bicycle: If you stop pedaling—if the EU stops evolving, and its members stop driving it forward with political visions and new legal instruments covering new areas—the bicycle will fall over. This is a real worry shared by many Europeans, who are convinced that Europe should put further enlargements on hold, regroup, digest previous enlargements, and do something about the rejected Constitutional Treaty. A growing number of voices are saying out loud that Europe should stop beating about the bush and define clearly where its borders lie. In September 2006, Nicolas Sarkozy joined the taboo breakers when, in a speech, he said: "We must declare who is European and who is not!" The Balkan nations, Iceland,[56] Norway, and Switzerland are part of Europe; therefore, they can join the EU if they wish to. Others, including Turkey, of course, are not; therefore, they can at best only enjoy a special partnership with the EU. Membership is out of the question.

The EU is fundamentally a practical manifestation of traditional integration theory; thus, it has evolved from a customs union first into an internal market covering millions of economic sectors and then into a monetary union. For a few months, it seemed that it would make a significant symbolic step toward becoming a political union. Then came the French and Dutch NO to the Union's most ambitious political project yet: the European Constitution. The model of linear evolution crashed spectacularly, not least because Western Europeans were scared by the breakneck speed of enlargement dictated by the political elite. Hardly had people digested the ten newcomers from 2004 when Bulgaria and Romania were in already in 2007, with Turkey approaching quickly on the radar screen. Enlargement is not the most popular project in Europe; it is rejected by close to 60 percent of Germans and Austrians. At the same time, popular support for EU membership also keeps falling in the new member states; in the mid-1990s, almost 80 percent of Poles expressed a belief that EU membership was a good thing; ten years later, only half as many did. In 2000, an impressive 75 percent of Croats polled in favor of their country's accession to the EU (the only candidate enjoying the majority backing of the Western European public); but in 2005 only 36 percent were still in favor. As we have seen, many factors contributed to the rejection of the EU Constitution, but oddly none was really directly connected to the Constitution itself but rather to member states' domestic political, social, or economic weaknesses. In the face of all these difficulties, the European Union will find the way—according to the bicycle allegory—to save as much of the Constitution as possible. And with the Lisbon Treaty, it really did a very good job.

The big question is how further EU enlargements are going to change the course and face of European integration. Over the course of the coming decades, the change could be dramatic, as far as the operation and ethos of the EU are concerned. The prospect of Croatia's accession will by definition provoke the amendment of the Nice Treaty—the current Founding Treaty—because the present rules cap Union membership at twenty-seven. The prospective accession of Turkey and the other many hopeful would-be entrants could induce even deeper changes. One of the key questions that must be answered is what Europeans want integration to do for them. The kind of pan-European socioeconomic architecture that the citizens of the continent's nations want for the future will determine how future waves of enlargements are handled.

Several schools of thought are clashing over this issue. One would like to see a more intense institutionalization of European integration, another wishes to move toward a political union of European peoples, and yet another extreme camp sees no role for integration other than ensuring free trade and economic liberties. The end of the Cold War made it blatantly obvious that stability—political, economic, or security—is something that the EU can offer neighboring countries without giving them full membership, which is a cheaper form of regional stability that puts less strain on the core project of integration. The economic motivation to press on with enlargement has dwindled because the EU has already established some form of economic cooperation with almost all the European countries, thus bringing to the forefront alternatives to full membership, such as special reinforced partnerships. So far, there has been no precedent for a country acceding to the EU without full rights as a member, apart from temporary transitional periods. Staying out of a certain aspect of integration has been more of a stigma than a success. Second-class membership has fundamentally been a solution requested by second-class members, which the Central and Eastern European countries found hard to swallow but which will become a much more crucial issue in the future.

Until now, with some exceptions—such as the single currency and the Schengen Agreement, which eliminates all internal border controls between its signatories—the EU's geographic enlargement ("widening") has always gone hand in hand with its functional expansion ("deepening"). Thus, new members always signed up to all aspects of integration and pledged to accede at an early stage to those functional areas that they could not join upon accession (typically, the euro zone). Yet obviously, beyond a certain point, geographical enlargement and functional expansion (or maintenance) can no longer be coupled. For the decades ahead, Europe will need to come up with a new evolutionary model. As we have seen, the EU's 2004 enlargement from fifteen to twenty-five members did not destabilize it. Although it fell short of the dream of revitalizing the European economy, it had a beneficial impact, even if ever so slight. The single most important fallout of the 2004 enlargement was that it launched a widespread political and social debate on redefining Europe. Enlargement did come as somewhat of a shock to the Western European public, which—unfortunately—was often exacerbated by populist politicians. The tensions stirred up by the Iraq war and American statements about "old" and "new" Europe only added fuel to the fire.

The EU enlargements of the future—if there are going to be any—will be very different insofar as they will force the EU to really redefine itself. Turkey's accession has a huge potential to revitalize the continent's economy in the long run, but carries an equally big risk of potentially destabilizing the Union politically. That is why Europe must have a clear model and vision for the future before embarking on the next rounds of enlargements, which will bring a standoff between a developed and an undeveloped region. The developed region cannot be expected to give up its market rules; the undeveloped one cannot be expected to fully adopt and implement the hundred thousand pages of the *acquis communautaire*. The center cannot be expected to allow the workers of the periphery in or to finance a new Europe stretching from the Atlantic all the way to the Middle East.

When elaborating future EU enlargement strategies, it must be clarified whether enlargement is an instrument of expanding the area of European prosperity or of ensuring regional stability. The original motivation behind European integration was to create peace and security, by putting Germany and France at the same table with other Western European nations and making war between them practically impossible. This plan worked; Europe's nations were united in a friendly club. Of course, it helped immensely that the United States contributed a lot of money and the Cold War stimulated cohesion. As a bonus, the peaceful coexistence of democracies brought unprecedented prosperity to Western Europe.

The situation is radically different today. The European center has never been more stable and cooperative, the Cold War stalemate is long gone, and there are many ways—military, political, economic, and cultural—to manage conflicts near the borders of Europe. It is legitimate to ask whether the unstable states on Europe's periphery ought to be given full EU membership just to stabilize them, knowing that they are unlikely to contribute much to prosperity but will certainly make the EU's functioning more complicated and cumbersome (e.g., for decisionmaking). Or should the EU instead offer them free trade, investment, and targeted aid? There have been many suggestions on how to overhaul the EU's European neighborhood policy to intensify relations by expanding the policy to a "European Commonwealth of Nations." This could result in a special relationship between the EU and associated states, covering a customs union, certain financial transfers, and wide technical coordination but not the single currency, employment, or any decisionmaking role. This European Commonwealth could have its own decisionmaking bodies and other organs and even speak with a single voice on the international scene.

Future EU enlargements could also have a major influence on public opinion about the EU itself and put into a new perspective the EU's key credos, such as solidarity (i.e., regional policy) and its complicated but fair (i.e., positively discriminating in favor of small states) decisionmaking procedures. Despite all these challenges and dilemmas, it is most probable that the geographical expansion of European integration will continue in the coming decades. As the global race intensifies, regionalism is set to grow in strength and the EU is set to continue enlarging, which will not leave the model of integration unchanged. In the long run, the EU will be able to choose from at least three main roads, which I would describe as two-speed Europe, flexible Europe, and network Europe. All three of these models would mean a break with the present, coherent, "monolith Europe" model, in which the same Community standards apply to all EU members, which are all fully involved in functional expansion. Whichever road Europe goes down on, ultimately the choice will be prompted by enlargement.

Two-speed Europe is not a newfangled idea; social analysts and politicians have been toying with the idea for a while, but it has been in the news more often recently. The concept of a two-speed Europe is rooted in the recognition that in a wider and more heterogeneous Europe, it is increasingly difficult for member states to develop at the same pace; therefore, states that want to and can push ahead with integration faster than the rest should be allowed to form a pioneer group that bring those areas (e.g., foreign policy, social policy, or taxation) under Community competence that other states would rather keep for themselves.

The fundamental problem with this two-speed model is not that some member states wish to proceed with integration faster than others, because the door is open to all that want to join later on. But what if the leading pack wants to go not just faster but in a different direction from the rest? This could create all sorts of problems, especially if the hard core attempted to build a protective wall around a completely different socioeconomic model. Just imagine if the credo of such a core Europe was to follow the outdated social model, protect national champions (large, partly state-owned incumbents), prevent tax competition, and seek introversion driven by a fear of globalization and protectionism. Would potential new member states or the Nordic countries ever want to join such a group? This is rather unlikely, just as it is unlikely that such an arrangement would do much good for the continent's competitiveness.

Of course, this example is a fictitious work of my imagination, but because of recent developments, it is not completely plucked out of the air. At the moment, the European center is wary of new members in a number of ways; politicians and analysts often point the finger at Central and Eastern Europe and use European dumping as a scapegoat. The EU's new member states, with their cheap workers and lower-than-average social standards, are supposedly guilty of "social dumping" and of encouraging a "race to the bottom." In fact, they are the family cat on whom everybody takes out their anger, when the real culprits are the Indian tiger and the Chinese dragon. Another characteristic of this two-speed model is that any move toward a political union—which is most likely in this particular model—will necessarily happen in core Europe, among the members of the avant-garde group.

Flexible Europe is similar to the previous model insofar as it would entail cores, or alliances, whose members would move ahead more quickly with integration, leaving the others behind. Participation in such a core group would be voluntary and open to newcomers or any country that changes its mind. There are examples of this already in place; just think of the euro or Schengen. The difference, compared with the previous model, is that instead of a "leading pack" and a "laggers' group," there would be several ad hoc, flexible partnerships, each formed for one specific area, and much less institutionalized than in the two-speed model.

This flexible model would not require any major legislative changes, because the Nice Treaty already allows for "enhanced cooperation," on two conditions: (1) At least one-third of the member states must be involved, and (2) it must remain open for participation to all the other member states. It goes without saying that such enhanced cooperation cannot run counter to the EU's common values. This form of flexible integration could have some disadvantages, however; it could add to the complexity of the EU and, in the worst-case scenario, could encourage certain member states to dismantle a valuable part of the existing rules. Informal intergovernmental alliances are not unprecedented; for example, there are three EU members—France, Germany, and the United Kingdom—vis-à-vis Iran; five

EU members—France, Germany, Italy, Spain, and the United Kingdom—cooperating on terrorism; and the seven signatories to the Prüm Treaty on police cooperation and information exchange—Austria, Belgium, France, Germany, Luxembourg, the Netherlands, and Spain.

Theoretically, this could mean that the EU's Constitution is formally divided into several parts—a central Founding Treaty, which all members sign, and other sectoral treaties (e.g., Home Affairs, Foreign Affairs, the euro), which would remain optional. The clash of the prowidening British and prodeepening French positions has left its mark on the history of European integration, but the question has become theoretical; the Union is enlarging at a pace that defies imagination. The EU's enlargement is definitely happening too quickly for its member states to digest. No wonder that an increasing number of people are asking this question: Where are the limits of the EU's capacity to absorb new members? More and more observers believe that, without clearly defining the borders of Europe, it will be impossible to regain the support of citizens for the European project.

In the European Union of twenty-seven members, the chances of adopting a new Founding Treaty are dwindling fast, and thus the Union's decisionmaking procedures and its political architecture must be reformed, at least to allow countries that want to push ahead faster to do so. An obvious choice for the avant-garde group would be the euro zone, which would not necessarily mean that they should aim for a political union. That would make it considerably easier for the United Kingdom to jump on the bandwagon. I have already referred above to the difficulties of closer cooperation in the area of fiscal harmonization, but enhanced cooperation should not be ruled out in justice and home affairs or defense either.

Flexible integration could play a major role in maintaining support for enlargement and alleviating the fear that further enlargement would weaken the EU's institutions and its solidarity. Moreover, in a more flexible Union, applicant countries would be more willing to accept longer transitional periods, delaying their full participation in certain Community policies, which would also considerably reduce the costs of enlargement and sugarcoat future enlargements for the skeptics.

Network Europe would be the most diluted, least cohesive of the three models, applicable in the distant future, when the borders of Europe have been extended beyond the continent's geographic frontiers. In this model, Brussels would act as the main center of coordination where the basic rules are set, and it would be surrounded by several subregional centers of cooperation. The credo of this form of integration could be a free market as a bare minimum, but members would be allowed to go much further in harmonization and coordination. Even an avant-garde group could have a place in network Europe, in which case the voting system would positively discriminate in favor of the core group, except for decisions on the most fundamental issues. Enlargements would have new strings attached—not only long transitional periods but even permanent exclusion from certain policies, which would institutionalize second-class membership. The Mediterranean Union, an alliance between the Southern European EU member states and the North African and Near Eastern countries—which was proposed by Nicolas Sarkozy in 2008, partly to find a way out of the Turkish deadlock, but was later watered down by Germany—would have been something very close to this network Europe concept.

Whichever road the European Union takes, it must recognize two things. First, in the long run, the right answer to globalization is EU enlargement. Second, enlargement requires a carefully planned and appropriately flexible long-term strategy. It is one thing to determine what forms of cooperation the EU allows for its members, and it is another—more revolutionary—thing to control the extent to which it allows its external partners to take part in common policies and decisionmaking. Not to mention how much enhanced partnership would satisfy partners aiming for full membership—something tells me, not very much. No matter which model Europe chooses, its boundaries will certainly become blurred in the coming decades.

Europeans need—more than ever—a strong and efficient European Union, which promotes their interests and values and is not fearful about the challenges of globalization. Such a Union does not have to be a political union. Europeans must not allow orthodoxy to cloud their thinking and put form ahead of content. It would be a big mistake for Europeans to first decide which model they want to build—two-speed Europe, flexible Europe, or network Europe—and then tailor their common values and principles according to the chosen model. The process should work exactly the other way around. Thus, Europeans must first decide what they want Europe to do for them, what they want from European integration, and then build a model suited to the task. Politicians will need to concentrate on this issue; in fact, some of them already started a while ago. The French president, Sarkozy, went one step further; he wanted to set up of a group of "wise men" with the mandate to conceptualize Europe's future, with special attention to the definition of its final borders. What happened instead was the setting up of a "reflection group" with no mandate to "define" the frontiers of the European Union.

As I said above, I am convinced that a two-speed Europe is the best option. This model is flexible enough to cater to those EU members that cannot or do not want to move as fast as the others. At the same time, it guarantees that a strong, coherent, internationally visible political Europe will be born as the core of the continent's integration.

* * *

Further Reading

For basic knowledge of the European Union, a good guide is Nicholas Moussis, *Access to the European Union: Law, Economics, Policies* (Brussels: European Study Service, 2003). On European identity and culture, I recommend William Outhwaite, *European Society* (Cambridge: Polity Press, 2008). On the complex institutional functioning of the EU, a helpful source is Helen Wallace and William Wallace, eds., *Policy-Making in the European Union*, 4th ed. (Oxford: Oxford University Press, 2000).

On the euro, its functioning, and its future options you can consult Simon Tilford, *Will the Eurozone Crack?* (Brussels: Centre for European Reform, 2006); and S. Adam Posen, ed., *The Euro at Five: Ready for a Global Role?* Special Report 18 (Washington, D.C.: Institute for International Economics, 2005). A veteran German banker's essays on the euro and politics are also useful: Otmar Issing, *Economic and Monetary Union in Europe: Political Priority versus Economic Integration* (Frankfurt: European Central Bank, 2001); and Otmar Issing, *Europe: Common Money—Political Union?* (Frankfurt: European Central Bank, 1999).

With regard to EU foreign policy, I recommend Eneko Landaburu (a high-ranking EU official), "Hard Facts about Europe's Soft Power," *Europe's World* (Brussels), Summer 2006. On enlargement, I recommend Olli Rehn (the EU's commissioner for enlargement), *"Europe's Next Frontiers,* Munich Contributions to European Unification 14 (Baden Baden: Nomos, 2006); and Paola Subacchi, *What Does a Larger EU Mean for the European Economy? Looking at 2005 and Beyond,* Conference Paper (London: Chatham House, 2004), http://www.chathamhouse.org.uk/publications/papers/download/-/id/527/file/9642_081104subacchi.pdf.

On EU–United States relations, an interesting view about the ever-deeper divide between the two regions is given by Jeffrey Kopstein and

Sven Steinmo, eds., *Growing Apart? America and Europe in the Twenty-first Century* (Cambridge: Cambridge University Press, 2008). The relations between Europe and China (besides routine EU-China dealings) are rather poorly documented, but for a good comprehensive overview from culture through economics to politics, see David Shambaugh, Eberhard Sandschneider, and Zhou Hong, eds., *China-Europe Relations* (London: Routledge, 2008). On EU-China relations in general, a useful source is the *EU-China Observer*, the monthly bulletin of the College of Europe in Bruges, Belgium.

Chapter 5

Europe 2050

This chapter endeavors to grasp the essence of European integration. Also, building on the evidence presented in the previous chapters, it seeks to look into the future—assessing the outlook for the old continent and, in a broader sense, that for the West.

What Is the EU?

The European Union lacks the most important features of a nation-state—an army, a significant budget, a cultural identity. But it does have a very sophisticated legal system that binds together all its member states and common institutions. This section looks at the dimensions of the EU's identity.

The Street of the Law

Rue de la Loi—Street of the Law, the main street of the EU district in Brussels—is by day the scene of a unique tableau: diplomats inching forward in stop-and-go traffic in their CD-licensed BMWs, European Commission interns (*stagiaires*) riding along its red bike path ringing their bells to scare the news-hungry journalists out of their way, lobbyists chasing officials on their daily trip around the European Council's and European Commission's many buildings. I wonder how many of them ask themselves: What is the European Union?

Brussels is a combination of two very different worlds. On the one hand, it is a European city with a nice but not too impressive center, green parks so numerous that most continental capitals pale in comparison, and run-down districts inhabited mainly by immigrants. There is nothing surprising in this.

On the other hand, Brussels is also home to a unique world, the only postmodern mini-state, commonly referred to as the EU Quarter. All capitals have government districts, but this one is different. This is a world of "Franglais" or "Frenglish," where sentences begin in French and end in English, and where nobody is surprised if a French noun is followed by an English verb. This is a world where ambassadors often spend all night arguing whether an "and" should be replaced by an "or." And this is a world where, when prime ministers have two minutes in the elevator, they decide on the spending of billions of euros or the fate of EU accession countries.

Brussels' EU Quarter is wedged between the historic city center and the posh suburban residential areas, almost like an arm of the old Brussels reaching out toward the east. Downtown Brussels and the EU Quarter are connected by two four-lane, one-way streets, both constantly blocked by traffic jams, except for late in the evening. The Rue de la Loi leads the endless lines of cars from the EU institutions to the center, while the Rue Belliard channels traffic in the opposite direction. On the side streets, there are endless rows of boring, gray office blocks housing corporate offices or European Commission services. One such battered building is home to the Directorate-General for Agriculture, which annually distributes and manages funds equivalent to about one and a half times Slovakia's gross domestic product (GDP). A few meters down the street, another modest if slightly more modern office building houses rigorous officials who show little mercy when making the final decision about billion-dollar mergers or handing out hefty fines. This glass-and-concrete building houses the Directorate-General for Competition—the EU's competition watchdog, dreaded even by Bill Gates, the world's richest man and cofounder of Microsoft, which the directorate fined $500 million in 2004 and another $250 million two years later. In 2009, the European Commission imposed another $1 billion fine on an American firm; this time it was Intel, which was found guilty of breaching the EU antitrust laws.

At one point, both streets disappear and continue underground—this is the Rond-Point Schuman, dominated by the EU Council and Commission headquarters buildings on opposite sides. The Council's building, named after Justus Lipsius (often referred to as the Tomb of the Pharaohs), serves as the venue for meetings between heads of government and ministers. Across the street stands the recently refurbished Berlaymont Building where, on the thirteenth floor, you will find the office of the man with the world's most difficult job: the European Commission's president. Law is the cement that binds modern Europe together.

Hundreds and hundreds of warpaths crisscrossing the highway of history have led us to the Street of the Law. And many intellectual streams have brought Europe this far: Christianity, Greek philosophy, Roman law, the Renaissance, the Reformation, the Enlightenment, the modern notion of the nation-state, and the fight for the respect of human rights. In the early years of feudalism, Europe, the Western world, was much less developed than China, the Muslim world, or the Byzantine Empire. In 969, when the ambassadors from Otto I—then head of the German-Roman Empire, which never possessed any real power during its millennium of existence—presented their credentials to the Byzantine emperor, he did not know whether to laugh or get angry at the insolence of these "wretched western barbarians."

The shared faith of Christianity and the appearance of the common enemy in the shape of Islam in the seventh century did create some sense of European-ness, but its importance should not be overestimated. After his unsuccessful attempts at uniting Europeans against the Ottoman Empire, Pope Pius II asked, "Who can understand all European languages and know the traditions of all European nations? Who could mediate between the English and the French? Who could unite the Genoese and the Aragonese, or the Hungarians and the Czechs?" Paradoxically, the appearance of Islam not only helped the development of a European identity by uniting the continent against this common enemy but also because most ancient scientific achievements were transmitted to feudal Europe by the Muslim Arabs. An emblematic moment for Europe came in 732, at the Battle of Poitiers, when the Frankish ruler Charles Martel fought off the tide of Arabs, pushing them back beyond the Pyrenees, and thereby prevented the "Islamization" of Europe. This would later allow Charlemagne—Martel's grandson, the Father of Europe (pater Europae)—to begin the integration of Christian Europe. His imperial seal read Renovatio Imperii Romani.

The elementary symbolic power of Charlemagne is best illustrated by the everlasting Franco-German debate over whether he was French or German. His reign and empire were short-lived (just like those of Napoleon and Hitler, both of whom attempted the integration of Europe a thousand years later on the two sides of the Rhine, however peculiar or terrible their means may have been) and Europe's peoples fought numerous wars in the centuries thereafter. Europe only managed to rid itself of the Muslim threat eight hundred years later with King John III Sobieski's 1683 victory near Vienna, which also marked a turn in the course of events; as Christian states grew in strength, they gradually overpowered the Muslim world. As a consequence, Europe began defining its identity vis-à-vis Russia, which took over as the center of Orthodox Christianity.

In the meantime, during the Reformation, "Western Europe" was torn apart along religious lines as the reformed church emerged with its many variations. The Enlightenment and the Industrial Revolution further reduced the role of the church and accelerated the pace of secularization and the separation of church and state. But there was no sign of a similar evolution in Muslim areas and, in some places, little has changed up to today. The merely religious opposition of the two civilizations was transformed; they now had completely different approaches to statehood. In Charlemagne's era, Europe signified a loosely defined geographical area that shared a certain degree of nostalgia for the Roman Empire. Almost a thousand years would need to pass for that to change.

The first known map showing Europe's peoples with uniform symbolism dates from 1544 and bears the title *Europa in forma virginis.* A young woman—Europe—is pictured, with Spain as her head, Italy and Denmark as her arms, France and Germany as her body, and Bohemia as her heart. She has the Eastern European countries (Hungary, Prussia, Lithuania, and Russia) under her belt, and some countries under Turkish rule at the time (Albania and Bulgaria) are also featured.[1] Europe did not exist in a political sense at the time, but the shared religion and common traditions surrounded the continent's countries and drew its cultural borders. The idea of the Roman Empire, of "uniting civilized lands under a single ruler," was never lost, and Latin continued to provide linguistic cohesion for a long time. In the seventeenth century, after the first war to merit the "world" adjective—the Thirty Years' War—modern Europe was formed, and political states and center-periphery relations ossified between East and West.

By the early nineteenth century, when the continent's nation-states emerged, it became natural to refer to "Europe" and "European civilization." But the process of defining European civilization as a continent—with the world's most advanced culture and economy, and as the only place where freedom existed—began earlier, during the Enlightenment. France created the prototype of the modern constitution, which later served as a model for many European peoples. Liberalism and the establishment of the constitutional system went hand in hand in Europe.

This was, of course, no coincidence; it came as a direct consequence of European social architecture and development, which—in addition to the absolute monarch—had always granted the nobility a high degree of autonomy, guaranteed by law the security and inheritability of private property, and thus favored the formation of an autonomous middle class. Europe had come a long way by the end of feudalism, but it was still far from global dominance. Only in the age of early capitalism did Europe became a leading region of the world in intellectual, economic, and geostrategic terms alike.

Capitalism presupposes civil values and industrialization, which require not only political reforms and economic modernization but also—first and foremost—free, diligent, and enterprising citizens. According to Max Weber's narrative, the evolution of this type of person was largely shaped by the ideology of the Reformation, primarily the Calvinist version.[2] Originally, Calvinist teachings said that God chooses those sinful souls whom he will save from eternal perdition. But such a dogma is not the best way to encourage followers to work hard. Realizing this flaw, Calvinist theologians introduced a loophole: God may not communicate to you whether you are predestined for salvation or damnation, but he gives you one clue: Those who work hard for economic and financial success can be more certain of salvation. Thus, you should work hard, compete fairly, be rational, increase your wealth, not be wasteful, believe in yourself, and know that you can only count on yourself. At the dawn of the development of civic society, the forerunner of the liberal ideology appeared, with the—nowadays bizarre-sounding—aim of "obtaining" the freely given grace of God Capitalism was born, and with it also came animosity against the purpose-oriented, seemingly cold, and arrogant ideology of liberalism.

The other main ideology of the Reformation, Lutheranism, differs from Calvinism in many aspects. Lutherans do not trust the propriety of human motivations and thus believe that social institutions ensuring the welfare of society must be concentrated in the hands of the state and not in the hands of self-organized civil society. In Lutheranism, political governance (i.e., the state) is entrusted with the task of building a welfare state. No one can be certain—even if they do their best—of living in prosperity as a result of their hard work. Consequently, there is a need to redistribute wealth so that everyone gets their fair share, not only the most needy. For Lutherans, work is not the declaration of divine grace but the redistribution of God's gifts.

This book has attempted to delineate the various European socioeconomic models and sociopolitical approaches, because their reform is the key to the continent's success. The previous paragraphs hopefully make it clear how deeply the different socioeconomic models are rooted in the traditions of Western Europe. When creating their own model, countries are remarkably faithful to their different religious and social traditions. And it is also apparent just how deeply rooted are the ideological conflicts between liberalism and social solidarity in Europe.

What Is a Hermaphrodite Good For?

Recently, a close acquaintance bluntly told me that the European Union is only good for those on its payroll, that Brussels is just a bureaucracy of overpaid good-for-nothing officials. Such views are by no means rare. A more sophisticated observer would tend to say that the European Union is the symbol of crushed illusions and unfulfilled expectations. But both of them are wrong and unaware. I am not implying that there is no room for criticism: The EU is far from being the most perfect of all worlds; much could and should be improved. As long as war in the EU remains in the category of science fiction (thanks to Franco-German reconciliation), as long as Europeans hardly have to slow down when crossing borders driving along six-lane highways, and as long as they can freely study, shop, do business, or work in any other EU member state, one should not make the mistake of speaking evil of the EU only because it is boring, its decisionmaking is cumbersome, or it does not double people's salaries overnight.

On television, I often see reporters and invited public figures competing as to who can put down the EU better, saying things like: "If X or Y European politician can come out with such statements, what is the EU good for?" From time to time, the extreme foolishness of Brussels-made rules resurface in public discourse, causing either public hilarity or dismay. Surely you have heard the urban legends of Brussels regulating the size and curvature of bananas and cucumbers. My personal favorite was the nationwide concern in Hungary—a poppy-seed superpower—that the EU would ban poppy-seed cakes following the nation's accession to the Union. Perhaps it is naïveté or perhaps it is a lack of knowledge that leads people to confuse the important with the spectacular. European integration can take a lot of battering; but we must not confuse the odd political statement from Brussels or from any other capital with the essence of the European Union. Helping people to comprehend this distinction was one of my aims when I decided to write this book. People have nothing to be ashamed of. The former U.S. secretary of state, Madeleine Albright, supposedly once said that, to understand how the EU works, one needs to be either a genius or at least French. There is some truth in this; and this is partly the reason for the lack of interest in and the animosity toward the EU.

Jacques Delors, the former European Commission president, called the EU a UPO—an unidentified political object. The former Italian premier, Giuliano Amato, called the EU a hermaphrodite, whose institutions and operations blur the line between interstate and federal organizations. In an interstate organization, it would be the EU member states, whereas in a federal organization, it would be the Union's common institutions that have the right and competence to make decisions directly influencing citizens' lives. Amato believes that we must accept this unique creature as it is—first, because it is the result of decades of natural evolution based on the balance of political power; and, second, because it works rather well, despite its peculiarity. The EU is a blend of the primacy of European Community law and soft (nonbinding) cooperation based on voluntary coordination and mutual learning. Its hermaphroditic features were quite apparent in the failed EU Constitution, which proposed a double-hatted foreign minister: On the one hand, the Union minister for foreign affairs would be the vice president of the federal Commission; on the other hand, he or she would act as the foreign policy high representative of the intergovernmental European Council.

The question is to what extent this hermaphrodite will come to resemble a federal organization. This will need to be decided according to what is best for Europe. The institutional construction of modern Europe has always been a gradual process. Europeanization began in nonsensitive areas where European Community action was beneficial for all, and then it spilled over into newer and newer areas. The European Union's founding states first pooled their coal and steel sectors; then came a wider harmonization of their economies, then the customs union, and so on, and so forth.

Undoubtedly, the EU is much more than the typical international organization; it has many common policies and institutions whose role is to promote cooperation among its member states and enforce its common rules. In political and institutional terms, it is one of a kind—unique—an evolving experiment unprecedented in history. Its peculiar dual nature (interstate or suprastate, pragmatic or purpose-made institution?) is illustrated by the common misnomer "a federation of states," which is pure nonsense in political science. Since the seventeenth century, it has been taken for granted that an alliance of states can take two roads: (1) a federation, whose member states cease to have sovereignty and for which a common parliament legislates according to a common constitution; or (2) a confederation, whose member states retain their sovereignty and for which common legislation is adopted unanimously by their representatives. The EU is a hermaphroditic "third road." The question is: Where does it lead?

We have seen that public acceptance of the EU is not evident at all. Some say that people, mostly youngsters, think that the EU is a pseudodemocracy, a remote bureaucratic government, and that is why the whole project has lost its idealism and appeal. Maintaining a peaceful and prosperous continent is simply taken for granted, not "sexy" anymore. Others claim that the European Community was, basically and necessarily, undemocratically planned and implemented by farsighted visionary politicians who fixed their eyes on history's horizon, not on opinion polls. The EU is sick of too much democracy, which is suffocating its development. Clearly, these are radically differing views about this UPO.

From 1948, when the General Agreement on Tariffs and Trade was created, until 2000, more than two hundred regional trade agreements were concluded among nations, more than half of which failed. In contrast, the project of the European Economic Community has proven to be a uniquely successful venture. Regional integration is considered successful if, for its members, it is worth harmonizing their rules at the international (regional) level. According to theory, doing so pays off for every trading country without a perfect institutional structure. Obviously, no country has the perfect institutional setup, and all European countries are active traders. But there is one more ingredient for success: observance of the rules, which requires well-functioning common institutions that can enforce the rules. Europe has created its well-functioning institutions to manage its hermaphroditic life.

The politicians of the European Union's member states like to point the finger at Brussels as the source of all troubles, as if "Brussels" had forced the new rules upon them—rules that may occasionally mean sacrifices for a sector or society as a whole. In most cases, in national politics, Brussels is only used as a red herring to divert and neutralize public fury; in fact, national ministers were present when the decision was made, and they voted in favor of it, because deep down inside they agreed with it. By relocating decisionmaking to a distant Brussels, politicians save themselves an awful lot of inconvenience by not having to fight such battles on the fields of domestic politics. However, member states are often accused of defending "national interests" in "Brussels" against "European interests." With the exception of really blatant cases, distorting the facts and turning them into such accusations is rather bizarre; after all, that is what democratically elected national governments are supposed to do. And we have come full circle, back to the EU's hermaphroditic nature and the difficulties of being objective in our assessment.

The American and German national federations both also began with economic cooperation, but in their cases this was quickly followed by a political union not hindered by linguistic or cultural differences and strongly divergent national identities—unlike European integration. The EU was created in the first place to guarantee peace through common economic action. This was not an overambitious project, and it was not a political mission to unite the continent by sacrificing national sovereignty. However, as European integration unfolded, the EU's member states gave up more and more of their sovereignty. They did so because it served their interests—an argument rammed home by economic operators lobbying for more economic freedom and more free markets. Their inclination was further reinforced by the realization that, through integration, they could boost their international profile and beef up their role in a globalizing world. As we have seen, European integration is more than just the lowest common denominator of its member states' positions; the European Community has important instruments at its disposal for motivating and enforcing, from elaborating common European programs to the jurisprudence of the European Court of Justice. Integration—which, in practical terms, means the intensification of links between member state politicians, officials, companies, businesspeople, intellectuals, and students—is a process of mutual learning, a self-generating phenomenon, that enhances further cooperation.

The key motivation for the creation of the EU was to ensure peace between France and Germany, the two biggest continental powers. European integration was instrumental for achieving peace and stability, but one should not underestimate the disciplinary potential of the Cold War and the U.S. nuclear shield. Uniting the peoples of Europe has also contributed to increasing prosperity, although, after World War II, the free world from America to Asia also seemed to be rolling in wealth. European integration played a role in the proliferation of the concept of liberty, even if that role was marginal; neither the Mediterranean revolutions nor the collapse of the Berlin Wall were directly triggered by EU policies. All the EU did was to consolidate the newly democratic states (first Greece, then Portugal and Spain, and most recently the Central and Eastern European countries) by granting them membership. Thus, Europe's role is primarily consolidation and partly facilitation. It consolidates—but does not create—peace, freedom, and economic development. There have been, are, and will be many different answers to the question of what the EU means and what is its main function. Some consider it the stabilizing force behind peace in Europe and the guarantor of economic freedoms. Others see it as the forum for discussing and implementing member states' interests. Still others view it as the forerunner of the European dream of a United States of Europe capable of playing a dominant international role. There are politicians who say we have enough Europe as it is, and there are those who wish to breathe new life into the project.

"What does the EU say about that?" is a question that I am often asked by representatives of various chambers, professional associations and interest groups, and "laypeople." Most often, my answer is the same, "Nothing," which usually surprises them. The secretive, antidemocratic EU is just as much of a popular myth as the omnipotent EU. And it is nothing more than a myth—in many areas of life, the EU has no competence; and in many, it does not even have an "opinion." The EU law, the *acquis communautaire,* may amount to a hundred thousand pages, but even that is not enough to cover everything. Often, the EU's role is merely to complement national policies. The hard core of Europe uses the euro, a common single currency; "Brussels" enforces cartel rules on its own authority; the customs union has been in existence for almost four decades; and European Community principles are present in a multitude of fields. Transportation, fisheries, health care, consumer protection, visa policy, and foreign policy now all function according to partially harmonized rules. National governments are bound by the Stability and Growth Pact, which prohibits overspending even in election years. To what extent these rules are respected is another but—as we have seen—crucial question.

But let us remember that European laws—apart from the rulings of the independent Court of Justice—are adopted by the member states and not by "Brussels." So the omnipotence of "Brussels" is a myth after all, not only because "Brussels" generally means the Community of member states but also because Community competences are very weak in many areas of life. The pillars of nation-state sovereignty are guarding the borders, running the country, and building a political and social system. These are areas in which Brussels still has no say. On top of that, the Union does not have a federal budget that would enable it to perform statelike tasks; nor does it have any customs authorities, army, police, or diplomatic corps (diplomats working at Commission delegations do not represent member states). Such functions and officials are present here and there in embryonic form, but their importance is dwarfed by member state capacities. The EU does not levy taxes; the idea of financing the EU budget from a Community tax pops up from time to time, but even if it becomes a reality, it will be a low-rate tax. In the overwhelming majority of cases, the member states must transpose Community rules into national law; implementation is the task of national public administrations, and enforcement falls upon national courts. The EU administration in Brussels employs about 30,000 officials, a hundred times less than the number of people working in the U.S. federal administration, which explains why the member states continue to play a key role in keeping the EU machinery moving. For instance, the French National Assembly spends roughly 70 percent of its time transposing EU law into national legislation.

The impact of European integration varies immensely from one area to another; moreover, the European social scene is virtually nonexistent, and political systems are also structured on a national basis. Political parties, trade unions, nongovernmental organizations, and the media are all national, despite the fact that there are at least ten thousand lobbyists around Brussels. There is no such thing as "European public discourse"; citizens are by and large indifferent toward the European project, and public opinion is preoccupied with national political and social issues. Those who are interested in or are supportive of the European project typically belong to the social or political elite. A popular explanation for this public indifference is the theory of democratic deficit, which argues that the Europe-wide apathy is caused by the antidemocratic ways of "Brussels." Citizens feel they cannot influence European decisions because they are made by a remote elite of technocrats and not by their directly elected representatives.

Once could heave a sigh of relief if this were Europe's biggest problem. But I am afraid the problem is far greater. It seems unlikely that democratic involvement would excite people's curiosity in EU affairs overnight, as indicated by the poor turnout in elections for the European Parliament, the Union's only directly elected body. (Paradoxically, as the European Parliament's role has grown in EU decisionmaking, voter turnout has fallen.) I agree with the opinion that the theory of democratic deficit is exaggerated; decisions are made by the European Council, where representatives of democratically elected national governments sit, and by Parliament, where directly elected members sit. The European Commission, where the technocrats of whom the public is suspicious sit, is mostly confined to the role of the initiator, making proposals but not making decisions. Moreover, in key areas that have the biggest direct impact on people's lives (taxation, education, social policy, and the budgetary redistribution of wealth), the EU only plays a marginal role, and hence democratic control does not need to be as scrupulous as control over a "normal" government.

The truth is that, for most people, European issues fall way behind domestic affairs. The root cause of the apathy toward the EU—though not a problem in itself—is that there is no such thing as a "European people." Germans are interested in familiar, domestic affairs, just like the Finns or Italians. A 2005 survey showed that while 40 percent of Europeans feel attached to Europe, 90 percent feel the same sentiment toward their home country or hometown.[3] The situation is further complicated by the complexity of the "European equation": Political debates cannot be simplified as ideological clashes of right versus left or power struggles of government versus opposition. At the European level, British Labourites may have a very different position from French Socialists. How do you define government and opposition in the European Council? And what in the world is this Commission, anyway?

One must ask simple questions to get clear answers. Is there a European dream? Fundamentally, if we define this as the dream of average Europeans, there is no such thing. There might be German or Lithuanian dreams, but generally people do not dream about the EU. The American dream is very simple; it boils down to this: freedom, success, wealth—I can be whatever I want—it is all up to me. There is a kind of European dream—the dream of Europe's elite about a successful and peaceful continent. And this dream has already become reality, but the people of Europe have acknowledged it without much enthusiasm. With this little bit of brainstorming, I have simply tried to illustrate how close the European project is to the citizens of the EU member states—or rather, how distant it is from them. I do not believe in a future built on dreams. And I do not believe that a European identity needed or needs to be constructed artificially. History shows that such attempts are doomed to fail. The great architect of European unity, Jean Monnet, once said that if he could start European construction from scratch, he would begin with culture and not the economy. How fortunate that he did not get a second chance.

Europe is a nascent project forged from political compromises and based on a common legal system. Despite thousands of years of cohabitation, Europe's peoples do not have any common traditions, living myths, identity, language, or image that they try to project to the rest of the world. A Fleming will refuse to speak French outside Brussels, and an average Walloon could not speak Flemish to save his life. There are still many open questions. And the EU's future—let alone its ultimate goal—is far from defined.

The Two Camps and the Key Compromise of Europe

When I was halfway through writing this chapter, a friend phoned. He is a leading EU diplomat, and as such a defender of national interests, but also a committed federalist. After we exchanged "merry Christmas" and "happy New Year," we turned to our favorite topic: the United States of Europe. He compared Europe to an expectant mother bearing a political union for a baby. The only question is the time of birth. Premature labor could be fatal for the fetus; late delivery could be the end of both child and mother. In other words, if the EU embarked upon the venture of building a political union prematurely, it would certainly lead to failure—as has happened before. Conversely, procrastinating about the creation of the political union would lead to European disintegration. In the middle of this dilemma, federalists are divided over the question of whether the right time has come or not.

However, the real disagreement is over whether Europe is expectant at all. Does it carry the possibility and necessity of a political union? Many say NO. I happen to believe the answer is YES, followed by a big BUT. Let me explain. A considerable proportion of the EU's member states, public opinion, and intellectual elite reject the idea. Mentally, Europe is not yet ready for political union. First, it does not have common European traditions, identity, or language. Second, member states have very different ideas about what they want from the European Union and what economic and social model would be ideal. Third, an EU of twenty-seven members—and still enlarging—would be physically impossible to convert into a political union, which raises the possibility of a two-speed or multispeed solution— although this is like a red flag to most countries that are likely to be left out of the vanguard.

Talking about two "camps" is not a new concept. There are very different sets of views concerning the essence of European integration, all of which have been part of theory and practice for decades. Of these various views, the functionalist and federalist schools of the second half of the twentieth century have had the most effect on the understanding of European integration. But it is more than a question of different theories as the two schools clash daily on politics and the economy, and as they give very different answers to the extremely topical question "How to proceed from here, Europe?" The two schools of thought have served as ideological bases for competing strategies of integration—the British model versus the French model. The functionalist school tries to use the empirical facts from the early years of integration and generalize them for theoretical purposes;

the federalist school tries to justify the final goal. The functionalist explanation uses mainly economic concepts; the federalist one is more political.

Thus, federalism sets the final political goal and carefully plans the constitutional steps that will lead to its attainment. Conversely, functionalism proceeds in specific, successive—primarily economic—steps. Federalism would like to see national power concentrated in the hands of the integrating bodies, whereas functionalism wishes to raise the activities of nation-states to a higher, international level. Federalism would curtail national sovereignty and condemn nationalism. The goal of pure federalism is to unite states by constitutional means, whereas functionalism aims to establish the framework for socioeconomic prosperity through the cooperation of participating states and common organizations. In federalism, states and governments are the principal actors of integration, but in functionalism subnational entities such as economic operators or lobbying groups are the main actors. In federalist theory (which is more unified than the numerous offshoots of functionalist theory), legal regulation plays a key role, but for functionalism legislation is only one of the instruments of integration.

However, these two camps are merely abstractions; reality is much more complex. In "Brussels," where in addition to political affiliation, nationality and national traditions also make a difference, everything becomes more complicated and interconnected. Nevertheless, here I will attempt to describe the two actual camps whose members are arguing about the point and future of European integration.

In one camp, we find the federalists dreaming about a political alliance or union of European states. It is slightly puzzling, but this camp has in its ranks those who believe in maintaining the welfare state and—with a few (but important) exceptions—leftist politicians and opinion leaders. This camp is characterized by economic seclusion, protectionism, and sentiments of antiglobalism (if not openly hostile to globalism, the federalists at least interpret it as a serious threat). The economic policy of this camp is largely Keynesian, stressing the interventionist role of the state—even of monetary policy, if need be. This camp is typically against enlargement, because it could dilute the European Union or ultimately even cause it to disintegrate. Its adherents' worldview is fundamentally political; they see political decisions, regulation, and institutions as the engine of growth and development. They are devout advocates of building a political union. For them, political union is the ultimate objective, which can be achieved by political means—that is, through a top-down approach, just as the big steps in European integration more or less have always been made.

The second camp is the free marketers; we can call them liberals, if you like. Their approach is fundamentally economic. Accordingly, they see the role of the EU as creating and guaranteeing market rules. For them, the EU's enlargement is an opportunity to extend the pan-European market rather than a menace, because they are not worried about reduced political cohesion within the Union. In their political affiliations, they are a varied bunch, mainly comprising liberals and right-wingers. Some of them could be labeled Euroskeptics. They favor flexible solutions to integration and hold national sovereignty dear. They oppose the idea of a political union, because for them European integration is a rational alliance between member states to unite their forces and pool their resources in order to achieve their goals more efficiently.

There are countless oddities in the worldviews of the two camps that we could use to illustrate the misconceptions people have about "Europe." It is puzzling that the left—normally so keen on solidarity—is opposed to the EU's enlargement. It is equally puzzling how important national sovereignty is to the liberals, who generally try to reduce the state's role to a minimum. For supporters of political union, eliminating social disparities is a key objective, so that not only markets but also citizens would benefit from the European project. However, this again raises the idea of where the boundaries of this Europe lie if the poorer new EU member states—where workers earn one-fifth the wages of their Western European counterparts, not of their own free will but due to prevailing circumstances—can be accused of social dumping and even threatened with having their EU cohesion funding frozen. And similarly, where is this Europe that competes openly and with a united front on the world stage when proposals for a minimum level of European harmonization are vetoed time and again? As I have said, Europe is not prepared for political integration, either socially or mentally. The political concepts and worldviews that developed within the nation-state framework tend to get muddled up in "Brussels."

The significance of political affiliations is becoming more and more important in the political decisions of the European Parliament, which illustrates the coming of age of this institution in terms of European politics. Although the nationality of the members of Parliament remains a decisive factor at election time, the traditional right/left split is often increasingly tangible in debates and decisions. Market regulation seems to be the great divide; the left wants more rules, but the right and the liberals want fewer. Because the EU is not a proper state and does not redistribute incomes, the traditional "left versus liberal/conservative" clashing point of how much national income to pump back into the welfare system cannot be relevant. The European Union does not redistribute money (or does so only at a very low rate); it makes rules.

Accordingly, the ideological collision between the two sides makes itself manifest in the field of rules: what for, and how many? In Brussels, the "much regulation, strong control versus a liberal laissez-faire system with few rules" antagonism goes well beyond economic philosophy. In the world of Brussels and Strasbourg, things are very different from the EU member states' political framework. The choice between more or less regulation is not only a choice of economic and social policy but also a choice between more or less "Europe." In other words, it is a choice between a "minimum" program guaranteeing freedom of markets on the one hand and a "maximum" program leading to political union on the other. And it is this operating logic encoded into the system that leads to Europe's biggest dilemma —to the atavistic opposition of the two camps and the fact that neither camp can be right. Although one is on the right road, what it wants is precious little for Europe's survival; the other means well, but it is on the wrong road. The liberals—who want to liberalize markets, boost competitiveness, modernize the unsustainable social model, and have an economic and social policy capable of adjusting to the requirements of "turboglobalization" (see chapter 2)—fundamentally reject a closer union of the EU's member states (although this is a bit of a generalization and thus may be misleading) out of fear that a political union may end national sovereignty and that its protectionist rules may paralyze competitiveness, the real key to future prosperity. The left and the federalists want closer political cooperation in Europe, but for all the wrong reasons; for them, the objective of political integration is to perpetuate the welfare model, which—as we have seen— is doomed to fail in the long run.

Thus, Europe faces what is probably its most crucial intellectual and political challenge: how to make the self-proclaimed saviors of national sovereignty (the Euroskeptics, if you will) understand that, without closer political cooperation, Europe could not only fall behind the rest of the world but might even become destabilized in the age of repeated EU enlargements. And how can the federalists, insistent on the welfare model, be made to realize that in today's world of cutthroat competition, when billions are entering the global labor market from the East, the achievements of that welfare model must be trimmed back. Unless it does this pruning, Europe's fate will be sealed, it will be heading for disaster, and it will never get the support for a political union of those member states with a noncontinental mentality.

Agreement on reforming the European socioeconomic model is the key precondition to taking the first step toward successful political integration. Once there is such agreement, those involved can start thinking about the timing, members, and operating principles of political integration. But in the absence of a consensus on the basics of reform, political union will not strengthen the continent and may even become a source of tension. The key to Europe's further development is finding and amalgamating competitive content with an operable form. Yet this does not imply that Europe should copy the American socioeconomic model, which leaves practically 50 million people without social security.

Moreover, as far as the form of union is concerned, the European Union does not need to turn itself into a traditional federation of states, which could lead to a situation of internal secession by some members states if all of them do not agree to federate. Finding a competitive social and economic model and an operable form is paramount to saving the European Union from dilution, while ensuring the necessary degree of flexibility to keep an increasingly heterogeneous club together. A competitive economy and a form of integration guaranteeing the European Union proper weight on the international political scene could mutually reinforce each other. But one question cannot be avoided: What is the purpose of the EU—free trade or a future Community of nations with a political union and common identity? There is no need to rush into answering this question, and a dogmatic answer is the last thing Europeans need. First, one must pose another question: What would be best for Europe and its half billion citizens?

Interlude: Epilogue

Otmar Issing, a former senior economist at the European Central Bank, once wrote: "Surely there are economists whose reputation hinges on their gloomy forecasts and who are thus terribly disappointed if the predicted disaster does not happen."[4] The old monetarist's words put a smile on my face; he is so right. Then I asked myself: Will I be annoyed if the demographic time bomb does not blow up social welfare and national budgets in Europe? Will I be sad if Europe does not fall behind in international competition due to its flagging competitiveness and overregulation in the labor market? Will I fret if a German engineer invents a method to generate energy from hydrogen or wind a hundred times more efficiently than now, solving Europe's energy dependency problem overnight? Will I lose face if the American market model collapses due to social tensions and politicians on the other side of the Atlantic start copying our ways? Will I be unhappy if China learns the basics of social policy and geopolitics from us?

The answer to all these questions is NO. I would love to see all these things happen. I would be glad to have my book referred to as one of the many products of the "doomsday cult" of the turn of the millennium, and to have Europe alive and kicking, leading the world by example. I wish it could happen that way; but that is a rather unlikely scenario. The course of events will soon take a turn for the worse, unless we start taking the problems seriously. I would gladly believe Stephen Haseler when he says that the European social model that limits the unscrupulous autocracy of capital will continue to develop and its global success will overshadow the glow of American raw capitalism, especially in the eyes of the American public, changing their understanding of the world and values. Europe will set the trend to follow for the United States and maybe the entire world—he claims. His is a nice but unrealistic vision.[5]

Everyone is entitled to an opinion, but all opinions should be taken with a bit of healthy skepticism. I am no exception; you should take my views with a pinch of salt. Proving someone wrong is the most exciting intellectual challenge for any thinker. At this moment, I am convinced—and I have tried to support my position with hundreds of facts and figures—that my views on the seriousness of the perils endangering Europe's future and how to manage them will stand the test of time. Nonetheless, I welcome anyone who can prove me wrong—with facts and figures, of course.

In 2050, theoretically, Europe could be a success or a failure, rich or poor, an exemplary cultural node or a miserable open-air museum. What will it be like, or what could it be like? That is what the final section is about.

The Picture in 2050

What will Europe and European integration look like in 2050? This is a very difficult to answer. Nevertheless, the most important and decisive factors can be identified, and a few probable models can be sketched. One thing is certain: The global world order is already changing, and in the coming decades it could change quite dramatically.

A Letter from My Son

Let us suppose that my son, who will be fifty years old in 2050, will still write to me, and that I can still read, and that letters still exist as a mode of communication. Provided that all those things hold true, his letter to me could be something like this:

Dear Father,

I will soon visit the city-state of Brussels to conduct an interview with the president of the United States of Europe on the situation and prospects of the United States of Europe and the Pan-European Federation of States. This is my first major assignment since I was appointed head of Shanghai University's Media Institute in Frankfurt. It won't be easy asking the European president sensitive questions at such difficult times. That is why I am asking for your help and advice. If you have some time, please give me a video call. Until then, let me briefly outline how I see things. The European president is in the hot seat; the central states—those that have introduced the common currency—are under pressure from strong centripetal forces, which are dwarfed by the tension induced by the cohesion of the State Federation. The Asia Minor Alliance, the Eastern member of the Pan-European Federation of States, has become very unstable due to the Eastern and Southern immigration flows and the Turkey-Armenia conflict.

On top of all that, Ukraine no longer accepts Turkey's dominant role in the Alliance. The situation inside the Mediterranean Alliance is even worse; hostilities between its members have resumed for the first time since Muslim pacification, with more and more countries questioning Egypt's informal leadership. Due to the depletion of oil reserves and the failure to modernize during the good times, several members now face a bleak outlook for the future. The president of the Asia Minor and Mediterranean Alliance, as the vice president of the Pan-European Federation of States, has considerable powers on pan-European issues, which members of the Central States of Europe will not tolerate much longer.

As long as the stability of the two alliances on the periphery could be taken for granted, the central states were more inclined to delegate decisionmaking competences to the peripheral states. The modern network-Europe model that evolved following the economic crisis and huge social shock of the 2010s has been working without any major glitches, although the United Kingdom proved to be difficult to integrate at first.

When a statement by the British heir to the throne had to be subtitled for American audiences to understand what he was saying, the British suddenly realized that ties with their special transatlantic friends had weakened. This realization, triggered by a series of incidents, came as quite a shock to them, and for a good while they were unable to choose between the two sides of the Atlantic.

Finally, in the second half of the 2010s, as part of a compromise package (which gave Turkey privileged status but ruled out its full membership), the United Kingdom decided to opt for full integration into "core Europe" and introduce the single currency, thereby relinquishing its aspiration to enter into some special state federation with the United States. The Great European Compromise was born, and it included these key points: creating a multispeed Europe, setting the ultimate frontiers of "core Europe," adopting a European Constitution, continuing with "flexible" enlargement (flexible meaning not leading to full membership), organizing Europe into regional suballiances, and carrying out a radical reform of "core Europe's" social and economic models to make them competitive.

The new Europe worked like a charm and, by reinforcing its unity in foreign policy, it could even compensate geopolitically for the further strengthening of China. Europe came to play an important role in the pacification of deteriorating Sino-American relations. Muslim radicalism subsided in Europe, partly thanks to the political success of the new Union. The economic reforms of the late 2010s met with great social opposition in "core Europe," which reinforced the power of "Brussels," as members saw the federal central government as the sole guarantor of painful reforms. Public acceptance of the Union fell to unprecedented lows; hardly a year went by without at least one extremist national party initiating a country's withdrawal from the Federation. The European economy regained its competitiveness, although still lagging somewhat behind Asia and the United States—and consequently social tensions eased.

This heralded the dawn of a new era: the golden age of the 2020s and 2030s. There were minor economic crises and even local wars, but Europe's economy remained in good shape, the reformed pan-European institutions worked satisfactorily, and relations with the United States were characterized by partnership and close cooperation. In the late 2030s, things took a turn for the worse: with the internal problems of Chinese society (rapid aging, staggering social differences, and the roughly 50 million women "missing" by the turn of the millennium due to mass abortions of female fetuses), the stability of this continent-sized country showed signs of cracking, and its international policy became erratic.

In turn, the United States began acting as an aggressive world power again. In the meantime, the pension time bomb exploded in Europe; as it turned out, the reforms two decades earlier were insufficient to guarantee long-term sustainability. Climatic conditions, after decades of slow gradual change, drastically worsened. Despite the apprehension, few concrete steps were taken. The world should have taken the signs much more seriously—for example, when, in December 2006, an ice shelf of 11,000 square miles broke off the Arctic ice shelf near the Canadian coast. Europe was overrun by masses of predominantly Muslim climatic refugees, leading to serious social conflicts both with the "aboriginal" Europeans and with descendants of former immigrants who had become secularized and assimilated into mainstream society. The central "core" closed itself off from the landslide social changes happening on the periphery of Europe.

The first telltale signs of disintegration in the Pan-European Federation of States appeared. The world order was becoming fragmented and polarized. A declining Russia moved toward China, while the traditionally friendly relations between Europe and India turned cooler as a consequence of turbulent conditions on the Asian continent. However, the primary source of tension in the world was the deepening conflict between China and the United States. Long years of economic recession and political tensions followed until, in the late 2040s, a new fragile world order emerged: the Pax Sino-Americana. It was built on the balance of power and not cooperation, mistrust rather than mutual goodwill, but still it was welcomed with a sigh of relief.

In this world order, Europe could only play second fiddle to the United States, but remained a trusty sidekick of its Atlantic neighbor. Another factor contributing to Europe's weaker role, in addition to the collapse of the multipolar and cooperative world order, was its loosening internal cohesion. The multilayered pan-European model was on the verge of disintegration; social tension mounted. In a nutshell, this is the history of the past few decades—at least in my interpretation. In the interview, I would like to ask the president how he sees the future, the chances for climbing out of this slump. What do you think I should ask him? (Who knows, if the interview turns out well, I may even turn it into a book.)

I hope your synthetic heart transplant went well, etc.

Oliver

Frankfurt, January 7, 2050

The Three Graces and the Three Demons

Fewer than 800 million people have the fortune to be living in a wealthy country in better-than-average conditions. These fewer than 1 billion people populate fewer than 20 countries—mainly North American and Western European ones—where the per capita GDP varies between $25,000 and $35,000. Five billion people live in 110 poor countries, where the GDP is below $8,000 per head.[6] History teaches us that whether a country becomes rich or poor is determined by a handful of easily definable factors such as technology, geographical location and conditions, and a society's degree of civilization, ethics, and institutions. As history progressed, institutions (including the legal order and the unwritten rules governing society) became increasingly crucial to success. One of Europe's strengths has been its developed legal order and institutions, which evolved over the course of centuries and served as a model for the rest of the world during Europe's global hegemony. They still serve as an example for those European societies that wish to join the continent's modern integration project, the European Union built on law and institutions. In the 1980s, people began writing off the United States and watched in awe at Japan's rise and its mercantilist model, which has since plunged into a deep crisis. Then the tables were turned, and the United States again became the model to follow. Today everyone fears the Chinese dragon and pities Europe, but the tables could be turned again, just as they were a few decades ago. It would be silly to be defeatist, but trivializing the world's current problems would also be a grave mistake.

History has taught Europe that the Three Graces of peace, prosperity, and democracy usually go hand in hand. Likewise, so do the Three Demons of war, poverty, and totalitarianism.

As we saw above, the world had already lived through an age of global capitalism from the mid–nineteenth century to World War I. In those decades, capital, goods, persons, and information moved completely freely in the capitalist world. Moreover, the global gold standard worked well with all the countries—except China and Persia—that were participating by the turn of the century. The rate of growth was staggering, people lived better and better, poorer countries were catching up with the leading pack, modern corporations—I would venture to say, the predecessors of today's multinationals—were born, and everybody believed the miracle would never end. But something did go wrong. There were enormous political tensions beneath the surface, the Balkans were a tinderbox, the Franco-German rivalry grew worse, and as Germany was growing in strength and finding itself again, it demanded a place at the table of colonial powers.

However, there were also less spectacular reasons for the collapse, which could serve as a lesson for us today. In the first liberal era, the world suddenly found itself interconnected by a web of globalization—economic relations became completely free overnight, and there were no more obstacles to the free movement of goods. Due to this unrestricted movement, Europe was inundated with agricultural products from the New World, causing extraordinary existential problems for European farmers, who produced at higher costs. Antiglobalism sentiments rose, but in the absence of multinational companies with great lobbying powers or of a class-conscious working class and with democratic rights limited, governments had a relatively easy task managing the situation. Wage cuts or layoffs did not cause grave political turmoil at the time. Workers and farmers had to put up with whatever global competition threw at them; at least, that was the official political position.

After World War I, which broke out because of political and social tensions, representative democracy was strengthened, and the first steps were taken toward creating a welfare state in an attempt to alleviate social tensions. In hindsight, we now know that these attempts failed, but with the welfare constraints in place, politicians could no longer ignore the negative effects of global liberalism. Global capitalism did not create the problems— poverty, totalitarianism, and war—but it did ignite the world economy, quickly connecting economies on different continents and thereby inducing extremely rapid changes in social processes. Apart from the geopolitical situation of the time, the root of the problem was that governments failed to realize the necessity of managing these social processes. We are currently living in the second wave of globalization in the modern age. Many factors have changed radically, but there is one lesson we can learn from history: In an age of rapid changes, it is essential that politics respond quickly by taking appropriate measures.

United Kingdom–led global capitalism failed, and the age of global wars arrived, but the emergence of the United States gave the world another chance to start from scratch. It remains to be seen whether the America–led global capitalism of the twenty-first century will share the same fate as the one led by Britain in the twentieth. Europe has a decisive role to play in shaping the future of global capitalism economically, politically, and intellectually. Currently no other potential threat could match the disastrous consequences of the disintegration of today's economic world order, if that should happen.

At the height of the nuclear threat in 1955, John von Neumann, the Hungarian-born mathematician and father of the modern computer, posed this question in the title of an article for *Fortune* magazine: "Can We Survive Technology?" He believed that the human qualities required to survive were patience, flexibility, and intelligence. He wrote about reliance on these three qualities at a time when European integration was only in the offing. The Coal and Steel Community, created to pacify Germany, was already in existence, but the treaty establishing the European Economic Community—which later became the European Union—would not come until a few months later. Now, a half century later, nuclear war is not our biggest headache by far, but we still need patience, flexibility, and intelligence—and lots of them, especially in Europe, which is under geostrategic, social, or economic pressure. Impatience leads to the death of democracy, Europeans' most important value; and who would know this better than Europeans. Without flexibility, Europeans will get sucked down by the ever-faster whirlpool of turboglobalization. And intelligence is what Europe needs to see its future, challenges, and options realistically—in other words, to reinvent itself for the twenty-first century.

In the early years of the third millennium, Europe has no idea what to do with its Union or where its frontiers lie. As we have seen, these two issues are interrelated. Some say that the Union will save the nation-states, while others believe just the opposite: that the nation-states will come to the rescue of the Union. Whatever the case, at present there are no credible alternatives to European integration as a guarantor of prosperity and security in Europe.

The first generation of modern Europeans created peace on the continent in the wake of two world wars. The second generation created the single European market and prosperity in the Cold War years. The task of today's generation is to identify a model and future for European integration that will enable generations to come to enjoy the two common European achievements in the age of turboglobalization. Productivity and competitiveness are incomprehensible concepts for the person on the street. Prosperity, peace, and democracy are much more tangible, but we must never forget that they are the result of hard work, the rule of law, and free enterprise and not of luck, conquests, or marauding neighboring peoples.

Europe—it seems—is a journey, not a destination. Decades ago, Robert Schuman wrote in his memoirs: "Europe is in search of itself; it knows that its destiny is in its own hands. . . . Lord, let it not miss the decisive opportunity, the last chance."[7]

Crisis, Reform, and an Empty Center

Since 2008, the word "crisis" has not been an abstract concept. The time comes when changes—in other words, reforms—are needed. Society and the economy go through rapid changes, which some see as an opportunity but most fear as a danger. The result is wavering public trust, a chronic refusal of the political elite and institutions, and a widening gap between the elite and the rest of society. The welfare model, which was created to prevent the terrible social trends of the interwar period from coming again, has fallen into a deep crisis, together with the social peace built on the contentment of the middle classes.

This 2008–9 global financial and economic crisis was further aggravated by the economic and social tensions caused by immigration and a hysterical fear of globalization. For many people, globalization—or, to use the terminology of antiglobalists, unrestricted markets and raw capitalism—is embodied by the European Union. (The EU is indeed one of the engines of globalization, but demonizing it together with globalization is an erroneous misconception and a delusion.) It is no accident that European integration is being increasingly rejected, alongside a general rejection of the political mainstream. On political orders "from above," Europe's nations had to abandon their national identity—meaning security and prosperity—to reinforce Brussels' power, and they even had to tolerate poorer nations being financed to the detriment of their "own" national budget.

For a society, it is always difficult to swallow the bitter pill of being the first generation in decades to be worse off than the previous one—especially when faced with the problems caused by Muslim immigrants and the constant threat of terrorism. Moreover, Brussels deprives them of the sweet remedy of nationalism, and it allows increasingly suspicion-inducing countries, whose dirt-poor workers will flood the labor market, to join the EU. At times like this, populist politicians have nothing to do but sit back, relax, sip their cocktails, and bide their time. And this is exactly what responsible politicians must not do. However difficult it is to convince the public of the necessity of reform, they must try; and if they fail, they must try again. Luxembourg's prime minister, Jean-Claude Juncker, once said that all European politicians know what needs to be done, but they have no idea how to get reelected once they have carried out the necessary reforms.

Seemingly, there is still time to procrastinate, but that will not last long. It is arguable what balance Europe should strike between coldhearted liberalism and tender social democracy, between change and preservation, or at what pace the reforms should be introduced, but the changes cannot be postponed much longer. Europe's responsible parties—the Social Democrats, Christian Democrats, and Liberals—cannot sit idly twiddling their thumbs while voters are being attracted to the extremes of the political spectrum. The political pendulum swings left and then swings right—a phenomenon always welcomed by the victorious side. It is business as usual. But finding that the center has become empty is not business as usual. If the center loses its grip on voters concerned about the future, Europe will face a political climate change.

Some of the worrying signs are already visible. In the Dutch election of late 2006, Maoist and ultra-Christian political parties that were hostile to globalization and the EU grew considerably in strength while centrist parties suffered serious losses. The hitherto-tolerant left-leaning lower middle classes were welcomed with open arms by the far left, while the formerly tolerant right-leaning upper middle classes, together with voters weary of immigrants, found the promises they were looking for on the extreme right. Dutch society expressed its opinion in a firm voice—it had had enough of enlargement, globalization, immigration, the EU, and everything else that the centrists preach. Public sentiments are similar in most Western continental countries; society has stood up against the political elite, which will remain unchanged until the center can come up with a credible and convincing vision for the twenty-first century. Unfortunately, this is a vicious circle; reform-advocating center parties have less and less room for maneuvering to implement reform programs, whereas a failure to carry out the reforms will lead to further deterioration in the political climate.

For a long time, the Germans and the French believed that the welfare state would last forever, just as the citizens of ancient Rome two thousand years ago were convinced of the eternity of their empire. They could not have been more wrong. Many European firms are leaders in their sector, but more of them need to learn to be successful internationally, not only in the domestic market. The good people of Western Europe, who are usually fervent supporters of protectionism, must open their eyes and see that it is not their jobs their governments are protecting, only the management of national champions.

Polls show that 84 out of 100 Germans are afraid that their company will be relocated to a new EU member state and that they will lose their job as a result. The full application of the EU's four freedoms has become problematic with Eastern European enlargement, which has created huge disparities in income levels. It is not by chance that Hungary, a zealous advocate of free labor markets when it joined the EU, introduced restrictions on the movement of Romanian workers upon its neighbor's accession to the EU.

During the 2008–9 global crisis, popular fears further intensified; and as unemployment soared, many Europeans started to feel insecure. The 2009 European Parliamentary elections clearly showed the fear and frustration of the Europeans, in two ways. First, the level of voter participation turned out to be the worst since the Europeans started to elect their European members of Parliament by a direct and universal vote. More important, this election reinforced the radical (antidemocratic, anti-EU, anticapitalist, anti-Semite, and xenophobic) parties to an unprecedented extent.

It would be wrong to say that there are no reforms. Most EU member states have been making efforts for years to modernize their pension systems, update protective employment rules, and slowly but surely dismantle the walls of the traditional welfare state. Even in "unreformable" France, changes are beginning to take place. One example is the reform of the central bank's own pension scheme in November 2006. The central bank—which was deprived of its monetary policymaking competence with the introduction of the euro—has a ridiculous seven trade unions, which first resisted any change to the scheme, originally established in 1800 by Napoleon. In the end, six trade unions came around to the idea of reform and agreed to raise the retirement age from fifty-five or sixty to sixty or sixty-five years. Germany is undertaking much deeper reforms within the framework of its "Agenda 2010" and so-called Hartz reforms for paying the long-term unemployed, but its decisionmakers also occasionally take one step forward and two steps back. Thus, it was decided that the unemployment benefit for the elderly should increase, which will make a €700 million dent in the federal budget annually. At the same time, the new Swedish government trimmed trade unions' powers and introduced tax cuts to boost competitiveness.[8]

Some segments of European social democracy have sounded the warning bell, denying the need for the welfare state and to trim union rights or lower taxes. One of their main arguments is that, in reality, Europe's productivity is not far behind that of the United States but only reflects Europeans' preference for more spare time. (Undoubtedly, there must be some truth in this.) The problem with this theory is that productivity is not Europe's only problems—so are low growth rates and unemployment. On top of that, official productivity figures are distorted by the fact that many low-productivity jobs do not exist or are unfilled because of the high minimum wage. What the continent is experiencing is more than just a transitional slump in its economy. That this is more than a cyclical downturn is indicated by the fact that Europe started falling behind the United States when its economy should have been booming as a result of new economies of scale in the completed internal market.

In a common economic area and a common monetary zone, it would be completely sensible to carry out a common reform process. But as long as economic policy remains the competence of national governments, it is not quite that obvious. We cannot talk about coordinated reforms even in the euro zone, and the EU's member states often embark on reforms and modernization without a comprehensive reform strategy. The first steps are usually the ones that are likely to meet the least public opposition, and often reforms end there. It is by no means easy to carry through a fundamental overhaul of the economy, because it may run against the interests of numerous social groups and thus trigger widespread—occasionally violent—resistance. The potential disadvantages and losers can usually be quickly and easily determined, but the winners are more difficult to identify, and the advantages tend to make themselves felt over a longer period of time. When the economy soars, governments let the good times roll and loosen the purse strings to buy themselves a reelection. When the boom is followed by a bust, it is too late for officials to roll up their sleeves and get on with the reforms. In this vicious circle, member states badly need to be able to blame the reform measures on Brussels but also need to have it help them coordinate their reform efforts. The added value of synergy lies not only in the exchange of best practices but also in common or parallel reforms, which can reinforce each other and have a multiplier effect, particularly within the euro zone.

The European Union itself is in dire need of reform. Its institutions could do with more than the usual facelift, and it would do no harm to also revamp its activities and mentality. Important decisions lie ahead for the Union: determining the fate of the common foreign policy and common defense policy, and relaunching the institutional and decisionmaking reforms stalled by the rejection of the Constitution. The budget needs to be reformed and turned into a future-oriented, forward-looking financial instrument focused on areas fostering competitiveness, such as research and development and high-quality education, instead of agricultural policy, which now mainly subsidizes large farms. The budgetary review planned for 2008–9 would be an excellent opportunity to refashion European finances. The EU's budget may only amount to 1 percent of its total GDP, but it reflects political priorities, and thus, first and foremost, the European family of peoples must sort out what areas deserve its financial support in the twenty-first century.

The End of Global Capitalism?

As of this writing, it is 2009, and the world is in a financial and economic crisis. There is anger aimed at incompetent and corrupt financiers, and rightly so, but what is more worrying is the wave of populist, anticapitalist outbursts. Interventions at international forums reveal how globalization and the basic principles of capitalism are hated on every continent.

However, this hatred of capitalism must have been held back until global capitalism was apparently successful and beneficial. Now it can be set free. Bashing the "Washington Consensus" is just à la mode right now. The French president called on the leaders of the world in September 2008 to hold a summit to build a regulated capitalism to replace the failed global financial system. At the same time Henry Paulson, then the U.S. secretary of the Treasury, declared that raw capitalism is dead, and the *Washington Post* wrote about the "end of American capitalism." The United States used to be a global economic model, say the critics, but the recent crisis-induced, radical change in its economic policy—massive state intervention—could shift the balance of how other governments conceive and manage their economic systems. The hands-off brand of capitalism is now being blamed for the trouble. America, the showcase country for capitalism, is in the middle of an identity crisis. Governments on both sides of the Atlantic will be busy probably spending colossal amounts in the coming years cleaning up the mess, applying Keynesian remedies and putting their economies on a healthier track. U.S. president Barack Obama, right after his election, began to push a comprehensive program of social and economic reforms (alternative energy, health care, and education) beyond an immediate emergency economic stimulus package. Economists have estimated that the U.S. budget deficit could more than double, to almost $1,000 billion, within a year. Nevertheless, both the rules and the international system need to be overhauled. It is true that today nobody would laugh along with Ronald Reagan at his favorite joke, which goes like this: "What are the most terrifying nine words for the Americans? The answer is: 'I'm from the government and I'm here to help!'"

"Liberalism is over"—educated people say this so easily and en passant, as if they were talking about the weather. Europeans have been hearing this statement so often that it has become somewhat of a platitude. Those who believe in the end of liberalism are right in a way, because they usually look at it from a political perspective. In the EU member states and the other nations of the Western world, the fundamental liberal objectives have been attained; the citizens of these nations have social and economic freedom, everyone is equal before the law, and democratic institutions are stable. Consequently, liberalism has run out of breath in the political context. Francis Fukuyama was wrong; history did not end, but the political curiosity of liberal democracy did, because no one—apart from extremists—dares question the above principles.[9]

My understanding is that liberalism is not a political concept but a choice of values. That is why I stated at the beginning of this book that, despite all the challenges it faces, liberalism is not dead. If we look at it this way, the triumph of liberal values resulted in the supposedly waning importance of self-proclaimed liberal policy.

Those who lament this cannot see the forest for the trees. The future is much more problematic, because these values (whether represented by any political party) are going to be in real danger in the coming decades in Europe. Many even predict the end of liberal capitalism—the Western model —as such.

The United States–Europe axis is still the dominant force in globalization. However inconvenient it may be to admit, these two regional centers of the West are the ones "doing" globalization. The Americans, of course, play a much bigger role in shaping things, but Europe remains their economic focus. In 2004, the transatlantic economy generated a total output of $3 trillion, while the trade disputes widely reported by the media amounted to no more than 1 to 2 percent of that volume. It is a common misconception that Americans and Europeans mainly invest in poor countries. They invest considerably more in each other's economies than they do in developing or emerging Asian markets. Formerly, U.S. and European companies produced at home and sold overseas, but this trend has been reversed in the last decade and companies now tend to relocate production itself to the other side of the Atlantic. Global companies are increasingly dependent on the success of their subsidiaries. In 2005, Siemens had 900 companies it owned completely and another 400 in which it had a majority share. The same figure for General Electric was 8,000. In terms of doing business abroad, the

U.S. economy is clearly Europe oriented; in 2004, roughly 60 percent of its foreign direct investment (i.e., investment with the aim of setting up companies)—to a total value of $100 billion—arrived in Europe. American exports to China that same year were worth $50 billion, compared with U.S. exports worth $60 billion to Spain and $205 billion to Germany.[10]

In addition to investment, bilateral trade was also significant; in 2004, its value was close to $50 trillion. Europeans invested $100 billion in American securities, which equaled the revenue of European subsidiaries of American companies. Chinese affiliates of U.S. firms generated income equal only to one-third of Irish and one-fifth of Dutch subsidiaries of American firms. The majority of American expatriates work in Europe, and vice versa. U.S. companies employ twice as many people in their German subsidiaries as in their Chinese ones. About 60 percent of research and development not carried out on American soil is outsourced to Europe, and the same ratio holds the other way around. And if all these statistics have not convinced you of the global dominance of the transatlantic axis, then one last figure should do the trick: There are more European investments in Texas alone than American investments in China and Japan combined.[11] The main axis of globalization is clearly the one spanning the Atlantic Ocean. The Internet has opened up new horizons for small and medium-sized enterprises by allowing them to become international players, and it has also reinforced the role of English as the lingua franca of Western civilization.

The dynamism of China does pose the possibility of a shift in focus. But there is an even more important question behind all this: Will global capitalism be able to cope with globalization? Could China's triumphant return on the back of turboglobalization—after a millennium of seclusion and humiliation—mark the end of the second age of globalization? Is China the twenty-first century's Germany, which demands a seat at the top table, and will it destroy modern global liberalism? China is starting to behave like a Western capitalist country on the international stage. It does not really have any other option. The Chinese company TCL, the world's second-biggest manufacturer of television sets, took over Thomson of France only to close it down to rid itself of the loss-making burden. The profit earnings of Lenovo also fell by 85 percent after it had acquired the personal computer division of IBM. The reasons for these business mistakes could vary from bad management to insufficient knowledge of Western markets. Whatever the case, China will soon become a global player and, as such, it could be in for some nasty surprises in a game that is about more than just producing at low cost and enjoying the benefit of a booming economy due to investment by Western firms. In other words, China has yet to "go fully global." The question is what ripples it will make in the process. China has already accumulated huge potential: a currency reserve worth more than $1 trillion (40 percent of its GDP), with 70 percent invested in U.S. Treasury bonds.[12] But what if China decides to turn the screws and apply pressure on the United States through its currency reserve, just as Russia is playing its gas trump card? If something like that were to happen, it could harm not only America but also its biggest economic partner—Europe.

The Western world is the greatest beneficiary of globalization. The European Commission estimates that globalization could boost the EU's wealth over the next fifty years if Europe manages to make the most of it. Nevertheless, certain groups in Western society—the so-called worrying middle class—are terrified by globalization. Disregarding these fears would be a big mistake and could easily backfire.

The second, American scenario of globalization is different from the first one in many aspects; it evolved much more slowly, and with much stronger social checks. Today's Western societies are highly developed, self-organizing democracies, and today's social welfare provisions (even in the United States) have created a real social democratic paradise compared with what Europe had to offer a century before. The problem is that the entry of China, India, and other important players into the global market has also meant the entry of 2.5 billion workers into the labor market, which is an unprecedented, historic development—even if its impact is somewhat counterbalanced by the fact that these 2.5 billion people have also become global consumers. This can mean two things. On the one hand, it opens up new horizons for capital investment and improves profit prospects; on the other hand, cheap Asian labor leads to the devaluation of the Western workforce and weakens its negotiating position. In the short run, this formula applies: Western capital and Eastern labor will combine forces, and as a result corporate profits will soar, real wages in the West will fall, and Eastern wages will increase. Calculations comparing the profit-to-wage ratios before and after the turn of the millennium verify this prediction. The question is whether Western society will be able to cope with these changes and wait patiently until the world economy finds its new balance and whether Western political elites will be able to conduct an economic and social policy that calms the waves of turboglobalization without resorting to protectionism, which would be detrimental in the long run. Decisionmakers on both sides of the

Atlantic find themselves in a difficult position as capital becomes increasingly mobile and is easily enticed to high-growth Asian markets where costs
are considerably lower. That is why raising the minimum wage always carries the risk of inducing more firms to relocate.

There are also protectionist inclinations outside Europe. The United
States, the leading player of globalization, resorts to protectionist measures
quite regularly, mostly under pressure from powerful lobbying groups. The
closed-door policy is part and parcel of American political culture, just as
much as the open door policy. (This is best illustrated by the 2006 decision
to limit the role of foreigners in the management of U.S. airlines.) As we
have seen, today's world is characterized by serious economic and financial
imbalances, primarily because the United States consumes more than it
should and China keeps its currency weaker than it should. The question
arises: How long will global openness be good for the United States from a
geostrategic and national security perspective, if China benefits the most?

George Soros warned during the global crisis of 2008–9 that a rising
American protectionism could disrupt the world's economy and plunge it
into a recession or worse. The first age of globalization ended in failure because of bad and late political responses.[13] The current global capitalist system also faces many pitfalls of an economic, ideological, religious, and
geopolitical nature, as well as growing social dissatisfaction. The world has
not flattened out, and the end of history—the eternal age of global capitalism—has not arrived. Earlier in this book, I said that recent events, such as
the failure of the Doha Round and corporate scandals, will not bring globalization to a standstill. This is true, because at the micro—that is, company—level, the integration of the world economy is happening at a staggering pace. Yet what the coming decades will bring in international politics
is a completely different question. If the stakeholders in globalized capitalism fail to manage their domestic problems properly and do not cooperate
internationally, the system could fall to pieces. The global capitalist order
is no longer confined to Europe, the United States, and Japan, but—however bizarre it may sound at first—now includes China, which only makes
the task at hand more complicated. To make it even worse, the global capitalist order suffered a dramatic blow in 2008. It is in the West's strong economic and geopolitical interest to repair it. In the meantime, we must bear
in mind that globalization was made possible by a series of political decisions in America, Europe, and China. And if the political wind changes,
globalization can be undone.

The Decline of Europe and the West?

According to Voltaire, "In the age of decline, people find the easiest way to do things, they are too lazy to see their projects through, they have grown disgusted with real art and fancy the bizarre instead." Someone told me that I should not bother with the publication of this book because the subprime crisis and the global economic downturn in 2008 were only the start of a genuine paradigm change, which heralds the end of the capitalist world order.

For many, the twilight of Europe is part of a more general decline, that of Western culture. The West, and within it Europe, has been inundated by alienation, the absurd, postmodern denial, the whining of existentialism, the spirit of nihilism, and a generally negative attitude toward knowledge, science, institutions, social cohesion, political and international organizations, globalization, and the European Union. Full emancipation has led to a denial of Western values; a denial of, or indifference to, the Western view of the world; and a denial of all forms of authority or objectivity. We are continuously bombarded with statistics like this: In 1972, fewer than one in ten British children grew up in a single-parent family, but this ratio has increased to one in four, and almost every second child is born out of wedlock. Take any American bestseller about "Europe," and it will depict Europe as too sophisticated and too soft, as the mother of Western civilization on her deathbed whose days are numbered. Even though I do not share this deep pessimism, one cannot help but notice the warning signs in today's Western societies.

Civilizations do not have clear territorial boundaries; they continuously change, develop, are born, prosper, and then fail. According to Samuel Huntington's popular paradigm, the future will be determined not by traditional nation-state-based clashes but by the conflicts of different civilizations.[14] If he is right—and what we are witnessing is more than just a simple postcolonization geopolitical reshuffle with formerly subordinated countries in search of their place in the new world—then the coming decades will be crucial for the West.

Western civilization developed in Western Europe in the eighth century and went on to conquer first North America and then other parts of the world, such as Australia. Western civilization is defined by common values, ideologies, and development trends rather than by its peoples, religions, or geographical areas. It has been characterized by the rule of law; the separation of church and state; Catholic and Protestant roots; civil society representation; representative democracy; individualism; and, more recently, by industrialization, urban life, the sanctity of private property, modernity, social mobility, self-organization, emancipation, prosperity, quality education, and democracy. Some of these features are present in other civilizations (Muslim, Chinese, Indian, Japanese), but never all of them at the same time. This is what makes the West the West.

According to Huntington, Western civilization was at its peak when the Western powers held most of the world under colonial rule. Since then, Western civilization has been on the retreat in many respects (in terms of territory, relative military and economic might, superior prosperity), while the Islamic and Chinese civilizations have been gaining strength. The West, and within it Europe, is under threat from these two—self-proclaimed superior—civilizations that deny several fundamental Western values, such as individualism and democracy. The possibility of serious conflicts with an increasingly self-conscious Islamic culture cannot be ruled out, and the clashes between Western liberal democracy and Marxist ideology could pale in comparison, Huntington writes.[15] Let me add an interesting fact: In a 2006, poll one in three young British Muslims approved of the London Underground bombing of July 2005.[16]

Huntington also considers China's rise to power a threat, arguing that China is predestined to act as an empire and become an even greater menace than the Germany of Emperor William II. It is therefore in America's interests to prevent China from dominating the Asian continent single-handedly, just as Germany's dominance of Europe was prevented in the twentieth century.[17] The geopolitical balance is shifting quite rapidly. The success of the Beijing Olympics in August 2008 followed soon after by the collapse of Wall Street is symbolic. America needs the dollars held by China to survive, and the West needs the booming Chinese economy to keep rolling.

The big question is whether Europe will be able to withstand this double crunch. The West will probably lose its global hegemony, ending the division of "the West and the rest," both in public thinking and in practice. However, Western values and institutions have profoundly penetrated certain rival civilizations (with great variations of impact), and thus a sudden dethronement is unlikely to happen. The key sign of decline—as historical examples illustrate—is not territorial or demographic loss but "social decline," indicated by lax work ethics, worsening social apathy toward public affairs, hostility toward equal burden sharing, increasing cynicism and corruption among political leaders, the devaluation of fundamental values, and intellectual coarsening.

It may be worthwhile to continue the comparison with the Roman Empire, this time focusing on its collapse. First of all it, should be noted that although the Roman Empire was formed in Europe, its ideology and mentality were very different from that of post–World War II European integration, based on voluntary cooperation and free markets. Rome was a true empire held together by military power and built mainly from appropriated resources and by conquest. Rome did not have a proper budget; its revenues came from looting neighboring peoples and from proceeds from conquests, which stymied technological progress and the development of its own industry. Many believe that this was what caused its disintegration. The empire had to spend vast sums on maintaining its borders, which could only be done by relying on barbarian mercenaries paid with revenues from sky-high taxes.

People began to lose their faith in the Roman Empire as famine became frequent, corruption and decadence spread like a disease, social differences and regional disparities widened, and unemployment and inflation rose. The empire lost its cohesion economically, politically, and spiritually. The appearance of the Germans, many of whom had served in the Roman army, was the last straw. As citizens sank into lethargy, they no longer knew why they should defend the dilapidated empire, which meant less and less to them. In 476, the German commander Odoacer deposed the last Western Roman emperor, Romulus Augustulus. Weeds grew over the roads; townsfolk abandoned the cities; trade declined; artisans closed their shops; fields were left to lie fallow, unploughed, and barren; the countryside was infested with bandits; and the seas swarmed with pirates. In the meantime, Christianity was spreading quietly, and there was no stopping it.

In his book *Imperium: A Novel of Ancient Rome,* Robert Harris draws an interesting parallel between Rome and the United States. In 68 BC, there was a terrorist attack against Rome, which had been thought invincible up to that point.[18] Rome's port at Ostia was set on fire, the consular war fleet was destroyed, and two prominent senators were kidnapped. Such was the panic that the good people of Rome invested Pompeius Magnus with extraordinary power to conduct the "war on terror," thereby voluntarily curtailing their own civil rights, which in turn opened the way for rolling back democracy and centralizing power.

Back to the future—Europe is sinking. In the eyes of many Americans, it has become a decadent, lazy, and insignificant "country," facing a slow and painful end due to its own softness and its catastrophic demographic prospects. Today, Europe is home to more than 11 percent of the world's population, but by 2050, this proportion will have fallen to 7 percent, while the number of Muslims will have trebled.[19] To make things worse, many Americans believe that in the hour of need following the terrorist attacks on the United States, Europe turned its back on its transatlantic ally. In 2003, the U.S. secretary of state, Condoleezza Rice, is said to have advised President George W. Bush to "punish France, ignore Germany, and forgive Russia."

In the realm of the world's leading powers, a rivalry between the United States and Europe in the field of their policy vis-à-vis China could be potentially dangerous if it becomes divisive, which is not an unlikely scenario. The United States increasingly looks upon China as a threat, while Europe is beginning to see China's emergence into the ranks of the global powers as an opportunity. This is not accidental, but the time may come when Europe must make its choice, which could cause tension. This is thus one more reason to have substantive dialogue between the two Western powers. Having said this, obviously the optimistic "Plan A" works on the premise of China becoming a peaceful member of the new world order, and probably adopting a somewhat softer policy toward Europe than the United States, with its global hegemony. Europe has already twice smashed through the gate of China. In the fifteenth and sixteenth centuries, China welcomed barbarian missionaries from Europe with apathy; in the nineteenth century, Europe sent troops instead, which then humbled the proud Chinese. Hopefully, both sides have learned their lessons, and they will do business differently now that China is knocking on the gates of the West. Asia must also face its internal conflicts. China is not the only country in the continent aspiring to a key regional and/or global role, it has two more contestants to reckon with. The fundamental idea behind Europe's reunification was to stifle Franco-German rivalry. The project succeeded in a few decades, with a help from Europe's transatlantic friend. Pacifying Chinese-Japanese and Chinese-Indian rivalry will probably take much longer, if it is possible at all. The European example of strong regional integration is there to copy, and Asia would to well to follow suit.

The development of the Asian countries shows some peculiar features. Since World War II, some have been walking the road of democracy, and some (in fact, most) have taken the road of economic liberalization while resisting democracy. The second group has had more success; economic reforms, modernization, and preparing for globalization have been easier for the quasi-tyrannies, while the countries that have pursued democracy have developed more slowly or sunk into chaos due to weak institutions, an unstable economy, and the lack of a civil society. Nevertheless, Western values have spread all over Asia, of course always with a local twist. Countries that we used to call the third world not long ago are making progress—or at least changing—at an astonishing speed. Dubai, Saudi Arabia, and Qatar are investing billions of dollars in construction projects. But all that glitters is not gold. The fashionable group of countries known as the BRICs—an acronym for Brazil, Russia, India, and China, the key emerging economies —is far from homogeneous. China and India are investing in the future, have leading global companies, and are making the most of their intellectual resources, while Brazil and Russia are enjoying the windfall profits generated by high prices of raw materials. Even so, by the middle of the twenty-first century, only one of the world's top six economic powers will come from the West.

What are Europe's prospects in this situation? What can we expect on this continent, which has had by far the greatest number of leading powers per square kilometer throughout history? We know that pluralism and diversity are important European values, which have deep historical roots. We also know that European unification has never succeeded or remained sustainable, except during short periods of conquest. There has never been a single power that could have dominated the entire continent, and we feel the consequences—positive and negative—even today. This is partly due to the continent's fragmented geography, the fact that Europe is made up of many territorial units with differing geological and geographical conditions. Lowlands divided by mountain ranges and barren hills enclosed by vast forests make it difficult to unite the continent by military means alone. This facilitated the development of dozens of separate cultures and administrations, which induced competition—a key element of European civilization. This competitive environment produced a number of global powers, which came to dominate the world in successive centuries. As a result, by the end of the nineteenth century, Europe had irreversibly left its cultural mark on all the Earth's continents.

In a military sense, Europe was undefeatable because it was never united. Moreover, the European powers were always the biggest "troublemakers" in history, waging countless wars against each other. The appearance of the Ottoman Empire and of the Soviet Union were perhaps the two most important exceptions, when European countries to some extent joined forces against the outside world. The Soviet threat was the second menace from the northeast; until the Crimean War in the mid–nineteenth century, the quickly developing Russian Empire had been a potential threat to the West. Then the West, led by Britain, quickly disposed of this menace: Russia's growth was simply light years behind that of the West. For instance, in 1830, Britain's GDP per head was double that of Russia; fifty years later, it was four times as much. Soviet imperialism in the twentieth century and the Cold War redrew Europe's power map completely. By the second half of the twentieth century, it became clear that a fragmented continent was more of a disadvantage than a blessing.

Two momentous occasions of the last two decades have brought significant changes in international relations, not only in geopolitical terms but also in terms of focus. The first occasion bringing these changes was the end of the bipolar world resulting from the end of the Cold War, which rearranged the balance of power and shifted the emphasis from military and power politics to civil aspects, such as human rights, terrorism, the environment, and climate change. The second occasion was the advent of turboglobalization, which delivered a blow to traditional geopolitics based on national and military alliances by pushing economic factors and players to the forefront of international relations. As a consequence, certain doctrines and institutions—such as NATO, the symbol of Western "brothers-in-arms" —found themselves looking for a new place in a new world.

The question Europeans need to answer is what is Europe's place in this new international system of doctrines, institutions, and relations. Accepting that Western culture is now and will continue losing ground in the coming decades—which could lead to the realization that global culture is a thing of the past—Europe could benefit from the new world order in many ways. In the brutal, force-based Cold War era, Europe's strongest nation, Germany, was divided and thus unavoidably condemned to an obviously subordinate role. Now, however, Europe could have much to gain in the new world, partly because power-based politics has been devalued and other softer factors are becoming more important, and partly because Europe is evolving into an ever-larger regional federation—no longer caught between the two poles of a divided world. But to make the most of this opportunity, Europe must be able to demonstrate much more unity in foreign affairs. I do not believe in utopian predictions that the world will become a set of self-organized regional alliances. Nor do I believe that a global federation of states with real, meaningful content will be created. However, the absence of such alliances and federations will only enhance the relative weight and role of Europe on the international stage, especially when a Eurasia holding three-quarters of the world's energy reserves is becoming an increasingly significant part of the world.

This, however, does not change the fact that there is no European identity. Moreover, a European identity cannot be shaped on the basis of old national identities, precisely because they run counter to a common single identity. For the British, the Hundred Years' War fought with France remains an important historical memory, just as the Battle of Verdun is for the French. Such cultural memories are difficult to leave behind or integrate into a common European memory. The absence of a common language is another sensitive issue. Obviously, without a common language, or at least without a dominant language spoken by all, there can be no common identity. Logically, this common language could only be English, which one day could become the communication channel for a common European media and public arena. Unfortunately, the trends are unfavorable; the pan-European idea was more important for postwar generations, whose memory of the war years helped them understand the alternative to cooperation. Subsequent generations, who have benefited more from integration, do not have that understanding, and as they take the benefits of European integration for granted they become increasingly skeptical toward it.

Eighteenth-century France gave the world the ideological underpinnings of a modern, democratic, and constitutional state. Nineteenth-century Britain gave the world the model of a modern and flourishing global economy. And twentieth-century Germany provided the world with the example of how to build a successful society and welfare state from ruins. The question is open: What will twenty-first-century Europe give the world? Or should Europeans not aim that high and just be happy if Europe survives the twenty-first century?

After World War II, the United States built the "free world" based on the ideas of liberty, the rule of law, and international cooperation. These ideas put at least as much pressure on the Berlin Wall as did the U.S. proposal for Star Wars missiles. Empires, even the most successful ones, collapse in the end. But successful ideas always survive.

What Will Have Become of Europe in 2050?

Mark Twain once said that prophecy is a difficult art, especially when it is the future you have to predict. Many polemics about the future of the world popular at the time of my PhD studies now seem like futile academic reflections. One example was the polemics between those who foresaw the end of the nation-state and the creation of a world government and those who believed that the odds were in favor of nation-states maintaining their role. The polemics are just as interesting today as they were then, but they have lost their relevance. So many things have happened in recent years, and so much more is yet to come, that sterile scientific theories about the future of governments and politics in the new world order are dwarfed by the topical and pressing issues interwoven in our daily lives in thousands of ways, such as global warming, migration, megaterrorism, and the 1 billion Asian workers about to enter the global labor market. For Europe, one such acute problem is the future of its own regional integration.

As we have seen, the European Union is far from being a proper state. It does not have any political or military powers and, due to the divergent interests of its members, it is not a serious force to reckon with on the global scene. Europe might be using its self-generated identity as a soft power to conceal its weakness as a military power, which may be a useful and workable doctrine until a serious international conflict arises. Also, it is unclear how the proposed nuptials of the two hermaphrodites—the EU, a confederation showing federation-like features; and Turkey, a country Westernized by fire and sword—will turn out. And it is unclear whether the Franco-German axis, once the driving force behind European integration, will ever regain its momentum and significance. That is only likely to happen within the context of a smaller "core Europe." I have pointed out several times throughout this book that it is unclear what vision the EU has for the future. This lack of a vision has been an effective weapon in the hands of people proceeding with integration slowly but surely; as long as it is boring, unattractive, and undefined, it does not provoke those EU member states that are opposed to deeper integration. This has also led to a fear of a "creeping Brussels," which keeps extending its power slowly but with steadfast determination and keeps enlarging, up to as many as thirty-three members by 2020.

Let us now take a look at the various theories circulating about the future of European integration.

The EU has come to a crossroads. Its destiny will be determined first by the outcome of the fight between federalists and believers in the nation-state; second by its ability to modernize, which will be determined by the outcome of the competition between different European models and by the upsurge of liberalism; and third by the efficiency and public support of European institutions. Among the external factors that will shape the continent's future are global competition; Europe's relations with China, America, and Russia; and Europe's responses to the global trends outlined at the beginning of this book. As far as the answer to the "How to proceed from here?" question is concerned, there are several viable alternatives. The two-speed, network, and flexible models for European integration described in chapter 4 more or less correspond to the musings of the Economist Intelligence Unit.[20] The most probable scenario forecasts a slowing down of integration but rules out the possibility of backtracking. The fight between profederalists and antifederalists will continue, but without any winners or definitive solutions. The EU's institutions will refrain from forging new policies but will widely apply existing legislation. Eventually, some elements of the EU Constitution will be adopted, which will make the enlarged Union more effective and manageable.

There are also much less realistic speculations, which reckon that the EU or its key policies will disappear. They predict that European Community's powers will fall back upon the member states, except in areas directly linked to the operation of the single market; otherwise, further market liberalization will come to a halt. This scenario foreshadows a pruned budget with expenditures below 0.5 percent of GDP and a streamlined bureaucracy. And there is an "anarchist" scenario, according to which events will unfold the following way: Single market rules will be disregarded, and the institutions responsible for enforcement will be paralyzed.

The evolution of a multilayer "Fortress Europe" is also not unthinkable. This would involve a group of "pro–social Europe" EU member states forming a closely knit hard core on the basis of the Founding Treaties in force, surrounded by a more loosely integrated outer layer. The core group would enact protectionist measures combating relocation and would introduce new minimum wages. Corporate tax rates would be aligned as part of fiscal harmonization. Transitional measures on the free movement of labor would be extended and further tightened.

Finally, there is the rather improbable "Phoenix" scenario, which forecasts Europe's sudden recovery, deepening integration, and new European policies. In this scenario, these elements would come under the Community's umbrella: minimum requirements on social protection, agreement on minimum corporate tax rates and action against tax evasion, further deepening of the internal market, and the extension of mandatory Community rules to new economic and financial areas.

The future of the EU, a hermaphrodite in constant transformation and facing myriad dangers, is of interest to many. But even the most gifted analysts can only outline divergent alternatives, which are best summed up as "anything could happen." Nevertheless, their best guess is a scenario leading to Europe's disintegration brought about by a deep social crisis caused by immigration, and aging population, and deepening competitiveness.

There are several other models—some rather utopian—for the EU's future development, which I briefly set out here.[21] In the "victorious markets" model, a United States–led global free market is completed, and the EU loses its international role and slowly disappears; corporations become the key actors of the international order, competition is the rule of thumb, social disparities widen, and the state plays a limited role. In the "hundred flowers" scenario, regions and microregions are remarkably invigorated, and the EU disappears due to its inability to push through its policies of centralization against the will of regional self-organizations. In the "turbulent neighborhood" scenario, the EU crumbles under the pressure of masses of immigrants arriving from Africa and the East; this model is characterized by terrorism, civil wars, organized crime, and the extreme right's climb to power, while European institutions and civilization lose ground. The "creative society" scenario—despite what the name suggests—does not bring heaven on Earth; this world is troubled by permanent social unrest and by antiglobalization and anticapitalist demonstrations, and the evolution and enlargement of the EU are frozen. Finally, there is an "optimistic" scenario; a successful EU takes up the torch, modernizes its economy, trims back the unsustainable welfare state, and properly manages immigration and neighborhood policy.

The Copenhagen Institute for Futures Studies outlines four different scenarios for the future of Europe. The first, the "cooperating nation-states" model, is a continuation of what we have today. There are enhanced economic cooperation and weak cooperation in the political, foreign policy, and social policy areas; and the member states remain powerful within the Union, which reinforces protectionism and blocks further enlargement. The second scenario—"Europe's corrosion"—envisages the end of European integration and the collapse of the monetary union; the member states go on operating in smaller and looser alliances, Brussels becomes largely superfluous, and some member states emerge as winners from this rupture, while others are plunged into economic and social crisis. In the third scenario—bearing the fancy name "Intertwining Europe"—the role of the member states diminishes and slowly disappears as Europe's peoples are integrated culturally; cooperation is not nation based but builds on intertwining towns, cities, regions, nongovernmental organizations, and enterprises, with the EU having the role of coordinator for this happy and peaceful self-organized world. And last but not least, the fourth scenario promises a proper "European state," a federation with a common president and Parliament, enabling the EU to become a true global power.

It would be difficult to call any of these scenarios realistic. However, there are also several truly visionary models out there, which are often quite farfetched, such as the one for a new "Western Empire" uniting the regions of Western civilization in a multicontinent state in order to maintain the balance of power between rival civilizations.

Personally, I would put my money on the "network Europe" scenario as the most likely one, provided that Europe does not collapse before that. In this model, European integration goes beyond the geographical boundaries of Europe, with Brussels as the main center, coordinating and adopting the fundamental rules; and "core Europe"—the monetary and political union, with a common president and Parliament—is surrounded by several subregional centers of cooperation.

Ten Recommendations for "Europe"

In the coming years, Europe needs to preserve its prosperity, enhance its growth, and reinforce its international position in a more and more unsustainable world and in a rapidly changing geopolitical environment. The following ten recommendations form more than just a slightly arbitrary to-do list. I have tried to enumerate the tasks that become topical at various stages of European integration and to indicate their varying degrees of priority.

First, Europe must not be afraid of globalization and the rise of the new world order; instead, it should try to make the most of it. There are so many things going on at the same time in Europe that parallel developments become entangled, which may cloud some people's thinking. The many phenomena to which Europe is exposed are often negative or evoke fear—including a stumbling economy, excessive unemployment, sudden waves of EU enlargement that seem to happen without warning, Turkey's candidacy for EU membership, massive immigration, terrorism, and the rise of China—and all manifest themselves in the notion of "globalization." Thus globalization has become the object of—or has even come to embody—social unrest and anxieties in Western Europe, which is misleading and harmful and could therefore seriously distort Europeans' view of the world and their place in it. In the long run, this could amplify detrimental and potentially self-harming political and economic reflexes. Yet contrary to public belief, Europeans cannot close themselves off from globalization, particularly because the European economy is one of the engines driving it. Along with managing short-term social tensions, those European leaders truly serving society must enable people to understand that globalization—to be precise, the global integration of markets—actually serves the interests of Europe's economy. Europeans must learn not be afraid of change; they must do their best to preserve the values of European culture. Europeans should aim to set global standards and play a prominent role in establishing the rules of the postcrisis world order—a new world order of more international rules but no less freedom, of more institutions but no less global interaction.

An open and cooperative Europe is crucial for the rest of the world, especially for the United States, with which Europe not only has the most intense and comprehensive economic ties but also shares the most important cultural and societal values. It is clear that Europe's destiny is not solely a European story but also a story of the Western world.

Second, Europe must choose substance over form—it must focus less on institutional issues and more on finding a viable socioeconomic model. The question of European institutions and decisionmaking procedures is indeed an important one—especially for this ever-changing economic-political union, this unique hermaphrodite that is the EU. However, it is even more important to have something to manage, to ensure the long-term stability and success of the EU, which requires a reformed, modern, competitive socioeconomic model. Of course, this does not mean that Brussels should create a common, central European model. It is up to the EU's member states, particularly those continental ones with decisive economic weight, to overhaul their unsustainable welfare systems, while Brussels plays a supportive and consultative role.

One can safely state that in the long run, it is probable that the liberal American model, the social European model, and the Asian mercantilist model of China will get closer to each other. Unless a dramatic shift occurs in the geopolitical order, each model will cherry-pick those elements from the other models that help enhance competitiveness and social satisfaction. Europe will get somewhat tougher; America will get somewhat milder.

Third, Europeans must come to a clear agreement on the role, mission, and boundaries of the European Union. The mission of European integration has always been understood in various ways, and people continue to define it differently. For decades, this was not a problem because, as the European Union evolved and its functions changed, everyone got a bit of what they wanted—whether federalism, a looser association of states, economic integration, or political union. These times seem to be over once and for all. With the end of the Cold War, the cohesive force binding Europe together has weakened, and several other developments have also rearranged the face of Europe. The same developments that have generated fear of globalization are mercilessly undermining the top-down, managed, but continuous and linear evolution of integration. The stability of European construction hinges on a number of questions, and the task of answering these cannot be deferred any longer. Europeans must clearly define the function, future, and ultimate objective of Europe as well as its functional and geographic boundaries. Naturally, these factors are all interrelated. If Europe's function is that of a well-oiled regional economic alliance, or a common market with limited political dimensions, then its functional borders do not need to stretch beyond the economic market.

Conversely, because the European Union is not a political union, only an economic alliance, its geographic borders can be arbitrary. However, if Europeans are aiming for a closely knit political union, then a too-heterogeneous group is obviously unworkable, which not only rules out the full membership of countries not traditionally considered to be part of Europe but is also likely to lead to a multispeed Europe. Consequently, clearly defining the EU's ultimate aim may induce extraordinary changes in the future of integration, and Europeans must proceed with caution. The question is: How long can integration continue to operate in its traditionally slow, unobtrusive, apolitical manner?

Another question is what the European Union's choice regarding its enlargement would mean for the rest of the world. An integrated Turkey—with a special membership status that did not grant all the rights or impose all the obligations of full-fledged membership—could make Europe, the Middle East, and the whole world safer.

Fourth, Europe must reinforce its international profile and thus needs a single foreign policy. Irrespective of the ultimate goal of integration, Europe must speak with one voice to the rest of the world. Europe is an economic giant staggering on wobbly feet, the disadvantages of which are so obvious that they require no explanation. Naturally, a move toward political integration would benefit more united international action. But there are other ways to achieve results, for example, by reviving the relevant elements—a European minister of foreign affairs, a common diplomatic service—of the rejected EU Constitution. One of the key elements of success depends on aligning the French and British positions, and not only in foreign and defense policy. Europe would also need single representation in foreign trade, which would be best achieved by reinforcing the role of the euro zone and of "Mr. Euro" (see chapter 4). The United States might feel uneasy because of an ever-more-prominent European currency, but in foreign policy it has already started to realize the need for a stronger and more capable Western ally.

Fifth, Europe must place competitiveness at the center of its policies. Amid cutthroat global competition, both EU member states' and European Community strategies must have competitiveness as their centerpiece. Some leading member states, however, persist in wanting to maintain their competitiveness by means of protectionist measures, which has nothing to do with real, performance-based competitiveness. Protectionism is only a provisional solution; a mollycoddled economy accustomed to the lukewarm coziness of protected markets will inevitably be swept away by the flood of competition when the levee finally breaks. The bedrock of competitiveness is competition itself, which inspires performance, progress, and innovation. Having completed its internal economic integration, Europe must now open up to the world and allow its economies and industries to become global players.

Times of crisis are tough tests of openness, both politically and economically. In today's troubled global economic climate, the worst-case scenario would be if the United States and Europe were to start a protectionist competition against China or each other.

Sixth, Europe must finish building a true single internal market and preserve the stability of its monetary union and its common currency. The single European market is one of Europe's untapped potentials. The remaining obstacles must be dismantled. The single currency is the pinnacle of economic integration, and even though it was created through political decisionmaking, it is stable and rests on solid economic foundations. Maintaining the currency union of a dozen countries whose economies are so different is not a boring "autopilot" job, especially in times of recession. The rules and institutions of the monetary union are under constant and heavy criticism, even while Brussels and the EU member states are engaged in the Herculean task of fully enforcing them. The euro may be Europe's brightest success story and its most important common symbol, but at the same time it is much more than that; it holds the key to the economic stability of the euro zone and is a potential lever of Europe's international role. At first, many called the euro the sibling of political union, and some still await the other sibling's birth. Yet one way or another, preserving the single currency has become one of Europe's top jobs.

The euro has a great track record so far. Therefore Europe, with its strong new currency, has the chance to lead the world into a new dual or multicurrency era in the medium term, which would be the start of a new world economic order. The outcomes of these possibilities are nevertheless still quite difficult to predict.

Seventh, Europe must focus its intellectual and financial resources on managing its essential economic and social challenges, such as the security of its energy supply, its aging population, and immigration. Europe is trapped; due to its aging population, the ratio of retirees to active wage earners will double. People find it easier to cope with modest living conditions than to experience falling living standards. The members of today's generation will be the first ones to be worse off than their parents, and this trend will probably continue in coming decades. Drastic reforms will need to follow, and solutions will be required for dealing with a growing number of immigrants. Europe is also trapped due to its energy dependency. It must do two things. First, it must modernize its economy and improve energy efficiency. Second, it must elevate energy policy to the forefront of its foreign policy and negotiate with energy-supplying countries in a more effective and united manner.

Europe's long-term security risks—energy dependency, demography, and so on—are significant. For these issues, Asia and Africa pose big challenges to Europe—Asia with respect to the energy supply and general economic competitiveness, and Africa with respect to migration. The coming years will reveal whether Europe can manage these risks appropriately, which to a large extent will influence tomorrow's geopolitical landscape.

Eighth, Europe must pursue a multilateral and consensual world order. Europe has had enough hard-bought experience playing second fiddle in a bipolar world based on mutual distrust and power politics. The creation of a multilateral world order will serve the interests of Europe as well as the whole world, whose focus and potential crisis zone will lie in Asia. A Sino-American bipolar situation would probably not be consensus based but rather divisive and filled with tensions. It is therefore of global interest to forge a multiplayer, more "complex" world order. How effective Europe's "soft power" approach—used successfully vis-à-vis the EU's neighboring applicant countries—would be on the global scene remains a big question.

The unipolar moment of U.S. hegemony is over, while China is on the rise. A "Group of Two," whereby the world order would be defined by potentially conflict-ridden United States–China relations, would not only be problematic for Europe but also harmful for the whole world.

Ninth, the feeling of European-ness must become stronger among Europe's citizens. The job description is self-explanatory: No matter how well European institutions function, they are operating in a vacuum unless the "project Europe" they are running can rely on popular support, fondness, or at least some kind of shared identity. I have deliberately avoided saying that "Europe must strengthen European-ness," because it will not work like that. The feeling of European-ness can only become stronger as a result of a long process; one-time public campaigns can achieve very little. There must be a cross-cutting element in federal and national policies to improve the situation. However, it is of paramount importance to avoid the pitfall of trying to build a common European identity on the basis of the cozy feeling of being shielded from globalization. European integration has always been a top-down, elitist project. If, in 1950, European voters had been asked to decide whether they wanted a Coal and Steel Community, there would probably not be an EU today. However, these days, the public cannot be circumvented when deciding on crucial questions of integration. In the words of Jacques Delors, "People must be made to fall in love with Europe." It is of course much easier to say than to do.

Tenth, Europe must have more efficient institutions. The Europe of Six is a thing of the past; the club's membership could soon swell to thirty. Community institutions are a unique "Laocoön Group," one of a kind in the whole wide world, incomparable in comparison with anything that nation-states or other international organizations have devised. These common European institutions churn out legislative acts by the hundred, providing work for millions of civil servants Europe-wide. Although the EU is seemingly always pressed for time, laws can sometimes take as much as a decade to adopt. European institutions have developed in parallel with the geographical and functional enlargement of integration. During the last few years, the number of member states has almost doubled, which means that the EU must respond to the new situation. At the same time, due to the rejection of the Constitutional Treaty, institutional and decisionmaking reforms have yet to be made.

These reforms remain all the more necessary; the principles and solutions laid down in the draft EU Constitution are resurfacing after being shelved for a brief period of reflection. It does not matter if we call it the Constitution, or by any other name. One day, Europe should have a legal tool to make its integration deeper, and its international voice stronger for the good—I believe—of the whole world.

The Old Lady and the Bull

I did not want to write an "I-am-telling-you-the-truth" type of book, with punchy statements. I do not believe in finite history, in flat planets, or in everlasting superpowers. I mistrust everyone who tries to explain the ultimate truth to me. Ultimate truths in economics or in political science tend to change in every decade, and sometimes even more frequently. I imagined that my readers would appreciate this approach as well.

I began writing this book on a sunny morning on the Dalmatian Coast and finished it on a rainy evening in Brussels. In the months between, I visited chilly Scandinavia, the frivolous French Riviera, and post–World Cup, football-crazy Germany. I witnessed the glamour and glitter in the cities of Western Europe and the palpable poverty in the rural towns of Eastern Europe. I saw the lush lawns of suburbia and the filthy alleys of ghettoes, walked along the cobbled streets of thousand-year-old city centers and through the towering office buildings of European corporations, smelled the confined air in cluttered rooms of research centers, gazed up at state-of-the-art skyscrapers, wondered at the exhibits in museums, drove on the tarmac of German autobahns, drank beer in centuries-old smoky pubs in Brussels, and sipped tea in central European coffeehouses.

Thus, I saw a small slice of the continent called Europe. I met many Europeans and some "foreigners." I listened to gobbledygook supported by econometric heavy artillery about how there was nothing wrong with the continental model and read politically motivated, contemptuous pamphlets confuting the "neoliberal mantra of this age," namely, that Europe should reinforce its competitiveness and productivity and realize that its welfare system needs to be adjusted to the new environment of the age of globalization. I read prophecies about Europe's decline due to its pathetic weakness by both European and American authors. Wherever I looked, it was apparent that the old continent was in turmoil. Those who care about the destiny of European integration are looking for the way of the future because everybody—including people who prefer to ignore the problems—feels that we are witnessing the end of a long era. Europe has arrived at a crossroads, which involves the identity and future of the European Union as much as the choice of socioeconomic models made by Western European countries.

A bigger problem than the worrisome—at times defeatist—tone of these conversations across the continent is the fact that public discourse on Europe is largely limited to the elite, while the masses continue to ignore European issues. It has become clear that it is increasingly difficult to maintain an elitist approach to the European project, but we have yet to see active participation—and especially positive commitment—by the whole of society. Europe must overcome this logjam, but the usual propaganda will not do the trick. History teaches us that the cohesion and identity of a group, people, or region is reinforced when they face a common external threat. This is another trap, however, because the majority of the public looks upon both the United States and globalization as threats. It would be a historic mistake to forge a European identity built on the animosity toward these "threats." As a consequence, enormous responsibility rests on the shoulders of Europe's intellectual and political elite.

Europe feels threatened in many ways: its economy and competitiveness by China's emergence, its social peace by Muslim immigration from North Africa, its role in international relations by the overpowering presence of the United States. In response to the "Chinese threat," Europe may resort to protectionism, sealing off its doors and hiding from globalization behind them. This scenario could become reality if the political center fails to make society understand that such an extreme leftist economic policy would be untenable and would send Europe sliding downhill. Rising social tensions caused by the growing Muslim population could bring grist to the mill of extreme-right political forces if Europe's political mainstream is unable to face the question honestly and allows xenophobes to move into, and fill, the empty space of the unavoidable social debate and soul searching. I do not need to spell out to what this could lead; Europe has seen it happen before. Anti-Americanism, which is gaining ground, confuses short-term aspects with Europe's long-term interests. It is nonsensical for the two key bastions of Western culture—due to real or unreal contemporary political consider-ations—to forget or even deny their common roots, common fundamental values, and their belief in democracy, social justice, and liberty, which tie them closely together. Whatever the political conditions of the time, they belong to the same ideological family.

For the sake of European integration, it is important for Europe to put its own house in order by answering several crucial questions about its pres-ent and future: What is the aim of integration? How far can Europe's bor-ders stretch? How close should integration be? Should Europe insist on a homogeneous integration whereby all members proceed at the same pace? And more important: Europe must choose a socioeconomic model that is competitive and successful in the long run and can ensure prosperity for its enterprises and citizens in the twenty-first century. The key policy chal-lenges of the twenty-first century are preventing a potential clash between ascending and descending civilizations; handling the rise of Asia; dealing with global threats like climate disasters, energy, and water scarcity; and creating new global rules and a new multipolar order, where Asia as well as

Europe has an important role to play. Or is John Gray right, and simply "those who control oil and water will control the world"?[22] Time will tell, but I believe the world is not that simple and that hard work, creativity, and vision can make a difference. Sometimes—actually, fairly frequently in the EU's history—crises do the job. I would not be surprised if the EU's constitutional deadlock and the 2008 global economic meltdown push Europe in new directions, such as political union and multiple-speed integration. Both are necessary to get Europe out of stagnation, move it ahead, and enable it to be successful.

I have attempted to provide insights into the key challenges facing Europe, which comprise dangers and solutions like the many layers of an onion. We have peeled the layers off the onion, which has brought tears to our eyes, but it is time to face the facts. The future holds many opportunities as well as difficulties and losses—that much is true. But introversion is the wrong response; Europe would be making a big mistake if it attempted the impossible and tried to shun globalization and cooperation with the rest of the world instead of turning it to its own advantage and making the most of it. The new world order of globalization, with the Asian rise, is like a raging bull, charging around the planet. Europe must mount the bull and ride it before it rampages roughshod over her.

*   *   *

Further Reading

On the general understanding of the European integration, I could recommend Paul Magnette, *What Is the European Union? Nature and Prospects* (London: Palgrave Macmillan, 2005). Also for this subject, it could be helpful to see Andrew Moravcsik, "In Defence of the Democratic Deficit: Reassessing Legitimacy in the European Union," *Journal of Common Market Studies* 40, no. 4 (2002): 603–24.

On the general question of the decline of the both the West and Europe, see the extraordinary book by Jacques Barzun, *From Dawn to Decadence: 500 Years of Western Cultural Life* (New York: HarperCollins, 2000). Also very interesting is Jeffry Frieden, *Will Global Capitalism Fall Again?* Bruegel Essay and Lecture Series (Brussels: Bruegel, 2006).

As for the future of Europe, useful contributions are Centre for European Reform, *EU 2010: A Programme for Reform—Manifesto* (Brussels: Centre for European Reform, 2006); and Tuomas Heikkil, ed., *Europe 2050: Challenges of the Future, Heritage of the Past* (Helsinki: Edita Prima, 2006).

There are many books with bold statements as regards the future role of Europe and the EU. Almost all of them choose a simplistic concept, and the function of the book's narrative is to underpin this—usually bombastic—vision. Nevertheless, it may be interesting for students studying European affairs to study these contradictory concepts as well. Jeremy Rifkin discusses how the European dream will eclipse the American one in his book; see Jeremy Rifkin, *The European Dream: How Europe's Vision of the Future Is Quietly Eclipsing the American Dream* (Cambridge: Polity Press, 2004). According to John McCormick, the next superpower will be the EU, mostly relying on soft power; see John McCormick, *The European Superpower* (London: Palgrave Macmillan, 2007). Stephen Haseler thinks similarly; see Stephen Haseler, *Super-State: The New Europe and Its Challenges to America* (London: I. B. Tauris, 2004). Another author with a similar opinion is Mark Leonard, *Why Europe Will Run the 21st Century* (London: Fourth Estate, 2005). Finally, a more balanced assessment is given by David P. Calleo, *Rethinking Europe's Future* (Princeton, N.J., Princeton University Press, 2000).

In general, I recommend consulting the regular bulletins and special issue papers of the Brussels-based think tanks, such as Bruegel (www.bruegel.org) and the Centre for European Policy Studies (www.ceps.be).

For statistical data on Europe, I recommend Eurostat, the statistical department of the European Commission (http://ec.europa.eu/eurostat). For poll results, see Eurobarometer, the EU's polling service (http://ec.europa.eu/public_opinion/index_en.htm).

Notes

Notes to Chapter 1

1. These data are from forecasts by the Organization for Economic Cooperation and Development and by the European Union; see Attila Marján, ed., *Az Európai Unió gazdasága* (The economy of the European Union) (Budapest: HVG Kiadó, 2006).

2. Martin Wolf, "Comment and Analysis: Why Do English-Speaking Countries Perform Better?" *Financial Times*, January 25, 2005.

3. Ibid.

4. "Agrifood" is the business of producing food agriculturally, rather than through hunting, fishing, etc.

5. See D. Wilson and R. Purushothaman, *Dreaming with BRICs: The Path to 2050*, Global Economics Paper 99 (New York: Goldman Sachs, 2003), http://www2.goldman sachs.com/ideas/brics/book/99-dreaming.pdf; and Marján, *Az Európai Unió gazdasága*.

6. European Commission, *Green Paper: Confronting Demographic Change—A New Solidarity between the Generations*, COM (2005) 94 (Brussels: European Union, 2005).

7. Ibid.

8. European Commission, *Green Paper: A European Strategy for Sustainable, Competitive and Secure Energy*, COM (2006) 105 (Brussels: European Union, 2006).

9. Francis Fukuyama, *The End of History and the Last Man* (New York: Free Press, 1992).

10. George Soros, *George Soros on Globalization* (New York: PublicAffairs, 2002).

11. These liberal economists include Paul Samuelson and Alan Blinder; see, e.g., Gabor Steingart, "The End of Globalization?" *Spiegel Online*, December 11, 2007, http://www.spiegel.de/international/world/0,1518,522628,00.html.

12. Thomas L. Friedman, *The World Is Flat: The Globalized World in the 21st Century* (New York: Penguin Books, 2006).

13. Valéry Giscard d'Estaing, *A franciák* (The French) (Budapest: Európa könyvkiadó, 2002).

14. Robert Schuman, *Európáért* (For Europe) (Budapest: Pro Pannonia Kiadói Alapítvány, 2004).

355

15. Greenspan was quoted by Kara Scannell and Sudeep Reddy, "Greenspan Admits Errors to Hostile House Panel," *Wall Street Journal Online,* October 24, 2008, http://online.wsj.com/article/SB122476545437862295.html.

16. Alan Greenspan, "Testimony of Dr. Alan Greenspan, Committee of Government Oversight and Reform," U.S. House of Representatives, October 23, 2008, http://oversight.house.gov/documents/20081023100438.pdf.

17. Bernanke was quoted by Peter Baker, "A Professor and a Banker Bury Old Dogma on Markets," *New York Times,* September 20, 2008, http://www.nytimes.com/2008/09/21/business/21paulson.html.

18. Stiglitz was interviewed by Kiyoshi Okonogi of *Asahi Shimbun,* November 5, 2008, as quoted by the Share the World's Resources Web site, http://www.stwr.org/global-financial-crisis/joseph-stiglitz-crisis-points-to-need-for-new-global-currency.html.

19. See Paul R. Krugman, "Is Free Trade Passé?" *Economic Perspectives* 1, no. 2 (Fall 1987): 131–44, http://math.stanford.edu/~lekheng/krugman/trade6.pdf.

Notes to Chapter 2

1. Paul Kennedy, *The Rise and Fall of the Great Powers* (New York: Random House, 1987); for the interview with Kennedy, see John Crace, "Paul Kennedy: Neocons' Worst Nightmare," *The Guardian,* February 5, 2008.

2. These data are from the United Nations Statistics Division; see http://unstats.un.org/unsd/default.htm.

3. See Jane Jacobs, *The Economy of Cities* (New York: Random House, 1969).

4. This section uses data from Jessica Williams, *Fifty Facts That Should Change the World* (Cambridge: Icon Books, 2004); Worldwatch Institute, *State of the World 2005: Redefining Global Security* (New York: W. W. Norton, 2005); and Ray Hammond, *The World in 2030* (Paris: Éditions Yago, 2007).

5. Nicholas Stern, *The Economics of Climate Change* (London: Her Majesty's Stationery Office, 2006).

6. European Communities, *Statistical Portrait of the European Union 2007* (Luxembourg: European Communities, 2007).

7. Samuel P. Huntington, *The Clash of Civilizations and the Remaking of World Order* (New York: Simon & Schuster, 1996).

8. Martin Wolf, *Why Globalization Works* (New Haven, Conn.: Yale University Press, 2005).

9. Daren Acemoglu and A. James Robinson, *The Economic Origins of Dictatorship and Democracy* (Cambridge: Cambridge University Press, 2006).

10. Thomas L. Friedman, *The World Is Flat: The Globalized World in the 21st Century* (New York: Penguin Books, 2006).

11. In this section, I cite many statistical data given by Wolf, *Why Globalization Works.*

12. Zentrum für Europäische Wirtschaftsforschung, "New Channels of Business Cycle Transmission Are Gaining Importance," ftp://ftp.zew.de/pub/zew-docs/zn/en/zn032002.pdf.

13. Friedman, *World Is Flat.*

14. Eliot A. Cohen, "World War IV," *Wall Street Journal,* November 20, 2001.

15. Joschka Fischer, "Europe's Calamity: A Commentary," *New Europe* (Brussels), June 22–28, 2008.

16. World Bank, *Globalization, Growth, and Poverty: Building an Inclusive World Economy* (Washington, D.C.: World Bank, 2002).

17. Food and Agriculture Organization of the United Nations, *The State of Food Insecurity in the World* (Rome: Food and Agriculture Organization of the United Nations, 2005).

18. Wolf, *Why Globalization Works.*

19. World Bank, *Globalization.*

20. These data are given by Daniel S. Hamilton and Joseph P. Quinlan, eds., *Deep Integration: How Transatlantic Markets Are Leading Globalisation* (Washington and Brussels: Center for Transatlantic Relations and Centre for European Policy Studies, 2005).

21. These data are from the World Trade Organization.

22. Wolf, *Why Globalization Works.*

23. Jean Pisani-Ferry and Bruno van Pottelsberge, *Handle with Care! Post-Crisis Growth in the EU,* Bruegel Policy Brief (Brussels: Bruegel, 2009).

24. Mark Leonard, *Why Europe Will Run the 21st Century* (London: Fourth Estate, 2005).

25. These are statistics from the Organization for Economic Cooperation and Development; see http://www.oecd.org/statsportal/.

26. Pascal Lamy, "The Future of the World Economy: What Place for EU Industries?" introductory remarks, Conference on the Insertion of European Industry in the International Division of Labour: Position and Perspectives, European Commission, Brussels, 2005.

27. Statistics from the Organization for Economic Cooperation and Development.

28. Martin Wolf, "Comment and Analysis: Why Do English-Speaking Countries Perform Better?" *Financial Times,* January 25, 2005.

29. The fifteen pre–2004 enlargement EU members are Austria, Belgium, Denmark, Finland, France, Germany, Greece, Ireland, Italy, Luxembourg, the Netherlands, Portugal, Spain, Sweden, and the United Kingdom. The data here are from Eurostat, the European Commission's data Web site, http://ec.europa.eu/eurostat.

30. Wolfgang Hirn, *Kína, a nagy falat: Miként változtatja meg életünket Kína felemelkedése* (China, the big bite: How China's rise changes our lives) (Budapest: HVG Kiadó, 2006).

31. Ibid.

32. See European Commission, *Brain Drain Study: Emigration Flows for Qualified Scientists* (Brussels: European Union, 2003), ftp://ftp.cordis.europa.eu/pub/indicators/docs/merit_exsum.pdf.

33. Paul Magnette, *What Is the European Union? Nature and Prospects* (London: Palgrave Macmillan, 2005).

34. The data here are from various sources, including Eurostat, the International Monetary Fund, and the World Trade Organization.

35. Hirn, *Kína, a nagy falat.*

36. Ibid.

37. See Ted C. Fishman, *China Inc.* (New York; Scribner, 2005).

38. These data are from several newspaper headlines.

39. Ibid.

40. Chicago Council on Global Affairs, *Global Views 2006* (Chicago: Chicago Council on Global Affairs, 2006), http://www.thechicagocouncil.org/UserFiles/File/POS_Topline%20Reports/POS%202006/2006%20Full%20POS%20Report.pdf.

41. Hirn, *Kína, a nagy falat.*

42. For more on the Chinese corporate sector, see Fishman, *China Inc.*

43. The data and in this subsection are from Gucharan Das, *India Unbound* (New Delhi: Penguin Books, 2000), and from several newspaper articles.

44. These data are from the United Nations Statistics Division.

45. Ibid.

46. These are Eurostat data.

47. Ibid.

48. See International Labor Office, "Child Labour in Asia and the Pacific," http://www2.ilo.org/wcmsp5/groups/public/---asia/---ro-bangkok/documents/publication/wcms_099511.pdf.

49. These data are from BBC reports.

50. The data in this subsection are from Das, *India Unbound,* and from several newspaper articles.

51. The data here are from business news sources.

52. Harry G. Broadman et al., *Africa's Silk Road: China and India's New Economic Frontier* (Washington, D.C.: World Bank, 2007).

53. D. Wilson and R. Purushothaman, *Dreaming with BRICs: The Path to 2050,* Global Economics Paper 99 (New York: Goldman Sachs, 2003), http://www2.goldman sachs.com/ideas/brics/book/99-dreaming.pdf.

54. See International Institute for Strategic Studies, "The Pentagon Eyes China's Military," *Strategic Comments,* July 2005, http://www.iiss.org/publications/strategic-comments/past-issues/volume-11-2005/volume-11-issue-5/the-pentagon-eyes-chinas-military/.

55. These are Eurostat data.

56. See Leonard, *Why Europe Will Run the 21st Century.*

Notes to Chapter 3

1. Anthony Giddens, Patrick Diamond, and Roger Liddle, *Global Europe, Social Europe* (Cambridge: Polity Press, 2006).

2. Wilhelm Röpke, *Emberséges társadalom: Emberséges gazdaság* (Human society and human economy), (Budapest: Aula, 2000).

3. André Sapir, "Globalisation and the Reform of the European Social Models," *Journal of Common Market Studies* 44, no. 2 (June 2006): 369–90.

4. On the four models, see ibid.

5. Ibid.

6. See Stephen Haseler, Werner Abelshauser, Evelyne Gebhardt, Jean-Marc Ayrault, Patrick Diamond, Mircea Geoana, Giuseppe Vacca, and Jo Leinen, "The European Economy: Some Reflections," *Social Europe: The Journal of the European Left* 2, no. 1 (July 2006); and Sapir, "Globalisation."

7. For more on this, see Brigita Schmögnerova, *The European Social Model: Re-*

construction or Destruction—A View from a Newcomer (Bonn: Firiedrich Ebert Stiftung, 2005).

8. See Sapir, "Globalisation"; André Sapir et al., *An Agenda for a Growing Europe: The Sapir Report* (Oxford: Oxford University Press, 2004); André Sapir, ed., *Fragmented Power: Europe and the Global Economy.* Brussels: Bruegel, 2007; and selected EU documents at the European Commission's Employment, Social Affairs, and Equal Opportunities Web site, "Flexicurity," http://ec.europa.eu/social/main.jsp?catId=102 &langId=en.

9. These are Eurostat data; see http://ec.europa.eu/eurostat.

10. Organization for Economic Cooperation Development, *The OECD Jobs Study: Facts, Analysis, Strategies 1994* (Paris: Organization for Economic Cooperation Development, 1994), http://www.oecd.org/dataoecd/42/51/1941679.pdf.

11. Philippe Herzog, "Anxious France Overwhelmed by the Challenges of Reform," *Europe's World* (Brussels), Summer 2006.

12. These are Eurostat data and media information.

13. See Globescan, "20-Nation Poll Finds Strong Global Consensus: Support for Free Market System but Also More Regulation of Large Companies," http://www .globescan.com/news_archives/pipa_market.html. -

14. Dominique Moisi, "The Need for Reform in France," *Financial Times,* October 13, 2006.

15. Nicolas Sarkozy, *Testimony: France, Europe and the World in the Twenty-first Century* (New York: Pantheon Books, 2007).

16. Commission pour la Libération de la Croissance Francaise, *Rapport de la commission pour la libération de la croissance francaise: 300 décisions pour changer la France* (Paris: Commission pour la Libération de la Croissance Francaise, 2008), http://lesrapports.ladocumentationfrancaise.fr/BRP/084000041/0000.pdf.

17. Giddens, Diamond, and Liddle, *Global Europe, Social Europe.*

18. See Sapir et al., *Agenda for a Growing Europe.*

19. This was widely reported in the business press.

20. These data are from Haseler et al., "European Economy."

21. These data and those that follow are from Fredrik Bergstörm and Robert Gidehag, *EU versus USA* (Stockholm: Timbro, 2004).

22. See Bruce Bawer, "Perspective: We're Rich, You're Not; End of Story," *New York Times,* April 17, 2005, available at http://www.cepr.net/err/nytimesarticles/2005_ 04_17wealth.htm; and Daniel J. Mitchell, "What Can the United States Learn from the Nordic Model?" *Policy Analysis* (Cato Institute), November 5, 2007, http://www.cato .org/pubs/pas/pa-603.pdf.

23. Bergstörm and Gidehag, *EU versus USA.*

24. See selected EU documents at the European Commission's Employment, Social Affairs, and Equal Opportunities Web site, "Flexicurity."

25. These are UN forecasts; see United Nations Statistics Division, "Size and Structure of the Population," http://unstats.un.org/unsd/demographic/sconcerns/popsize/ default.htm.

26. European Commission, *Green Paper: Confronting Demographic Change—A New Solidarity between the Generations,* COM (2005) 94 (Brussels: European Union, 2005).

27. Ibid.

28. Ibid.
29. Ibid.
30. Ibid.
31. Ibid.
32. Ibid.
33. Ibid.
34. European Commission, "EU Employment Report and Social Outlook Monitoring Report," February 2009, http://ec.europa.eu/social/main.jsp?langId=hu&catId=89&newsId=457.
35. This information was reported in the business media.
36. European Commission, *Green Paper: Confronting Demographic Change.*
37. Ibid.
38. Ibid.
39. These data are from the European Commission's Directorate-General for Economic and Financial Affairs; see http://ec.europa.eu/dgs/economy_finance/index_en.htm.
40. European Commission, *Green Paper: Confronting Demographic Change.*
41. See U.K. Pensions Commission, *Report by the U.K. Pensions Commission* (London: U.K. Pensions Commission, 2005), http://news.bbc.co.uk/2/shared/bsp/hi/pdfs/30_11_05_exec_summ.pdf. Also see U.K. Pension Service, "Pensions Commission Releases New Report on Pension Reform," http://www.thepensionservice.gov.uk/aboutus/2005/nov/pensionscommissionreport.asp.
42. U.K. Pensions Commission, *Report.*
43. The descriptions here and above of the pension systems and reforms of EU member states use data from EU official sources (Eurostat and European Commission documents) and the business press; see the notes above.
44. Tomorrow's Company, *The Ageing Population, Pensions and Wealth Creation* (London: Tomorrow's Company, 2006), http://www.tomorrowscompany.com/downloads%5CAgeing%20Population%20Exec%20Sum%20FINAL.pdf.
45. European Commission, *Green Paper: Confronting Demographic Change.*
46. Ibid.
47. Ibid.
48. These data are from the International Labor Organization, the United Nations, and Eurostat.
49. Marie-Claude Blanc-Chaléard, "L'immigration: Une histoire francaise?" (Immigration: A French Story?), *Homme et Libertés,* January–March 2005. See more statistics in two documents on the European Commission's Freedom, Security, and Justice Web site, "1 January 2003: National and Foreign Population in Eu25 Member States," http://ec.europa.eu/justice_home/doc_centre/asylum/statistics/docs/population_by_citizenship_2003_en.pdf, and "Crude Rate of Net Migration 1990–2002, per 1000 Population," http://ec.europa.eu/justice_home/doc_centre/asylum/statistics/docs/migr_rates_en.pdf. Also see the European Migration Network's annual reports on asylum and migration statistics at http://emn.sarenet.es/Downloads/prepareShowFiles.do;jsessionid=0ED5C2D819049AC65C47FCD57BD1CD03?directoryID=110.
50. Moisi, "Need for Reform."
51. These data are from a European Commission press release.
52. This is according to estimates debated in the media.
53. See Blanc-Chaléard, "L'immigration"; and Jacques Bichot, "Immigration: Quels

couts pour les dépenses publics?" (Immigration: What cost for the public budget?), *Les Notes* (Institut Thomas More), February 2006, http://institut-thomas-more.org/pdf/81_en_NoteITM6BichotFr2.pdf.

54. Bichot, "Immigration."

55. These are EU statistics, from Eurostat and the European Commission's Directorate-General for Justice, Freedom, and Security.

56. For more information on the new EU immigration package, see European Commission, "Package of Measures to Reinforce Solidarity between Member States and the Fight against Illegal Immigration" (press release), http://europa.eu/rapid/pressReleases Action.do?reference=IP/06/1026&format=HTML&aged=1&language=EN&gui Language=en.

57. International Energy Agency, *World Energy Outlook 2006* (Paris: International Energy Agency, 2006).

58. Ibid.

59. These data are from the European Commission, *Green Paper: A European Strategy for Sustainable, Competitive and Secure Energy*, COM (2006) 105 (Brussels: European Union, 2006); and IEA statistics.

60. European Commission, *Green Paper: A European Strategy;* and IEA statistics.

61. Ibid.

62. This is based on information from the IEA and press sources.

63. Vladimir Putin, "Europe Has Nothing to Fear from Russia's Aspirations," *Financial Times,* November 22, 2006.

64. This is based on information from the IEA and press sources.

65. European Commission, *Green Paper: A European Strategy;* and IEA statistics.

66. Ibid.

67. Ibid.

68. Ibid.

69. International Energy Agency, *World Energy Outlook 2006.*

70. Ibid.

71. See the ITER Web site, www.iter.org.

72. For more on this, see European Commission, Climate Action Web site, "The Climate Action and Renewable Energy Package: Europe's Climate Change Opportunity," http://ec.europa.eu/environment/climat/climate_action.htm.

73. This is an IEA forecast.

74. World Economic Forum, *Global Competitiveness Report 2009–2010* (Geneva: World Economic Forum, 2009), http://www.weforum.org/pdf/GCR09/GCR20092010 fullreport.pdf.

75. See Martin Wolf, *Why Globalization Works* (New Haven, Conn.: Yale University Press, 2005); and Martin Wolf, "Comment and Analysis: Why Do English-Speaking Countries Perform Better?" *Financial Times,* January 25, 2005.

76. Wolf, *Why Globalization Works;* Wolf, "Comment and Analysis."

77. McKinsey Global Institute, *Reaching High-Productivity Growth in France and Germany* (Dusseldorf: McKinsey & Company, 2002).

78. Bill Saporito, "How We Became the United States of France," *Time,* September 21, 2008, http://www.time.com/time/nation/article/0,8599,1843168,00.html.

79. For more on this see André Sapir et al., *An Agenda for a Growing Europe: The Sapir Report* (Oxford: Oxford University Press, 2004).

80. Bergström and Gidehag, *EU versus USA.*

81. For more on this, see André Sapir, ed., *Fragmented Power: Europe and the Global Economy* (Brussels: Bruegel, 2007).

82. Organization for Economic Cooperation and Development, *Economic Survey of the Euro Area, 2007,* Policy Brief (Paris: Organization for Economic Cooperation and Development, 2007).

83. The Eurobarometer Web site can be found at http://ec.europa.eu/public_opinion/index_en.htm, and the surveys in question can be found at "How the Europeans See Themselves: Looking through the Mirror with Public Opinion Surveys," http://ec.europa.eu/publications/booklets/eu_documentation/05/txt_en.htm.

84. William W. Lewis, *The Power of Productivity: Wealth, Poverty, and the Threat to Global Stability* (Chicago: University of Chicago Press / McKinsey & Co., 2004).

85. These data are from a survey by the Aspen Institute and the Economist Intelligence Unit in 2005, reported in the business media.

86. Anita Roddick was quoted in the *Financial Times,* November 14, 2006.

87. For more on this, see the EU documents related to the Lisbon Program, which can be found at the European Commission's Growth and Jobs Web site, http://ec.europa.eu/growthandjobs/european-dimension/index_en.htm.

88. Jean Pisani-Ferry and André Sapir, *Last Exit to Lisbon,* Bruegel Policy Brief (Brussels: Bruegel, 2006).

89. See European Commission, *Creating an Innovative Europe: Report of the Independent Expert Group on R&D and Innovation Appointed following the Hampton Court Summit and Chaired by Mr. Esko Aho* (Brussels: European Union, 2006), http://ec.europa.eu/invest-in-research/pdf/download_en/aho_report.pdf.

90. See Sapir et al., *Agenda for a Growing Europe;* and European Commission, *Facing the Challenge: The Lisbon Strategy for Growth and Employment, Report from the High-Level Group Chaired by Wim Kok* (Brussels: European Union, 2004), http://ec.europa.eu/growthandjobs/pdf/kok_report_en.pdf.

91. For the latest update of the Eurochambers report on competitiveness, see Eurochambers, *What Foundation Does Europe Need to Ensure Its Global Competitiveness? A Time-Distance Study* (Brussels: Eurochambers, 2009).

92. For more on this, see the EU documents related to the Lisbon Program.

93. Ibid.

Notes to Chapter 4

1. The Eurobarometer Web site can be found at http://ec.europa.eu/public_opinion/index_en.htm, and the surveys in question can be found at "How the Europeans See Themselves: Looking through the Mirror with Public Opinion Surveys," http://ec.europa.eu/publications/booklets/eu_documentation/05/txt_en.htm.

2. See the Eurobarometer Web site and "How the Europeans See Themselves."

3. See "EU Citizens Want One European Parliament Seat in Brussels," http://www.bmbrussels.eu/images/upload/pr_eu-widesurvey30may.pdf.

4. See the Eurobarometer Web site; and "How the Europeans See Themselves."

5. See the Eurobarometer Web site; and the survey archives, http://ec.europa.eu/public_opinion/archives/eb/eb65/eb65_fr.pdf.

6. European Commission, "Completing the Internal Market: White Paper from the Commission to the European Council (Milan, 28–29 June 1985)," http://europa.eu/documents/comm/white_papers/pdf/com1985_0310_f_en.pdf and http://europa.eu/documents/comm/white_papers/pdf/com1985_0310_f_en_annexe.pdf.

7. See European Commission, "Europe 1992: The Overall Challenge [Summary of the Cecchini Report], SEC (88) 524 final, 13 April 1988," available at http://aei.pitt.edu/3813/01/000209_1.pdf.

8. Ibid.

9. European Commission, *The Internal Market: Ten Years without Frontiers* (Brussels: European Commission, 2002), http://ec.europa.eu/internal_market/10years/docs/workingdoc/workingdoc_en.pdf.

10. See Jean Pisani-Ferry and André Sapir, *Last Exit to Lisbon,* Bruegel Policy Brief (Brussels: Bruegel, 2006). Also see Juan Delgado, *Single Market Trails Home Bias,* Bruegel Policy Brief (Brussels: Bruegel, 2006).

11. The data given here are from the European Commission.

12. Copenhagen Economics, *The Economic Importance of the Country-of-Origin Principle in the Proposed Services Directive* (Copenhagen: Copenhagen Economics, 2005).

13. European Commission, "Results of the Competitiveness Council of Ministers, Brussels, 11th March 2004 Internal Market, Enterprise and Consumer Protection Issues," Press Communiqué, March 12, 2004, http://europa.eu/rapid/pressReleasesAction.do?reference=MEMO/04/58.

14. European Commission, *Financial Services Action Plan,* COM (1999) 232 (Brussels: European Union, 1999), http://ec.europa.cu/internal_market/finances/docs/actionplan/index/action_en.pdf.

15. For the Internal Market Reviews and other related documents, see the EU Single Market Web site, http://ec.europa.eu/internal_market/strategy/index_en.htm#agenda.

16. See also André Sapir, ed., *Fragmented Power: Europe and the Global Economy* (Brussels: Bruegel, 2007).

17. See the EU Single Market Web site.

18. Pisani-Ferry and Sapir, *Last Exit to Lisbon.*

19. Robert Mundell is quoted by S. Adam Posen, ed., *The Euro at Five: Ready for a Global Role?* Special Report 18 (Washington, D.C.: Institute for International Economics, 2005).

20. Fred Bergsten, "The Euro and the Dollar: Toward a 'Finance Group of Two'?" in *Euro at Five,* ed. Posen.

21. Sapir, *Fragmented Power.*

22. Daniel Griswold, "'Bad News' on the Trade Deficit Often Means Good News on the Economy," *Free Trade Bulletin,* no. 14, January 11, 2005, 1–3, http://www.freetrade.org/pubs/FTBs/FTB-014.pdf.

23. The data given here are from the ECB and the International Monetary Fund.

24. These are ECB data.

25. These are European Commission data.

26. HSBC, *European Meltdown?* (London: HSBC, 2005).

27. See Jean Pisani-Ferry et al., *Coming of Age: Report on the Euro Area,* Bruegel Blueprint 4 (Brussels: Bruegel, 2008).

28. Quoted by Posen, *Euro at Five,* 181.

29. Jean Pisani-Ferry and André Sapir, *Last Exit to Lisbon,* Bruegel Policy Brief (Brussels: Bruegel, 2006).

30. Ottmar Issing, *Europe: Common Money—Political Union?* (Frankfurt: European Central Bank, 1999).

31. Kishore Mahbubani, "Europe Is a Geopolitical Dwarf," *Financial Times,* May 22, 2008.

32. These data are from the European Defense Agency; see its Web site, www.eda .europa.eu.

33. See Joseph Nye, *Soft Power: The Means to Success in World Politics* (New York: PublicAffairs, 2005); and Joseph Nye, *Bound to Lead: The Changing Nature of American Power* (New York: Basic Books, 1991).

34. See Robert Kagan, *Of Paradise and Power: America and Europe in the New World Order* (New York: Alfred A. Knopf, 2003).

35. M. Stephen Walt, *Taming American Power: The Global Response to U.S. Primacy* (New York: W. W. Norton, 2005).

36. Andrew Moravcsik, "In Defence of the Democratic Deficit: Reassessing Legitimacy in the European Union," *Journal of Common Market Studies* 40, no. 4 (2002): 603–24.

37. Joschka Fischer, "Europe's Calamity: A Commentary," *New Europe* (Brussels), June 22–28, 2008, 1.

38. These data are from the European Commission, *Enlargement, Two Years After: An Economic Evaluation* (Brussels: European Union, 2006). For a more recent assessment, see the 2009 Eurobarometer survey on enlargement, *Views on European Union Enlargement: Analytical Report,* http://ec.europa.eu/enlargement/pdf/press_corner/ publications/eurobarometer_feb2009_analytical_report_20090506_en.pdf.

39. See, e.g., European Commission, *Enlargement;* and Katinka Barysch, *Enlargement Two Years On: Economic Success or Political Failure?* Briefing Paper (London: Centre for European Reform, 2006).

40. For more on this, see Barysch, *Enlargement Two Years On.*

41. European Commission, *Enlargement.*

42. Ibid.

43. Ibid.

44. Ibid.

45. In 2010, crisis-torn Ireland might not seem to be the ideal model country. Nevertheless, Ireland's fast modenization in the 1990s is worth studying by new member states undergoing socioeconomic transition.

46. European Commission, *Enlargement.*

47. Ibid.

48. Ibid.

49. Géza Gárdonyi, *Egri csillagok* (Eclipse of the crescent moon), available in Hungarian at http://mek.oszk.hu/00600/00656/html/.

50. These are Eurobarometer data.

51. These data are from the European Commission's Freedom, Security, and Justice Web site; see "1 January 2003: National and Foreign Population in Eu25 Member States," http://ec.europa.eu/justice_home/doc_centre/asylum/statistics/docs/population _by_citizenship_2003_en.pdf, and "Crude Rate of Net Migration 1990–2002, per 1000 Population," http://ec.europa.eu/justice_home/doc_centre/asylum/statistics/docs/migr_

rates_en.pdf. Also see the European Migration Network's annual reports on asylum and migration statistics at http://emn.sarenet.es/Downloads/prepareShowFiles.do;jsess ionid=0ED5C2D819049AC65C47FCD57BD1CD03?directoryID=110.

52. These points are based on the European Commission Directorate-General's enlargement information.

53. Ibid.

54. Fischer, "Europe's Calamity."

55. Jacques Barzun, *From Dawn to Decadence: 500 Years of Western Cultural Life* (New York: HarperCollins, 2000), 103.

56. The economic crisis has pushed even Iceland to apply for EU membership in 2009 to find a safe haven inside the Union.

Notes to Chapter 5

1. This map has been evoked by many authors; e.g., see Miroslav Hroch, "A Europe of Nations," in *Europe 2050: Challenges of the Future, Heritage of the Past,* ed. Tuomas Heikkila (Helsinki: Edita Prima, 2006).

2. See Max Weber, *The Protestant Ethic and the Spirit of Capitalism,* trans. Talcott Parsons (London: Routledge, 2004; orig. pub. 1930).

3. This is from a 2005 Eurobarometer poll; see "How the Europeans See Themselves: Looking through the Mirror with Public Opinion Surveys," http://ec.europa .eu/publications/booklets/eu_documentation/05/txt_en.htm.

4. Otmar Issing, *Europe: Common Money—Political Union?* (Frankfurt: European Central Bank, 1999).

5. See Stephen Haseler, *Super-State: The New Europe and Its Challenges to America* (London: I. B. Tauris, 2004).

6. These data are from the United Nations.

7. Robert Schuman, *Európáért* (For Europe) (Budapest: Pro Pannonia Kiadói Alapítvány, 2004), 152.

8. This information is from press reports.

9. Francis Fukuyama, *The End of History and the Last Man* (New York: Free Press, 1992).

10. See Daniel S. Hamilton and Joseph P. Quinlan, eds., *Deep Integration: How Transatlantic Markets Are Leading Globalisation* (Washington and Brussels: Center for Transatlantic Relations and Centre for European Policy Studies, 2005).

11. Ibid.

12. The data here were reported by the *Financial Times.*

13. For more on this, see Jeffry Frieden, *Will Global Capitalism Fall Again?* Bruegel Essay and Lecture Series (Brussels: Bruegel, 2006).

14. Samuel P. Huntington, *The Clash of Civilizations and the Remaking of World Order* (New York: Simon & Schuster, 1996).

15. Ibid.

16. More precisely, 16 percent of British Muslims considered the bombers' cause just, 13 percent said they should be considered "martyrs," and 6 percent believed that they were acting in accordance with the principles of Islam. These data were reported

by the U.S. Institute of Peace, "British Counter-Terrorism after the July 2005 Attacks," http://www.usip.org/resources/british-counter-terrorism-after-july-2005-attacks.

17. Huntington, *Clash of Civilizations.*

18. Robert Harris, *Imperium: A Novel of Ancient Rome* (New York: Simon & Schuster, 2006).

19. European Commission, *Green Paper: Confronting Demographic Change—A New Solidarity between the Generations,* COM (2005) 94 (Brussels: European Union, 2005).

20. Economist Intelligence Unit, *Twenty Questions on the Future of Europe: The EU after "Non" and "Nee"* (London: Economist Intelligence Unit, 2005), http://www.eiu resources.com/mediadir/default.asp?PR=300001830.

21. These models have been widely publicized and debated in the EU's think tanks; see, e.g., Centre for European Reform, *EU 2010: A Programme for Reform—Manifesto* (Brussels: Centre for European Reform, 2006).

22. John Gray, "Those Who Control Oil and Water Will Control the World," *The Observer* (London), March 30, 2008, http://www.guardian.co.uk/commentisfree/2008/mar/30/fossilfuels.water.

Bibliography

Acemoglu, Daren, and A. James Robinson. *The Economic Origins of Dictatorship and Democracy.* Cambridge: Cambridge University Press, 2006.

Ackerman, Bruce. *We, the People: Foundations.* Cambridge, Mass.: Harvard University Press, 1991.

Aghion, Philippe, et al. *Higher Aspirations: An Agenda for Reforming the European Universities.* Bruegel Blueprint Series 5. Brussels: Bruegel, 2008.

Albright, Madeleine. *The Mighty and the Almighty: Reflections on Power, God, and World Affairs.* London: Pan Books, 2007.

Bailyn, Bernard. *The Ideological Origins of the American Revolution.* Cambridge, Mass.: Harvard University Press, 1992.

Barysch, Katinka. *Enlargement Two Years On: Economic Success or Political Failure?* Briefing Paper. London: Centre for European Reform, 2006.

Barzun, Jacques. *From Dawn to Decadence: 500 Years of Western Cultural Life.* New York: HarperCollins, 2000.

Bawer, Bruce. *While Europe Slept: How Radical Islam Is Destroying the West from Within.* New York: Doubleday, 2006.

Beetsma, Roel, and Xavier Debrun. "The New Stability and Growth Pact: A First Assessment." *European Economic Review* 51, no. 2 (2007): 453–77.

Bekouche, Pierre. "The Mediterranean Union's First Step Must Be a Two-Way Energy Deal." *Europe's World* (Brussels), August 2008.

Bichot, Jacques. "Immigration: Quels couts pour les dépenses publics?" (Immigration: What cost for the public budget?). *Les Notes* (Institut Thomas More), February 2006. http://institut-thomas-more.org/pdf/81_en_NoteITM6BichotFr2.pdf.

Bergström, Fredrik, and Robert Gidehag. *EU versus USA.* Stockholm: Timbro, 2004.

Blanc-Chaléard, Marie-Claude. "L'immigration: Une histoire francaise?" (Immigration: A French story?). *Homme et Libertés,* January–March 2005.

Blanchard, Olivier. *The Economic Future of Europe.* NBER Working Paper 10310. Cambridge, Mass.: National Bureau of Economic Research, 2004.

Blankley, Tony. *The West's Last Chance.* Washington, D.C.: Regnery, 2005.

Boeri, Tito, Agar Brugiavini, and Lars Calmfors. *The Role of Unions in the Twenty-first Century.* Oxford: Oxford University Press, 2001.

Broadman, Harry G., et al. *Africa's Silk Road: China and India's New Economic Frontier.* Washington, D.C.: World Bank, 2007.

Brook, Elmar. "How to Rescue the CFSP." *Europe's World* (Brussels), Spring 2006.

Brown, Peter. *The Rise of Western Christendom: Triumph and Diversity AD 200–1000.* Cambridge, Mass.: Blackwell, 1966.

Buchanan, Patrick J. *The Death of the West: How Dying Populations and Immigrant Invasions Imperil Our Country and Civilization.* New York: Thomas Dunne Books / St. Martin's Press, 2002.

Calleo, David. *Rethinking Europe's Future.* Princeton, N.J., Princeton University Press, 2000.

Calmfor, Lars. *What Remains of the Stability Pact and What Next?* Stockholm: Swedish Institute for European Policy Studies, 2005.

Centre for European Reform. *EU 2010: A Programme for Reform—Manifesto.* Brussels: Centre for European Reform, 2006.

Christiansen, Thomas, and Emil Kirchner. *Committee Governance in the European Union.* Manchester: Manchester University Press, 2000.

Commission pour la Libération de la Croissance Francaise. *Rapport de la commission pour la libération de la croissance francaise: 300 décisions pour changer la France.* Paris: Commission pour la Libération de la Croissance Francaise, 2008. http://lesrapports.ladocumentationfrancaise.fr/BRP/084000041/0000.pdf.

Copenhagen Economics. *The Economic Importance of the Country-of-Origin Principle in the Proposed Services Directive.* Copenhagen: Copenhagen Economics, 2005.

Craig, Paul, and Gráinne de Búrca. *EU Law: Text, Cases, and Materials.* Oxford: Oxford University Press, 2003.

Das, Gucharan. *India Unbound.* New Delhi: Penguin Books, 2000.

De Grauwe, Paul. *On Monetary and Political Union.* Leuven: University of Leuven Press, 2005.

Debeljak, Ales. *Európa, európaiak nélkül* (Europe without Europeans). Budapest: Napkút Kiadó, 2005.

Debrun, Xavier, and Anthony Annett. "Implementing Lisbon: Incentives and Constraints." In *Euro Area: Selected Issues.* IMF Country Report 04/235. Washington, D.C.: International Monetary Fund, 2004.

Delgado, Juan. *Single Market Trails Home Bias.* Bruegel Policy Brief. Brussels: Bruegel, 2006.

Dierick, Frank. *The Supervision of Mixed Financial Services Groups in Europe.* ECB Occasional Paper. Frankfurt: European Central Bank, 2004.

Dixon, Mike, and Howard Reed. "Tony Blair's Opportunity: An Anglo-Social European Model." Open Democracy Ltd., July 27, 2005. http://www.opendemocracy.net/democracy-europefuture/society_2705.jsp.

Duhamel, Alain. *Le désarroi français* (The French Disarray). Paris: Plon, 2003.

Economist Intelligence Unit. *Twenty Questions on the Future of Europe: The EU after "Non" and "Nee."* London: Economist Intelligence Unit, 2005. http://www.eiu resources.com/mediadir/default.asp?PR=300001830.

Elias, Norbert. *The Civilizing Process: The History of Manners.* Oxford: Blackwell, 1978.

Eschke, Nina, and Thomas Malick. *The European Constitution and Its Ratification Crisis: Constitutional Debates in the EU Member States.* ZEI Discussion Paper C156. Bonn: Center for European Integration Studies, 2006.

Eurochambers. *What Foundation Does Europe Need to Ensure Its Global Competitiveness? A Time-Distance Study.* Brussels: Eurochambers, 2009.

European Commission. *Brain Drain Study: Emigration Flows for Qualified Scientists.* Brussels: European Union, 2003. ftp://ftp.cordis.europa.eu/pub/indicators/docs/merit_exsum.pdf.

―――. *Enlargement, Two Years After: An Economic Evaluation.* Brussels: European Union, 2006.

―――. *Financial Services Action Plan.* COM (1999) 232. Brussels: European Union, 1999. http://ec.europa.eu/internal_market/finances/docs/actionplan/index/action_en.pdf.

―――. *Green Paper: Confronting Demographic Change—A New Solidarity between the Generations.* COM (2005) 94. Brussels: European Union, 2005.

―――. *Green Paper: A European Strategy for Sustainable, Competitive and Secure Energy.* COM (2006) 105. Brussels: European Union, 2006.

―――. *Working Together for Growth and Jobs: A New Start for the Lisbon Strategy.* Communication to the Spring European Council, COM (2005) 24. Brussels: European Union, 2005.

European Communities. *Statistical Portrait of the European Union 2007.* Luxembourg: European Communities, 2007.

European Union. *Public Finance, 4th Edition.* Brussels: European Union, 2008.

Fagerberg, Jan, David C. Mowery, and Richard Nelson. *The Oxford Handbook of Innovation.* Oxford: Oxford University Press, 2005.

Fishman, Ted C. *China Inc.* New York; Scribner, 2005.

Fischer, Joschka. "Europe's Calamity: A Commentary." *New Europe* (Brussels), June 22–28, 2008.

Food and Agriculture Organization of the United Nations. *The State of Food Insecurity in the World.* Rome: Food and Agriculture Organization of the United Nations, 2005.

Freeman, Richard B. "Are Your Wages Set in Beijing?" *Journal of Economic Perspectives* 9, no. 3 (1995): 15–31.

Frieden, Jeffry. *Will Global Capitalism Fall Again?* Bruegel Essay and Lecture Series. Brussels: Bruegel, 2006.

Friedman, Thomas L. *The World Is Flat: The Globalized World in the 21st Century.* New York: Penguin Books, 2006.

Giddens, Anthony, Patrick Diamond, and Roger Liddle. *Global Europe, Social Europe.* Cambridge: Polity Press, 2006.

Giscard d'Estaing, Valéry. *A franciák* (The French). Budapest: Európa könyvkiadó, 2002.

Glania, Guido, and Jürgen Matthes. *Multilateralism or Regionalism? Trade Policy Options for the European Union.* Brussels: Centre for European Policy Studies, 2005.

Gnesotto, Nicole, and Giovanni Grevi. *The New Global Puzzle: What World for the EU in 2025?* Paris: Institute for Security Studies, 2006.

Hagen, Jürgen von, and György Szapáry. *Monetary Strategies for Joining the Euro.* Northampton, Mass.: Edward Elgar, 2004.

Hamilton, Daniel S., and Joseph P. Quinlan, eds. *Deep Integration: How Transatlantic Markets Are Leading Globalisation.* Washington and Brussels: Center for Transatlantic Relations and Centre for European Policy Studies, 2005.

Hammond, Ray. *The World in 2030.* Paris: Éditions Yago, 2007.

Harris, Robert. *Imperium· A Novel of Ancient Rome.* New York: Simon & Schuster, 2006.

Haseler, Stephen. *Super-State: The New Europe and Its Challenges to America.* London: I. B. Tauris, 2004.

Haseler, Stephen, Werner Abelshauser, Evelyne Gebhardt, Jean-Marc Ayrault, Patrick Diamond, Mircea Geoana, Giuseppe Vacca, and Jo Leinen. "The European Economy: Some Reflections." *Social Europe: The Journal of the European Left* 2, no. 1 (July 2006).

Haseler, Stephen, Detlev Albers, and Henning Meyer. *Social Europe: A Continent's Answer to Market Fundamentalism.* London: Metropolitan University Press, 2006.

Heikkila, Tuomas, ed. *Europe 2050: Challenges of the Future, Heritage of the Past.* Helsinki: Edita Prima, 2006.

Herzog, Philippe. "Anxious France Overwhelmed by the Challenges of Reform." *Europe's World* (Brussels), Summer 2006.

Hirn, Wolfgang. *Kína, a nagy falat: Miként változtatja meg életünket Kína felemelkedése* (China, the big bite: How China's rise changes our lives). Budapest: HVG Kiadó, 2006.

Hobsbawm, Eric. *The Age of Capital, 1848–1875.* New York: Vintage Books, 1975.

———. *The Age of Extremes: The Short Twentieth Century, 1914–1991.* London: Michael Joseph, 1994.

Holland, Stuart. *Towards a New Breton Woods: Alternatives for the Global Economy.* London: Spokesman, 1994.

Huntington, Samuel P. *The Clash of Civilizations and the Remaking of World Order.* New York: Simon & Schuster, 1996.

International Energy Agency. *World Energy Outlook 2006.* Paris: International Energy Agency, 2006.

International Monetary Fund. *Advancing Structural Reforms: World Economic Outlook, April 2004.* Washington, D.C.: International Monetary Fund, 2004.

Issing, Otmar. *Economic and Monetary Union in Europe: Political Priority versus Economic Integration.* Frankfurt: European Central Bank, 2001.

———. *Europe: Common Money—Political Union?* Frankfurt: European Central Bank, 1999.

Jarosz-Friis, Anna, and Lykke Friis. *Countdown to Copenhagen: Big Bang or Fizzle in the EU's Enlargement Process?* Copenhagen: Danish Institute for International Affairs, 2002.

Jones, Alison, and Brenda Sufrin. *EC Competition Law: Text, Cases, and Materials.* Oxford: Oxford University Press, 2004.

Kagan, Robert. *Of Paradise and Power: America and Europe in the New World Order.* New York: Alfred A. Knopf, 2003.

Kamp, Karl-Heinz. "It's Not the Demise of the West but Its Rise." *Europe's World* (Brussels), Summer 2008.

Kennedy, Paul. *Grand Strategies of War and Peace.* New Haven, Conn.: Yale University Press, 1991.

Khanna, Parag. *The Second World: Empires and Influence in the New Global Order.* New York: Random House, 2008.

Kopstein, Jeffrey, and Sven Steinmo, eds. *Growing Apart? America and Europe in the Twenty-first Century.* Cambridge: Cambridge University Press, 2008.

Lamy, Pascal. "The Future of the World Economy: What Place for EU Industries?" Introductory remarks, Conference on the Insertion of European Industry in the International Division of Labour: Position and Perspectives, European Commission, Brussels, 2005.

Landaburu, Eneko. "Hard Facts about Europe's Soft Power." *Europe's World* (Brussels), Summer 2006.

Landes, David S. *The Wealth and Poverty of Nations.* New York: W.W. Norton, 1998.

Leonard, Mark. *Why Europe Will Run the 21st Century.* London: Fourth Estate, 2005.

Lewis, William W. *The Power of Productivity: Wealth, Poverty, and the Threat to Global Stability.* Chicago: University of Chicago Press / McKinsey & Company, 2004.

Magnette, Paul. *What Is the European Union? Nature and Prospects.* London: Palgrave Macmillan, 2005.

Mahbubani, Kishore. "Europe Is a Geopolitical Dwarf." *Financial Times,* May 22, 2008.

Marján, Attila. *Európa pénzügyei* (Europe's finances). Budapest: Sanoma Budapest, 2005.

———, ed. *Az Európai Unió gazdasága* (The economy of the European Union). Budapest: HVG Kiadó, 2006.

Masci, David. "An Uncertain Road: Muslims and the Future of Europe." Pew Forum on Religion and Public Life, October 2005. http://pewforum.org/docs/index.php?DocID=60.

McCormick, John. *The European Superpower.* London: Palgrave Macmillan, 2007.

McKinsey Global Institute. *Reaching High-Productivity Growth in France and Germany.* Dusseldorf: McKinsey & Company, 2002.

Molnader, Per, and Allan Gustafsson. *Coming of Age? Economic Management of the European Union.* Stockholm: Swedish Institute for European Policy Studies, 2003.

Moravcsik, Andrew. "In Defence of the Democratic Deficit: Reassessing Legitimacy in the European Union." *Journal of Common Market Studies* 40, no. 4 (2002): 603–24.

Naumann, Klaus, et al. *Towards a Grand Strategy for an Uncertain World.* Lunteren, the Netherlands: Noaber Foundtion, 2007.

Neyts-Uyttebroeck, Annemie. "It's Time Governments Told the Truth about the EU." *Europe's World* (Brussels), Summer 2006.

Nicolaides, Phedon. "A Theory of Regulatory Integration." *Intereconomics,* January–February 2006, 37–43.

Nicolaïdïs, Kalypso. "Europe and Beyond: Struggles for Recognition." Open Democracy Ltd., February 21, 2006. http://www.opendemocracy.net/faith-europe_islam/recognition_3288.jsp.

Nicoletti, Giuseppe, and Stefano Scarpetta. "Regulation, Productivity, and Growth." *Economic Policy* 36, no. 1 (April 2003): 9–72.

Offe, Claus. *Reflections on America: Tocqueville, Weber & Adorno in the United States.* Cambridge: Polity Press, 2005.

Olson, Mancur. *Power and Prosperity.* New York: Basic Books, 2000.

Organization for Economic Cooperation and Development. *Economic Survey of the Euro Area, 2007.* Policy Brief. Paris: Organization for Economic Cooperation and Development, 2007.

Outhwaite, William. *European Society.* Cambridge: Polity Press, 2008.

Palánkai, Tibor. "European Integration: Theoretical Relevances of Our Integration Maturity." *Journal of Public Finance* 2 (2006).

Philippon, Thomas, and Nicolas Véron. *Financing Europe's Fast Movers.* Bruegel Policy Brief. Brussels: Bruegel, 2008.

Pisani-Ferry, Jean, and Indira Santos. *Reshaping the Global Economy.* Bruegel Policy Contribution Paper. Brussels: Bruegel, 2009.

Pisani-Ferry, Jean, and André Sapir. *Last Exit to Lisbon.* Bruegel Policy Brief. Brussels: Bruegel, 2006.

Pisani-Ferry, Jean, and Bruno van Pottelsberge. *Handle with Care! Post-Crisis Growth in the EU.* Bruegel Policy Brief. Brussels: Bruegel, 2009.

Pisani-Ferry, Jean, et al. *Coming of Age: Report on the Euro Area.* Bruegel Blueprint 4. Brussels: Bruegel, 2008.

Porter, Michael E. *The Competitive Advantage of Nations.* New York: Macmillan, 1990.

Posen, S. Adam, ed. *The Euro at Five: Ready for a Global Role?* Special Report 18. Washington, D.C.: Institute for International Economics, 2005.

Rehn, Olli. *Europe's Next Frontiers.* Munich Contributions to European Unification 14. Baden Baden: Nomos, 2006.

Riés, Philippe. *L'Europe: Maladie de la démocratie.* (Europe: The illness of democracy). Paris: Garret, 2008.

Rifkin, Jeremy. *The European Dream: How Europe's Vision of the Future Is Quietly Eclipsing the American Dream.* Cambridge: Polity Press, 2004.

Röpke, Wilhelm. *Emberséges társadalom: Emberséges gazdaság* (Human society: Human economy). Budapest: Aula, 2000.

Rostoványi, Zsolt. *Az iszlám világ és a Nyugat* (The Islamic world and the West). Budapest: Corvina Kiadó, 2004.

Sapir, André. "Globalisation and the Reform of the European Social Models." *Journal of Common Market Studies* 44, no. 2 (June 2006): 369–90.

———, ed. *Fragmented Power: Europe and the Global Economy.* Brussels: Bruegel, 2007.

Sapir, André, et al. *An Agenda for a Growing Europe: The Sapir Report.* Oxford: Oxford University Press, 2004.

Saporito, Bill. "How We Became the United States of France." *Time,* September 21, 2008. http://www.time.com/time/nation/article/0,8599,1843168,00.html.

Sarkozy, Nicolas. *Testimony: France, Europe and the World in the Twenty-first Century.* New York: Pantheon Books, 2007.

Schmögnerova, Brigita. *The European Social Model: Reconstruction or Destruction— A View from a Newcomer.* Bonn: Firiedrich Ebert Stiftung, 2005.

Schuman, Robert. *Európáért* (For Europe). Budapest: Pro Pannonia Kiadói Alapítvány, 2004.

Shiller, Robert. *The Subprime Solution: How Today's Global Financial Crisis Happened, and What to Do about It.* Princeton, N.J.: Princeton University Press, 2008.

Simai, Mihály. "The World Economy and Europe at the Beginning of the 21st Century." *Development and Finance* (Quarterly Hungarian Economic Review) 1 (2006).

Stern, Nicholas. *The Economics of Climate Change.* London: Her Majesty's Stationery Office, 2006. http://www.hm-treasury.gov.uk/stern_review_report.htm.

Strasser, Daniel. *The Finances of Europe: The Budgetary and Financial Law of the European Communities.* Brussels: European Communities, 1992.

Subacchi, Paola. *What Does a Larger EU Mean for the European Economy? Looking at 2005 and Beyond.* Conference Paper. London: Chatham House, 2004. http://www.chathamhouse.org.uk/publications/papers/download/-/id/527/file/9642_081104subacchi.pdf.

Tack, Lieven. "Monetary Policies of the Fed and the ECB." College of Europe, Warsaw, 2002.

Tilford, Simon. *Will the Eurozone Crack?* Brussels: Centre for European Reform, 2006.

Tomorrow's Company. *The Ageing Population, Pensions and Wealth Creation.* London: Tomorrow's Company, 2006. http://www.tomorrowscompany.com/downloads%5CAgeing%20Population%20Exec%20Sum%20FINAL.pdf.

U.K. Pensions Commission. *Report by the U.K. Pensions Commission.* London: U.K. Pensions Commission, 2005. http://news.bbc.co.uk/2/shared/bsp/hi/pdfs/30_11_05_exec_summ.pdf.

Van Ham, Peter. "America's Rising Anti-Europeanism." *Europe's World* (Brussels), Spring 2006.

Verhofstadt, Guy. "Only a New 'Political Core' Can Drive Europe Forward Again." *Europe's World* (Brussels), Summer 2006.

Wallace, Helen, and William Wallace, eds. *Policy-Making in the European Union,* 4th ed. Oxford: Oxford University Press, 2000.

Walt, M. Stephen. *Taming American Power: The Global Response to U.S. Primacy.* New York: W. W. Norton, 2005.

Weber, Max. *The Protestant Ethics and the Spirit of Capitalism.* London: Routledge, 2001.

Westaway, Peter. *Modelling Shocks and Adjustment Mechanisms in EMU.* EMU Study. London: Her Majesty's Treasury, 2003.

Williams, Jessica. *Fifty Facts That Should Change the World.* Cambridge: Icon Books, 2004.

Wilson, D., and R. Purushothaman. *Dreaming with BRICs. The Path to 2050.* Global Economics Paper 99. New York: Goldman Sachs, 2003. http://www2.goldmansachs.com/ideas/brics/book/99-dreaming.pdf.

Wolf, Martin. "Comment and Analysis: Why Do English-Speaking Countries Perform Better?" *Financial Times,* January 25, 2005.

———. *Why Globalization Works.* New Haven, Conn.: Yale University Press, 2005.

World Bank. *Globalization, Growth, and Poverty: Building an Inclusive World Economy.* Washington, D.C.: World Bank, 2002.

Worldwatch Institute. *State of the World 2005: Redefining Global Security.* New York: W. W. Norton, 2005.

Xiang, Lanxin. "China and Europe Together Could Break the Mould of Global Politics." *Europe's World* (Brussels), Summer 2006.

Zakaria, Fareed. *The Post-American World.* New York: W. W. Norton, 2008.

Index

energy supply, 175; and U.S.-Russian relations, 255–56
redistribution rates in welfare system, 125–26
Reformation, 306
reinsurance sector, 53
relocation of production: to Asia, 52; and Deutsche Bank, 99; to Eastern Europe, 227, 276; and European social models, 129; from Germany, 327–28; and minimum wage hike, 334; trans-Atlantic, 331. *See also* outsourcing
Renault, 186
renewable energy sources, 169–70, 178
Rentokil Initial (office services company), 151
research and development (R&D): and "brains market," 87; in China, 94; and European Institute of Technology, 195; and European social models, 133, 143; European spending on, 8, 85, 86, 196, 200; financial instruments as support of, 194; in India, 99; in magic triangle, 194–98, 203; and Microsoft, 181; outsourcing of, 332; and patents, 190; and reform, 329; U.S. spending on, 88, 131
Ricardo, David, 17
Rice, Condoleezza, 338
"Riester pension," 154
The Rise and Fall of the Great Powers (Kennedy), 25
Roddick, Anita, 193
Roman Empire: collapse of, 15, 270–71, 337; and European identity, 305; and Islam, 49; as political union, 265; and Turks, 284
Romania, accession to EU of, 275
Rome, Treaty of (1957), 122
Romulus Augustulus, 337
Röpke, Wilhelm, 120
Rowling, J.K., 92

Rumsfeld, Donald, 57, 254–55
Russia: in customs union, 77; democracy in, 113; economic development in, 339–40; and energy supply, 172–76, 177; European borders of, 290–91; and foreign policy, 257; and globalization, 38–39; Orthodox Christianity in, 305; population in, 26

SAP (company), 87
Sapir, André, 138, 199, 236, 248
Saporito, Bill, 185
Sarkozy, Nicolas, 68, 137, 251, 288, 293, 299
Scandinavian Monetary Union, 230
Schengen Agreement (1985), 294, 298
Schuman, Robert, 21, 325–26
sectors. *See individual sectors, e.g., information technology (IT) sector*
Security Council, UN, 134, 250, 253
Sensex (Indian stock exchange index), 99
Serbia, globalization and, 35
services, freedom to provide, 217–18, 226
Services Directive, 223–24, 276
service sector, 84, 98–99, 185
Sharia law, 161
Shell, 83
Siemens, 280, 331
Singh, Manmohan, 110
Single European Act, 215, 217
Skype, 46
Smith, Adam, 118, 186
"snake in the tunnel" arrangement, 231
social cohesion, European model of, 119, 121, 123
"social decline," 336
Social Democrats, 327
social dialogue, 120, 167, 184
social dumping, 276, 297, 316
"social market economy," 119–20